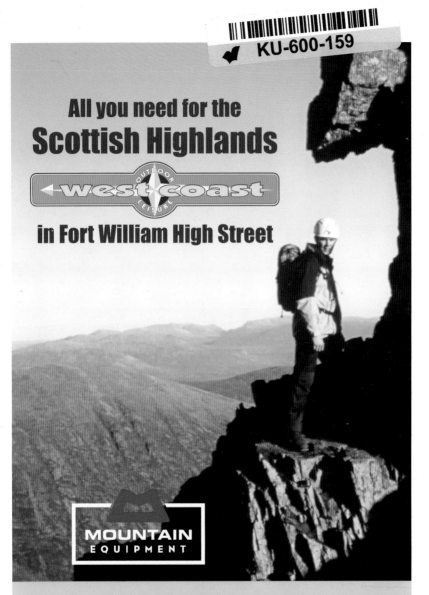

THE SCOTTISH MOUNTAINEERING CLUB JOURNAL

| Vol. XXXIX | 2005 | No. 196 |

THE FAR END OF THE FAR CUILLIN

By Iain Smart

I EMERGED from the BMC hut in Glen Brittle one brilliant June morning as the brief shadow of the night was fading over the northern hills. The rising sun was just catching the dew drops weighing down the grass, each drop photo-multipying the oblique sunlight into a star, achieving effortlessly and in abundance the effect artfully-cut diamonds strive for; try as they may, such artifacts can never be as good as the real thing. The birds were singing, the force of gravity had been turned down to a peep and the midges were off duty. Aesthetically, it was a full house, four aces on a king, if not the fabled five aces that are said to occur occasionally in skilled hands or in rare transcendental moments – a morning like this seemed to be one of them. As an extra bonus I was all by myself without a companion to disturb the local geometry of space-time.

I intended to contour along the base of the Cuillin to Garsbheinn, come back along the ridge as far as Coire Grundda and return to the splendours of the BMC hut where some slices of filet mignon, assorted mushrooms (morels, ceps and the ordinary ones), new potatoes and mild onions awaited me – a simple repast after a long day on the hill. Oh yes, there was also a bottle of claret, more expensive than I could prudently afford.

I was off to Garsbheinn because it is the least popular of the Cuillin summits, yet has one of the best panoramic views of the wide sea to the south and west, the dragon's back of the Cuillins to the north and beckoning Blaven and the receding horizons of the mainland hills to the east. I was going to spend a long time on the summit just enjoying being alive. I would relax with a loaf of bread, a flask of wine, a book of verse and if I needed a 'thou' or two beside me dreaming in the wilderness I could summon someone up from the richly-populated mansions of the past to share the enjoyment.

One thing I wanted to do was to look down on Soay and remember the day we had tried to get across there to work for Gavin Maxwell in his shark fishery. The arrangement was for us to light a fire on the Skye shore

The Inaccessible Pinnacle from Sgurr Thearlaich, Skye. Photo: David Ritchie.

at 2pm on an agreed day and they would come across to pick us up. In spite of a large smoky fire, nothing happened. As we walked disconsolately back to Glen Brittle Maxwell's shark-catching motor torpedo boat sped into the Sound of Soay from the west with a scraggy, sardonically smiling shark no more than 10ft. long lashed to its side – their total catch for a week. Gavin Maxwell had been operating the fishery for a year or two and after a period of success basking sharks for some inexplicable, Osgood-Mackenzie-like reason had all but vanished. Consequently, there was no work to be had on Soay. There was a telegram to that effect waiting for us at the hostel when we returned. So we had to make do instead with midge-bitten toil cutting bracken around the struggling foot-high Sitkas that now in their maturity dominate the glen.

And so that morning I started off with a spring in my step but after half-an-hour or so slowed to a trudge; it was after all more than 60 years since my first visit. By conserving energy I arrived at the summit in fairly good nick and spent the afternoon there enjoying my flask of wine and book of verse and letting my mind out of its box to soar around looping the loop and enjoying its freedom. It turned into a hot shimmering afternoon and I did a sort of *après midi d'un faune* for a couple of hours, followed by a substantial zizz in the shade of a rock.

As I was about to bundle and go I was disturbed by the arrival of two youngish men. We greeted each other and agreed on the superb weather. They dumped their rucksacks and modest rack of chocks and runners, then started admiring the view pointing out landmarks to each other and arguing over some of them. Then taking out their picnic they reverted to the conversation they must have been having when they arrived. They seemed a pleasant couple, light on their feet and obviously fit. Then one of them gave me a second look.

"Didn't we once meet a couple of years ago in the Nevis Hut?" he enquired. "You helped us during our retreat from a debacle on the Orion Face."

This could only be the man who was the prime mover on that memorable occasion. I reported the events of that night in the Journal a few years ago (*SMCJ*. 1996, xxvi, 187, p7). Their party of four had straggled down from the Ben in darkness and blizzard and I had offered them shelter in the hut. You may possibly remember that an interesting little bit of theatre unfolded with a colourful *dramatis personae* that included Maggie, the dark dominatrix and the Storm Goddess whose name I never discovered, the *deux femmes sans merci* who spiced up the evening and, of course, there was the hapless Harry. Mike, the leading man on that occasion still had a slight Australian overlay to his Scottish consonants and vowels and the same relaxed genial manner.

"Yes, how could I forget? It was quite a night. That was a remarkable bottle of brandy you had. I remember it well."

"We expected to hear from you again. Did you lose our telephone number?"

"No, I lost my nerve. All that nonsense you talked might have been true. I don't take risks any more. I try to be happy as I am." I said, sententiously.

You may remember they had come out with some plausibly implausible story about their ability to sustain life beyond its natural span, enough to be highly entertaining science fiction. They had been great company for an evening and, toned down a bit to make it believable, the evening had made a good story for the Journal.

"I am disappointed in you," he said, cracking open a can of beer and handing it to me.

"Well, let me introduce you to my friend Dirk here. He is a sailing man. Mostly square riggers. He's old-fashioned but much sought after nowadays by training ships."

I exchanged how-do-you-dos with a pleasant man of middle height, rugged appearance, fair hair, blue eyes, a broad smile and a notably firm handshake. It appeared they were off Dirk's boat anchored in Portree. It wasn't a full square rigger he said apologetically. Well not really. His present vessel was a brigantine. Squaresails on the foremast only. Easier to handle with a small crew. He and Mike were having a day off. They had just done the main ridge in a leisurely 10 hours from Sgurr nan Gillian by way of the Pinnacle Ridge and were going back along the ridge to descend to Glen Brittle via Coire Lagan They were to be picked up at Glen Brittle House that evening by one of the crew.

"Join us for a bite to eat," he invited indicating a spread of crusty bread, sausage and relish he had laid out on a stone. I accepted, more to be sociable than anything else. I tried to make some mileage with Dirk, reminiscing about the Centennial Yacht Meet and the joys of sailing in state-of-the-art ships of yesteryear. We rambled on but it was an unequal conversation. Rounding the point of Sleat or even Barra Head was a pussy cat compared to the Cape of Good Hope.

"I'd like to see your yacht," I said to change the subject from my embarrassingly inadequate sailing experience.

"She is not a yacht – she's a brigantine!, a real ship," he exclaimed banging me on the head with the remains of the baguette in mock huff. "Usually, I use a belaying pin to correct remarks like that. Be grateful that there isn't one handy."

And so at their invitation I travelled back along the ridge with them in a late afternoon of purring warmth. We conversed easily together, mostly about history and literature. They were both scholarly souls very well read with a breath-taking historical perspective. I kept up with them conversationally fairly well, but I started to lag increasingly far behind on the uphills. The verve of the morning had gone. I reverted to my own leisurely, great-grandfatherly plod. They waited for me at the bottom of the final ascent to Sgurr Dhu.

"Here we must part. It was nice to meet you all again," I said offering a parting handshake. They declined the gambit. Mike made the suggestion that since it was such a fine evening we all saunter slowly to the Thearlaich-Dhu gap I could join them in a rappel down the short side and then go back down to Coire a'Ghrunnda from the bottom of the gap. It sounded sensible and I was enjoying their company, so I accepted and we plodded communally onward.

I managed the rappel into the gap with a fair show of residual competence. We sat companionably at the bottom, sharing some chocolate. Dirk said it would be really easier for me if I kept on the ridge and went back to Glen Brittle down the stone shoot and home by Coire Lagan in their company.

"We can all go together. No need to hurry. The sun is still high and the colours will get better as the shadows lengthen."

The offer was confirmed by Mike: "We'll give you a top rope. It would be a pity to miss the view from Sgurr Alasdair on an evening like this. It will be worth the effort."

I've seen the day I could have led the steep side but now I knew I didn't have the strength or control to get up under any circumstances. It would be too humiliating to be hauled up like a sack of potatoes. So, I declined. "No thanks, I'll just rest here a bit and then wander back in my own good time. One of the joys of maturity is that you know how to take your time," I added, not too convincingly.

Mike looked at me appraisingly and then produced a flask and some small nesting metal cups not much bigger than thimbles from his rucksack.

"Okay then let's have a final dram afore we go."

"Is it that stuff again? I don't mind if I do. A little snort would do me good."

"It's not exactly the same stuff, but it's pretty good."

Whatever it was, was strong – bitter with a pleasant herbal taste, a bit like Gamle Dansk, the Danish pick-me-up. We continued to chat companionably. At one stage they were arguing together about something to do with the next stage of their voyage and I poured myself another dram without being asked. I don't think they noticed.

A few minutes later I heard my own voice saying: "I've got a good idea. I'll just lead this pitch then we can all go down to the hut and you can have dinner with me before you drive back to your yacht, I mean brigantine. I have some good wine and a bottle of Old Brora." They exchanged a worried glance.

"Steady on old fellow," said Mike. But I was already tying on the rope.

Then they gave each other a meaning look. Hendrik nodded: "Let him try," he muttered under his breath. "Let's see what he can do. We can catch him when he falls." I think they both moved to cushion my fall on the first move.

The fact was that I climbed the nasty smooth side with confidence and some aplomb. The rock was much smoother than of yore and unsightly grey, green, greasy limpopo chalk marks were everywhere. Nevertheless, I went up like a competent 20-year-old. I could feel parts of my nervous system, dormant for 50 years, emerging from retirement. My fingers read the rock like brail and my eyes transmitted data about the geometry and texture of the coming rock. My nervous system integrated all this information, optimised the configuration of my body in relation to the pull of gravity and the expected frictional properties of each hold and organised the sequence of action of the appropriate muscle groups, checking that they could exert the required power. I seemed to be just coming along for the ride. It was a bit like driving a perfectly tuned aeroplane, operating under an efficient autopilot. I got to the top before I was ready, belayed expertly and brought the others up.

"That's a bloody good dram you have in that flask," I remarked as we untied.

"We'll have to watch you," Mike replied. "I thought I saw you have a second shot of that stuff. You shouldn't have done that. Never mind. We'll make sure you get home alright."

"What do you mean 'get home all right'? I've never felt better."

"I am sure you haven't. Not for years anyway. I mean what you have just done has a cost. The stuff you just knocked back opened up blood vessels in brain and muscle and is even now emptying your liver of glycogen and catabolising your brown fat reserves. When we get back to the hut you're going to have to keep off alcohol and take aboard as much glucose and skimmed milk as you can to protect your liver and let it resynthesise its energy stores.

"I thought it was supposed to be a 'magic' elixir'," I said provocatively.

"You obviously don't know what magic is," he replied. "We can't break the Laws of Thermodynamics. You always get less useful energy out of a system than you put in. Free energy is a misnomer. In the end you have to repay the bill with interest even if you happen to be a magician."

"Tell me more," I asked fascinated by this tutorial on the metaphysics of physics but any further exposition was interrupted by Dirk.

"Enough of this babble," he said. He had finished coiling the rope and was preparing to go. "There is some magic to be made on top of Alasdair on an evening like this. Let's go where the magic will actually happen."

We wandered on and spent a full hour on the summit while the sun got lower, the colours richer and the shadows longer. It was one of those Aphrodite moments when the mind and the world get fankled up together. This is an interesting subjective state to be in. Nevertheless, I have little doubt the great wide world out there was completely indifferent to the fact that our nervous systems were transmuting all the mindless radiation it was emitting into a thing of beauty and a joy for ever. Although we take it for granted the ability to do this is profoundly magical. I remarked as much to the other two. They asked if I was sure I had got it the right way round.

Then we picked our way lightly down the great stone chute into Coire Lagan, loped with long strides over the great elephantine boiler plates of the coire floor and on through the rough bounds of the lower glen in the luminous afterglow of a summer gloaming.

When we got back to the hut they accepted my invitation to dinner.

"Show me your stuff and I'll cook," said Mike. He saw the mushrooms which I had left re-hydrating in a bowl. "I'll make soup. Dried ones like these have better flavour as soup."

He sat me down, took out some gadgets from his rucksack and clipped something on to my wrist which displayed my blood pressure and the rate and character of my pulse. Then he had a look in my eyes with a little ophthalmoscope. "I never travel without one, he explained: "The retina is the only place you can actually see blood vessels. Yours are alright. Your circulation seems up to it. I am just being careful. Just checking your tyre pressures, as it were."

"Now go and pour Dirk a dram," he directed as he unpacked more things from his rucksack. "Chat about derring-do on the high seas with him. You'll find him interesting. I'll bring you a liver-saving drink in a few minutes."

Dirk was an impressive character. He seemed to have sailed everywhere but he was appropriately foggy about dates. Most of his stories seemed a bit old-fashioned. He told them with grace and interpretive skill. He listened appreciatively enough to my story of going through the Corrievreckan and the Grey Dog but it couldn't match his story of being dragged southwards by the Benguela current through the teeth of a full gale blowing in the opposite direction in a full-rigged ship without an auxiliary engine.

I was reminded of a similar experience some years ago. At a formal dinner I was seated next to someone because we were both pilots. Our host obviously thought we had a lot in common. "How many hours do you have," my neighbour asked after we had introduced ourselves.

"Two hundred," I replied, quite pleased with myself.

"Is that all? I have 40,000." He had been chief test pilot for the RAF and had once got a Vulcan bomber out of an inverted spin. The rest of the evening he talked to me about chess – not playing it but about the set he was carving from hippopotamus teeth harder than ivory; each piece representing a figure from Eskimo mythology. The significance of each he explained to me in some detail. I saw the full set later; it was exquisite. After years of experience in this sort of thing. I have learned to enjoy the rewarding experience of being an eternal pupil. I learned a lot about life on the high seas in big ships.

Mike came through with a drink in a pint mug.

"You must get through two more of these tonight," he announced.

It wasn't bad stuff – smooth, warm, milky, redolent of honey with a prolonged, rich, nutty après gout. A little later he came back with a couple of bowls of mushroom soup and garlic bread which he and Dirk supped with great enjoyment. Mushrooms, he explained to me between spoonfuls, had toxins which my liver couldn't handle in its present state. I went off and boiled the new potatoes, grilled the filet mignons and returned with the bottle of claret. This they partook of with relish, commiserating with me but assuring me, while I sipped my liver-protecting posset that it was for my own good.

The hut was full of climbers noisily reliving the near-death experiences they had confronted during the day. To escape from the clang of decibels we moved outside to a green bit above the road, they with their coffee and drams, me with my third posset. It was a lovely soft summer night with enough breeze to keep the midges away.

"Tell me," I said: "What was that stuff you gave me up on the ridge? Was there amphetamine in it? Are you a couple of junkies just keeping going on performance-enhancing drugs?"

"Of course not," Mike replied matter of factly. "We are not escapists, at least not in that sense. We are just knowledgeable about replacement therapy. We are no more junkies than a diabetic is for taking insulin. We have just learned how to use replacement therapy for a greater range of conditions than diabetes. Aging is a deficiency of the renewal systems and can be controlled. We know how to keep collagen from gumming up the system and the elastic tissue in the body healthy. We are pretty good at tweaking neuro-transmitters and keeping mood at its optimum. You tune the engine of a car or the sails of a boat for optimum performance, don't you? You do that as a matter of course. Why not tune your mind and maintain your body in optimum condition just like you would a car or boat?

"Sounds logical, but how long can you go on for?"

"In theory, indefinitely, but accidents do happen. Harry Nieve for example – the chap you met in the CIC hut – is no longer with us. He was in the twin towers on 9/11. We can only do physiological longevity. We haven't cracked immortality yet."

"But we are working on it," interjected Dirk, raising his glass and getting a disapproving look from Mike.

"Okay, but don't you get bored being on holiday all the time. Aren't you just a couple of self-indulgent playboys? There must be more to life than climbing and sailing endlessly round the world."

"Bored? With such a remarkable thing as life? Bored with having an intellect that has hardly been used?"

He then enlarged on the challenges of what he called 'the fifth stage of learning', the period in our later years when we actually began to learn something. Even if we have gained a reasonable pass in the University of Life most of us are denied admission to this great experience, due to the lamentable inability of our deteriorating support systems to keep body and mind in decent nick for more than the trivial period of a few score years.

"Well why do you risk all this by dangerous activities like climbing and sailing?"

"We climb and sail because both require route finding and calculating risk under stress and have no rules except those imposed by the laws of nature – wind and tide and gravity – against which there is no appeal. Apart from the enjoyable adrenalin-buzz, it is the perfect practical metaphor for us. It helps to steady our nerve for route finding at the wild frontier of the fifth age. We are no longer exploring the edge of our climbing ability. We have done all that. We climb well within our ability. We have new unknowns to explore."

He and Dirk expanded on this theme for a couple of hours in the deepening summer dusk. However, I won't bore you any more on these matters. This is after all a mountaineering journal and not a text book on the wild frontier of creative living beyond three score years and 10.

The session ended about midnight when we saw the headlights of a car coming down the glen.

"That must be Gourlay," said Mike rising and dusting himself down.

As we walked back to the road Dirk looked at the impeccable sky.

"The weather is stable. There isn't going to be much wind," he said sniffing the air. "No good for sailing. Why don't we just stay and do a climb tomorrow? Our friend here and Gourlay would make good climbing partners."

The car arrived and I was introduced to Gourlay, a big genial rough-hewn man who turned out to be the ship's engineer. ("We have an auxiliary engine nowadays," Dirk explained, having the good grace to look shamefacedly at his boots).

Gourlay exuded competence and had a handshake like a friendly velvet vice. The weather report he brought was good for the next 12 hours; then an Atlantic front was due to arrive. It was decided to grab the good weather while it was on offer and make an early start.

The Wild Frontier Of The Fifth Age:

We managed to squeeze in to the hut for a few hours to get away from the dew that was settling over us. A few hours later as dawn's left hand was in the sky and the first birds were tweeting tentatively we left quickly without breakfast, except I had to drink something rather neutral tasting. The dew-laden grass was seeded with pearls gleaming silver-grey in the directionless light – there were no shadows yet. A few strands of mist decorated the black skyline of the Cuillin. The attention to detail that morning was immaculate. We moved fast through the fields of pearls as they transmuted into diamonds under the first sunlight. The rolling flanks of grass and heather gained texture from the first long shadows and oblique shafts of sunshine. I was moving easily and seemed to have lost weight.

At the entrance to Coire Lagan we paused to appreciate the ambience and have breakfast. We looked out over the sea to Rum of the fretted skyline, to Canna of the golden sunlit cliffs and over the Minch to the Long Island, to green Barra of the waves and fair Uist of the songs, all bright in the sunlight and set in a sea patterned in blues, greys and silver. For breakfast, I had another pint of the rich emollient mixture Mike had been feeding me with the night before. He also tested my tyre pressures and had a cursory look at my retinal vessels, pronouncing my systems to be operationally satisfactory. I remarked on how well I was feeling and asked why I was so spry and light on my feet after all yesterday's activities and so little sleep. He explained that I had used up my brown fat and had now switched over to converting the fat in my spare tyre into energy. My fuel tank was emptying, that was why I felt as if I had lost weight. But there was nothing to worry about unless I started running on empty and he wouldn't allow that to happen.

We split into two teams. Gourlay and I were to do *Cioch West* and *Integrity*. Dirk and Mike would do the *Direct* and the *Crack of Double Doom*. We would meet at the top. Gourlay insisted I lead the first pitch. The last time I tried a few years ago I couldn't get off the ground. This time I had the power and control to climb with easy competence. I had the feeling that mind and body, liberated from the shackles of age were really enjoying themselves. Physical competence in my 20s had been great but its return 50 years later was even better. Physical well-being was now a mere vehicle for something much more exhilarating. I was more comprehensively aware of the surrounding world than I'd ever been before; a strange sense of intellectual adventure had arrived. You know these pictures made of incomprehensible wiggly coloured lines that were fashionable a few years ago, the ones if you look into them a certain way, a three-dimensional scene, otherwise completely invisible, appears. It was a bit like that.

We reached the Cioch and sat there for half-an-hour just enjoying being alive. Gourlay was a good companion. He seemed to have a comprehensive practical understanding of how things worked. The old familiar feeling of being outclassed returned and I adopted my accustomed role as pupil, listening to accounts of everything from the deficiencies of the old British

Seagull outboard engine to the working of molecular nano-machinery. He wasn't a boring pedant merely the willing provider of asked-for information

En passant he explained how the brain worked. Ordinary computers, he pointed out, are hard-wired, use electronic current, generate too much heat and have to be programmed. The living brain uses the much more subtle system of ionic current and comes hard-wired with a program already installed donated by your ancestors. We are dragged through the first part of our lives as our inherited program makes us conform to its priorities. As you have no doubt noticed we don't always approve of what our inherited program is doing with us. That is because we have so much surplus circuitry that we are capable of exerting quality control on our behaviour – which of course is over-ridden if it becomes too sophisticated and gets in the way of survival. Our soft wiring is configured by our culture and education and tends to become hard-wired. Dogma is a particularly deep and irreversible conversion from soft to hard-wiring. As you know once you get down to someone's hard-wired dogma, appalling behaviour can result. Here he glanced westwards to the scene where the hard-wired dogma of the psychopathic Calvin had destroyed so many songs and stories. He also muttered: "Alas, poor Harry," presumably referring to the demise of the chap I met so briefly in the CIC hut.

Reclining in the sunshine on the top of the Cioch like an intellectual Bacchus he explained further: Once our inherited program has been run through we, as individuals, are redundant. Our body has done its biological job and is ready to be recycled. However, this is also the beginning of a golden age. Once we are freed from the tyranny of our biological program we are left with a mighty intellectual engine which, biologically speaking, is surplus to requirements. The tragedy is that just as we become free to use these latter-day processing skills our support systems start to fail. The brain is a demanding organ; it needs more oxygen and glucose than other tissues to work efficiently. Like Moses we see the promised land, but don't have the metabolic wherewithal to enter.

He went on like this for quite a bit. I was fascinated. But I won't bore you any more. I know this is a mountaineering journal. I am only trying to describe a day out on the Cuillin as it actually happened.

Back at the climbing we addressed *Integrity*, a well-named climb of uncompromising verticality which previously would have tested me to my limit but now was so well within my physical and mental competence that I sang as I climbed. It was so exhilarating to be operating well within the limits of my ability instead of continually husbanding my aging resources to make them last. We met the others at the top and continued towards Sgurr Alasdair. I really enjoyed the bad step on Sgurr Sgumain; an out-of-balance move I found amusing. The last time I had been there was in winter with Malcolm a few years ago on a windy day with snow drifting around our knees. We didn't have the strength to get up. This time I scarcely paused.

And so on to Sgurr Alasdair and Sgurr Thearlaich. On a spur looking out over the Coruisg side we stopped for a prolonged lunch. Mike explained in his usual matter-of-fact way that life originated as one of the many back eddies in the downward energy flow of the universe on its way to absolute zero. A back eddy by definition contravenes the Second Law and uses energy to create order.

"Life is a self-propagating back eddy, a special type of wave phenomenon," he declared airily pointing to the lichens on the rocks and a passing raven which croaked wisely in confirmation. (This was probably a coincidence.) The particular retrograde surge which produced life configured a chemistry that was capable of utilising energy to propagate itself and to create other retrograde waves of increasing orders of complexity. Imagine a swirl in a mighty river with a standing wave going against the current. Life is the crest of a retrograde energy wave with an edge ruffled like a Mandelbrot set. It is distinguished by each wave, before it dies, harnessing more energy from the ambient universe to generate and diversify yet other retrograde waves of increasing complexity – evolution is, I think the appropriate term. We, he indicated Dirk and Gourlay, are just able to keep our own particular little wave going for longer and we know how to make this psychologically bearable by building on our hard-wired desire to explore the unknown. We are the opposite of Buddhists who strive to put the mind into the neural equivalent of zero degrees Kelvin where everything is still and, as far as we know nothing much happens except happiness. We feel we have more interesting things to do then await terminal recycling with minds in tranquil neutral. Breaking the Second Law of Thermodynamics is, of course, the Original Sin, a capital offence carrying a mandatory death penalty. We have just negotiated a longer stay of execution than most."

Seeing my dismay, he said: "For goodness sake cheer up. Don't you understand that the ability to have a conversation like this is a miracle? It's like making an irreversible move over an overhang into unknown problems possibly beyond our capacity to solve. We are trying to find a route on a new mountain where all the usual rules are invalid, where everything is unpredictable. You must remember what that was like – the exhilaration of pushing yourself into the unknown, the creative excitement of making the great irreversible move. The wild frontier of the fifth age is where the action is. Just think of it, no guide books, no artificial aids, no leaders, no foreknowledge of what is beyond the metaphorical overhang."

We passed the next hour or two in silence and comfortable companionship, each of us utilising energy from the surrounding universe to surf along on the fractal edge of our own little wave. We reassembled ourselves a couple of hours later at what seemed to be the appropriate time and continued along the ridge via King's Chimney and the Inaccessable.Pinnacle and then down the long shoulder of Sgurr na Banachdich to the glen. The weather by then had begun to change, the air turning sultry and close. Tall anvil-headed cumulus clouds approached from the south-west. The sun developed a halo; colour and relief slowly drained from the landscape. Normally, this would have made me depressed but this time I seemed to interpret it as a different sort of splendour.

At the hut I pressed them to stay for another meal, but they just asked for a pot of coffee and then they'd be off.

"We have a lot to do," Dirk explained. "I have to get the ship ready for a new voyage. We are hoping to navigate through a barrier of treacherous metaphors and explore the uncharted seas beyond."

I am not sure what he meant by this. He did smile as he said it. Maybe he was pulling my leg.

Before he left Mike tested my tyres again and left me some stuff I was to take in decreasing doses over the next few days added to a posset of skimmed milk and honey with a grating of nutmeg. He warned me to follow closely the instructions he was leaving and in a few days I would be back to my old self again.

"Sorry about the pun, but here is my card with my e-mail address. Contact me in a few weeks if you like and we can have more discussions about this and that." Once again he waved his hand about airily

As we sat having our coffee, the bad weather front arrived and the rain started. Nevertheless, they insisted on leaving. I saw them to the car. Curtains of warm, grey rain swept past in the special Skye manner and thunder rumbled around here and there in the gloom. We rapidly shook hands. Both Gourlay and Dirk said they hoped to see me again soon. After they got in there was an impressive display of lightning followed closely by a *basso profundo* roll of thunder. Mike must have seen the expression on my face. He rolled down the window and said: "Don't look like that. This extravagance has nothing to do with me. It's too theatrical. I'm embarrassed."

They drove off in a cloud of spray turned silver by a wan shaft of sunshine that momentarily appeared. I ran back into the hut into the smell of wet clothing, tinned soup and someone's burning toast. Mike's card was damp and the print discreetly small. I was about to start looking for my glasses when I found I could read it easily without them.

(My eyesight seemed to have improved.) The card read: michaelscott@aikwoodpharmaceuticals.com.

I really don't know what my next move should be. Contacting them again is tempting, but there are so many practical difficulties in deserting the doomed ship of your own generation.

ALEXANDER M. KELLAS: EVEREST FORERUNNER

By George W. Rodway

INTRODUCTION

Dr Alexander Mitchell Kellas, 1868-1921, a pioneering Himalayan explorer and mountaineer who spent nearly the last 20 years of his working life as a member of the chemistry faculty at the Middlesex Hospital Medical School in London, died of illness during the 1921 British Mount Everest Reconnaissance Expedition. He was born in Aberdeen and educated at Aberdeen Grammar School.

In 1889, Kellas went to Edinburgh to study for two years at the University and the Heriot-Watt College. He then moved on to University College, London, where he obtained his BSc in 1892. Kellas stayed on for several years as a Research Assistant to the chemistry professor Sir William Ramsay (of noble gas fame) at University College before going to Heidelberg University in Germany to study for his DPhil degree, which he received in 1897.

As a boy, Kellas had become fascinated with the hills, walking and climbing first among the Grampians, then later in Wales and on the Continent. This love for the hills drew Kellas to another academic chemist and well known mountaineer in Ramsay's laboratory at University College, London – J. Norman Collie. During the 1890s, Kellas and Collie made several climbing trips together to the British hills and the Alps. It is very likely that Collie was instrumental in introducing Kellas to the possibilities for exploration and mountaineering in the Himalayas.[1]

Kellas remains to the present day a surprisingly unknown figure despite his noteworthy contributions to high altitude physiology and exploration. He was almost certainly the first person to apply state-of-the-art knowledge of high altitude physiology to field investigations at altitudes above 6000m. Additionally, it is extremely likely that he had spent more time above 6000m than anyone on earth by the time of his death in 1921. He undertook no fewer than eight expeditions to the greater ranges during a Himalayan career that had its inception in 1907.[2]

Without doubt, one of the most far-reaching contributions Kellas made to Himalayan mountaineering is that he was among the very first Europeans to recognise the natural mountaineering talents of Himalayan natives, and he was almost certainly the first to rely extensively on them as sole climbing companions during numerous extended high altitude explorations and climbs in the Sikkim and Garhwal Himalaya.

Some of Dr Kellas's obscurity can certainly be attributed to his retiring disposition, not caring to publicise his high altitude physiology and mountaineering accomplishments with other than a few articles in publications such as the *Geographical Journal* and *Alpine Journal*. Many of these articles have been 'lost' to history and are virtually unknown today. As well, unpublished material written by Kellas concerning a little-known proposed expedition to Everest in 1915-16 had resided in the files of Henry R. Kellas (nephew of Alexander M. Kellas) for many decades until John B. West unearthed it in the 1980s while researching the life of Alexander Kellas. West's research led to the first extensive review of Kellas's climbing and scientific achievements to appear in English.[2, 3]

This article aims to not only present in print, for the first time, a portion of the 1915-16 Everest proposal that pertains to mountaineering, but to explore Alexander Kellas's involvement in other important events leading up to the 1921 Everest Reconnaissance. Kellas's 1920 scientific expedition to Kamet in the Garhwal Himalaya will be the specific focus, as the results and conclusions of physiological observations made at high altitude during this venture had important implications for the attempts on Everest in the years that followed. However, it is probably not an exaggeration to suggest that some important lessons learned on Kamet died with Kellas, only to be resurrected several decades later.

THE 1915-16 MOUNT EVEREST PROPOSAL

Prior to the first successful penetration of the inner sanctum of Everest in 1921, British explorers and mountaineers had for more than two decades shown a serious interest in planning a reconnaissance expedition to the mountain. Several months before the initiation of hostilities that marked the start of the First World War, Colonel C. G. Rawling, the surveyor who had identified Everest for the first time from the north during the 1903-04 Younghusband mission to Lhasa, proposed a reconnaissance of Everest from the north to commence in the year 1915. This was to be followed by an attempt on the summit in 1916. Although this scheme necessarily had to be shelved because of the outbreak of war, it had gained the approval of the Alpine Club and RGS, and Kellas drafted a proposal of expedition activities and personnel. Kellas had by 1912 made several mountaineering ventures in the Sikkim/Tibet border area while exploring the region north of Kangchenjunga,[4-6] and was arguably more familiar than anyone with, not only the physical approaches to Everest, but with the physiological problems associated with attempting to climb it, as well. A portion of the proposal for a 1915-16 expedition follows (quoted verbatim):

"Mountaineering: The expedition proposes to examine Mount Everest with a view to ascertaining the possibility of climbing it and to reach the highest point attainable. The experience of the Duke of Abruzzi, Colonel Bruce and others of recent years in the Himalaya has upset many of the old views as to the limits of attainable altitude. It may well be that Mount

Everest is unclimbable on the north side by any mountaineer however skilled, or that, even if the mountaineering difficulties are not insuperable, the altitude makes human advance impossible. These questions however have not yet been settled, and it is the aim of the expedition to do something towards their solution.

Plan of the expedition:

Line of approach: The intended route is a direct one: from Darjeeling to Gantok, the capital of Sikkim, and thence due north to Khamba Dzong (in 1903 the temporary headquarters of the Tibet Mission). From Khamba Dzong a westerly route will be taken until the slopes of Mount Everest are reached.

Area of investigation: The work will be limited to the block of country bounded on the north by the Brahmaputra, on the south by the border line of Nepal and Tibet, and on the west and east by the 86th and 88th meridians of E. Longitude.

Date of operations: The routes out of Sikkim will be practicable about the middle of May 1915, which will allow of the expedition being in the neighbourhood of Mount Everest not later than the middle of June.

Anticipated progress of the work: During the first four months – that is from July 1st to October 31st 1915 – the following work should have been accomplished: the formation of the zoological, botanical and geological collections; the investigation of the deflection of the plumb line, and most of the magnetic and meteorological observations; the triangulation of all visible peaks, and a complete topographical survey of the immediate neighbourhood; a large scale plan of Mount Everest, which, together with the photographs, will show which of the routes hold out the best prospects to the climber. Possibly an altitude of 20,000ft. will have been reached, but it is unlikely that any greater height will be attained during the first year. In November 1915 the expedition will return to India to work out the results of the past season and prepare for a return to the same district in 1916, when the scientific work will be completed and the whole efforts of the expedition will be concentrated upon an effort to ascend Mount Everest.

Personnel:

The leader of the expedition will be Major C. G. Rawling CIE. (Companion of the Indian Empire), Somerset Light Infantry. In addition to important journeys in other parts of the world, Major Rawling has travelled in Tibet on five separate occasions, and in northern Tibet has explored and surveyed 40,000 square miles of unknown country. He was employed throughout the Tibet Mission under Sir F. E. Younghusband, and was in command of the Gartok expedition from eastern Tibet to the sources of the Brahmaputra, Sutlej, and Indus. He is familiar with the Tibetan language.

As medical officer, botanist and entomologist, Mr. A. F. R. Wollaston, if his services are then available. Mr. Wollaston has travelled extensively in the Sudan, central Africa, the Pacific and New Guinea, and had fulfilled the same duties with notable distinction on three separate expeditions.

As chief Surveyor and officer in charge of the survey, plumbline and magnetic operations, Captain H. T. Morshead R. E., Survey of India, whose services have been lent by the Surveyor General of India. Capt. Morshead accompanied Capt. F. M. Bailey in the successful exploration of the lower Brahmaputra and reached to within three days march of Lhasa. He will be assisted by a native surveyor.

As transport officer and photographer, Lieutenant J. B. L. Noel, East Yorkshire Regiment. This officer has had considerable experience on the frontier roads of Sikkim and is familiar with mountain transport.

A meteorologist (with approval of the Director General of Observatories).

An officer or assistant of the Geological Survey of India (with the approval of the Director General).

A Tibetan interpreter from the Magistrates Court at Darjeeling (with the approval of the Government of Bengal).

Three Alpine climbers, one of whom will be Mr. A. M. Kellas. In the Himalaya, Mr. Kellas has made the first ascents of Chomiumo (22,450ft.), Kangchenjau (22,700ft.), Powhunri (23,180ft.), and Langpo (22,800ft.). Two other members of the Alpine Club, and it is hoped that Dr Longstaff may also join this expedition. A Swiss guide will be added who has had experience in Himalayan climbing. The members of the expedition destined for the attempted ascent of Mount Everest will only join during the second season.

A staff of Gurkhas, Bhutias, and Tibetans.

Cost of the expedition:
It is anticipated that the total expenditures on the expedition, including wages, travelling expenses, transport, food, equipment, and instruments will reach 4,500 pounds sterling for the first year, and 2,500 pounds sterling for the second year – a total of 7,000 pounds sterling."

Even though war put a reconnaissance of Everest on hold, whenever the opportunity presented itself during the years of the First World War, Noel would visit Kellas in his chemical laboratory at Middlesex Hospital to talk about Everest. During these discussions, Kellas told Noel "many things that have never been made known about his plans and work concerning the mountain".[7]

In *Through Tibet to Everest*, Noel described Kellas as "a pioneer in every sense. He established new records in Himalayan travel and climbing and in feats of physical endurance. Furthermore, he pioneered in ideas and methods."[7]

Everest Forerunner – Alexander M. Kellas. Royal Geographical Society.

Noel relates how Kellas had "worked out a plan to lay depots of food in uninhabited high valleys west of Kangchenjunga by means of his own trained Sherpas, and of his hopes of reaching Kharta, crossing the river and going up to the eastern glaciers of Everest by the Kama Valley, escaping the watching Tibetans."[7]

Apparently, so detailed was the plan, and so confident was Kellas that he could reach Everest (Noel had seen Kellas's reconnaissance photos of the aforementioned area), that Noel had agreed to accompany him on this adventure "as soon as the War was finished and we could both get away".[7] However, this proposed "furtive private raid", as Noel termed it, never came to fruition after the end of the war. It would be rather intriguing to know what had prompted two experienced Himalayan travellers such as Noel and Kellas to seriously entertain the idea of a "private raid" on Everest after obviously giving careful consideration to the planning of a reconnaissance for 1915. Unfortunately, Noel does not discuss his thoughts regarding this issue in *Through Tibet to Everest*.[7]

Kamet 1920:

Aside from the author's recent article in a scientific journal,[8] no one has revisited in any detail what was the first field study of its type at Himalayan altitudes – A. M. Kellas and Henry T. Morshead's 1920 Kamet Expedition. This undertaking by Kellas and Morshead was unique because it specifically emphasised investigation of the practical difficulties inherent in climbing at very high altitudes. During this endeavour Kellas carried out the first rigorous tests of the value of supplementary oxygen for climbing at high altitude.

Kamet (7756m.) lies in the Garhwal Himalaya on the Indian-Chinese (Tibetan) border approximately 300 km. north-east of New Delhi and roughly 75 km north-west of the more famous Nanda Devi, 7816m. Kellas and Morshead's 1920 visit to Kamet was Kellas's third attempt at the peak, and late arrival of scientific equipment from England delayed their climbing and research plans until well into the late summer and autumn. Their highpoint on Kamet in 1920 was Meade's Col, just over 7100m. Kellas had hoped to use Meade's Col as a high camp for an attempt on the summit and as a platform for physiological studies, but his porters could not be persuaded to camp there because of the excessive late season cold.

In a letter written in February, 1916, Kellas remarked that as preparation for Everest: "A preliminary expedition to Kamet, on which a camp could be formed at 22,000ft. (6705m.) or over would be of great value in order to gain experience regarding effects of prolonged camping at 22,000ft. (6705m.), suitable diet, etc."[9]

He also realised that "the oxygen necessary for the work of ascent is the difficulty" in considering the first ascent of Everest.[9] By December 1918, a few short weeks after the armistice of the war, the RGS had resumed

Jim Lowther on the approach ridge to the Lammergeier Spire, Miyar Glacier, Lahul, India. Photo: Graham Little.

Miyar Nala peaks. Photo: Alastair Matthewson.

official contact with the Secretary of State for India, stressing the need for support of scientific-oriented high altitude exploration. Understanding that an expedition to Kamet was to be organised as the first step in the operations aimed at the eventual conquest of Everest, the Government of India agreed to lend technical and logistical support to Kellas's proposed high altitude physiological investigations in 1920.

Kellas started for Kamet from Darjeeling on June 25, 1920. Morshead joined him several weeks later in the Garhwal. By September 8, the expedition was camped very near the actual base of Kamet on rough glacial detritus at 5639m. Illness of the expedition's porters at Camp 4, at 6400m., delayed progress from September 11-18. A day after establishing Camp 5 at 6700m on September 19, Kellas, Morshead, and three native porters from the village of Mana reached the maximum elevation attained by the expedition, Meade's col, 7140m. (which is the prominent saddle between Kamet and Ibi Gamin). At this point, the porters refused to ascend farther. The group descended to Camp 5 that afternoon, and the next day the porters refused to entertain the idea of moving a camp up to the saddle, alleging that the 'winter storm' was due.

Morshead bade farewell to Kellas on September 22, and turned his steps toward home, his leave from the Survey of India coming to an end and the season now too far advanced for further efforts at the highest altitudes. Regardless of the disappointments encountered during the expedition, Morshead had nothing but praise for the few Bhotia (Sherpa) porters of the higher Himalaya that Kellas had employed: "On rock they can climb like goats, while on ice they readily learn step-cutting. It appears very doubtful if the present-day expense of importing Alpine guides can ever justify their employment in future Himalayan exploration."[10]

Looking for an opportunity to complete several physiological experiments, Kellas eventually settled for a camp at approximately 5486m. on a considerably smaller peak to the north-west of the Bagini Glacier. After a week's worth of experimental work at this location, Dunagiri village was regained on October 16, with Kellas eventually returning to Darjeeling on November 9, after an absence of four-and-a-half months.

Notable scientific results and observations of the expedition included the very first field tests of the value of supplementary oxygen for climbing at high altitude. Preliminary experiments on Kamet at 6400m. confirmed that the oxygen tanks sent from England were unsuitable, but not until Kellas reached the 5486m. camp on a smaller peak to the north-west of the Bagini Glacier (after Kamet was abandoned) was there an opportunity for systematic experiments designed to determine the usefulness of the oxygen tanks for practical climbing work. During the week of work in the vicinity of the 5486m camp, climbing trials with the oxygen tanks were carried out over three different courses. Regardless of the course undertaken, the porters that Kellas managed to enlist for these experiments had consistently greater elapsed times *with* supplementary oxygen from the cylinders than without. He concluded, no doubt rightly, that "the cylinders are too heavy for use above 18,000ft., and below that altitude they are not required."[11,12]

Additionally, tests of 'Leonard Hill Bags' containing Oxylithe also yielded interesting results. Professor Leonard Hill of University College, London suggested that Kellas carry out practical climbing trials using rubber bags containing Oxylithe (sodium peroxide), which produces oxygen when water is added. The most intriguing experiment that Kellas performed with the Hill bags involved continuous breathing from the bag during ascent.

Kellas indicated that during these trials "the gain while using oxygen was quite decisive, the advantage being up to 25%. This again was to be expected, and clearly indicates that light oxygen cylinders…might be of considerable value as regards increase of rate of ascent at high altitudes."[11]

Conclusion:

The 1920 Kamet Expedition provided strong support for the use of supplementary oxygen at high altitude, provided it could be supplied in a relatively lightweight form. After Kellas died on the approach march to Everest in June of 1921, insufficient interest and technical expertise in the oxygen systems guaranteed neglect of the apparatus by other expedition members. Just as the 1921 British Mount Everest Reconnaissance Expedition was catching its first glimpse (quite literally) of Everest, Kellas met his untimely demise due to illness in early June, near Kampa Dzong, in Tibet.[13] George Mallory described the scene of his burial on a hillside south of the village: "It was an extraordinarily affecting little ceremony, burying Kellas on a stony hillside – a place on the edge of a great plain and looking across it to the three great snow peaks of his conquest (Pauhunri, Kangchenjhau, and Chomiomo). I shan't easily forget the four boys, his own trained mountain men, children of nature, seated in wonder on a great stone near the grave while Bury read out the passage from I Corinthians."[14]

Of the other personnel who were listed in the proposal for the 1915-16 Everest Reconnaissance Expedition, Major Rawling became General Rawling and also suffered an early demise when he was killed in the early days of the First World War. A. F. R. Wollaston and H. T. Morshead both participated in the 1921 Everest Reconnaissance Expedition. Wollaston assumed the duties of expedition naturalist and physician, while Morshead was one of the two surveyors that mapped the area around Everest as well as the mountain itself. Morshead was also part of the climbing team (including Mallory, Somervell, and Norton) on Everest in 1922 that pushed through the 8000m. mark for the first time, though Morshead, unfortunately, had to turn back just short of the team's highpoint. Both

John Noel and Tom Longstaff accepted invitations to join the 1922 British expedition to Everest. Longstaff served as the medical officer and naturalist of the expedition and Noel was along as the official photographer and cinematographer. Noel also returned to Everest in the capacity of official photographer and cinematographer for the 1924 attempt.

Thanks to the efforts of George Ingle Finch, the second summit attempt of the 1922 Everest Expedition was able to utilise supplementary oxygen with reasonable success. However, the lessons learned about oxygen use at high altitude during Kellas's trials in 1920 and on Everest in 1922 were not fully applied to subsequent Everest expeditions of the 1920s and 1930s. Not until the early 1950s was supplementary oxygen for use in high altitude mountaineering once again the subject of intensive investigation. Mountaineers were, by this time, prepared to exploit the more efficient supplementary oxygen systems then available, as well as an improved understanding of human physiology, in order to successfully tackle the troublesome 'last thousand feet'[15] of Everest.

REFERENCES

1. Mill C. Norman Collie – A life in two worlds: Mountain explorer and scientist 1859-1942. Aberdeen: Aberdeen University Press, 1987.

2. West J. B. A. M. Kellas: Pioneer Himalayan physiologist and mountaineer. *The Alpine Journal* 1989/90;94:207-213.

3. West J. B. Alexander M. Kellas and the physiological challenge of Everest. *Journal of Applied Physiology* 1987;63:3-11.

4. Kellas A. M. Mountaineering in Sikkim and Garhwal. *Alpine J.* 1912;26:52-54.

5. Kellas A. M. The mountains of Northern Sikkim and Garhwal. *Alpine J.* 1912;26:113-142.

6. Kellas A. M. A fourth visit to the Sikkim Himalaya, with ascent of the Kangchenjhau. *Alpine J.* 1913;27:125-153.

7. Noel J. B. L. Through Tibet to Everest, chapter 5. London: Arnold, 1927.

8. Rodway G. W. Prelude to Everest: Alexander M. Kellas and the 1920 High Altitude Scientific Expedition to Kamet. *High Alt. Med Biol.* 2004;5:364-379.

9. Kellas AM. Correspondence to A. F. R. Wollaston. London: Alpine Club Archives, February 27, 1916.

10. Morshead H. T. Report on the expedition to Kamet. *Geogr. J.* 1921;57:213-219.

11. Kellas A. M. Dr Kellas's expedition to Kamet. *Geogr. J.* 1921;57:124-130.

12. Kellas A. M, Morshead H. T. Dr Kellas's expedition to Kamet in 1920. *Alpine J.* 1920/21;33:312-319.

13. Howard-Bury C. K. Mount Everest: The reconnaissance, 1921. London: Arnold, 1922.

14. Robertson D. George Mallory. London: Faber & Faber, 1969.

15. Ward M. The first ascent of Mount Everest, 1953: The solution of the problem of the 'last thousand feet'. *Journal of Wilderness Medicine* 1993;4:312-318.

THE PEAK OF THE QUARTERS

By Bob Richardson

A YEAR after I left school (working for £160 a year) I had managed to acquire a 'Commando' rucksack, a pair of boots and a groundsheet. My mother made me a sleeping bag from an old quilt and I borrowed my father's Primus stove and a couple of dixies. When my holidays came at the end of May I took the train to Spean Bridge and hitch-hiked as far as Invergarry.

The road was quiet and by the time I had walked to Tomdoun it was getting dark. There was an old stable at the back of the hotel where the road to Cluanie started over the hill. It had no door and a cobbled floor but it was shelter, so I laid my groundsheet on the cobbles and got into my bag. But the floor was cold and hard and after a while I got packed and walked on into the darkness. By the time I reached the bridge over what was then the Loyne River, it was raining hard and I crouched down behind a buttress of the bridge inside my cycle cape. Once more, after a while, discomfort and restlessness got me going again and I rounded the side of Creag a'Mhaim as a faint light was becoming apparent under the cloud.

As I was heading for Glen Affric, I decided to cut the corner and went down the track towards Cluanie Lodge. In those days the glen had not been flooded and I had hoped to cross the river and head directly towards the pass of An Caorann Mor. As was often the case in the Highlands there was a light left burning in the lodge but I stayed well away to avoid awakening the dogs. Down at the river I found it too deep and, uncertain of fording it in the half-light, turned wearily to head back up to the road. Shortly afterwards, I walked into a bog-hole and got soaked to the waist. Back on the road, I skirted Cluanie and turned down the road to the start of the track through to Glen Affric. At least there was daylight under the ever-present mist as I trudged through the pass towards the Youth Hostel at Alltbeithe. The hostel was listed as "open during summer months" but was empty and padlocked. I went over to the old stable at the back to find another cobbled floor. But it had a roof and walls and I could light the stove and cook a meal.

I lay on top of my sleeping bag and tried to sleep but the burn running outside the door played the old trick of sounding like human voices as the wind shifted and eddied. Several times I was so convinced that I went to the door, unfamiliar then with the mimicry that water and wind can produce. Sometime that afternoon, bored and not yet exhausted enough to sleep, I wandered up the slope behind the stable.

I had no definite intentions, just passing time by walking slowly under the mist in a type of landscape that was still strange to me. The slope levelled off after a bit and I found myself in a shallow corrie. Above me the slope steepened again and I thought of going back but continued on up. I climbed into the mist and eventually found myself on a ridge. I had started with no intention of reaching the summit but now I turned left and continued along the mist-obscured ridge. Somewhere along it, cold, fatigued and feeling for the first time that presence which hills have in mist and half-light, I stopped. In my solitary and weary state Sgurr nan Ceathreamhnan had overawed me. I turned back down the hill towards the cobbled floor and the thin sleeping bag. This time I could sleep on the hard floor and the burn didn't talk to me again until the next morning.

Next day, I walked down the glen then up over Mam Sodhail to Carn Eige. Coming down the ridge of Sgurr na Lapaich there was sunshine on its lower slopes. Lying in the sun, looking down on the loch and the pine woods and feeling warm for the first time in two days, I began to think there might be elements of pleasure in this hill-walking business.

Another night on the cobbles and then I went westwards to Glen Lichd and out to the Youth Hostel at Ratagan. The next day I went over the Five Sisters in light mist and occasional snow. Blue sky showed just above my head but the mist was faithful and never deserted the ridge. Back down in the Glen, the local policeman gave me a lift down the road and told me Everest had been climbed. The flags put out at Invershiel for the Coronation hung limp and wet. The next day I went out over the south ridge below the Saddle and down to Kinlochhourn. When I was about a half-mile along the Barrisdale track, I was hailed from the shore by a keeper in a boat who had just landed a couple of lads on their way back from a dance at Arnisdale. He gave me a welcome sail down to Barrisdale and, as there was still plenty of daylight, I continued on to find a bothy at Loch an Dubh-Lochan. The next day I went over the pass to Carnoch and then out eastwards to Glen Dessary. At Loch Arkaig I found the second sunshine of the trip and a road-repair gang. I lay in the sun until they finished their shift and then bounced on the back of their lorry all the way back to Fort William. And that was my first long trip into the hills.

I was back in Glen Affric the next year, at the start of a transit from Cluanie to Dundonnell, but the mist hung over the hills again and I left the Peak of the Quarters to brood under its cover. Over the years, I was conscious that I had unfinished business – but failure has its uses. It did me no harm to have a memory of the way in which I had been defeated, psychologically as much as physically, on that final ridge.

Nearly 50 years later I finally realised that if it were to be done, it were best done soon (if not quickly). This time I came from the north with an over-ambitious plan to sweep the summits from Bidien a' Choire Sheasgaich, then do the round of Loch Mullardoch to finish on the summit of the Peak of the Quarters. I had a bivvy bag, self-inflating air mattress, a good sleeping bag, lightweight gas stove and about four days food and whisky. What I did not have was youth. I went in by the track from Achintee to Bearneas bothy on a very hot day and on the climb up from Loch an Laoigh my plans fell apart. The heat, the decrepitude of age and the weight of my pack combined to tell me firmly that my days of scampering the hills had gone and another day like this might just about be terminal.

As I was lying resting on the summit of Lurg Mor a pair of Munro-baggers appeared, so after a brief courtesy chat, it was off down south-eastwards to cross the river and thread the bogs to reach the track from Patt Lodge to Iron Lodge. Farther up the Allt coire nan Each there is a nice little grassy island which provided a luxurious bivouac site. In the morning the mist was down so I lay in comfort until it began to clear. From Loch Moicean I went south over the bealach and crossed the river.

The ridge over Mullach na Dheiragain and on to Sgurr nan Ceathreamhnan stretched out in front. I climbed slowly to reach the ridge and at last I could see the summit. Coming down the ridge were two Englishmen who were doing the round from Iron Lodge where they had left their bikes. (You're never alone with a Munro.) I wandered on in clear weather to reach, at last, the summit of the Peak of the Quarters. It had taken me most of my life to get there but now it felt like just another summit. There was no elation and I couldn't even be bothered to search in my sack for my whisky supply. Another bivouac (in rain this time), another day and Ben Attow and then the road would lead me to the bar at Loch Duich Hotel. The Peak of the Quarters had taught me two lessons and I didn't much like the second one.

COMING OF AGE ON THE LAMMERGEIER SPIRE

By Graham E. Little

The ageing process is a matter of compromise, about balancing ambition and ability. To pretend it isn't happening is a sure-fire route to frustration and suffering.

Descending to base camp at the foot of the Miyar Glacier, I sensed Jim's disappointment, we had failed on The Orange Tower and I had reneged upon our plan to try the big mixed line on the north face of Point 5760m. Both my physical prowess and my tolerance of risk were in question — in truth my body was tired and my head just wasn't in it. Peaks and rock towers all around us yet we had achieved so little. Jim had every right to be annoyed with me, yet he was both tolerant and philosophical. After all, reaching a top is fine but the icing on the cake, our exploration and appreciation of this magnificent mountain world has the deeper value. All the same, there was a sense of unfulfilled business. It called me, siren like, as I drifted into deep sleep.

The pleasures of family and home are just ten days away and I keenly anticipate them. We have only three days left at base camp before a walkout down the flower decked Miyar Nala. Clearly, we can't just sit around for three days! Our friends, Kevin and Brian, are heading down the valley to do some rock climbing on the flanking slabs. I catch Jim gazing up at the splendid unclimbed rock spire high above the east flank of the Miyar Glacier that had immediately caught our eye on arrival at base camp ten days ago. There really is no debate – we have to climb it! The plan is simple; we will get as close to the base of the spire as possible, bivouac, climb it the following day and then descend. Dan Singh, our head Kumaoni porter, is willing to carry our hardware up to the bivouac, allowing me the benefit of a relatively light load.

The ground leading up to the foot of the spire is much more complex than it appeared from base camp. We are forced to set up our bivouac at about 4800m, well below the foot of the spire and to the south of a rock ridge bounding an apron of wet slabs. Before heading down, Dan Singh joins us in some heavy engineering to create something approaching a level bivi ledge on the boulder strewn slope.

Jim and I agree that it would be wise to undertake an afternoon recce of the approach ridge in preparation for tomorrow's attempt of the spire. The nagging doubts are returning, my base camp enthusiasm is on the wane, but I keep them to myself. As I scramble up the narrow, scree filled gully towards the little col on the ridge above, I decide to adopt a 'pitch at a time' tactic and see how it goes. From the col we solo a short distance until the ridge narrows to a near knife-edge. Roping up, I ease past a perched flake and then climb an awkward step to reach the edge of a wide gap in the ridge. Jim descends to the foot of the gap and dumps one rope and most of the rock gear. I note that the wall on the other side of the gap has no easy line. As we reverse down the ridge, a great bird glides below us, wide wings stroking the air in effortless glide. The ease of the lammergeier's flight contrasts with my own feeling of clumsiness. It is *of* the mountains; I am *in* the mountains.

Our bivi site slips into deep shade as Jim cooks up a splendid dinner of soup, tortellini and smoked fish. We slip into our sleeping bags at 6pm, the clearing sky promising a cold night. Jim is soon asleep. I lie gazing up at a dazzling star filled firmament. I watch and think for hours before gliding with the lammergeier on the wings of dream sleep.

Jim wakes at 5am. I lie white and cold in a sharp frosted bivi bag. Our water bottles are frozen. Jim makes breakfast — the hot fruit tea encourages me to get moving but I eat some noodles with little enthusiasm. The first ten minutes out from our ledge is mind over body stuff as I battle with leaden legs and morning phlegm. However, I soon get into a rhythm. Moving over familiar ground, through the shadows of the sharp dawn light, we return to yesterday's gear cache. Jim leads a fine, long groove pitch out of the gap and I follow with the clumsy sac. Jim volunteers to take the sac and I hand it over without compunction. Clicking into route finding mode, I weave an intricate line up slabs, grooves and chimneys until the angle eases back and snow patches merge into a well-frozen snowfield. I edge and kick up the steepening neve, using my nut key as a surrogate ice axe. After nearly four hours of hard labour we gain the slabby foot of the spire's west face at an altitude of about 5150m. It is a good feeling.

I take the first pitch and run out nearly 60m on beautiful, easy angled grey rock. It is covered with a battery farm of chicken heads making the climbing embarrassingly easy. Jim leads on through to the top of a short vertical wall that defines the obvious gash that separates the lower third from the upper two thirds of the face. Nearly kneecapping myself when a large flake slides off, I climb down into the gash to belay at the foot of a squat pinnacle. Jim climbs a snow/ice groove to a narrow neck on the upper side of the pinnacle. The sun warms us as we swap big boots for rock shoes. I run out 60m up poorly protected but pleasant slabs. Sitting on the exposed belay, a biting north wind chills one side of my body whilst a weak sun warms the other. Gathering clouds soon shut out the sun's rays and by the time Jim joins me I'm chilled to the bone. Jim leads through and up into the 70m corner that is so obvious from below. The climbing is immaculate though much easier than we had anticipated. Donning my thermal top, I carry on to the top of the corner, taking great care not to dislodge a stack of poised blocks at the belay. As I watch Jim climb the final pitch, it becomes clear that the weather is about to break, the midday sky darkening around us.

The summit is perfect, a narrow spine of orange and grey granite, wildly overhanging a snow gully far below that separates our spire from its parent peak. At only 5350m. we are on top of the world! Churning grey clouds soon mask our deep view into the Miyar Nala. It is time to get down.

We down-climb and abseil to the gash in a rising wind and quickening snow flurries. The snowfield gives a soft landing and we swiftly slip-slide to the top of the rocks. Snow flurries merge as I solo down wet slabs and chimneys. In descent, I am in command, the survival gene switching into overdrive. The terrain is treacherous, yet I am in my element. The rock steepens as we approach the wide gap. I wait for Jim and we agree that it makes sense to abseil down into the gully demarking the north side of the approach ridge. A 60m abseil, down wet ropes, takes me through a veil of whiteness towards the grey gully.

It is as in my dream, the great bird drifting past again, it's wide wing feathers heavy with wet snow, unreal and surreal, yet of this place. I am as close as I can ever be to the world of the lammergeier.

Jim and I plunge unroped down the gully, the soggy snow sucking at our tired legs. 'This is the place to climb out', Jim says with absolute confidence. I know that he is right. The steep, icy groove is not easy but we are going home and nothing can stop us. As if pre-destined, we arrive at the notch in the ridge that overlooks our bivi site. Jim starts to down-climb the greasy rock. 'It makes sense to abseil', I insist. He knows that I am right. Soon we are stuffing wet gear into wet sacks and then heading down.

I am tired, and have to fight a strong desire to sit down. Snow covered boulders do their best to break me, but I plug on, just keeping Jim in sight. As we loose height, the terrain gets easier and a strange yellow light settles around me. Jim waits at the lateral moraine but I urge him to press on. As I stagger over the terminal moraine towards base camp, young Homu Singh runs towards me, offering to take my sack. I refuse, but I am warmed by his offer.

Many brews, a good meal and a glass of whisky in hand soon banish fatigue. The effort of a twelve-hour non-stop climb and descent is in the past, our success and return are in the present. There have been many similar occasions in my life, yet this time I have come of age. I have taken many risks yet I am still alive. It is the end of a perilous journey, a journey of seduction and beauty, yet a journey where many friends have died. I know that Jim is pleased with our ascent. It is modest in the greater scheme of mountaineering achievements but it has a perfect feel, as if symbolising all that is best in this crazy game.

Walking down the long stretch of the flower splashed Miyar Nala, I think of many things.

The expression 'quit while you're ahead' comes into my head and puzzles me. I decide that the importance of winning sits at the root of this expression. It is very clear to me that mountaineering is not a sport, is not about winning, but is a way of life. It must co-exist with other ways of life. Striking the right balance between the lives we lead is the key to fulfilment. Age of course must be factored into this balance. Through ageing we gain experience, sometimes understanding and rarely wisdom. Satisfaction and survival come from the right equation of effort, risk and reward. The equation will be different for every individual and is ever changing. I now see the way ahead.

I feel a sense of profound equilibrium at this place in time. A flight of glossy-winged choughs rise up from the dung splattered flats ahead of me. They wheel and call as if complaining about the disruption to their beetle-eating breakfast. This is all new, yet there is a strong sense of deja vu. The walk in, the climb and the walk out — they are the journey of life.

Jim catches up with me and we walk down the valley together, through the resin-rich pines and then across the footbridge to the dusty road-head.

Summary: Thoughts on ageing and climbing plus a description of the first ascent of the Lammergeier Spire, 5350m, above the east flank of the Miyar Glacier, Lahul, India, by G. E. Little and J. Lowther, May 22, 2004.

A GUIDE'S TALE

By Davy Gunn

June 1974:

GUIDING was confined to an elite few within the Glen and these few mostly in the employ of the old fox or his 2ic who was 'Big Ian' Nicholson at that time. Many were recruited on an *ad hoc* basis when business was brisk. Notables being the likes of Fyffe, Spence or Dave Knowles.

At that time I was a mere youth, not tempered by attempting hard men's climbs and harder drinking in the Clachaig's wee snug after hours. One climb above all was revered both from behind and in front of the bar. This was partly out of convenience. Like the hindquarters of an elephant described by Bill Murray, starting only 10 minutes from the bar door 'The Gully' could be accomplished either solo before 12.30 Sunday opening, or roped between two-thirty and six-thirty, usually by a mixed company of barman/maid and customer. It is fair to say 'The Gully' was well known to us.

Walking down the village one Saturday a passing car stopped and the driver wound down his window inquiring if I knew of a local guide for hire. A couple of names were passed to him and the chosen route asked. When the reply came that it was none other than 'The Gully' I offered my services, for a reasonable fee of course.

So I was hired, but not before my clients revealed that they were a professional couple, betrothed, that they belonged to a 'socialist mountaineering club' and were happy to support the local proletariat, but not at excessive cost. We settled on a less than princely sum, perhaps due to my obvious youth and assumed lack of experience which, in reflection, was the correct assumption. I went home to collect my climbing gear.

My kit at that time was by modern standards very meagre, dances, ceilidhs and girls taking priority. So, as an aspiring bergfuhrer I assembled my worn out rack at the foot of The Gully. 300ft No 2 Viking nylon donated by Robin Turner after an abseil lesson off his cottage roof, a pair of new Lionel Terray boots from Hamish, as mine had been stolen from Kingshouse after a rescue in Ravens, and the most modern harness of its age – the ubiquitous Whillans. This, along with a set of nuts attached to wire hawser, a selection of pegs and several slings in bright pink tape concluded the ironmongery for the ascent.

It had not rained for a month but never the less it would not have occurred to me to wear rock boots, even though I had a pair of EBs donated to me by Sandy Whellan's a local policeman. The Gully is a boot climb. That's how Bill Murray did it and you always emulate the footsteps of the master.

We started The Gully at its root via a pitch shown to me only the Sunday before by one of the barmen. This pitch is walked past by most but I thought that, as I was getting paid for the job in hand, a refund might be requested should all available rock not be included in the ascent. It went very well, with the pair climbing very fast and alarmingly competently, in parallel on the twin No. 2 weight nylon ropes. During conversation it became apparent that 'proper guides' were hired on a regular basis by the couple, indeed the previous weekend a 'proper guide' had been secured in the Llanberis Pass for the same rate as I, and three of the classics of the pass including the renowned *Wrinkle* had been successfully ascended.

By now the haze of morning had become a black menacing shroud of early afternoon and soon the occasional very large plop of rain fell. By this time we had passed the lower greenery and had arrived in the more austere surroundings of the crux slab above the 'Great Cave'. The atmosphere was oppressive and it was clear that it was going to become very wet. We passed an 'ICE' roadsign complete with metal post, put there the previous year by some pranksters on a fresher's weekend. The slab was climbed and soon we were at the redoubtable 'Jericho Wall' which at that time was pitch 7 or 8 if you included the lowest pitch. I regaled them with stories of derring do and an account of the early history of the gully, and of course a few rescue stories to enhance the atmosphere. It clearly had the desired effect, as they were keen to push on and seemed apprehensive. This was further heightened when the rain started in earnest and they realised this was a deluge. How quickly the atmosphere changed from overcast and dry, to heavy rain, mist and gloom.

Could the aspirant bergfurher pull it out of the bag without needing the services of the rescue team to which he was apprenticed? Afterburners on and it was all go, as I had no wish for ridicule from Messrs Thompson and Nicholson who always felt compelled to give their apprentice rescuer/ climber a hard time.

Each pitch was dispatched at full speed with a full blown thunderstorm breaking around us and with the prospect of drowning and falling as a combined incentive the pair climbed well, despite being visibly terrified and soaked to the arse. So credit to them as I was feeling a burden of responsibility way beyond my 17 years. We topped out after a five-hour ascent, 30-odd pitches, more than 1700ft. of climbing and in a reasonable time for a roped party of three. Some parties have taken upwards of 14 hours and in one case two full days. For us, all that remained was the knee wrecker down to the pub and a beer by the fire.

Two hours later, a bedraggled crew, we arrived at the pub. They reluctantly bought me a beer (I was underage) and complemented me on a fine, though short, day. As the day was 'shorter than they had in the Llanberis pass', the speed of ascent 'rushed' and the climbing 'inferior', they said they had discussed the fee and felt that it should be halved. So, barely enough cash for a decent piss-up was handed over to the naive bergfurher, who there and then decided that the people's flag was 'brightest pink, and not as red as he might think'. Guiding might not be a career for him after all.

DUNGEON DAYS

By Stephen Reid

WHEN I started climbing in 1978 it was as if I had discovered true
enthusiasm for the first time in my life. Here was a pastime that was really
exciting, well, as exciting as one wanted it to be anyway. So many new
places to discover, so many climbs to do and so many new friends to do
them with! And yet little over a decade later I was seriously in danger of
becoming rather jaded. By then I was living near Penrith and had exhausted
just about all possibilities round about, up to my maximum leading grade.
And though discovering a new route gave the occasional extra buzz, good
new routes at sub-E3 level in the Lake District were as common as hen's
teeth. One winter's evening, as rain lashed the window panes, in a moment
of inspiration, I fetched a road atlas, a pile of guidebooks, and a large
whisky and soda, sat at the old pine table in the kitchen, and weighed up
possibilities for exploration.

To the west lay the Lakes, hardly *terra incognita*. To the south and east,
Lancashire and Yorkshire were if anything even better explored, and the
same could be said for Northumberland in the north-east. To the north lay
the Borders and Dumfries – I'd already had several excursions to Clifton
and Meikle Ross but was not aware of anything much else thereabouts
worth visiting. In fact, only to the north-west was there any glimmer of
hope. Here lay a region that in over a decade I had never heard another
climber mention – the Galloway Hills. A glance through the 1986 SMC
guide revealed a crag with routes four pitches in length, but with only five
of them – the mysterious-sounding 'Dungeon of Buchan'. Reasoning that
any crag so big must have room for at least another line or two, I made an
early start on my next available spare day and drove to Glen Trool intending
to make my way to the Dungeon via Craignaw – a distance that, with my
Lakeland experience, I expected to be a longish but straight-forward day.
However, I soon discovered that a path in the Galloway Hills is not like
any path in the Lakes, in fact, it isn't really like a path at all, and I slithered,
stumbled and cursed my way up the Gairland Burn to the silver-sanded
shores of Loch Neldricken and then on to the craggy summit of Craignaw.

And yet, and yet, and yet... there was an extraordinary magic about the
place: the wildness and the ruggedness and the massive emptiness of it
all. Something about its rawness that immediately touched my soul in a
way the Lake District for all its beauty never had. Like many before me, I
fell completely under its spell. From the northern end of Craignaw I could
not only see the wide wilderness of the Silver Flowe with its glittering
treacherous tear-shaped pools, the Merrick and the Range of the Awful
Hand, and southwards to the deep dark blue of the Irish Sea, but also, to

the north, Dungeon Hill. And though the rapidly disappearing winter day put a stop to any closer approach, I saw enough to know that a return visit would be worthwhile, for the south-east face of the hill was a mass of steep clean grey granite, turned golden by the lingering rays of the setting sun.

All that long summer, Joe Grinbergs and I spent our days off driving north from Penrith and then cycling up and down seemingly endless forestry tracks along the River Dee and Cooran Lane, and in between, sounding out and climbing new routes on the fantastic south-facing cliffs of the Dungeon. What are now recognised to be almost classic (albeit obscure) climbs such as *Heir Apparent* (HVS) with its E3 *Direct Finish, The Colonel's Corner* (HVS), *Incy Wincy Spider* (E2), and *Bannockburn* (E1) were just a few of our dozen new routes. Later on, I visited the crag with others, including the late Dave Wilson who added the impressive *Parcel of Rogues* (E3). Of all the climbs on the crag, it is perhaps *The Colonel's Corner* that most parties of reasonable ability will opt for on their first visit. The initial huge corner pitch is the crux and gives sustained and well-protected climbing, though more than the usual rack of Friends is needed to maximise this. A long mix of slabby bridging and jamming moves leads, without much rest, to a slight respite in the form of a small sloping footledge under a slim groove. Here any number of wires can be placed until one feels safe enough to pull out left with a steep lunge for sanctuary in the form of a good ledge and easier ground from where a fantastic belay is soon reached. Time to pause and enjoy sweeping views of the desolate Silver Flowe with its pattern of pools shimmering in the morning sun like gilded islands, the abode of huge blue and yellow dragon flies, strange white-flowered water plants, and who knows what creatures of nightmare lurking in the depths. The next pitch is straight-forward but logical enough, a wending up the crag by little grooves and short steps to a commodious ledge beneath the highest part of a steep band of granite that bars the way ahead. Numerous interchangeable short lines exist up this band, but the way we went on the first ascent is the best and the most exciting. A crack forms the start, but it becomes unattractively earthy, and is soon quit for the bulging wall/arête on its right where a succession of invisible jugs reduces an apparent E2 to a pleasant VS. On the first ascent 60m. ropes allowed us to gain the final headwall in one pitch, but, for those with more standard gear, an interim spike belay and a heathery scramble saves the day. This top wall is impressive, no more so than to the left where the bottomless free-form flake of *Heir Apparent* and the compelling top crack of *Cyclopath* are enough to make any climber's pulse quicken, but our route lies on the right where two huge stacked rounded blocks test your jamming ability to the full before a short, awkward and highly exposed groove provides a suitably testing key to gaining the fine flat summit with its superb views, north to the Dry Loch and the Dungeon Stone, west to the Rhinns of Kells, and south as far as the eye can see, line after line of dim and distant blue hills, growing ever dimmer as they grow more distant. When we first did the route, my father, whose own climbing career had been cut short by the small matter of having to fight Rommel in North Africa, had just collapsed and died while landing a salmon on the banks of the Tay. The name suggested itself immediately, and I am sure he would take great pleasure in knowing how many people have enjoyed 'his' climb.

In the years since then, I have become rather intrigued that earlier visitors to such a superb crag didn't make more than one or two fleeting visits, and in particular did not pick the obvious plum of *The Colonel's Corner*, which was even mentioned in the 1986 guide as a "steep unclimbed diedre". If one discounts the extensive scrambling activities of J. McBain in the early part of the last century, and the exploratory ramblings of Edred Corner around the same time, the first route recorded on the Dungeon was *Cooran Buttress* by Jim Simpson, Jean Ractcliffe, Gordon Waldie and Mary Shields in September 1955. The route was Waldie's in conception; he had spotted it from the Backhill of Bush, but Simpson, although new to the sport, was the stronger climber, so he and Jean went first, while Waldie brought up the inexperienced Mary on a second rope. Interestingly they graded it V. Diff. at the time, but by comparison with other routes of that grade today, it fully deserves its Hard Severe. Years later Jim returned and soloed the route, but he and Waldie never really felt the urge to explore the Dungeon further. To them, the Highlands and the Lakes held a stronger pull, and Galloway was reserved for off days in the autumn. Indeed, Waldie's tone when he wrote up the climb in the SMC journal of 1958 was almost apologetic.

"The disconsolate climber, enervated by the balmy climate of Galloway and preserving his nails on its lush vegetation, might well consider selling his rope to the Solway boatmen," he began, before admitting that "while tramping the moors in search of good trout fishing" he might just find the chain of granite hills between the Merrick massif and the Rhinns of Kells "worthy of exploration".

Over a decade passed before that inveterate explorer of outback Scotland, Graham Little (then living in Girvan), together with Jimmy Dykes, visited the crag in April 1968, and made the first ascent of *The Highwayman* (HVS), a fact that, being very young, new to the climbing scene, and unaware of the protocol, he didn't record at the time. This superb four-pitch route was done in big boots and with only a couple of sling runners – no mean achievement. Although he vaguely recalls climbing a few other short things around this time. Little only returned once and that was to solo *The Highwayman*. The resulting near death experience when a large

Dave Wilson, belayed by Bill O'Connor, on the first ascent of Parcel of Rogues (E3), Dungeon of Buchan, in 1991. Photo: Stephen Reid.

flake came off in his hands, combined with his impression of the crag as rather vegetated was enough to turn his attention elsewhere. Almost another decade passed before April 1976 when a youthful Andrew Fraser, Donald Gibson and Willie Todd (all teenage school students from Dumfries) forced their way up the vegetated *Cooran Gully* with the moral assistance of 60ft. of hemp rope recently liberated from their Scout Hut and a few pegs. Not being put off by this heathery experience, Fraser returned several times to the crag. An attempt to straighten out *Cooran Gully* was abandoned due to a rucksack containing the vital rockshoes being dropped from halfway up the route. Then, with Todd, Mike Burgess and Davie Walker, he went back in 1978 to climb *Roraima,* a series of variations on Waldie's *Cooran Buttress*, though they were unaware of this at the time. Emboldened by success on this rather overgrown line, Fraser embarked on an ascent of the cleanest sweep of rock he could see, the slabs of *The Highwayman*, though again the team were unaware of the existence of any route there. However, with their minimal equipment and experience, the rounded cracks proved far too scary, and a traverse right was made onto what later became the line of *Heir Apparent*, before finally a long traverse back left was made onto *Roraima* and safety. On another visit, in June 1984, he soloed the superb four pitch *Traitor's Gait* (MVS) before having a narrow squeak when he fell trying to solo *Cooran Buttress* in order to work out how it compared with *Roraima.* Fortunately, he managed to grab the heather ledge he landed on – but understandably it rather put him off returning to the Dungeon, besides which university and work kept him away from the area for many years. When I questioned him recently as to why, knowing how good the crag was, he hadn't gone back, he said that he, and he suspected Little, and latterly the Fotheringham/Whillance, team had all been put off by what they perceived would be a lot of gardening, his ethic at the time being to climb on sight from the ground up. In fact, this was mainly a misconception – certainly as far as Cooran Buttress goes, and of all my new routes done there in the last 13 years, only two required much gardening, and that still minimal.*The Colonel's Corner* needed a large caterpillar of turf removing from the first 20ft. of the first pitch, and *Cooran Chimney* was relieved of a huge turf cornice that overhung the crux pitch. Other than that, all our new routes on Cooran Buttress were climbed ground up on sight, the only other major exception being the E3 Direct Finish to *Heir Apparent* which I top-roped prior to leading, due to the fact that the top half of the pitch, which included the 5b crux section, was completely devoid of protection for about 40ft. Dungeon Buttress was a different matter. Many of its jamming cracks required removal of considerable bilberry growth prior to an ascent. This was not difficult though – a quick abseil with an old ice axe running down the crack lines being all that was required.

Graham Little on pitch 3 on the first ascent of The Highway Man (HVS) in 1968. Photo: Jimmy Dykes.
First ascent of The Colonel's Corner (HVS) in 1991. Stephen Reid on the first pitch. Photo: Joe Grinbergs.

Just before Fraser's solo of *Traitor's Gait*, the strong Lakeland team of Jim Fotheringham and Pete Whillance had visted the Dungeon, cycling in, and staying overnight at the Backhill of Bush Bothy. Fotheringham had noticed the crag while perusing maps of the area shortly after he first moved to the Lake District, and had made a solo visit to reconnoitre the possibilities. However, it took him some time to find anyone prepared to accompany him to such a remote area. When he finally teamed up with Whillance they only did two days climbing there, repeating and naming Little's *The Highwayman*, and also adding two excellent major long new routes, *Cyclopath* (E1) and *Saddle Tramp* (E2), the latter being the first climb on the Lion's Head. Although there were patently further routes to do, including the obvious line of *The Colonel's Corner.* Whillance soon moved on to harder things at Creag an Dubh Loch and Creag a' Bhancair, and Fotheringham became more involved in the Greater Ranges. Somehow he never quite got round to going back until he and I visited Craignaw in the winter of 2001-2 to climb the classic icefall of *Dow Spout* (II) and make the second ascent of *Silver Flow* (IV). (smcj 2003)

Finally, the tale of the Dungeon, and indeed climbing in Galloway, would not be complete without mention of Kenny and Ian Livingston from Castle Douglas. They made an early visit to the crag with a view to rock climbing, but went away empty handed as it was too iced up! It is a rare corner of the Galloway Hills that these two haven't visited, and a glance in the first ascents list of the new guide will show that they had sounded out several crags well in advance of their subsequent development.

By the end of 1991 I had made 10 visits to the Dungeon and, except for the line of *Cooran Chimney* that I returned for in 1993 with Doug Scott (an occasion notable for Doug's bike acquiring a puncture that necessitated him stopping to blow the tyre up every 400 yards on the way back to the car), I considered the place worked out, and started casting my eyes farther afield. To the north, the Tauchers sounded intriguing but our one visit was on such a dismal day that we never even saw the main crag. In fact, unbeknownst to Joe and I, Fraser and friends were developing this remote spot at much the same time that we were discovering the Dungeon. Craig an Eilte on Craignelder to the south yielded a few short routes, but its main wall looked too wet and mossy to bother with, and on Cairnsmore of Fleet, the long Spout of the *Clints Gully* which I climbed as a summer VS in 1992 with Adrian Moore and John Campbell, proved a much better grade V winter climb when I returned with Chris Bonington during a sharp freeze in 1997. But except for that final foray, and a repeat visit with Doug Scott two days later to catch the adjacent Grade IV icefall of *Smear Test*, I figured I had done all that was worth doing in Galloway.

Thus things might have stayed but for a chance meeting in 1999 with John Biggar from Castle Douglas. I had met John once before on the

Dungeon when Joe and I had turned up to what we rightly considered our crag, only to find two climbers busy repeating our new routes – one of them being John. At the moment of our arrival, his partner took a 40-footer off *The Highwayman* when a hold snapped, which luckily for us rather put them off further exploration for a while. But now it seemed John had found a secret crag, or at least a secret craglet, lurking in the woods, close to the road, and not far north of Newton Stewart. He had already done several easier climbs there, but his forte was expedition mountaineering and he had (reluctantly?) decided that a technical rock climber was required for the harder lines. Not knowing any technical rock climbers, he ended up with me instead. So it was that I was sworn to secrecy and introduced to Corwar. This single 30m. high buttress of superb south-facing crystalline granite gave us many happy days of cleaning lines of a thick carpet of moss and pine needles that the crag had acquired when it was surrounded by forestry. Fortunately, John had 'contacts', and the offending conifers had soon gone towards the Euro chipboard mountain, so now the crag is wonderfully clean and also has majestic views through a fine clearing in the woods. Routes soon followed, every one a gem. John had already put up some fine VSs and the heightist *Peach* (graded HVS/E1 depending on whether you are taller than 5ft. 10ins. or not) but there were still lines aplenty. The day we did *Corwar Wall* (HVS) and *Plum Line* (E2) was perhaps the best of many superb days. Corwar Wall was one that John had inspected earlier, but didn't really feel up to leading. A fine pitch with a reasonably straight-forward start to gain a leaning break: here an awkward move of the sort that, having done it you still can't quite work out quite how, allowed the edge of a niche to be gained. A lunge up for a jug and a strenuous hand-traverse before moving up to a resting place all proved jolly exciting, though it has to be said that the gear is brilliant. This is definitely not so on *Plum Line* which was one that I'd inspected earlier and didn't really feel up to leading. The line is cracking – straight up the centre of the buttress at its highest point via a shallow pink groove/niche at half height. The first crux would be gaining this niche and the gear looked poor to the point of non-existence. There was a horizontal hairline crack though and with great reluctance this was compelled into accepting the tips of two knifeblades by dint of a large hammer. To their left, a very shallow sideways wire did nothing to boost confidence, but, after much to-ing and fro-ing, the move was made and the pink niche gained by nose-grinding mantelshelf. Here a precarious rest was possible and a good wire helped to calm a pounding heart. The exit moves were if anything more technical, but better protection kept the to-ing and fro-ing to a minimum and huge holds on the final steep headwall allowed me to show off an impressive technique, noticeable by its absence lower down. Two more extremes to the right of *Corwar Wall* gave equally tricky moments before they succumbed. But eventually, even we had to admit that there was not a line left for us to squeeze in. Dave Armstrong later added an E4, and, in a remarkable re-enactment of the Dungeon/ Tauchers parallel development, while myself and John had our hands full at Corwar, Fraser and Ian Magill ignored the ban (since lifted) on climbing in the nearby Goat Park to surreptitiously develop Craigdews. While they discovered some nice pitches, and the rather broken crag has some good points going for it (like being south-facing and only 10 minutes from the road), it is really their goat-inspired route names that one remembers most, the best perhaps being *Cemetery Goats* and *Goats of Delirium.*

Around this time came a contact from the SMC – a guidebook writer for the Galloway Hills was sought for the next edition of the *Lowland Outcrops* – unsurprisingly there was hardly a queue for the job. Feeling a bit like a minor edition of Graham Macphee (who while writing the SMC Ben Nevis guide in the 1930s checked nearly every route on the mountain from his base in Liverpool), and with only the mildest show of reluctance, and a short lecture from Mr Prentice on not annoying the locals by under-starring their routes, I gracefully accepted the post, and cunningly obtained a vehicle permit for the forestry tracks on the grounds that I was "working in the area", a ploy that I had previously used successfully in Ennerdale. Actually, I should put in a word of praise here for Sandy White who, as Forestry Access Officer, could not have been more helpful or understanding. And the permit meant more than a chance of finding a willing victim to partner me on checking some swamp-bound midge-ridden vegetated horror in the Backhill of beyond. That victim, bless him, was Chris King, a man who I had climbed with a bit in the past. Self-employed like myself, he is more than happy to take days off at a moment's notice given a good forecast. He is also a much better climber than me, a point that proved very useful when he on-sighted Donald Gibson's superb *Delta of Venus* (E4) at Craigencallie, while the guidebook writer required a tight rope the whole way up. Finally, Chris seemed happy to go anywhere and climb anything, even to revisit somewhere like the Tauchers where he had already checked three heather-strewn bilberry-ridden routes only the week before. In short, he is the perfect guidebook writer's climbing partner, and not adverse to an early start either.

To be truthful, I wasn't very kind to Chris, and made him check the Tauchers, Craigencallie, and Clints of Dromore thoroughly, before letting him near the Dungeon of Buchan and its considerably cleaner and more extensive rock. The Tauchers did prove to have one superb route in Rob McAllister's *Behind the Mask* (E1), and a few others that could make a reasonable day, but it is unlikely that this remotest and most romantically wild of the Galloway crags will ever become popular unless vehicular access is allowed along the forestry tracks between Lochs Doon and Dee, and even then it is doubtful. Nonetheless, we dutifully checked every line, returning several times over to catch some of the slower-drying ones in condition. Wellies were *de rigueur* on the approach, and midge-nets as essential as rock shoes.

Respite from ankle-wrenching tussocky walk-ins came when we moved south to Craigencallie. All the major lines and new routes were checked, but though this crag is close to the road it too is unlikely to become that popular as most of its climbs are lichenous. Some routes though are very good, the aforementioned *Delta of Venus* (E4) being one of them. Also worth braving the adders and bracken for are Fraser's *The Empty Quarter* (E2), the excellent *Alligator* (VD), and the exquisite short pitch of *Thumbs Up* (VS).

At both the Tauchers and Craigencallie, we had added the occasional new pitch, but nothing outstanding. Mostly, we had spent many hours checking rather vegetated climbs. The Clints of Dromore though were more fun. Many people (including Waldie) have climbed on these pleasant south-facing granite slabs over the years, but few have left any record. I gathered together what notes I could and then set about repeating everything and filling in the gaps, of which there were plenty. Many years previously I had noticed a small steep buttress near the very left-hand end of the escarpment. Nothing was recorded here and Chris and I quickly covered the face, with route names like *Make My Day* and *Do You Feel Lucky?* punningly inspired by the Clints. The more major area of Central Buttress was also scoured and several pleasant lines added. Finally, and only two years after initial contact, an access agreement was wrung out of SNH. It was time to move on.

After a long day repeating everything on the short buttresses of Loch Grannoch Crag, and adding a few more problems for good measure, I finally had no excuse for not letting Chris in on the Dungeon. Meanwhile though, I had been sneaky, putting up two routes without involving him. Rob Thomas and I had sought out and repeated the original route of the crag, *Cooran Buttress*. This proved to be an excellent Hard Severe and certainly not deserving of its two-line dismissal in the old guide. It also revealed considerable possibilities for variation and so I returned with John Biggar, my wife Jill, and Mathew Thompson who had contacted me because he was staying near New Galloway and was short of a climbing partner. The result was *Cooran Buttress Direct*, a very enjoyable four-pitch VS with a crux 5a move to break through the long roof avoided by the original route on the top pitch. It was a beautiful day, and looking around the coire it was obvious that there were still new lines to do.

The following spring, Fraser announced that he and Magill were intending to visit the crag, and: "Would I like to come?" This pair had recently made the most of unusual winter conditions to snatch *Hell Freezes*

Over (IV), a winter ascent of Cooran Buttress mainly via the summer line of *Roraima,* so it seemed obvious new routes were in the offing and the invitation puzzled me at first, until I remembered my forestry track permit. Thoughtfully, they provided me with a climbing partner in the shape of Alasdair Gillies. The plan was to tackle the complex area of slabs and walls on the far right of the hill that had been designated "The Lion's Head" by McBain. While our first route was eventually summed up in the guide as "an interesting route on top quality heather with a little rock in places", we slightly redressed the balance by climbing the fine hanging arête high in the middle of the coire at a wind-swept HVS.

Meanwhile the 'A' Team, having already put up the three pitch VS of *Aslan*, a rather poor climb to start with but one that builds up to a superb finish, were not to be put off by encroaching dusk, and were spotted setting off up the slabs to the left of *Saddle Tramp* as we headed back to the car. The result was *Horns of a Dilemma* (HVS), the best of the more recent new routes on the buttress. The crux, on the second pitch, involves a rising traverse along parallel crack lines to a point where you have to choose one or the other: this is also the point where you discover the source of the route name. All the routes climbed that day were done ground up on sight, a particularly fine achievement in the case of Horns which involves bold and technical climbing. A month later, an FRCC meet at Newton Stewart provided the opportunity to glean valuable comments on grades and star ratings.It was noticeable that the first went up and the second down in indirect relationship to the commentator's jamming ability. Apart from providing an unofficial taxi service to the crag, Malcom 'Pike' Cundy and I repeated Monkey Puzzle, and then set off up a line of cracks to the left of that route and were pleased as Punch to emerge at the top of the crag with the first ascent of the four pitch *Castles in the Air* (HVS) in the bag.

So by the time Chris King got seriously in on the act it was already late in the year. John Biggar had been eyeing up a slab above the descent ramp from Cooran Buttress more closely than the rest of us, and realised that it contained quite a large expanse of clean rock that could quite easily be persuaded to part with several fine pitches of VS and below. While he and Linda cleaned up lines on what they later christened Silver Slab, Chris and I set off up the ragged crack to the right of the start of *Traitor's Gait.* Four disjointed, but good pitches, resulted in *Snakes & Ladders* (E1), named in honour of the adder which I had almost trodden on at the foot of the crag. It is a moot point as to which of us was most frightened. In October, we were back, checking *Horns of a Dilemma* on the Lion's Head, and going on to add our own climb of *Aughty Star.* This last was inspired by the obvious off-width crack cutting through the roof at the start of the traverse of the final pitch of *Aslan.* Below the off-width was a crack system, and below that a fine groove up the right edge of the initial slab of *Saddle Tramp* – we had our line. A quick abseil to remove some bilberry, and we had soon climbed the first two pitches to the good platform below the top pitch of *Saddle Tramp*. By now the wind had got up and it was bitterly cold, but, fortified by Chris's Friend 5, I set off up to the roof, which was all rather steep and more awkward than I anticipated, not to mention damp. A better climber than myself would have almost certainly overcome it with technique, as it was I just udged. But the udging was hard, and my fingers soon froze. I kept having to down-climb to the stance where Chris was starting to look more and more like a potential hypothermia victim. Spurred on by the thought that it would be highly embarrassing to have to have him rescued by the Galloway Mountain Rescue Team (Leader: Linda Biggar), it was on no more than my eighth or ninth attempt that I finally cracked it, somehow squirming up the extra inch that enabled a crucial finger hold to be reached. Even Chris grudgingly admitted that it wasn't a bad lead. We gave it E2 for the guide, though to be frank, it's anyone's guess. Later, we added a gentler and much longer alternative top pitch, taking a counter diagonal line *to Horns of a Dilemma*, and reducing the grade to a pleasant E1.

Later on, in October, John and Linda continued their development of Silver Slab, their best route being the rather extraordinary *Sprauchler's Groove*. This gives a sustained pitch of some of the most awkward VS crack and slab climbing I have ever done, protectable only by cunning cam placements.

Meanwhile, my final new route on the crag was to be yet another multi-pitch affair. Intrigued by a superb wide jamming crack just right of the start of Cooran Buttress, abseil inspection revealed independent climbing the length of the crag finishing up a groove in between the top pitches of Traitor's Gait and Cooran Buttress Direct. December was perhaps not the best month to choose for the ascent, for although a crisp, clear, and midge-free day, it was bitterly cold with verglas on the rock in places, but I was mindful of the pending expiry of my forestry track permit. In any case the climbing was not that hard, being easy VS, with the crux of each pitch well protected. *Bickerdike's Buttress* was named in memory of John Bickerdike, friend and fellow SMC member, whom I had been on two expeditions to Greenland with.

A period of hard freeze that winter allowed Fraser, Biggar, myself, *et. al.* to indulge in a tidying up and sorting out of various icefalls in the Galloway Hills, the most notable probably being Fraser and Magill's *The Lang Scot's Miles* (IV) on the Merrick, though the most memorable day for me was introducing Alan Hinkes to the delights of the classic *Dow Spout*, and then sitting by the Dow Loch at its top, not far from the summit of Craignaw, while he took a call on his mobile from Kathmandu. Towards the end of the summer, Chris King and I returned to Craigdews to pick the short plum of *Nanny State* (E2), the thin crack up the central slab of the crag that can be so clearly seen from the road – naturally it was Chris's lead. But really the guidebook was done, the manuscript sent off for editing to Davison and Prentice, and, all of a sudden, a most enjoyable chapter in my life had come to an end.

There are 270 rock climbs in the Galloway Hills section of the new Lowland Outcrops guide, a four-fold increase over the previous edition of 1994. Of these, I have climbed all but a dozen or so, and most of those that I haven't done are either insignificant, overgrown, untraceable, or all three. Moreover, I have had the amazing good fortune to have been 'in' on the first ascents of more than 100 of them. Little did I know what I was starting when that wet evening 15 years ago I sat down at the kitchen table with a pile of maps and guidebooks. It has been great fun to be sure, but more than that, it has been a real privilege.

Acknowledgements:
I am most grateful for the help of the following in compiling this article (though needless to say, while the information may be theirs, any errors are entirely mine): John and Linda Biggar, Jim Fotheringham, Andrew Fraser, Graham Little, Kenny and Ian Livingston, and Jim Simpson. I would also like to thank all my climbing partners over the years, and in particular John Biggar, Joe Grinbergs and Chris King, without whose company exploring the crags of Galloway would have been a lot less enjoyable. Finally, I would like to thank Tom Prentice and the SMC for giving me the opportunity to contribute to the guide.

Bibliography:
A Gallowegian Wander, Edred M. Corner (SMC Journal 1900-1901).
The Merrick and the Neighbouring Hills, J, McBain (Stephen and Pollock of Ayr 1929).
Rock Climbs in Galloway, A. G. Waldie (SMC Journal 1958).
Climbers' Guide to Central & Southern Scotland, Jerry Handren (SMC 1986).
Galloway Inner Sanctum, Graham Little (SMC Journal 1991).
The Dungeon of Buchan, Stephen Reid (FRCC Journal 1992).
Lowland Outcrops, Tom Prentice, Grahame Nicoll *et. al.* (SMC 1994).
The Spout of Clints and Smear Test, Stephen Reid (FRCC Journal 1998).
Dow Spout, Stephen Reid (SMC Journal 2003).
Lowland Outcrops: Rock & Ice Climbs, Edited by Brian Davison and Tom Prentice (SMC 2004).

A TALE OF THREE ACCIDENTS

By Adam Kassyk

COINCIDENCE is a funny thing. Lightning isn't supposed to strike twice in the same place, never mind three times. And yet...

The events described in this article occurred on three consecutive trips into the hills, more than 10 years ago. The first occasion was a weekend in January, which I spent at a cottage in Ballachulish with a group of climbers from the north of England. After a long day on the Ben I opted for a less challenging climb on the Buachaille the next day, and paired up with a lad called Nick with whom I'd never climbed before. We set out on an exhilarating morning. The sun sparkled on hard frozen snow and the air was crisp and penetratingly clear. The invigorating weather and the certainty of good conditions seemed to lessen the usually serious atmosphere of the Scottish winter. A hard climb the day before meant a late start, and perhaps a slightly more complacent attitude.

I was keen to climb Shelf Route, long an ambition since I had read Bill Murray's *Mountaineering in Scotland.* At a little step below the Crowberry Basin we met two climbers descending. One had been hit in the face by a big chunk of ice, and we commiserated with their misfortune to be forced to descend so early on such a perfect day. They asked for assistance to lower the casualty down the pitch, and it was nearly an hour later when we resumed our upward progress. It never occurred to us that this might be some kind of foretaste of what was to come. It was well after midday when I arranged the first belay in the icy shade at the foot of Crowberry Gully. When my turn came to climb I found perfect Glencoe conditions of neve bonded like concrete to the rocks. Above the first vertical wall I emerged onto a steep little snowfield. My partner was belayed above, part way up a very steep rock corner. An attractive snow ramp led round the corner to the right from my snowfield, actually the correct line for the Shelf, and I called up that we should take this route. In any event a party higher up the corner was sending a continuous stream of ice blocks down, making it a most uncomfortable place - and increasing the risk of a bloodied face, like the stricken climber we'd met below. Nick agreed, and set up an abseil.

I put a sling round a block, clipped my end of the rope in, and looked up to watch my companion complete his preparations for descent. I saw him lean back, and then time seemed to slow momentarily as he tumbled outwards in a slow motion with a shocked expression on his face. He bounced off the wall, gathered speed then shot past me, hit a projection like a springboard at the foot of the snowfield and shot into the air turning a full somersault before disappearing in free fall down the vertical drop below. The full impact of his fall must have been on the gully bed below, because when the slack rope came tight on my sling, I felt very little tension.

My immediate reaction was that he could not have survived a fall like that. Images of what I would find below, and of the aftermath, haunted my mind. I became pre-occupied with the question of whether to re-arrange the ropes so I could retrieve them after I descended. Somehow, recovering the ropes seemed pointless. With numbed emotions I prepared to descend. Once the abseil was ready I called down, in the rather unlikely hope that there might be some reply. A seeming deathly silence met my anxious calls. But then, to my great surprise and relief, a faint cry floated up. I rearranged the abseil so I could retrieve the ropes, and descended with my heart in my mouth, eyeing my abseil spike with wary caution.

I found my partner sitting in a hole in the snow. I didn't stop to ask whether he'd created it on impact, or it had already been there. His face was purple and blue, and his helmet was badly dented. I suspected his head might be as well. He was able to answer questions, and it was clear that he had lost consciousness briefly on impact, and might have a fractured skull. I quickly established that apart from extensive bruising and associated pain, there didn't appear to be any other obvious injuries, though his ribs hurt badly. I made him more comfortable, and talked to him, noting his reactions. He seemed lucid and I realised that his condition was improving, if anything. It was now late afternoon, and Nick quickly agreed to try to descend, belayed from above by myself, rather than wait for a rescue. However, there would be a clear risk of him passing out again as he stood unbelayed while I descended, and I looked around for some assistance.

Just at this point a party of three climbers appeared, roped together and moving alpine style, traversing across the steep snowslopes on the flank of North Buttress. I hailed them, to discover to my surprise that they seemed to be more relieved at having come across us. They had come up the lower part of North Buttress, were now lost, and were looking for Curved Ridge. Nor did they know the way down from here. There was some mutual benefit in joining forces, so we agreed that I would show them the way down, and they would help by securing my companion after each rope length of the descent.

My partner managed the descent surprisingly well, but the three assistant rescuers turned out to be a mixed blessing. They were reluctant to down climb and wanted to be lowered as well. Since we came across few belays on the lower part of the mountain I had to make it very clear that after events above I didn't want to rely on marginal abseil anchors any more than was absolutely necessary, and they had to down climb, whether they liked it or not. After six hours and ten rope lengths of painstakingly slow descent we reached the Waterslide and the path with some relief. The walking wounded was now walking remarkably well, without support, and seemed much recovered. I handed him over to his friends for the long drive to Leeds, where he checked into the hospital to be examined by a doctor who confirmed there were no serious injuries, and remarked how lucky he was to have escaped without any greater damage.

As to why the belay anchor came out when he abseiled, we never did find any satisfactory explanation.

Four weeks later I was making the long drive north from Manchester again, this time with an old friend who I hadn't seen for years. He shall remain anonymous for the sake of his reputation. As we caught up on the past, it transpired that he had never climbed on Ben Nevis, despite having made first winter ascents in the Alps and been up to 8000m. without oxygen. This serious omission from his CV was put right the following day with an ascent of Observatory Buttress. The Ben was in a suspiciously benign mood – the weather was settled, there was plenty of ice, we even found the occasional belay. Everything was just about as good as you could hope for. We descended Number Four Gully, far too early in the afternoon for a normal day in winter, with a sense of relaxation and achievement. The churned up windslab high in the gully gave way to icy neve as we dropped below the upper limit of the recent thaw.

It's a great pleasure to linger, and savour the high mountain atmosphere on those rare occasions one finishes a climb with time to spare. I paused in the dip by the lochan for a while, and then became aware that my partner had disappeared from view. It seemed a little strange that he had descended the snow slopes below so quickly. I sensed an odd disquiet as I looked down the sweep of icy snow, to where it disappeared from view into the left hand of the two gorges that drains Coire na Ciste through the lower rock barrier. My disquiet increased as I cramponed down the brick hard snow, to the lip of the gorge. Below me, the recent thaw had melted back the massive depth of the snow in the gorge to create a gaping chasm. There were seracs with vertical walls some forty feet high, and a waterfall somewhere deep in the abyss. Just where the snowslope narrowed and steepened into the gorge, a crevasse had formed across the full width of the slope, about a metre wide and two or three metres deep. My companion, looking very shaken, was trying to climb out of the crevasse, with some difficulty, having lost his axe.

It turned out that, having descended the windslab to the lochan, he had applied alpine thinking to the situation, and decided that since the snow should get softer with the loss of altitude, he could take his crampons off and glissade. Unfortunately, this being Scotland, the snow got icier instead (as so often happens when you climb all the way to the corrie on perfect alpine neve, only to find powder and crust on the cliffs). He had lost control of the glissade immediately, lost his axe trying to brake, and was well on his way towards terminal velocity and an untimely end. He was only saved from the icy jaws of the Ben by the appearance of the aforesaid crevasse.

All this had happened in a matter of seconds, which explained why I had noticed nothing.

Thankfully he was able to walk, but I still went through the usual checklist of questions, to discover quite a lot of minor damage, including possible cracked ribs and some worrying pain in his neck which restricted head movement. He effected a self rescue unaided, though rather haltingly and painfully, still visibly shocked at his brush with the grim reaper. It was a very thought provoking drive on the way south the following day. None of my friend's injuries were serious, though the damage to his neck took a long time to heal. He wasn't the first Himalayan veteran to have come to grief on the Ben. And sadly, since then, not the last either.

Another six weeks passed, to find me setting off from Glen Nevis, with the intention of climbing the North East Ridge of Aonach Beag alone. I might have been forgiven for assuming that I was unlikely to be involved in someone else's accident on this occasion. The mist was low and thick, and ridges, snowfields and gullies floated in and out of the fog. None of them matched my impression of what I was looking for, and I eventually gave up trying to locate the start of the North East Ridge, and found a direct way to the summit, up a vast snow field and a narrow arete.

The top of Aonach Beag proved to be a thoroughly disorientating place. Despite the mist the early spring light was uncomfortably strong, and with my eyes screwed up against the painful brightness it was even more difficult to tell where the whiteness of the snow ended and the whiteness of the sky began. Finding the col to the north, to Aonach Mor, was the proverbial needle in a haystack - a point feature surrounded by hazards for the unwary. At one stage I had to pace out three sides of a triangle, to establish the true angle and aspect of the slope - a real navigational challenge.

From the col I set out, counting paces for company, to cover the mile to the summit of Aonach Mor. I was saved the need for a sweep search for the summit cairn by the presence of a group standing beside it, four spectral figures in the shifting mist. The unreality of the situation was increased when they insisted they were on the summit of Aonach Beag. I disagreed, but they continued to insist. Eventually we agreed to differ, and I left them to the consequences of their navigational hypothesis. I retraced my steps for a short way along the ridge, then found the steep snow slope which led down into the upper part of Glen Geusachan, towards Glen Nevis. Coming out from the mist for the first time in several hours, I emerged into a bleak glen hemmed in between the walls of the Carn Mor Dearg arete and Aonach Beag, the lansdcape reduced to a dull monochrome by the thick mist and limited winter light. At the foot of the last snow patch I stopped to remove crampons and put away my axe. There is a moment, at the end of every winter season, when you take your crampons off for the last time. I lingered, reluctant to descend and leave behind this shadowy, fleeting landscape.

As I sat there, I became aware of a very faint sound, like birdsong. I sat very still, and strained to hear it against the wind and the sound of running water. There was something odd about it, for I did not associate birdsong with this high winter landscape. As I packed my rucksack, I felt uneasy. There was only one other thing it could be, and I couldn't go down without being sure. I dug out my own whistle. I couldn't remember what the international distress signal reply was, but I reasoned that it didn't matter, any regular and unmistakeably patterned sound would do. I sounded six blasts, and waited. Sure enough, a repeated sound was faintly carried and dispersed on the wind. A four letter word crossed my lips as I realised with a sense of *deja vu*, trouble again.

The south flank of Aonach Beag above me was a vast wall, crossed by a continuous barrier of broken cliffs, riven by gullies, shrouded in the mist, and an unfriendly place at the best of times. The sound came from somewhere in this complex and inaccessible area. I set off up the hillside, and in about twenty minutes I had spotted a figure in blue close to the cliff base, on some rubbly ledges. Thankfully he was easy to reach. The casualty was quite lucid, and I went through the now routine checklist of questions. He had a broken ankle or foot, and some other minor injuries. I learned he had fallen after becoming disorientated trying to find the way down. He had been sitting on these ledges for some time, and was now hypothermic. I gave him an extra jacket, some food, and made him as comfortable as possible. Then I set off to call out the rescue, running in plastic boots down the never ending descent to Glen Nevis. It took me an hour to get to a telephone, and it was a few hours later before the helicopter passed overhead to take him to the Belford Hospital.

Later, he wrote to me to say he recovered well and hoped to be back hillwalking. Afterwards, I realised that I was almost definitely the only person to have passed down that glen that afternoon, and I would have never heard the whistle if I hadn't stopped for some silent contemplation.

With hindsight it's always possible to analyse cause and effect. Certainly all three incidents were the result of a combination of circumstances, and some degree of human error. Yet what is striking is not the coincidence of timing, but the fortunate accidents of chance that prevented each incident from becoming a tragedy.

DANCING WITH STICKS

By Phil Gribbon

THIS is a tale of two stickies. They came and they went by chance. I had Sticka, and she had Stic an Dubh.

I had crossed the alpine cow pasture descending quickly to get food from the car parked 1000m. below at the Col de Saint Sorlin. I knew that my metabolism could falter without adequate calories, the first incipient symptom being a hammer-clasping of toes inside my boots and for which the impracticable cure was to walk backwards. I regretted that my breakfast in the frigid hut had been skimpy scraps hurriedly forced down in the pre-dawn light in a rush to get out and assemble the instruments before the sun came slanting and scorching on to the glacier.

It had been an excruciatingly chill night in the metal box, if designated perhaps appropriately as a Laboratoire de Glaciologie; this night of scientific dedication was just another factor that was helping to sap my reserves of energy. Now with the thermometers and radiation meters hopefully ticking away automatically, I could abandon the desolate site and flee downhill. I crunched off across the sparkling filigree of ablating surface crystals, stopped to listen to meltwater trickles seeping musically downwards, and glanced appreciatively at the vapourous scarf banner trailing gently off the summit of the Pic d' Etandard. It was time to go. Little did I know that Sticka was waiting for me on the pasture.

There was no sign of the cows anywhere on the open ground, but what was that in front of my path? A whitened sliver lay stretched on the grass sideways across my path. Naked to the core, stripped of every trace of bark, devoid of all her cambium, it was a freshly pared branch of a scrubby tree brought up by a patient herdsman to whittle while he watched his grazing beasts. Just what was needed, just the right length, thickness, weight and balance to make a good easy-to-carry walking pole, and better still, grown of nature's material and for free. With delight, with no doubt of her gender, I picked her up and admired the carefully carved grooved channel ringing her stem. You're mine now, Sticka, come with me to the hills. On a nearby scree and rock jumble an inquisitive marmot, perching stiffly upright and watching, whistled its note of acquiescence.

Later came the weekend when the lethal rains tracked hundreds of miles across Europe bearing the radioactive detritus from the stricken Chernobyl reactor to the far fringe of our westernmost mountains. Unaware, and as always out of sight and out of mind, they wandered higher up the slopes of Druim an Iubhair far above the rush of waters coming down from the great rocky corrie of Garbh Bheinn. It may have been springtime in Ardgour, with the call of the cuckoo in the freshly greened birches, but pockets of old snow still lurked in the recesses of its gullies. There were climbers of rocks over there. The sun held warmth and promise but showers were creeping across Loch Linnhe, sweeping a skiff of light rain over the hillsides. Coming up a grassy bowl and close to the ridge they came on a shepherd's crook, walking stick size with a genuine horn handle, just right for leaning on with a distant dreamy expression of contemplation, but now lost, abandoned, and age-mellowed and glistening with rain film laced with radioactive dust. Here lay Stic an Dubh, a helpmate for Sticka in a good Gaelic sort of way.

Twenty years went by, fleeting and passing, both rough and smooth, in their one-way passage through time. Faint memory fragments may be available if still stuck in cerebral cells, ready to be flushed along the neurons.

Quickly Sticka became a natural stravaigher. Although cut from a subalpine thicket and fated to whack the cows, Sticka now had been adopted to be a wild wandering companion. Ahead lay many moons of striding o'er hill and glen; sometimes these were memorable outings yet often it was run-of-the mill occasions, full of pleasure in their own right but building up into a generalised mental construction of a lifetime's intimacy with a mountainous microcosm of the highlands of the world.

Sticka had many jobs to do in her role as a long leggy prosthetic third limb and in her function as an advanced triangular zimmer prototype. She provided balance and support as I cautiously waded and prodded step by step across the hidden boulder-strewn bed of many a dark river gleaming faintly in the dusk. I wasn't too sure of the validity of the triangle of forces at work as her tip was rigidly plonked against isolated rocks amidst a swirling stream as I hopped dynamically from stone to stone, hoping there was always another semi-submerged stone to take me to the far bank. One skidding slip and I would be in deep doodoo, poised to tumble headfirst into undesirable wetness, one good bang on his head and he would float off downstream; it would be no problem for Sticka, she was buoyant, in a manner of speaking, but it never happened. Nonetheless, the flat metal ferrule at her tip with minimum friction on smoothed pebble surfaces provided sufficient confidence to sustain momentary equilibrium. Perhaps a splayed wooden tip would have been more stable but then her useful life would have been abrasion limited. It was a question of longevity and the used shotgun cartridges, red, blue or green, that I collected in quantity provided tip protection and better still they were just the correct dimensions to fit snugly over her tip.

Of course, such homemade ferrules didn't last long but there were plenty more lying about in pigeon-infested woods, grouse butts, and sites of pheasant massacres. Besides few of the high technological spring-loaded, telescopic, collapsible, basketed, buffered, metal-alloyed aid walking poles have golden brass replacable varicoloured tips. Sticka felt quite the model for an environmentally sustainable future, if shooting continued and trees were around to sop up nasty unfriendly gases.

There was another negative point about flat ferrules; they can't dig into hard néve, they can't chop steps or brake simple slips. However, they do add spice to a winter ridge walk, when an iceaxe should be a *sine qua non* implement. One of those recent winters when only the highest ridges hold remnant wraithes and brief white snowfields he took Sticka on an escapade to the far summit of Buachaille Etive Beag. Silly old fart, I thought, scuttering along an increasingly narrowing and icy ridge, the valley was far below but the summit was getting closer. The dice was rattling in its cup; would it toss and spin? A gamble based on a thin length of ageing wood gave false security and it was little better than nothing. I had lots of confidence able to win out the day, if treated with caution, so on I went with every nerve a-jangle and a sixth sense fluttering to every nuance. Tap the cairn, give thanks, and remember most care is needed in descent.

Early summer days were so different. It was a time of year when reluctant Munro compleationists are forced after years of procrastination to get out and get it over with, and then find themselves in limbo and blighted with what next to climb and tick. It is often prompted by erstwhile friends who chiefly wish to have a hooley on the heights to terminate someone else's addiction. They mark the big day by gobbling scrumptious cake through dram-washed teeth, and weaving the dance circle to ghettoblaster reels echoing over the Rough Bounds of Knoydart. There are strange sporting activities too. A roadside skier having been captured and persuaded to lug his downhill boards to the summit of Sgurr a' Mhaoraich overlooking Loch Hourn. Those capable soon took flight wearing his oversized boots to do a few stylish turns on the crystal mush of a remnant snowfield. Sticka stood ramrod stiff surveying the frolics with her chilly cartridge tip stabbed into the snow.

Celebrations over and spurred by a spurious sense of achievement they raced erratically down to the road by Loch Quoich. As the compleater engaged a gear and drove forward the unfortunate Sticka was placed in a Sir Walter Rayleigh cloak gesture across the path of the moving car. Inevitably the rounded wood was crushed between rocky road and rubber treads spelling trouble with a soft splintering splush. Sticka had been transmuted from squat solid staff to short seamed stick with her terminal six inches fanned into a brushy appendix fit only for the chop. Undaunted she still had many leagues to go in a new guise.

However, her existence was not always a bed of roses of gentle walks and exciting routes. There was one task that conscientiously fulfilled the useful role of a wombling scaffy prodder of littering articles thrown away by thoughtless, if selfrighteous passersby. Juice cartons, crisp packets, fag filters, chewed gum splodges, sweetie wrappers, poly bags, rubber objects, snapped laces, rusty apple cores, slowly fading orange peel and blackened banana skins were common fare, but their anathema was

Top left. Garbh Choire Mor, Braeriach snow beds – August 24, 1997.

Top right. Below Sphinx Ridge – September 17, 1996.

The Sphinx Ridge site in 2003 – snow melted on August.23, Photos: David Duncan.

reserved for those scrumpled wads of tissue paper, soft pink, sky blue, lime green or off white, that lurked in allegedly hidden recesses beside a path. Flick, prod, push, bury, removed from sight. Now walk on, hawk eyes sweeping the ground. Where is the next affront to environmental sensibilities?

Now that Sticka was shorter she had become more amenable and suitable for carrying in the sack, when required. She may have resembled a disguised radio aerial jauntily protruding skyward but she was out of the way and both hands were free to grasp rough gabbro indents or schisty pinches. Of course, there were snags, like the inability to toss a climbing rope in a back flick into a belaying waist stance without several spaghetti-like failures, or the limitation in tackling overhangs in damp chimneys. When sackbound there was always the risk that she would jump and decide to return to the bottom of a pitch when least expected.

We had not intended to get into the Thearlaich Dubh gap but the desired route had not appeared where we expected it so we had pottered on into a *cul de sac* cleft between twin walls. What master polisher had got his abrading fingers into the grooves slanting up the ridge? It had never been this way in our youth, but hordes of scuffling feet had stripped away any satisfactory holds to produce a frictionless bathroom tile texture. While we lingered and prepared our gear a strange rattling stone symphony accompanying a flung rope came tumbling into the gap to be followed by a rapidly-descending abseiler.

You are one of our admirable members, said we, and who is your pal? We were too late for their conversational answer as they floated up the short side, suggesting that they were frantically trying to complete the Cuillin Ridge before the forecast rains came.

With my leader ensconced above, the sack with its pallid aerial waggling on the wall was hoisted upwards. Mere optimistic faith had been expected to keep her balanced in the bag, but with an extra applied heave she left her home and leaped down the face spinning and singing her tremulous tone before tumbling out of sight into the dark northern abyss. This must be the time to say goodbye to Sticka, I thought, and moved cautiously to the edge of the gap. No, there she was lying retrievably on a chockstone. Hello, naughty Sticka, and don't do that again. The rain slowly started to filter down as she was hauled up tightly strapped in this time. It was all about to be the most undelightful day for climbing as the cats and dogs began pelting down.

Her last outing had taken Sticka to the veritable edge of the abyss. Few walking tourists have not approached the curving abruptness of the friable pitchstone cliff that stops uncannily at the brink of absolute nothingness. Beyond is unsubstantial air whence only dark birds dare to go, their domain the sweep of land that broaches from the far Cuillin to the tip of Ardnamurchan, all bound by blue shades of sky, mountains and ocean.

Missing a great day on the hill – Ling Hut Work Party taking a break from internal painting – Allan Davidson, Dave Broadhead, Willie Jeffrey, September 1994. Photo: Dave Broadhead.

Do not scamper, he thought, at the top of the Sgurr of Eigg! Feel a wee sense of a touch of the void. Top tap the concrete obelisk with the wand, mutter a prayer, circle circumspectly three times as goeth round the sun, turn your back and return to the shore.

I didn't enjoy following the gouged path downwards, the black claggy peat splodging out of falling imprints, splattering upwards in squirts of eroded muck. Why do the growing hordes of visitors follow in each others footsteps? It is the same on many Munro, Marilyn, or Uncle Ben Corbett an all with deep trenches and serpentine paths created on every worn popular hill in the land. Humans are not sheep that must follow each other in mindless plodding. Everyone is born to create his own trace in the world. Go gently and do not leave a footprint behind. Life is more than another tick in the book. We both felt about it much the same.

The end of Sticka and Stic an Dubh was unpremeditated and unexpected. They lay side by side on a wooden pallet on the pier at Mallaig. When the car returned to collect the baggage the sacks were packed away but the stickies were unintentionally left behind, alone, forlorn, now lost but not in a sense forgotten.

They may have drifted off with the next tide. Shipped on board a trawler to the discordant call of the gulls in flight over the rattling hawsers and the salted screeching machinery, wafted out on the scruffy pallet, pitched into a dripping hold, clobbered with blue plastic boxes, bedded down under lovingly folded nets, unwillingly bound for the deep waters of the Minch.

Their fate perhaps was to be cast quickly upon the waters, there to sink downward or to drift eastward, their choice to landfall on the barren shores of the lochs of Heaven or Hell.

Then again perhaps they had sailed away, and returned on the ferry back to the Small Isles. Thoughtfully dumped on the new elaborate pier at the Isle of Eigg, they would have looked for someone to claim them and accept their offer of shared companionship. They were waiting to join again into that fitful and seemingly endless dance across the hills of home.

WARMER CLIMATE AND SCOTTISH SNOW

By Adam Watson

ONE of the main attractions of Scottish hills is that they are snowier and icier than hills of the same height in England, Wales or Ireland. Their northern position brings them closer to cold air from the Arctic and Scandinavia. Since the late 1980s, however, winters have become milder, and skiing and winter climbing poorer. Snow patches in summer are smaller and less numerous, and fewer of them survive till winter.

Until recently, many people had heard of global warming but doubted it. Now there is no doubt. Since 1970, Arctic sea-ice has declined in area and thickness, and Arctic land has warmed at twice the average global rate. Six of the UK's hottest years on record have been since 1989. Glaciers are in rapid retreat, and skiing on some Alpine glaciers had to stop in 2003 because the heat wave exposed bare ice.

The Editor sought an account of events so far. After a review of climate change, I emphasise skiing because there are long runs of data, and snow patches because they are familiar on our hills and I have studied them.

Climate change since 1900:

Studies of climate change use many years of daily observations on surface air temperature, wind-speed and direction, sunshine, and rainfall. This is complemented by other data such as the widths of annual growth rings in trees, ice cores from the Greenland or Antarctic icecaps, and glacier advance or retreat. Snow patches respond more quickly to climate change than glaciers, and have been increasingly studied in a number of countries.

Since about 1920 the world's climate has warmed (e.g. Hulme and Jenkins). The rise globally and in central England has been 0.6˚C. The rate of warming has also increased, now 0.2C per decade. Continental land has warmed more than maritime Scotland, because land absorbs heat more than water.

A paper by Parker and others reported a cold period at the end of the 1800s and the start of the 1900s, substantial warming between 1920 and 1940, slight cooling of the northern hemisphere between the 1950s and mid-1970s, and warm conditions almost everywhere in the 1980s except in Greenland and the north-west Atlantic. In line with this, Parker and Folland noted cooling in north-west Britain since about 1960, especially in northern Scotland, and surface air temperatures on land showed a slight negative trend between 1967 and 1986, amounting in Scotland to -0.25C per decade or -0.5C overall (Jones). In the late 1980s the manager of a Scottish ski centre sought an overdraft from the company's bank, but the bankers were concerned about reports of global warming, and the manager then asked me for technical advice. After I sent the manager the scientific papers that showed slight cooling and he passed them to the bank, he got his overdraft.

Since then, Scotland and the rest of Britain have warmed substantially. Because the surface of the seas around us has warmed, winds from the Arctic or Russia are less cold than they used to be. I suppose that bankers would now less readily give overdrafts to Scottish ski companies.

The *Monthly Weather Report* of the Meteorological Office gives mean air temperature and other records at many stations. John Harrison of Stirling University analysed records in 1964-93 at eight Scottish stations, including two in high villages at Braemar and Leadhills. He reported a shift to a run of mild winters since 1987-88. Maximum and minimum temperatures had risen in winter, and yet more in spring. Summer temperatures had increased at almost all stations, and only in autumn was there little change. He found a trend to less sunshine and more rain in the west half of the country. Mayes reported heavier winter rainfall in the west, as far eastwards as the Monadh Liath, Drumochter and east Loch Tay.

Harrison wrote of "a remarkable cluster of years since 1987 with snow cover well below average" and a trend at most stations towards fewer days with air frost. Westerly winds blew more frequently and strongly in winter. He and others report a reduction in the average number of days with snow lying since the 1970s, at a rate of 12 days per decade.

Trends to warmer wetter winters and springs, and to more Atlantic gales have continued since 1993. Take the monthly mean air temperatures for Scotland in November 2003 to February 2005, for instance, and compare them with the 1961-90 mean (from Weather Log, in the Royal Meteorological Society's journal *Weather*). In November 2003 the temperature anomaly was +2.2C, and for December, January etc +0.4, +1.4, +1.2, +1.3, +2.1, +1.5, +1.0, +0.2 in a wet dull July, +2.0, +1.3, — 0.2, +1.8, + 1.6, +2.2, and +0.9 for February 2005.

The North Atlantic Oscillation helps us understand and explain our weather. The NAO index rests on the gradient in winter atmospheric pressure between a coastal site in the Azores and another in southwest Iceland. When there is a high anticyclone in the Azores and a deep depression at Iceland, the pressure difference is big and the index strongly positive. This produces a major Atlantic influence in north-west Europe, characterised by mild air, rain and strong winds as in the winter of 2003-04 and most of the 2004-05 winter. When the pressure difference is small and the index negative, a Continental influence produces a winter with cold air, low precipitation, mostly of snow, and less wind, with extreme cases in 1947 and 1963.

The 'oscillation' in the NAO comes about because the index oscillates over many years, runs with a positive index being followed by runs with a negative index. These oscillations have fluctuated around a long-term mean, but since the late 1980s the index has been atypical in being positive for far more winters than usual, and in reaching high positive peaks not observed hitherto. Wilby and others found that the number of blizzard days in Britain was negatively correlated with the index (e.g. few blizzard days when the index was high), and "changes in the atmospheric moisture budget over the North Atlantic since the 1960s, in particular after 1980, have contributed to the wetter/milder conditions in Scotland".

In October 2004 the Press reported abundant rowanberries, which a few folk at Scottish ski centres regarded as a portent of a snowy winter, but this was wishful thinking. The old wife's tale is that nature supplies many berries so that birds can survive the winter. Extra wishful thinking in Press comments last autumn was that an unusually early and big invasion of bullfinches and waxwings from northern Europe into Scotland was a sign of early snowy conditions soon to hit us.

Ignoring the auld wives' tales, the Meteorological Office last October predicted a milder-than-average winter for Scotland on the basis of the NAO, and stated that the prediction in the past had proved right in two winters out of three. In the event it did turn out to be milder than average.

In November-January the Azores anticyclone stayed unusually far north and blocked easterly winds from Russia. Atlantic depressions were forced round the north end of the anticyclone and caused mild air to raise midday temperatures in Moscow, Oslo and Helsinki far above normal. Also they sent strong gales, which caused much damage to houses in Scotland. In the Swedish boreal forest, normally subject to calm conditions in winter, one gale blew down the equivalent of three years' felling of timber. As each depression moved east past Scotland, it pulled in anticlockwise northerly winds from the high Arctic, bringing snow to Scottish lowland and hill, but usually only for a few days until the sou-wester blew again.

For a month after about February 10, there came a change, as very cold air from Siberia broke through to the whole of Europe. Just afterwards, the Azores high had moved so far north that it pulled in air from Greenland, which maintained the pool of cold air over Scotland. Snow lay continuously even on lower hills, and sometimes at sea-level.

In mid-March the Atlantic oven opened again. On March 15, it was still cold, and a ski manager at Glenshee was preparing pistes. Next morning the temperature had soared, and at Ballater rose to 19C with a severe gale blowing out of a cloudless sky. Much of the snow vanished within hours. By April 3, I had never since 1942 seen Lochnagar with so little old snow for that time of year. It looked more like July 3.

Skiing, winter climbing, and other snow sports:
Attempts to develop downhill skiing in Scotland failed in the 1930s, but four of the five Scottish ski centres began and expanded during the cooler 1960s-1980s. The fifth, at Aonach Mor, started in 1989 during a mild winter, and has struggled since, as have the others. The annual mean

temperature anomaly for Scotland (relative to the mean for 1951-1980) was above zero in the 1950s except for two years, whereas in the 1960s it tended to be lower, yet lower in the 1970s, and was below zero in four years of the 1980s up to the cold 1986. Surface sea temperatures around north-west Europe and Greenland in 1971-87 were up to 1C lower than in 1951-60. Hence Scottish winters had more snow in the 1970s and up to the mid-1980s.

In these decades, heavy snowfalls usually became consolidated, because freezing soon followed the brief thaws. Since then, there have still been heavy falls, up to an extreme of 75cm at Ballater on February 4-5, 2001 with a south-easterly storm, but the soft unconsolidated snow melted quickly in mild gales and heavy rain soon after. Good weather in recent years has seldom lasted throughout a winter day on high hills, and gales are so frequent that settled conditions for a long day's trip have become uncommon.

The milder winters have seriously affected Scottish ski centres, culminating in Glenshee Chairlift Co. having to sell its Glencoe centre in mid-winter 2003-04 and declaring bankruptcy in spring 2004. During autumn 2004, agents announced that the managers of Glenshee Ski Centre had bought the business, but they received very little taxpayers' money compared with other centres, and face a difficult crucial first two winters. At the end of January 2005, they told the Press that they were desperate, but the snowy month that came in mid-February saved them.

The number of skier-days (e.g. 10 skiers on two days amounts to 20 skier-days) fluctuates from one winter to another, with peaks in snowy winters and troughs in mild winters, but the general trend was upwards from the 1960s to the mid-1980s. The all-Scotland total of skier-days rose greatly from the early to the mid-1980s, peaking at 655 000 in 1986.

Then it reversed. Mackay Consultants had forecast that the total would rise from 707 000 in 1986-1987 to 1,009 790 in 1991-92 and that expansion of existing and new centres would be needed. In the real, not fantasy world, the totals for these two seasons proved to be 615,000 and 149,000! The three poorest, 1991-1992, 2002-2003 and 2003-2004, had roughly 150,000 each.

Instead of the occasional poor winter being quickly followed by snowy ones, since the late 1980s there have been more runs of two or three poor winters in succession. So far there has been no run of four poor winters at any ski centre, but 2004-2005 up till mid February was a fourth, and unless April is very good the recent winter is unlikely to be a shining success.

The number of skier-days is strongly and negatively correlated with the year, i.e. the later the year, the fewer the skier-days. As the total of skier-days plunged downwards, so did figures at each centre, save at the Lecht where they showed a slight upward trend in recent years when the others fell. Some expected the Lecht to be bankrupt first, because its runs lie at the lowest altitude. In this review it would be a diversion to explain this apparent anomaly fully. Reasons include smooth terrain and no boulders, thus allowing skiing on thin snow and also the effective trapping of blown spindrift by snow fences.

By dividing the number of skier-days at each centre by the total of Scottish skier-days, one can calculate each centre's slice of the total cake. The biggest percentage drop has been at Cairngorm centre, and the only increase at the Lecht. Comparison of percentages at each centre with the year reveals a strong negative correlation at Cairngorm centre.

There is a strong negative correlation between the percentages at Cairngorm and the Lecht, and a weaker one between Glencoe and Aonach Mor. These are associations of events, not necessarily cause and effect. Nonetheless, it is reasonable to suggest that certain centres affect others adversely, through competition for dwindling trade.

I have no quantitative data on ski-touring, but I am sure about the poorer conditions. Conditions on Aberdeenshire farms, woods, riverbanks and even sea-beaches used to be good for a few days each winter, and sometimes for weeks. I wrote (*The Scotsman*) that in most winters in the 1960s to early 1980s: "There were days when I could put on skis beside my house and skim for mile upon mile by the River Dee, or through woods where deep snow lay heaped on the trees. Each winter I had good afternoons skiing on low moors and hills such as Clachnaben, as well as excellent conditions for ski-mountaineering in the Cairngorms" and The Mounth in almost every winter. In recent years, tours on lowland have seldom been possible, and excellent conditions on high hills have been all too rare. Others tell me the same.

Snow conditions for sledge-dogs have worsened. The Aviemore Sled Dog Rally has had to use wheels in recent years, and again for some of its 2005 meet. The secretary of the Siberian Husky Club of Great Britain said (*Press & Journal*, 21 January 2005): "We have been running for more than 20 years – we keep trying to find snow and we never get it these days."

John Coyne near Banchory has recorded days when he trained his dogs on snow. During most winters in the 1970s, snow lay for most of the season, and he noted this in 1984-1985 and 1985-1986 at the start of his log. Since then, his daily records show 1995-1996 as best with 45 days, but two seasons had only four each, one had seven, two had nine, and 2004-2005 only one day up to January 31.

The milder winters have disrupted snow and ice climbing. *The Scottish Mountaineering Club Journal* for 2003 reported: "The winter of 2002-2003 will not be remembered as one of the great Scottish winter seasons….The West in particular suffered from a real lack of snow." And the 2004 Journal mentioned "lack of any significant snowfalls until late March (when it was too late)".

Snow patches on Scottish hills in summer:
In 1938 I became interested in snow patches and in 1974 began a standardised survey on land east of the A9. If visibility was good I included other hills to west Perthshire, Ben Nevis and the north-west Highlands, but haze, mist or rain sometimes hid them. John Pottie described a useful different method, noting in 1973-93 when the last snow in Coire nan Laogh of Ben Wyvis melted as seen daily from his home at Gollanfield. The date varied from mid -June to late August.

In my survey, the highest patch at the start of July was almost at the top of Ben Macdui, and the lowest at 600m south of the Lecht in one year. The density (i.e. number or total length of patches per sq. km of ground) was biggest in corries below the highest tops, the latter being too exposed to hold deep drifts. Each summer the longest wreath lay north-east of Ben Macdui. At the start of July in snowy years, it stretched more than 3km from near the summit to the hillside north of the Feith Buidhe waterfall. In the least snowy year, 2003, it was only 200m long, confined to the upper part of the corrie.

The number of patches at the start of July varied in 1974-1989 from 144 in 1981 to 2896 in 1977, and their total length from 5700m in 1976 to 91 900 m in 1983. The smallest number since was 31 in July 2003. The amount declined greatly from month to month, the mean number in 1974-89 being 1218, 281, 64, and 19 at the starts of July to October respectively, and the mean total lengths 40,300, 82,000, 15.000, and 400m.

The main factor accounting for variation in the number or total length at the start of August and later months was the number or total length at the start of July. Summer weather had little influence, save in rare exceptions where fresh snowfall substantially delayed the melting of old snow. In an extreme case, only two small patches remained in the hot late August of 1976, and I expected them to vanish. Then a severe snowstorm in early September buried them into October, ensuring their survival.

Data on snow were compared with temperature, wind and precipitation at Braemar and Aviemore. By correcting for known changes with altitude, we estimated the temperature, snowfall, and wind speed and direction at the higher altitudes where patches lay. Because most snow on Scottish hills falls in strong winds and then drifts on to sheltered lee slopes, the measure 'snow drift' gave an estimate of the directional supply of snow. The number and total length of patches at the start of July were correlated with winter and spring temperatures, and with calculated amounts of spring snow drift.

For 1974-2004 I have analysed the number of patches at the start of July on the plateau and high corries between Ben Macdui and Cairn Gorm, which is the snowiest part of the UK. Statistical analysis showed strong negative correlations with the year, i.e. a trend to fewer patches. The number of patches was positively correlated with the total of skier-days over the previous ski season, and with skier-days at Cairngorm and Glenshee centres.

Snow patches that survive till next winter:

Some snow on Ben Nevis and the Cairngorms was regarded back to the mid 1800s as permanent, not vanishing within living memory. Manley (*SMCJ* 1972) gave a useful historical account on long-lying snow in Observatory Gully at Ben Nevis. He evidently lacked personal experience of snow at Garbh Choire Mor on Braeriach, and understated its persistence relative to Observatory Gully. In the *SMCJ*, Berry recounted a year's study at Garbh Choire Mor, but incorrectly stated that snow vanished in 1947. Scottish mountaineer and Arctic explorer, Pat Baird, erected a weather station in 1955 north-east of Ben Macdui summit and studied the nearby snow patch. Between the end of April (maximum) and the end of September 1956 the vertical depth declined 'by over 27ft. – but there was still a foot or two left' as fresh snow fell.

In 1971-1996 I found all snow survivals east of the A9 and on Creag Meagaidh. The highest patch to survive in the Cairngorms was at 1255m. on Ben Macdui, the one studied by Baird, and the lowest at 935m. on Ben Avon facing Tomintoul. Many patches survived till winter in some years, e.g. the total length of them on my survey area amounted to 1210m. in 1983. Since 1996, John Pottie, David Duncan and I have extended coverage to all of the Highlands, and an annual account in *Weather* describes this.

All Scottish snow melted in September 1933, early September 1959, October 1996, and late August 2003. In 2004 only one patch survived till lasting snowfall, in the Cairngorms. Although fresh snow can fall in August or September, it usually melts quickly. To find the date of the first lasting snowfall requires frequent observations and sometimes extra trips to check whether fresh snow has melted. Since 1974 the earliest date has been 6 September 1976 and the latest 5 December 1983.

On Ben Nevis the most persistent snow lies at the top of Observatory Gully, on a sloping shelf covered with boulders, from the east wall at the foot of Gardyloo Gully westwards underneath the wall towards Tower Scoop. A less persistent one sits at the foot of Point Five Gully. Another has been largely overlooked and yet may be as persistent as at Observatory Gully, and has been recorded by us only in the last few years, below the north wall of Aonach Beag. On 20 October 2002, when snow had fallen, it exceeded the one at Observatory Gully. Snow at Aonach Mor often survives till winter in Coire an Lochain, and again the exact sites have been recorded only in recent years.

The UK's most permanent snow lies below Sphinx Ridge in Garbh Choire Mor, so deep that it covers much of the lowest pitch of the ridge in summer, including the hardest moves for a climber. The second most permanent snow sits nearby, below Pinnacles Buttress. Ciste Mhearad on

Cairn Gorm is the next most persistent snow-holding corrie in the Cairngorms. Snow has survived in one or more years at many other places in the Cairngorms, and sometimes on other hills including Lochnagar, Ben Alder and nearby Geal-charn, Beinn a' Chaorainn in Glen Spean, Creag Meagaidh, Sgurr na Lapaich and Toll Creagach. There are other hills where snow has survived more rarely.

Most of the surviving patches are in deep hollows facing northeast and to a lesser extent east or southeast. Much snow blows into these hollows from high ground to the south and round to northwest, especially with the prevailing wind from southwest, and avalanches contribute further snow at hollows on or below steep ground, including Ben Nevis, Aonach Mor and Beag, and Garbh Choire Mor. Very few surviving patches face west.

Most glaciers during the last glaciation faced northeast and carved out deep corries and other hollows with cliffs, which now trap blown snow and avalanche snow. Most corries have easterly aspects, especially the deepest corries and tallest cliffs, such as on Ben Nevis, Aonach Beag, Loch Coruisk, An Teallach, Creag Meagaidh, Loch Avon, and Lochnagar. Snow below tall cliffs that face north or northeast receives little sunshine and melts slowly, such as at Observatory Gully. Secondly, rounded slopes and plateaux towards the prevailing southwest wind are too exposed to hold much snow, so it blows into sheltered corries on the lee side. Thirdly, summer sunshine from the northeast occurs in the morning when air has cooled overnight, whereas sunshine from south round to northwest occurs during midday and afternoon when air has warmed.

Seton Gordon noticed in 1912 that snow at Garbh Choire Mor built up because of drifting from Braeriach plateau behind the cliffs and from a big gathering ground on the Moine Mhor to the southwest. Other examples with broadly similar features are Observatory Gully, Coire an Lochain of Aonach Mor, Coire Ardair, Coire Domhain on Cairn Gorm, Garbh Uisge Mor and Garbh Uisge Beag on Ben Macdui, and the eastern corries of Beinn a' Bhuird.

Three of us studied surrounding topography at 24 locations where snow patches survived in one or more years in 1974-89 (Watson, Davison & French). We wrote, 'A striking feature at surviving patches is the light wind or calm there, even on windy days. They are usually sheltered from prevailing southwest winds, and at some sites from almost all directions. The shelter is localised, such that there can be a gale only 50m away.' We used three topographic measures, fetch, topographic rise and leeward slope, measured for each of eight directions round the compass. For fetch we measured the distance of relatively flat ground, for topographic rise the total vertical rise of terrain, and for leeward slope the total horizontal distance of leeward slopes, in each of the three for 10 km upwind.

The number of years that snow survived at each location was correlated positively and significantly with fetch to the north-north-west and west-north-west, and with leeward slope to the south-south-west. Other analyses that combined different wind directions and topographic measures accounted for most of the variation in the number of years that snow survived. This still left some variation unexplained. We think that the highly localised topography of the snow-patch hollow itself may explain that, but this has not been studied.

REFERENCES:

Baird, P. D. (1957). Weather and snow on Ben MacDhui. *Cairngorm Club Journal 17*, 147-149.

Berry, W.G. (1967). Salute to Garbh Choire Mor. *Scottish Mountaineering Club Journal 28*, 273-274.

Gordon, S. (1912). *The charm of the hills*. Cassell, London

Harrison, J. (1997). Changes in the Scottish climate. *Botanical Journal of Scotland 49*, 287-300.

Harrison, J., Winterbottom, S. & Johnson, R. (2001). Climate change and changing snowfall patterns in Scotland. *Research Findings No 14*, Environment Group Research Programme, Scottish Executive Central Research Unit.

Hulme, M. and Jenkins, G. (1998). Climate change scenarios for the UK. Summary report. *UK Climate Impacts Programme, Technical Report 1.*

Jones, P. D. (1988). Hemispheric surface air temperature variations: recent trends and an update to 1987. *Journal of Climate 1*, 654-660.

Mackay Consultants (1988). *The future development of the Scottish skiing industry*. Unpublished report to Tourism and Leisure Division, Scottish Development Agency.

Manley, G. (1972). Scotland's semi-permanent snows. *Scottish Mountaineering Club Journal 30*, 4-15.

Mayes, J. (1996). Spatial and temporal fluctuations of monthly rainfall in the British Isles and variations in the mid-latitude westerly circulation. *International Journal of Climatology 16*, 585-596.

Parker, D. E. and Folland, C. K. (1986). The nature of climatic variability. *Meteorological Magazine 117*, 201-210.

Parker, D. E., Jones, P. D., Folland, C. K. and Bevan, A. (1994). Interdecadal changes of surface temperature since the late 19th century. *Journal of Geophysical Research 99*, 14373-14399.

Pottie, J. M. (1995). Scottish snowbeds: records from three sites. *Weather 50*, 124-129.

Watson, A. (2004). Disappearing mountain snow patches confirm warming trend. *The Scotsman*, 10 November, p.19.

Watson, A. Davison, R.W. and French, D.D. (1994). Summer snow patches and climate in North-east Scotland, UK. *Arctic and Alpine Research 26*, 141-151.

Watson, A., Davison, R.W. and Pottie, J. (2002). Snow patches lasting until winter in North-east Scotland in 1971-2000. *Weather 57*, 374-385.

Watson, A., Pottie, J. and Duncan, D. (2003). Five UK snow patches last until winter 2002-03. *Weather 58*, 226-229.

Watson, A., Pottie, J. and Duncan, D. (2004). No Scottish snow patches survive through the summer of 2003. *Weather 59*, 125-126.

Wilby, R. L., O'Hare, G. and Barnsley, N. (1997). The North Atlantic Oscillation and British Isles climatic variability, 1865-1996. *Weather 52*, 266-276.

A MOVING EXPERIENCE

By David Adam

THE pilgrimage had started on The Curtain. Queuing for communion service on Sunday morning at the pulpit of some vast and cold cathedral. Their Bibles were guidebooks with neat ticks or circles on each chapter that they had completed. Journeys there and back again were etched into that personal code, not even a date was scribed, no sign of the epic struggles that climbers seem to be able to recall. When I was young, I had a bird book with a tick list, once you had spotted a new bird you ticked it off and then it was forgotten history. Some climbers are like that.

"What's it called, Dave?" said Paul in a doubting Aberdonian tone, in between sucks on a barley sugar. "Em, I think it's something called, Fawlty Towers."

I couldn't be sure because the guidebook wasn't too sure either. Well, with a name like that it's got to be fun, anything to cheer us up during this foul Ben weather. The traipse up from the hut was in an easterly gale full of icy grit and the sudden shelter of the Douglas boulder was quiet and reassuring. Paul ploughed on upwards, through chest deep powder, to what looked like the initial groove line. The big, black owner of the boulder flew overhead with half a branch in his beak, a Noah's ark throwback in negative. "Barley sugar, Dave?" the offer was welcomed alongside grim thoughts of choking to death on this sugary carbuncle if I happened to fall off. "It's only grade two, in the guide." I spluttered. Experience had soured the imaginary bond of kindness between the mountain and the guidebook years ago. We had no guidebook with us and I was relying on vague memories gleaned from an abandoned one lying on the hut table that morning. One with precise tiny circles next to all the trade route climbs that the owner had worshipped on.

"This must be it, twenty feet right of West gully" I said, feeling like some displaced treasure hunter ready to dig for glory. Steep groove lines are not usually in the grade two category, but after all, this was the Ben. It was nice to feel some ice under the ever impatient front points after floundering around down there in snow that always seemed to encourage excuses to stop and go home. The groove opened up and steepened, my barley sugar had melted in time with the ice and I was scratching around on bare rock. The smell of metal on rock tingled through every nerve. This shouldn't be happening on a grade two. I whacked the Vertige into the one and only ice boss left, some two feet above me. Moved up on a wobbly leg and pulled out the axe at face level. A mad rush of water gushed out of the pick hole, like a demented garden hose. To get this far only to be the first man drowned on The Ben. Face, gloves, sleeves and oxters were soaked. Bung the hole, bung it. Desperate floundering and bridging to escape the oozing solved the problem, over the ice bulge and breast stroke thrusts sunk into deep snow above, led to a heavenly cave. A feeling of womb like insulation ensued and I crunched up what was left of my barley sugar. From my quiet nest I could spy the service in progress, out across on Cam Dearg the cave shrine was busy.

Stepping out left from the cave now, an escape from the bedlam of twisted ropes and a jostling, uneasy second, easier progress in true gully style was made. A further slabby groove offered up precarious high stepping and bridging. The Ben's tight lipped rock offered no cracks for protection and the ever scanning eye found no comfort in an ancient peg, just bare unwelcoming solidarity. Paul, who was still wondering what route he was on, came bounding up in desperation.

"You didn't waste any time there" I said.

"Dave, I'm bursting," came the exasperated reply.

"Eh, what do you mean?" I enquired, with a hint of suspicion in my voice.

"I need to empty my bowels now and can't wait" said Paul.

"Didn't you think about that this morning?" I said.

"I didn't need then," came the impatient reply. Unfortunately, we were in full view of our friends across on South West ridge, who were hassling us to take a photo of their leader at the crux move. A convenient deepening in the gully was chosen and contingency measures were thrown into action, involving dubiously removing one rope end and tying it on to the shoulder straps of his rucksack, so that he could remove his harness and perform.

"Will that be strong enough, Dave, I'll need to lean back on it a bit" said Paul.

"Can you take a photo?" shouted Mike from the South West ridge.

"No, we can't, he's having a crap." I bawled back at him.

"He's what?" said Mike, in a stretched Lancastrian accent, still struggling on the crux.

"He's having a crap," I shouted. Meanwhile, an embarrassed Paul emerged from the gloomy spindrift looking much better for his ordeal.

"I hope that you haven't mucked up any gear," I said. He had managed all this without taking his harness off.

"Naw, but that spindrift fair freezes yer backside", came the shivering reply.

Back in the groove I was stuck, well and truly stuck. My right knee was wedged like a chokestone in a wide crack below a final bulge. It wouldn't move at all and my left crampon was scratching on the opposite wall. Thoughts of how the rescue team might have to perform open-air surgery up here flashed before me. All the aerobic contortions that I could imagine were put into action, twisting, pulling, wiggling, all to no avail. Would a hydraulic ram fit into that crack? What about the cheap washing-up liquid down in the hut, that might slide it out. God, my knee could be here for ever. Thrutching up onto the flake gave my left crampon some grip again and I managed to put some weight back down on the knee. Pain had started and a cold dreary sweat had taken over. There's no way out of this, just a farce, a crazy cock-up from start to finish. Logic tried to step in. Treat your knee like a big hex. that's stuck in a crack, I said to myself push it back in the way it came and squeeze down. Don't want to leave it here, not on The Ben. It worked, it bloody well worked, my Scots bred meaness hadn't left me yet! The leg popped out all in one piece to great applause from my belly who quickly mounted the offending flake snout in a friction embrace. The freed right leg bated the crack again and The Ben snapped like a jumping dog but failed to bite. Paul came up, axe at the ready to amputate above the knee, I think he just might have.

Abseiling into Douglas gap was a dream and freedom, wallowing deeper and deeper into the soft comfort of thigh deep powder in West Gully. The sermon on The Curtain was over for the day, yet two climbers approached it. Helmets with head-torches on, the candle-lit procession for mid-night mass had begun. Down at the hut, a tented village was sprouting. Two dark skinned, oriental looking chaps were busy building a huge wall of snow around their tent. Paul and I shared brief, knowing stares and simultaneously blurted out,

"Eskimos"

Back in the hut, two huge rucksacks were taking up all the room on the bench.

"Oh, ye'd betta get thae boys in ere, it's their sacks, see," came the explanation from a Geordie prowling about. I marched out and whistled on the Eskimos, gesticulating about sacks and their removal. "Move now, sacks, yes." not the politest of welcomes, I suppose, if you've just flown in from Canada. Down they came and struggled with these massive sacks, squeezing them through the door. Time for the proving question.

"Eh, where are you from then?" I enquired in a nice sort of way, expecting a reply that might stagger even the most ardent of pilgrims. Baffin Island would have done.

"Canterbury, dear boy, Canterbury".

Fawlty Towers had lived up to it's name, and yet I cannot tick this one in the guidebook, after all, I might not have been there at all. One thing's certain, when the weather is bad and the conditions are foul on The Ben, I'll be back up that groove line for a fine mixed climb to rank alongside the best that any grade' two' can offer.

CLIMBING ABOVE THE WORM GRASS

By Geoff Cohen

IN THE 1970s I used to have to lecture in one of those characterless tower blocks, epitomes of dreary 1960s architecture, which the University of Edinburgh so cruelly bestowed upon its maternal city. My lectures were probably equally dreary. Emerging desiccated after an hour spent explaining index numbers, or some such exhilarating topic, I would pass by some tables set up in the basement where a rudimentary second-hand bookstall was arranged. The sellers were two delightful hippies, clearly permanent students, with little interest in large profits. I suppose they got most of their books from departing students and retiring academics. There were plenty of classics and course texts, but there was also a sprinkling of unusual gems. In this way I came across, for example, *In search of the Mahatmas of Tibet*, by E. G. Schary, a highly independent American who, in the early 1920s walked solo from Ladakh across the barren Changthang into central Tibet. Another author that caught my fancy was Peter Goullart, a Belgian who spent the inter-war years based in Shanghai. He would escape when he could to the hills of Yunnan in south-west China. His description of Lijiang fixed itself in my imagination, an ancient jewel of a town where exotic ethnic groups lived together harmoniously.

With a certain lack of initiative I made no effort to visit this region after China began to open to visitors in the early 1980s. It remained a kind of Shangri-La of the imagination. I was a bit like the famous physicist, Richard Feynman, who had a lifelong fascination with the republic of Tannu Tuva (a Siberian enclave close to Mongolia). Feynman read everything he could about Tuva, collected its stamps, talked about it to his friends, but never went there. Perhaps he preferred to retain it as a mysterious port for his voyaging imagination.

The stimulus that finally started me on the road to China was Tamotsu Nakamura's splendid series of articles and photographs of *East of the Himalaya*. 'Tom', as he is happy to be called, is an elderly Japanese mountaineer who has made numerous journeys of exploration in Eastern Tibet and South-west China, all meticulously documented. In 2002 I found myself in Greenland talking to Martin Scott of the Alpine Club about Tom Nakamura's exploits. We managed later to draw in Dick Isherwood, a very old friend of mine with long experience of the Far East, and Bill Thurston, an old climbing buddy of Martin's. We were all the wrong side of 55, and Martin and Dick were in their early 60s, so it was clear that a modest objective was called for. No Siguniang–like adventures for us, though we did get enthusiastic advice from Mick Fowler, as well as very generous assistance with maps and photos from Tom. Finally, we focused on Haizi Shan (Tibetan name Ja Ra) which appeared to be quite accessible, was not too high (5820m.), had a reasonably friendly looking North face, and was still unclimbed. This would not take me anywhere near fabled Lijiang, but at least I would dip a toe in south-west China and eastern Tibet. This was my first visit to China proper. I don't count the so-called SMC China expedition of 1988 which ventured only into Chinese central Asia where we saw far more Kirghiz and Uighurs than Han Chinese. This time we flew to Beijing and on to Chengdu where we had arranged to avail ourselves of the services of an adventure travel company. Chengdu was astonishingly modern and clean (cleaner than most British cities), and boasted climbing shops where we found good down clothing with western labels at Chinese prices! Since nearly everything these days seems to be made in China (even a future edition of *The Munros* apparently, if the Publications Company gets its way! Ed.) perhaps I should not have been surprised by this, nor by the vast Carrefour supermarket where we could select our hill food from among shelves stacked with Boddington's beer, French bread and less familiar Chinese spices and vegetables.

Leaving 40 miles of nearly empty new motorway that runs eastwards from Chengdu across perfectly flat, rich farmland, we drove in poor weather over a high pass and found ourselves back in more familiar Himalayan-type territory – steep, arid gorges and small towns at the confluence of turbulent mountain rivers. We spent our first night in one such place, Danba, lodged in a spanking new hotel, The Old Castle, where next morning we were presented with the traditional Tibetan white scarves by local beauties dressed in traditional costume, all recorded on video for the benefit, no doubt, of some tourist promotion.

However, when we reached base camp at around 3300m. the Tibetans who crowded around our embarrassingly large Land Cruisers were a rather different crowd, variously clad in all manner of ancient and modern dress, a few with the latest leather jackets and sunglasses, but most with traditional plain cloaks. The 10-mile valley we had driven up was fertile and well-wooded, with clear patches for pasturing yaks and a welcoming stream, probably rich in fish. Five minutes away was a large Tibetan encampment in the trees. Their tents were made of a blue and red striped sheeting that appeared ubiquitous throughout this part of Tibet. The community of maybe as many as a hundred people had established themselves there for the spring 'Worm Grass' harvest. This traditional Chinese medicine, made from a fungus that grows on dead caterpillars, is said to increase strength and cure back and knee pains, among many other excellent properties, and apparently forms the basis of the Tibetan economy in this region as it is only found in high mountain areas and commands a high price. Men and women, young and old, scoured the hillsides for this precious commodity using little trowel-like digging tools.

The north face of our mountain rose just a short distance away, looking very snowy above the first 1500ft. of forest. We could easily make out the route attempted the previous autumn by Neil Carruthers, following a moraine ridge to gain a broad snow shelf that ran parallel to the prominent and apparently straightforward east ridge. This pair from Hong Kong had reached the north summit but had not had time to go to the main summit, some half-mile farther on.

We spent our first day on an acclimatisation walk up to a stone bothy where a Tibetan family were living with their animals. With the aid of our friendly interpreter Xiao Mei we were invited in for tea. There was a swaddled baby in a corner, two pretty sisters, cheeks highly rouged (like all the Tibetan women) wearing long maroon coats made of modern fleece material and an old leather-faced man who turned his prayer wheel continuously. We were told we were the first westerners these people had seen.

Next day we decided on a reconnaissance. The first hour of our approach was on an excellent track used by the worm grass collectors. Families of all ages carrying kettles and picnic baskets as well as their trusty digging tools thronged the path. Noticing my pathetic pace the teenagers had a friendly laugh at me, imitating my laboured steps aided by trekking poles. They offered to carry my sack but I was too proud to accept. At a lake below our peak there were prayer flags everywhere, and the air echoed to the shouts of the picnicking groups. The lake was frozen solid on this visit, enabling us to walk on the edge and avoid the surrounding thick bushes, where the thin track was deep in snow. But above the lake our tribulations soon started. The most feasible route was through thick rhododendron forest where each step meant pushing aside strong-limbed trees then stepping through several feet of powder snow onto a base of slippery branches or icy rocks more likely than not to trip or trap the foot. With moderately heavy loads and unused to the altitude it was purgatory. I very much doubt I would have made progress at all had it not been for Dick's demonic energy, stamping a trail up to a refrain of curses. A little higher we got into a gully which avoided the worst of the forest but not the snow. After a short icy section we left a dump of food and gear by some characteristic trees.

Bruised by this preliminary skirmish we elected to let the snow consolidate for a while. We made a pleasant excursion to some hot springs. Finer than the well-known pools near Askole, these offered the perfect hot bath, the temperature constantly maintained, with a soft gravelly floor, a surface of bright green algae and backrest boulders perfectly placed to let us peruse the maze of couloirs high on the east flank of Haizi Shan. Another day began promisingly with a walk up to a high valley with fine peaks of 14,000ft. to 16,000ft., allowing me to daydream about carefree lightweight camping and weeks spent bagging these attractive Tibetan Munros with only the odd yak in the valleys for company. Sadly the dreaming was soon shattered. A party of Tibetans with a train of yaks was descending towards us from the Tagong direction. As Dick stepped aside to let them pass one of the mastiffs mauled him quite badly on both legs. We had heard of the savagery of Tibetan dogs, but this was my first encounter for real. The ripped flesh was worrying, but Xiao Mei assured us that rabies was unlikely and Dick patched himself up as best he could. A few days later we returned to the fray, taking five days' food and hoping that melting snow and improved acclimatization would carry us to swift success. Optimism was quickly deflated. The snow remained abominable and the first day we only reached about 100m. above our previous dump. It took us two more days to plough up a twisting moraine ridge and establish a camp at 5200m. We left a dump of gear about 250m. higher but then poor weather set in and we were forced to retreat to base and sit out a storm. Life here was enlivened by the purchase of large supplies of beer from a one-toothed Tibetan who kept a curious shop in a tent. Added to our copious whisky supplies and plentiful reading material, and the unfailing flow of food from our cook Jin-Jin and the ever cheerful Xiao Mei, base camp was not a place of austerity. Gaggles of Tibetans, especially the women, came frequently to stare at us, which gave us the privilege of staring back at them and sometimes photographing them. The ladies wore immensely colourful headdresses in orange and maroon, covered in jewellery, much of it looking remarkably like electrical insulators. I was sorry we couldn't invite them into our mess tent, but space was limited and the others seemed reluctant to give any sign of open house in case we were inundated.

On May 1, we set off again and this time reached our 5200m. camp in a single long day. But next day increasing breathlessness forced us to camp again only a little higher at our gear dump. We had originally hoped to carry the tents up the east ridge of the mountain to a col below the north summit. This would have given us a full day to do the traverse between the north and main summits, which appeared to be the only mildly technical part of the climb. But now, to avoid carrying loads any further I suggested trying to reach the summit in a day from this lower camp. 'Summit day' started with a plod in the dark up deep soft snow at quite a steep angle. From the east ridge at dawn we were rewarded with magnificent views over a cloud sea to the Minya Konka range – hundreds of mouth-watering unclimbed peaks in a land barely touched by mountaineers!

The ridge was steeper than I had expected – not technically difficult, but corniced and mighty exposed. It rose in waves, one beyond another, each concealing the hoped for summit. In a few places we could see faint outlines of the Carruthers party's footsteps from the previous October. Bill and Martin had, unfortunately, decided to descend from the ridge (Bill was not well), but Dick and I kept up a good pace and reached the north summit about 11am. At this stage I was full of optimism. Beyond was a short descent where a crevasse required us to don the rope at last, then an agonisingly slow plod along a horizontal section in deep snow. Confronted by an icy step that from below we had thought might be the crux, Dick took a belay and I stepped across a suspicious chasm to get onto the north face of the step. Front-pointing up this was not really difficult (maybe only 60°), but the altitude was telling. It took me ages to set up a belay at the top and when I had finished I had little confidence in it. The surface snow was meringue like and my laboriously hammered-in axe belay rattled around in a hole with only aerated ice of the cornice holding it in. I could not find anywhere decent for ice screws. Ahead was a narrow horizontal ridge, then another step very similar to the one we had just climbed but a bit longer. Beyond this the ridge rose at a gentler angle for only a short distance to the summit. For a fit young party it should have been less than an hour to the top. But we were not such a party. Dick, once among the best rock climbers in England, does not climb these days and did not seem at ease on this ground. I was not so put out technically, but was very aware of how slowly I was going and how easy it would be to make a mistake on this unforgiving ground, where safe belays seemed almost impossible to arrange. Pitching it at the rate we were going we reckoned it would probably have taken us four hours to go up and down the remaining few hundred feet. Had we had the sense to carry bivvy gear we might have continued. But in the event an elderly discretion won the day and we reluctantly turned our backs on the attractive pointed summit that seemed so tantalisingly close.

The descent from the north summit was down a glacier recommended by Carruthers as being easier than retracing the ridge. By now the weather had turned quite bad (another factor in our decision), with painful spindrift blowing everywhere. The glacier curved over convexly, forcing us to abseil off a snow mushroom. A little farther down after some awkward routefinding choices a similar abseil was called for over a steeper ice cliff. Luckily, the landing was on a broad soft snow shelf, for when Dick came down the mushroom decided to disintegrate when he was still 15ft. up, landing in a heap much to my embarrassment (as I had set up the anchor). The descent went on and on, as glaciers do, and was followed by a short rocky traverse to regain the snow shelf where we were camped. We reached the tents just as dusk fell, somewhat justifying the decision to retreat.

Next day's descent was long and even more purgatorial in the rhododendron forest as the gully was now too icy to descend. We had to slide down slippery rock slabs hanging onto tree branches. In the afternoon as we reached base the weather turned really bad, making us glad we had not bivvied the previous night or rested on our laurels in the tent. In fact, the next morning the base camp scene, normally a pleasant meadow was totally white and Christmassy, and Xiao Mei built a splendid snowman before the hot sun came out and burned it all away.

We had a few days left, but not enough for another attempt. Rather than wander among the much lower peaks we chose to take a trip farther west towards Tibet proper (the region we were in, though ethnically and historically Tibetan, is now part of Sichuan). This involved lots of driving and enough Buddhist monasteries to jade our appetites for sightseeing, but also offered the opportunity to cross several passes and get glimpses of some of the other barely touched mountain ranges in this part of China. The scope for new mountains and new routes is immense.

MINUS ONE DIRECT WITH THE DOC

By John Workman

SATURDAY 14, August 2004 – the fates threw me and Lex together for a day, *and a night,* on Ben Nevis.

We leave my house on Argyll Road, Fort William at 7am *sur la bicyclette* and puff and pant our way up the BA zigzags followed by a walk up the Allt a Mhuilinn trail in the pleasant warm sunshine. The Hill is unusually quiet – which is nice. The only other parties that we saw all day were the usual dribble of twos and threes on Tower Ridge and another pair on Observatory Ridge.

Our chosen route for the day is Minus One Direct (now E1) and it's described in the guidebook as one of the most enjoyable routes known to mankind, at its grade. We arrive in the basin at the foot of the vast Minus and Orion Faces to find water streaks down the lower part of the route. Too late now to change our plan, so we gear up and scramble up the first pitch. The routes here are 800ft. long, plus the finish either up or down North East Buttress. They have a very Alpine feeling, although the high summer rainfall this year has washed away the large patch of old névé that sometimes remains from one year to the next. Lex gets the honour of leading off and makes short work of a wet 4B crack that I find very awkward to follow. I put this down to the rucksack that I'm carrying, which, although supposedly only containing our approach shoes and spare jackets seems strangely heavy. I suppose it must be the water bottles and sandwiches that are causing the problem – or is it my aging bones and muscles. Anyway, I dump the sack at the belay and look up at the next pitch.

I climbed Minus One Buttress a long time ago – no comments please – when it was a 'Scottish VS.' On that occasion I was unable to lead the harder but better variation and we finished up the original line. Today I'm hoping that Lex and I will crack the Serendipity and Arête Variations.

I remember this next pitch (now given 4C), passing a block on a steep wall. Today, the usual way is running with water so I have to resort to a devious bypass on the left. This goes with a bit of a struggle and then I head off up some short walls looking for a 'great pedestal' – according to the guidebook. I arrive at the said pedestal and it seems fairly familiar but when we check the route description it says that I should have only climbed 25m. when in fact I've climbed 45m. Lex 'has a look' in the direction of where we think the next pitch might go but he returns saying it looks unlikely (aka impossible).

After a recent outing on Church Door Buttress with Mark 2 and The

Apprentice, where my memory served me very badly and took me up a blind and rather frightening alley, I'm beginning to doubt my route finding ability. To compound the problem, although we are at a great pedestal, there's another equally 'great pedestal' exactly 20m. below us. So, we decide to abb back down to it. Lex goes first, I follow, but when I get there the route description doesn't really fit and the line looks bloody frightening. Eventually, we decide to go back up to the first 'great pedestal' from where we'll either go up or down. All this palaver costs us a couple of hours, a couple of hours that will become significant later, as you will see.

Success! Lex tries again from the pedestal, makes some moves around an arête, finds evidence of previous passage and we climb the first crux – supposedly 5b, but I'd shade that down a grade. Next comes the Serendipity variation – across a fine steep slab, around another arête and up, then out of a groove by some unlikely looking moves – 5a. I'm very pleased to get my revenge on this one from 20-odd years ago.

Another 4c slab pitch takes us onto The Arête Variation and into the sunshine. This is good news and bad news, as they say. It's good to have the warm sun on our backs but it means that either we are quite high up on the route or it's getting late in the day. Another check of the guidebook reveals that we still have four pitches to go. The next one being the second crux 5b, and time *is* getting on, around 5pm I think.

This next pitch is a cracker. It traverses a steep slab underneath a very long narrow overhang. Halfway along you move up underneath the overhang and then bypass it on some underclings, arriving at an undercut arête and a stance with nothing below but several hundred feet of thin air. I make it, but unfortunately, drop a bunch of Lex's small wires into the thin air, trying to protect the moves under the roof.

It's a pity we decided not to take the camera. It must be one of the most photogenic bits of climbing I've done in recent years. Lex follows with the rucksack. He arrives safely at the stance and enthuses over the quality and exposure of the pitch. Next another 4c crack and yet another steep slab. I don't know whether it's my antics on the crux or the exposure that have got to Lex (or is it both?) but he gibbers his way very tenuously up the first few moves. He later admitted to having thoughts running through his head that his hands were too weak, the belay was going to fail, and that we'd both be taking a big dive through that thin air that I was talking about.

Eventually, he regains control and climbs another fine pitch. We manage to increase speed up the last two or three pitches as the grade falls away to 4b and then scrambling. The top of the route lands us on the second platform of North East Buttress, with still several hundred feet to go to the summit. We move quickly together up this easy ground, vanquishing the 'Man Trap' and 'The Forty Foot Corner' at pace. Even so, its 9.30pm by the time we reach the summit plateau in gathering gloom and mist. We have the customary handshake, and with wide grins, we pack away the gear, swig the last of the water and exchange painful rock shoes – aka 'stickies' so I'm told, although such a term conjures up an entirely different image in my head – for comfy approach shoes.

The mist is swirling in and we head off to find the nearest descent route – down the Cairn Mor Dearg arête.

"Time to get out torches," I say, but Lex, the foolish virgin that he is, has not only forgotten to trim his wick but has also omitted to bring a torch. He obviously hasn't been on enough expeditions with the Doc to learn that if there's one thing that you should take with you when out on the hill with me, it's a torch. Getting back on time and in daylight is a rare luxury.

We reach the bealach of the arête in the last of the gloaming. From here on down it's the visually impaired – I'm using a new, but somewhat dim Petzel Tika fibre optic torch - leading the partially sighted - Lex following behind in the vague light and shadows. We teeter and stumble our way down the interminable boulder fields of Corrie Leis at snail's pace. I now feel fully qualified to apply for any usherette position in any cinema in the land.

If the SMC guidebook hadn't given us that bum route description we'd have been well past the hut by the time it got dark and we'd have saved ourselves all this faffing about. Guidebook writers must be among the most-often-cursed people on the planet and we add our two penn'eth to the pot.

Boulder hopping in Corrie Leis even in the daytime often reminds me of John Main who, after soloing something probably quite outrageous on the Ben, a good few years back, slipped in the Corrie and dislocated his middle finger at the second joint. He had to walk alone, all the way down and into the Belford Hospital with the finger sticking out across the other fingers at ninety degrees to the proper angle. Ouch! So I'm always a bit careful about how I tread on the boulders on the Ben.

We reach the CIC hut around midnight and waste another half-hour or more searching for my rucksack that I'd left under an 'obvious' boulder. Finally, we make it to the bikes and we're relieved to slip into downhill freewheeling mode, arriving back at my house at 3.30am Sunday morning. That means it took us six hours to descend from the top of the Ben.

All this will no doubt has a very familiar ring to many of you who have chanced your arm on 'The Hill' with 'The Doc'.

Food, beer and Lex's inevitable whisky, combined with almost twenty hours 'on the hoof' soon reduce us to that pleasant semi-zombified state and we slope off to bed to sleep the sleep of the just. (Just off the hill that is).

We rose late on the Sunday and I'm thinking 'rest day' but Lex, after showering and breakfasting suggests a walk out – back to the foot of the route to search for the dropped wires. After my initial shock, I suspect that this is some precursor to a negotiation for the cost of replacing his lost gear but it turns out that he really does just want some fresh air and exercise. Before I realise what I've said, I agree to accompany him. So at noon we head off again on the bikes. It crossed my mind to suggest that if we were going that far then we should take a rope and climb Observatory Buttress but something – good sense or old age? – made me bite my tongue.

In the end we enjoyed another pleasant day together. We did find a couple of the wires but the main lot of them must be still somewhere up on the Minus Face. And good luck to anyone who comes across them.

Ambling our way down in the afternoon sunshine we chatted about this and that and remarked on the beautiful clumps of ling and bell heather that are in bloom everywhere. And how the white bog-cotton and dark yellow asphodels are making their appearance, which must mean the turning of another summer. Finally, we call in at the enigmatically named 'Ben Fong' takeaway for chips, but no ice cream, and then to the parting of the ways once more.

I'll be pointing out the 20m. error in the guidebook to the SMC. Strangely, the previous edition of the guidebook is correct, so they'll be putting this down to a printing error. It seemed at first as though it was going to spoil the day for a couple of Englishmen but in retrospect it actually made it more memorable. Having said that, Scots do go up there too, so I expect the SMC will be rectifying the error in due course, so as to avoid incurring the wrath of the natives.

GOLDEN JUBILING

A celebration of 50 years of the Ling Hut

By Dave Broadhead

OVER the years, the Scottish Mountaineering Club has gradually established a network of five huts, situated in some of the finest mountain locations in the country. This aspect of the Club's activities has required foresight, commitment and a lot of hard work from the members involved, and the generous support of others.

Custodians especially have taken on a never-ending round of booking inquiries, sending out keys, collecting dues, maintaining the buildings and organising work parties. It is not just SMC members who have benefited from this enormous effort, as the huts are available to members of all clubs. Climbers and hillwalkers from throughout Britain and beyond have used them as a comfortable and convenient base for enjoying the Scottish hills in all seasons.

To celebrate the Golden Jubilee of the Ling Hut, for many years the Club's most northerly hut, this article looks back through the pages of the Journal and some personal reminiscences.

In April, 1955, the Club opened its third hut, in Glen Torridon, the jewel of the Northern Highlands, an isolated cottage in a superb situation near the entrance to Coire Dubh Mor, separating Liathach and Beinn Eighe, two of Scotland's finest mountains.

Coulin Cottage at Lochan Iasgaic, Glen Torridon, has been leased to the club and is to be known as the Ling Hut. It has three rooms and there is a byre. It has been repaired and equipped. There are six beds. (1955-SMCJ 146)

The official opening of the hut was combined with the Easter Meet, based at Kinlochewe Hotel.

On Saturday 9th April 1955 thirty two members and guests – were present at the official opening – by Mrs G.T. Glover, who came up from Carlisle specially for the occasion.

...the President paid tribute to Willy Ling and George Glover, two great friends through whose generosity the hut has been established in the area where they did so much of their pioneering climbing. (1955-SMCJ 146)

The Journal of the following year featured two tiny photographs of the new hut. One was a typically solemn group shot of the opening ceremony, while the other showed a rather austere building with the familiar ugly steel security grills across the windows and a makeshift corrugated iron porch. George Peat (Conon Bridge) was first and longest-serving Hon. Custodian, from 1955-1967. AGM reports in the Journals of that era give some insight into 'housekeeping' issues.

Improvements have been carried out – a new kitchen stove, calor gas etc. Already 225 hut nights have been recorded, half of these during the spring. (1956-SMCJ 147)

The Ling Hut was again most popular about Easter. Coal has been delivered to the hut direct, by the volunteer help of Hector Cameron with the Coulin Estate tractor. (1958-SMCJ 149)

...only the porch requires attention (1960 – SMCJ 151)

No more mention is made of the porch, which disappeared into the mists of history. With no easy vehicular access, the problem of delivering fuel to the hut has always been a headache for Custodians.

A supply of coal waits expectantly at the road end. (1962-SMCJ 154)

The open fire also disappeared into history, replaced by total reliance on the familiar big red cylinders of propane for heating and lighting. Originally, these were delivered to the far side of Loch Iasgaich, then floated across and man-handled up to the hut, until the instigation of the biannual gas lift. This requires the organisation of slick teams of lifters and shifters at both ends of the brief flight, when time in the air means money. On the subject of hut economics, details of hut nights etc remain buried in the minutes of Huts Sub-Committee meetings, but Journal reports of Meets give an indication of the popularity of the hut with members. At the Easter Meet of 1960, based in Lochcarron, four people stayed in the hut, rising to five in 1963, based at Kinlochewe. A new Custodian, Charlie Rose (Alligin) took over in 1968, serving until 1971. An alarming AGM report noted:

...use of the Ling Hut fell remarkably (1968 – SMCJ 159)

Fortunately, this seems to have been a short lived trend, as the Journal editor explained in his introduction to the ever growing 'New Climbs':

Because of the volume of exploration in the Northern Highlands I have split the area into 3 divisions... (1970-SMCJ 161)

Roger Robb (Dingwall) took over the Custodianship in 1972, serving until 1974, continuing the tradition of gradual improvements to the building:

New Year Meet – A party of twelve members and guests enjoyed a comfortable and pleasant New Year...All were most impressed by the remarkable improvements in the hut's facilities and décor. The weather was mixed and the snow scarce. (1972-SMCJ 163)

Other incentives were dangled before Club members to encourage greater use of all the huts:

A rise in the Club subscription (to meet increased costs)......was coupled with an offer of free hut use which drew groans of dismay from the Custodians as they saw their only "perk" disappear. (1973 – SMCJ 164).

In Memoriam. Bill Young.

Huts Convenor from 1972-76......remarkable programme of renovation at all three huts...at Ling...the now standard sleep-shelf replaced the old squeaky uncomfortable two-tiered iron bunks. (2004 – MCJ 195).

Despite these enticements, the main deterrent to making the then long and arduous journey north was, of course, the unreliable weather.

Easter Meet...based at Kinlochewe with quite a few members and guests at the Ling Hut...the weather was somewhat mixed – very wet on Saturday. (1977 – SMCJ 168).

Easter Meet held at Kinlochewe Hotel and Ling Hut...despite the rough weather it was an enjoyable meet. (1979 – SMCJ 170).

Jim Anton (Contin) served as Custodian from 1975 to 1982. According to his obituary (1996-SMCJ 187) he was 75 when he took on the job. In contrast, his successor, Gerry Smith (Inverness) was the youngest, and sadly, the shortest serving Custodian.

The tragic death of Gerry Smith, while descending North East Buttress, after completing an ascent of Minus Two Gully came as a cloud to us all. (1983 – SMCJ 174).

Clive Rowland (Cawdor) stepped in to fill the breach, serving until 1987, and carrying out some major improvements with the help of Ken Hopper, a builder based in Plockton. Ken was a rare practitioner of that fickle trade who seemed to relish working on remote jobs in the hills.

Torridon Meet 17-19 May 1985 – Ling Hut. The hut was full for the whole weekend...12 members and five guests signed in...thanks to Clive

Rowland's magnificent kitchen cum common room, managed very nicely.
The weather was mixed. (1986 – SMCJ 177).

By now the outside of the hut was also much improved in appearance by the occasional coat of white masonry paint, making a distinct and photogenic landmark in the glen.

Translocation of Ling Hut. A member who is also a reader of Woman's
Own has drawn our attention to an advert in that prestigious publication
which shows the Ling Hut in full colour. The blurb avers the hut is the
home of Rory McTavish, that it is located on "a remote island" and that
Mrs McTavish will soon be receiving from the mainland a new kind of
porridge made of wheat and nuts and raisins (yuk). The club legal advisers
are looking into the possibility of royalties. (1984 – SMCJ 175).

The present author (Inverness/Muir of Ord) served as Custodian from 1987-1996. By now, upgrading of the A9 road had significantly speeded up the drive to Inverness from the south, and the single-track sections beyond were rapidly disappearing. Weekend visits from the Central Belt were now feasible, and a growing number of clubs booked the hut for their annual meets programme. The flush toilet was finally operational, improving the immediate surroundings of the building. Twelve sleeping spaces were now available on the two 'mattressenlager'in the main bedroom, with four more spaces in the Members Room reserved for Club members. The popular members key system made access easier, with demand high when word spread of good winter climbing conditions. Revision of the Northern Highlands climbing guides in the late 1980s resulted in a lot more winter climbing activity, and the discovery that good conditions were more common than previously thought.

Hamish Irvine (Aviemore) did a temporary one year 'locum' in 1997, enjoying it so much that this stretched to 2002 when Bill Skidmore (Lochcarron), the current Custodian, took over.

Recent improvements include a wooden floor and double-glazing. The latter enabled removal of the original mesh security screens, which always had nightmare implications in the event of a fire. Ling Hut still lacks some of the mod-cons such as showers and microwaves found in other huts, but for most users the magnificent situation more than compensates for the basic facilities.

In December 2004, a gas generator was carried in and a low voltage lighting system will finally replace the fragile (and expensive) gas mantles.

Although the Torridon hills have become much busier over the past 50 years, they remain as challenging and enjoyable to climbers and walkers. Long may the Ling Hut continue to contribute to that enjoyment. Thanks to Coulin Estate, Custodians past, present and future, and their many helpers.

NEW CLIMBS SECTION

OUTER ISLES

LEWIS, Butt of Lewis, Conspiracy Stack (NB 518 665):
A 20m stack is easily viewed 100m west from the lighthouse. Access by abseil
from rocks/stakes (not in situ) to a narrow channel that separates the stack from
the mainland. A large step across and difficult moves are made to a platform and
belay.

Northern Conspiracy 20m Hard Severe 4b. R.I.Jones, J.Sanders. 12th June
2004.
Climbs the landward (south) face by a left-slanting groove/ramp with an awkward
step left at mid-height to easier ground. Good climbing on good rock.

Trojan Wall (NB 518 665, mainly west facing):
Fifty metres south-west of the stack is a large geo which has a large landslip in its
south end. Trojan Wall is on the east side of the geo and is split into two tiers by a
large ledge that becomes a sloping ramp to the north-east and a tidal cave. The
lower tier provides some excellent routes on good rock and with good protection.
It is accessible between mid and low tide. Routes on the top tier are more limited
and the rock is loose beyond the area where routes are recorded. The wall can be
easily viewed from the cliff-top on the west side of the geo. The wall is split into
four distinct sections (from left to right) Seaward Buttress, Three Corner Buttress,
The Face and Right End Wall. Right of this the rock is loose and broken. Trojan
Horse takes a line just right of the corner that splits Three Corner Buttress and The
Face on the lower wall and the middle of wall of the upper tier.

Trojan Horse 24m Severe *. J.Sanders, R.I.Jones. 12th June 2004.
1. 12m Climb a left-slanting crack 2m right of the right-facing corner.
2. 12m 4a Climb the middle of the wall on the upper tier directly through a bulge.

Upper Tier (non-tidal):
Hidden Agenda 12m Severe. J.Sanders, R.I.Jones. 12th June 2004.
Climb the wall 2m right of Trojan Horse to a small overhang at mid-height. Pull
out rightwards into a right-facing corner and climb to the top.

Lower Tier (tidal), Three Corner Buttress:
Routes are described first leftwards then rightwards from the main corner beside
Trojan Horse (the abseil line). This is the third corner of Three Corner Buttress
when viewed from the west side of the geo.

Odysseus 12m VS 4c ***. R.I.Jones, J.Sanders. 12th June 2004.
The middle corner. Excellent climbing up the slightly right-trending corner 3m to
the left, with the crux saved for the last few moves.

Helen's Chimney 12m Hard Severe 4b *. J.Sanders, R.I.Jones. 17th June 2004.

The first corner. Climb the corner-crack and chimney 3m left of Odysseus.

Left of Helen's Chimney is a 5m wide wall undercut on its left-hand side.

Menelaus 12m HVS 5a **. R.I.Jones, J.Sanders. 17th June 2004.
From the right side of the face, pull on to the wall and trend slightly left and then straight up on good holds.

Agamemnon 12m HVS 5a ***. R.I..Jones, J.Sanders. 17th June 2004.
Two metres from the left of the wall, climb directly up on good holds and steep ground.

Gneiss Achilles but not as we know it! 12m Hard Severe 4a. J.Sanders, R.I.Jones. 17th June 2004.
Left of the wall is a large chimney. Climbs the left-hand corner of the chimney on adequate holds. Protection is poor.

Seaward Buttress:
Journey Over the Sea 25m E1 5a/b **. R.I.Jones, J.Sanders. 17th June 2004.
An awesome route that takes a line out of the chimney and across the overhanging wall in a rising traverse to the Seaward Buttress. From the belay of Gneiss Achilles climb up 3m, then traverse leftwards on a hanging slab to an exposed position above the sea. Pull strenuously up and left on to the face and continue up a left-slanting crack-line on easier ground.

The following routes are to the right of Trojan Horse.
The Wall:
Messing with the Achaeans 12m HVS 5a ***. R.I.Jones, J.Sanders. 17th June 2004.
Starts 2m right of Trojan Horse. Climb the centre of the wall direct through steep ground to a hanging niche. Pull through this on the left and to the top.

Don't Look a Gift Horse in the Mouth 12m E1 5b ***. R.I.Jones, J.Sanders. 17th June 2004.
Start 1m to the right of Messing. Climb up and rightwards above a right-facing overhanging corner. Pull up and rightwards through steep ground and climb the wall direct, trending right of the orange wall to the top.

Something About the Iliad 12m HVS 5a **. R.I.Jones, J.Sanders. 12th June 2004.
Four metres right of Gift Horse. Climb the wall to an overhang at 5m. Take this on the right and move up to a hanging right-facing corner. Climb the corner and pull out left on to the wall above and then to the top.

Right End Wall:
Who's Homer? 12m VS 4c. R.I.Jones, J.Sanders. 17th June 2004.
Climb a short pillar in the centre of wall and step right on to the hanging slab. Follow good holds in a rising traverse. Pull up and right into a niche and then up to the top with care.

BRAGAR, Ard Mhor Bhragair (NB 269 495):
Approach: Turn off the A858 at North Shawbost (Siabost bho Thuath) at a sign for Fibhig and An Carnan. Park a few metres before the end of the road by the peat stack. Go through a gate by a ruin in front of the most northerly croft and down to the boulder beach, then follow the cliffs along to the Aird, 15mins.

A superb complex crag of fine Lewisian gneiss at an average height of 25-30m. As usual hereabouts, the more seaward rock is near perfect, though there is some deterioration towards the back of the geodh. The first landmark is a pile of rubbish tipped into the first geodh west of the crag; an abseil or scramble into this geodh gives access to some of the climbs. The next landmark is Stac nan Eun (Stack of the Birds) which is a series of three pinnacles on a narrow ridge running out into the sea. A very old piece of rope on the southerly-most pinnacle indicates an earlier ascent. To the east of Stac nan Eun, beyond a narrow inlet, are the Back Walls, a sweep of black rock 30m high and sporting some fine lines. To the north of the Back Walls is the Lagoon, a tidal pond at low tide, in a calm sea. Just to the north of this is the wonderful Folded Wall, with a clutch of excellent routes on perfect rock.

Fifty metres to the south of the rubbish heap are the first routes, on a promontory which has a fine little triangular witch's hat stack and small island off its northern end. The first climbs described are on the north-west tip of this promontory and are reached by abseil from a little grassy bay on the headland.

Scrap Heap Challenge   30m   E1 5b. M. & K.Tighe. 25th June 2003.
A diagonal fault-line starts from the extreme north-west corner of the promontory, initially as a groove to a big ledge, then as a steep crack-line up the wall to the left of Rock Island Line. Start from a mid-way ledge if a big sea is running.

Rock Island Line   30m   E1 5b *. M. & K.Tighe. 25th June 2003.
Just around the corner (south) from Scrap Heap Challenge is a fine corner/groove-line, which runs the full height of the cliff.

September Rain   30m   HVS 5a **. M. & K.Tighe, H. & C.Clarke. 1st September 2002.
A few metres south again is another fine corner-crack. A tricky start leads to a mid-way ledge and interesting crack above. Fragile at the top.

Western Rib   20m   E2 5b/c. M. & K.Tighe. 25th June 2003.
The next smaller promontory to the west has a fine route up the nose (north end). A gentle slab leads to a fierce little quartzy wall and some big steps out right to finish. Descend down an easy gully to the west to get started.

Route descriptions continue now from the scrap heap, heading north, then east.

Stac nan Eun (Stack of the Birds)   300m   Mild VS **. M. & K.Tighe. July 2000.
Though not strictly stacks, these three pinnacles adorn a narrow ridge running north to south, joined to the mainland but with sea either side. Abseil from a fence post or scramble into Scrap Heap Bay and traverse along (150m) to below the lowest point on the ridge, between the northerly flat-topped pinnacle and the middle one (only possible at mid to low tide). Climb up into the col and bag the northern

pinnacle, which is a big flat-topped affair. Return to the col and head south over the next two pinnacles. An abseil was made from the central pinnacle down the west side, to ledges from where a gully/groove line was ascended back to the cliff-top at about Very Difficult.

The next crop of routes is at the northern end of the Back Wall, which is to the east of Stac nan Eun, across the intervening channel. Difficult to identify from above, though a good reference is a small 'rectangular-topped' non-stack almost opposite the northern end of Stac nan Eun, which, on closer inspection, has two arches underneath it; a biggish tidal pond, the 'Lagoon' lies to the north of here. There is a wee gap south of the non-stack followed by a wall, then another arched recess with a sloping Grey Rib at the south. Around the corner (south) on the Back Wall proper is a Pot Belly chimney come crack-line and two bottomless crack-lines. These are immediately opposite the northern end of the ridge holding Stac nan Eun.

Sea Dog   E2 5b **. M. & K.Tighe. 15th July 2000.
This is the most northerly and most feasible of the two bottomless groove-lines mentioned above. It does have a bottom but often greasy, so it was gained by an excellent traverse across the wall from the foot of Pot Belly, after which the groove is followed directly to the top.

Pot Belly   E2 5b **. M.Tighe, I.Lee, G.Anderson. 23rd May 2001.
The excellent pea-pod shaped chimney/groove line accessed by abseiling down the route or traversing around from the foot of the Grey Rib. Squirm up the pod with some difficulty, and squirm out of it with even more!

Grey Rib   Severe. M. & K.Tighe. 15th July 2000.
A big bay/chasm with an arched overhang its back (east). This route takes the rib on the seaward side of the southern end. A little delicate at times.

Arch Wall   VS 4c *. M. & K.Tighe. 15th July 2000.
An arch just south of the non-stack, and an atmospheric ledge down by the sea underneath it. This route goes delicately out right (south) and on to the fine open wall, followed to the top.

Children of the Sea   30m   E2 5b/c ***. M. & K.Tighe. 25th August 2004.
Abseil down to the sloping ledge, under the arch just south of the rectangular topped non-stack (as for Arch Wall). Go delicately up, and out right on to an exposed ledge at the bottom of the wall. Go right across the wall gently gaining height for 10-12m, then go more diagonally up right to a small ledge (guano) below the impending headwall. Climb the fabulous upper wall on big jugs and immaculate rock.

High Teas   Mild VS. M. & K.Tighe. 15th July 2000.
Exits up the back wall from under the arch (out eastwards). Atmospheric climbing.

North is a tidal pond, the 'Lagoon', which has a fine 20m wall at the back (eastern side). There is a good ledge at the bottom of this wall, immediately opposite the outflow of the tidal pond. The following route starts from this ledge.

White Magic 20m VS 4c **. M. & K.Tighe, J.Winter. 15th June 2004.
A broad diagonal quartz vein slopes left up the wall from the left side of the platform; follow it and the little wall to the top on improving holds.

North again is the fabulous Folded Wall, a sweep of perfect gneiss, climbable almost anywhere at VS/HVS. There are good ledges at the bottom, and a 'trench' runs below the face at the southern end. There is a Difficult descent at the southern end, between the Folded Wall and the Lagoon, and similar in a wee bay to the north, although an abseil is better. Routes from right to left (looking in).

Number 3 20m Severe **. M. & K.Tighe, H.Clarke. 20th July 2000.
Near the right-hand side of the wall, at about one-third height, the rock has folded into a number 3 shape. Fall across the trench at the bottom of the wall and climb the wall directly through the 3 or a metre to the right.

Goodbye Donella 25m Hard Severe *. M. & K.Tighe, H.Clarke. 20th July 2000.
Below and a few metres left of Number 3 is a small triangular calcified alcove. A curving fault-line runs through it, the full height of the cliff. Get across the trench and follow the fault all the way, getting out of the alcove being the crux.

Black Recess 25m Hard Severe **. M. & K.Tighe, H.Clarke. 20th July 2000.
Slightly higher, and a few metres left of the calcified recess of Goodbye Donella, is a black recess with quartzy veins in the black rock. Cross the trench below and head straight up through the recess to the top of the crag.

Sleeping Dogs 25m Mild VS ***. M. & K.Tighe, H.Clarke. 20th July 2000.
Start in the middle of the wall 5m left of the Black Recess and 5m right of Le Slot, below a small triangular groove and overhang at one-third height. Climb up into the alcove and pull over the small overhang on to the steep wall above on immaculate holds. Continue to the top trending slightly left, or right (better but harder).

Le Slot 25m HVS 5a ***. M. & K.Tighe, H.Clarke. 20th July 2000.
Almost in the middle of the main face, low down, is a 3-4m diagonal slot. Step across the trench onto the wall and climb the slot and the immaculate wall above directly to the top. An alternative start traverses into the slot from the right (easier at VS 4c).

The Scoop 25m HVS 5b *. M. & K.Tighe. 10th June 2004.
There is a concave depression in the upper part of the wall just left of centre. Start below this, 2m left of Le Slot, and climb the fairly bold fingery wall past a small triangular niche to a half-way ledge. Finish up the scoop.

Left Edge 25m HVS 5a ****. M. & K.Tighe. 15th July 2000.
A few metres left again from The Scoop and a similar distance in from the left edge of the wall (Edge of Distinction). An intricate series of moves up the fine lower wall; the steep upper wall, just left of The Scoop, is easier.

Edge of Distinction 25m VS 4c *. M. & K.Tighe, J.Winter. 10th June 2004.

The left edge of the main wall before it turns back into Kenny's Cavity. A bold move low down leads to an airy finish.

Kenny's Cavity   25m   Mild VS ***. M. & K.Tighe. 11th July 2000.
The excellent corner/groove line around the corner.

Octopod   25m   Severe **. M. & K.Tighe. 11th July 2000.
Start at the base of Kenny's Cavity and follow the curving crack-line for a few metres before heading straight up the gently bulging wall above on excellent jugs. A possible exit right at two-thirds height is better avoided by taking the quartzy wall directly above.

Squid   25m   E1 5b *. M. & K.Tighe, H.Clarke. 20th July 2000.
Start at the same place as Octopod but climb the much thinner curving crack below the main one to a ledge at half-height. Go up the wall into a shallow chimney and finish by a 3m flake-crack.

Snake Dyke   25m   E2 5b/c ***. M. & K.Tighe. 11th July 2000.
The superb diagonal fault leads to a ledge at half-height, followed by easier climbing up a brown groove.

After Snake Dyke the wall falls back into another small bay with a Difficult ascent/ descent in the back. Seaward (north) again is a smooth wall after which the crag peters out into the sea.
   Around the corner from the Folded Wall, i.e. on the north side of Aird Mhor Bhragair, there is a series of sea inlets and promontories guarded by a similar series of low-lying islands/skerries in the sea to the north, which almost mirror their landward neighbours. The channels have been numbered from 0 to 4, and the four skerries 1 to 4. 0 is the first channel 20-30m east from the Folded Wall area. The following route is on the north-east tip of this channel and the next three around the corner, on the north wall opposite Skerry 1.

Sgarbh Beag   25m   Mild Severe. M. & K.Tighe, J.Winter, N.McGoughan. 7th June 2004.
Abseil down to a good ledge at the north-east corner of Channel 0. Follow big flakes up and slightly left to a big ramp near the top. Finish up a groove in the wall above.

Crack and Slab   25m   VS 4b. M. & K.Tighe. 7th June 2004.
Climb the short groove and crack above the belay ledge, the most westerly line on this wall, to a ledge/ramp at mid-height. A delicate poorly protected slab leads to the top.

D Day   25m   HVS 5a/b ***. M. & K.Tighe. 7th June 2004.
Almost in the middle of the wall is a crack-line which runs up into a groove guarded by a short overhanging section (awaits an ascent). Follow the fine crack for a few metres and go left into the corner. Pull out and left under an overhang to a little pedestal below the final tricky wall. Sustained, well protected but a touch fragile.

Next is Channel 1 with Skerry 2 off the north-east side and a big sloping black slab on the west side at the mouth. On the east is a diagonal fault-line, starting at the seaward end and sloping up from left to right.

Frigate   25m   E1 5b **. M. & K.Tighe, Y.Colwell. 29th May 2001.
Abseil down to the bottom of the route or approach down a series of ledges around the corner on the north side of the promontory. The excellent little corner is tricky low down, but eases a little after half-way.

On the north wall of the promontory (opposite Skerry 2) is a fine broken corner-line about a third of the way along and opposite Channel 2:

Ken's Route   25m   VS 4c. K.Colwell, R.McLachlan. 29th May 2001.
This corner is rather more tricky than it looks, though the protection is good.

Chanel   25m   Hard Severe. M.Tighe, T.McLachlan. 29th May 2001.
Going east from here, the crag starts to overhang. Climb up under the initial overhang before traversing out right to avoid it.

Roberton's Jam   25m   E1 5b. H.Robertson, M.Tighe. 29th May 2001.
Follow the initial part of Chanel, but continue up the crack through the overhang.

There are fierce overhangs now at the eastern end of this promontory and opposite Skerry 3. The next two routes start around the corner on the west wall of Channel 3. Good view from the opposite (eastern side) of the channel. About 10m in from the seaward end of the wall is a vertical fault-line running the full height of the cliff. The following route starts at the bottom of the fault-line.

Black Sabbath   45m   E2 5b. M.Tighe, H.Clarke. 1st September 2002.
Go out diagonally right across the wall fairly low down to a little platform on the corner. Go around the corner and follow a diagonal gently overhanging crack-line to the top.

Plumb Line   25m   E1 5a. M. & K.Tighe. 16th June 2003.
Takes a fairly prominent line up the west wall (east facing) of Channel 3, 10m in from the seaward corner. Start at a notch below the fault just above the high tide mark. Go up and left a few metres to a prominent left-sloping ramp. Go straight up the groove above and exit left on slightly friable rock at 5a, or right up the steeper headwall on better rock at 5b.
The cliffs decrease in size to the east of Channel 4, which has a rusty van at its southern end. The first cliff east of Channel 4 is around 18m high, with a line of overhangs at the top. The three routes to date start from the extreme north-west corner of the promontory below an arête, on a wee ledge just below the high tide line (calm sea required).

Seal Play   20m   HVS 5a. M.Tighe, J.Cargill. 23rd June 2001.
From the ledge below the arête, go up a metre or so then right into the bottom of a recess/bay. Climb up the wall and the small diagonal groove on the right.

The Arête (HVS 5a *) has not been led. Protection is rather limited, making it a bold lead or a deep-water solo if the tide is in!

The Sting   20m   HVS 5a ***. M.Tighe, J.Cargill. 23rd June 2001.
The excellent crack just left of the arête can have a damp start but great protection and a tricky finish.

SHAWBOST, Rubha Bratach, Orpheus Wall:
(NB 240 473), Partly tidal, west facing.
Note: M.Garthwaite, R. & C.Anderson climbed around 10 routes in addition to these in 2004.
Approach: Park to the side of the road at the start of a track at NB 245 473. Follow the track to the west through a gate and after a few minutes leave the track and cross a fence using a style or gate. Turn to the north and follow this around to the west to drop down to below the wall. 10mins.
   The wall is characterised by a slightly overhanging 15m wall to the left of a corner, which is accessible at mid to low tide. To the left the wall is undercut and a short wall forms beneath this. The wall ends in a left-facing corner, which holds the crack-line of What Planet? Routes at this end are accessible at most states of the tide.

Blowin' a Gale   10m   HVS 5a. R.I.Jones, J.Sanders. 13th June 2004.
Climb the large left-facing corner for 4m. Step left to a niche and then right to a platform. Pull up into the hanging niche on the left and to the top.

What Planet Do You Live On?   10m   Very Difficult. J.Sanders, R.I.Jones. 13th June 2004.
Climb a large broken crack-line to the right of the left-facing corner.

Stolen Moments   10m   Hard Severe 4b *. J.Sanders, R.I.Jones. 13th June 2004.
Climb the arête to the right of What Planet to a hanging slab and crack.

Sirens of the Sea   12m   HVS 4c/5a ***. R.I.Jones, J.Sanders. 13th June 2004.
The wall right of Stolen Moments. Climb the wall to a niche below a leaning wall with a hanging arête on its right above. From the niche step right and climb the arête and corner above.

The next route takes a spectacular rising traverse from the bottom right to the top left of the main wall.

Orpheus   30m   E2/3 5c **. R.I.Jones (unsec). 14th June 2004.
Start at an inverted hanging V-groove towards the right end of the main wall. Pull up right before traversing left up a left-slanting ramp. Just before the end climb the wall above for 2m before traversing leftwards including a step down and a pull across to a small left-facing niche. Pull up under a small overhang which is taken on the left.

Rubha na Beirghe (NB 235 475):
Another fine esoteric little crag in a wonderful setting, the great sea arch of Stac a' Phris being just to the south. Five minutes south of the previous crag. A good mixture of routes, most of which require low tide and a fairly calm sea.
Approach: Park near the end of the road at South Shawbost (approx NB 245

474). Follow a peat track and then the coast out to the headland, which in times past has been walled off to create a fort. A longer, but no less pleasant approach can be made from Dalbeg.

Walking out on to the headland the first feature to be seen is a little fin of rock (Murray's Rib) jutting north and creating a fine east-facing slab 10m high. A sea-arch running through the headland exits below. Scramble out along the rib above the slab and descend (tricky) to a wee platform at the north end. Traverse back along the bottom of the slab and take the central crack-line, *Duck Egg* Difficult **, T.McLachlan, K.Tighe 29th May 2001; or the little corner, *Stowaway* Difficult **, Y.Colwell, M.Morris, 29th May 2001. The slab between and to the right of these routes can be climbed just about anywhere at Very Difficult or Severe.

Continuing west the headland becomes almost square with walls facing north and west dropping straight into the sea. The main fault/crack-line on the north side gives a fabulous route.

The Poacher 25m E1 5b ***. M.Tighe, H.Robertson, K.Colwell, K.Tighe. 29th May 2001.
Abseil down the line of the route to a good ledge at half tide. Climb the excellent corner-crack to a sloping overhang at three-quarters height. Pull over this going right, and so to the top.
Note: M.Garthwaite, R. & C.Anderson climbed around 12 routes in addition to this in 2004.

DALBEG BAY (Tidal):
There are four 10-15m sea stacks in the bay, one to the north and three to the south, which are easily assessable an hour either side of low tide. The southern stack is an easy climb up the landward face. The west and east stack are joined at the high tide mark. The western stack can be climbed by an easy wall at Moderate from where the stacks join. The outing can be extended to take in the western pinnacle with a difficult down climb (Difficult) from the top of the stack. The eastern stack has a cairn on the top and can be accessed by a scramble up the east side (assumed to be the line of first ascent; difficulty not known but no more than Difficult). The western wall makes for an enjoyable outing and holds the following route.

The Day the Whale Danced 20m VS 4b. R.I.Jones, J.Sanders. 14th June 2004.
Climb the wall to a large perched block. Pull around this to its left and belay (10m). An easy scramble is made to the top and summit cairn. Descent is by abseil from the belay.

GARENIN CRAGS:
The best starting point for these sea-cliffs is the beautifully restored Black House Village at Garenin itself (NB 193 443).

Tiumpan Head, Aird Mor (NB 192 453):
This fine crag is characterized by striking pink and black banding in the near perfect gneiss.
Approach: Follow the green and yellow posts of the heritage trail northwards from Garenin village to the top of Aird Mor (NB 191 451). Leave the trail here

and head north for a further 300m to arrive at the headland. A tiny rock islet, the Oyster Skerry, lies a few metres offshore. Routes are quite difficult to identify from above. The main feature is the big corner of Clais Mor, which is opposite the northern end of the Oyster Skerry and has a big smooth black boiler-plate slab on its south side. The following route is north of Clais Mor, the rest working south.

Clais Mor is in the back of a huge right-angled corner, the northern wall of which holds a chimney the shape of an elongated S. This gives the following route, which is best approached by abseil, though there is an approach from the north down black slabs (Difficult if dry).

Sinuous Chimney   30m   E1 5b *. M. & K.Tighe. 27th August 2002.
The deep S-shaped cleft a few metres left of Clais Mor. Make some steep moves up a rib on the right and layback around on to the face. This leads to somewhat easier climbing and better protection in the chimney proper.

Clais Mor (Big Corner)   40m   E3 5b/c ***. M. & K.Tighe. 26th June 2003.
The big corner-line gives an excellent tussle with very wide bridging and excellent protection.

Olive Oil   45m   HVS 5b **. M. & K.Tighe. 27th August 2002.
Start a couple of metres up Clais Mor where a ramp goes out right across the black wall.
1. 15m   Follow the ramp out right and make an airy move around the corner (difficult to protect the second).
2. 30m   Go up and left into a leaning recess and climb delicately up the slab to a steep exit on the left.

Olive Oil finishes above another excellent corner (English Spinach) which is the next big feature of the cliff after Clais Mor. The following route starts from a fine ledge at the bottom of this corner, just above the high tide line; approach by abseil.

Popeye   30m   HVS *. M.Tighe, I.Lee. 24th May 2001.
Start from the ledge at the bottom of English Spinach. Step left around the corner and climb a rib for 15m before going delicately left over an overlap to reach the corner of Olive Oil, which is followed to the top.

English Spinach   30m   E1 5b ***. M. & K.Tighe. 28th August 2000.
The fabulous corner.

There is another unclimbed slabby corner right (looking up) of English Spinach before the crag becomes more broken and the routes shorter. These routes are climbed from a big broken ledge system 8-10m above the sea, and are characterised by some striking white, orange and black vertical banding. Access by abseil.

Orange & Black   20m   HVS 5a *. M.Tighe, I.Lee, G.Anderson. 24th May 2001.
The fine jam crack at the left side of the wall (looking in), between the two very different colours of rock, leads to a mid-way platform. The continuation of the fault-line gives the crux right at the top.

The Bay   20m   Mild VS. M.Tighe, I.Lee, G.Anderson. 24th May 2001.

Climb a shallow bay in the middle of the wall, then a tricky little black wall and short diagonal fault (with a brownish-white quartz vein on the left), followed by easier ground to the top.

The Vein 20m HVS 5a. M. & K.Tighe, J.Cargill. 21st June 2001.
The eroded white quartz vein in the upper part of the cliff, just right of centre.

Black Honey 20m Severe *. M. & K.Tighe. 30th August 2000.
A few metres right of the vein is a fault-line containing unusual rough black honeycombed rock. Fine climbing on the unusual rock.

A' Bheirigh (Berie) (NB 187 451):
Several routes in the easier grades make it a good venue for the lower grade climber. Being only 500m south of Tiumpan Head, access is very similar. Once down a line of 8m bluffs just east of the headland, head up to the high point of the headland. The first route is a traverse line out on to the most north-westerly promontory. Scramble down on the north side until the traverse line can be seen 8-10m above the sea. The start is characterized by a bottomless chimney dropping into the sea.

The Gunnel 50m Very Difficult **. M. & K.Tighe. 30th August 2000.
Follow the traverse line going gently downhill. Arrival is at the neck of a little promontory jutting out to sea, the North Landing. On a calm dry day at low tide it is possible to continue the traverse right around the headland by going down into a boulder choke and up right over a keystone (greasy) on to a diagonal ramp-line. At Very Difficult, return. Otherwise there is a fine crag overlooking the North Landing.

Red Velvet 30m E1 5b **. M. & K.Tighe. 30th August 2000.
The central corner-crack line can be started via the following route (Ard Cuan) or by a short little wall immediately below the line.

Ard Cuan 50m VS 4c **. M. & K.Tighe, J.Winter, N.McCougan. 8th June 2004.
The diagonal crack-line that goes out left from the North Landing, crossing Red Velvet low down. Fine, exciting and well protected.

On the south-west side of the headland the cliffs are more broken and there is a myriad of little walls, chimneys and corners down to the sea. Going down (west) from the high point over yellow lichenous rock, there are two diagonal ramp-lines running towards the North Landing, the upper of which is a continuation of The Gunnel. Both ramps can be scrambled down at Moderate to Difficult. Towards the bottom of the lower one is a tunnel under a boulder; the following route starts here.

The Loom 40m Very Difficult **. K. & M.Tighe. 20th August 2000.
Go out on an exposed ledge on the wall above the tunnel and climb up to the second ramp-line. Finish by a chimney-corner line.

The Weaver 35m Very Difficult *. K. & M.Tighe. 30th August 2000.
About 10m back up the ramp from the previous route zigzag up the wall and head for a chimney in the upper part of the crag.

Creag Ruadh (NB 189 447):

A crag best seen from the opposite side of Loch Garenin, when three small 8-10m stacks can be seen close in by the shore overlooked by the 20-30m cliffs. The stacks are a swimming, rather than climbing challenge, though the central one is joined to the mainland by a precarious bridge. Approach as for the previous two crags, but turn left after 500m and set off around the head of Geodh Ruadh to the cliffs. The three stacks are the best reference points.

Gneiss Little Wall   20m   HVS 5b **. M.Tighe, J.Armour. July 1999.
About 50m south of the south stack, this fine wall is reached by abseil into a little rocky alcove (possible to traverse in to here from Geodh Ruadh). Go out left under a grey rock platform and pull up on to the wall (good protection).

Red Slab   20m   Very Difficult. M.Tighe, A.Gillespie. July 1999.
This is the diagonal slab overlooked by Gneiss Little Wall and just south of South Stack.

Marine Exposure   30m   VS. M. & K.Tighe. 28th August 2000.
A diagonal abseil past an overhang leads to an alcove immediately opposite the northerly most rocks of North Stack. Climb diagonally up left to the left edge of the overhang. Pull through this (good protection) and climb the steep wall and slab above.

Rubha Eacleit (NB 186 439):

Short (15-20m) but worthwhile. There is a fine Hard Severe at the north-west end and an excellent E3 5c *** crack up the front face, gained by a traverse in from the north.

Rubha Talanish (NB 179 437):

Approach: Park at the Garenin road end. Walk down through the village and go south along the rocky coastline to the headland of Rubha Talanish cairn, 50mins. A slightly shorter but less attractive approach is from the road end at Borrowston (NB 189 424), 20mins.

Doctor MacDonald's Farewell to Lewis   60m   Mild VS ***. M. & K.Tighe, H.Clarke. 21st July 2000.
The route lies on the fine black slab on the north-east side of the headland. Abseil down to a jumble of huge boulders at the bottom of the slab, just above the high tide line.
1. 30m. Make a tricky move up the little apron slab to gain a diagonal fault-line which heads up right to join the rib which delineates the north-east and north-west faces.
2. 30m. Follow the fine rib above via cracks and small corners to the top.

The following were sent by I.Small; the relationship to the above is unknown. Approach by abseil. Descriptions start from the right, seaward end. All routes climbed on 18th August 2001 by I.Small and A.Hume.

1. *Blackhouse Arête*   35m   Hard Severe. The prominent arête running straight down into the sea. Abseil to a small ledge above high tide. Climb the left side of the arête.

2. *Stormy Slab*   35m   VS 4c. Abseil to the same ledge as the previous route. Climb the slab to the right of the arête via grooves and a final overlap.

3. *Tigh Dubh*   25m   VS 4c. The corner-line at the left end of Stormy Slab. Abseil to a ledge at the base of the corner.

4. *Tents Away*   25m   E2 5b. The corner-line left again of the previous route. From the ledge climb a steep corner and transfer left to gain the main corner-line. At the final headwall, finish strenuously rightwards via a flake.

5. *Beached Whale*   30m   HVS 5a. The next large corner-line to the left. Abseil to a boulder-covered platform. Climb a steep corner and awkward diagonal crack leading left to the main corner; ascend this directly.

6. *Thatch Top*   30m   E2 5b. Climbs the prominent buttress with a double overlap at the landward end of the crag. Abseil to the platform. Climb a thin crack on the front of a large flake at the base of the buttress. Cross the overlap and gain a thin diagonal crack. Follow this through a second overlap, finishing up the fine headwall.

GREAT BERNERA, Campaigh:
Campaigh is one of a group of small islands off the north coast of Bearnaraigh Beag at the head of Loch Rog an Ear. No more than 500m long and 250m wide, it has a through tunnel at its narrowest point and a second tunnel close by to the south, known as Suilean Dubha (the black eyes). They are well seen from the east. There is no easy landing on the island and there is no water.

Geodh' an Tuill area:
The north side of the geo forms a very overhanging wall.

Yo Heave Ho   12m   E2 6a. H.Cottam (unsec). 30th May 2004.
Follows the most obvious weakness at the left end of the wall.

The next two routes are on the western end of the overhanging wall.

Inchling   12m   VS 4c. J.Wright, H.Cottam. 30th May 2004.
The right-hand crack direct.

Friggin' in the Riggin'   12m   HVS 5a. A.Norton, K.Archer. 30th May 2004.
The left-rising crack-line in the centre of the face to a precarious exit.

The next two routes are on The Pinnacle, well seen to the left and gained by following a dyke.

Bruichladdich   14m   VS 4c. J.Wright, H.Cottam. 30th May 2004.
Descend the dyke until below an overlapping block. Climb direct to this then traverse left into a groove. Up this until you can step left on the headwall to finish.

Tide & Timing   14m   VS 4c. A.Norton, K.Archer. 30th May 2004.
Named for the crossing of the dyke to reach the start! Climb the crack and wall direct.

The next two routes are on Wheeling Gull Wall, the west facing wall of the small geo, which runs into a cave on the south side of Geodh' an Tuill.

Wee Restorative   15m   HVS 5a. K.Archer, A.Norton. 30th May 2004.
The first corner on the left when looking at the wall. Abseil down to ledges then climb the corner direct, nice.

Crabwalk   15m   E2 5b. H.Cottam, J.Wright. 30th May 2004.
Abseil down Wee Restorative to a small triangular platform to the right. Climb up and right to join the hanging corner; follow this to finish.

Platform Bay Area:
On the north side of the island is a large bay with a low tide platform at the back. The following route lies in a corner at its right end, gained from the same area as The Pinnacle.

Railsway   12m   E1 5c. H.Cottam, J.Wright. 30th May 2004.
The obvious clean hanging corner with a horizontal rail just above half-height.

The next routes are on the main, west-facing wall of Platform Bay; this was the only area where care was needed with exits because of loose rock at the top. The wall is divided into two distinct sides by a central corner. Access is by abseil down the corner.

Heart of Oak   18m   E4 6a. H.Cottam (unsec). 31st May 2004.
Start from the big ramp below the big corner. Climb the corner with an overlap at two-thirds height.

Gall, Wisdom & Guile   30m   E1 *. A.Norton, K.Archer (alt). 31st May 2004.
1. 16m 5a Follow the corner formed by the ramp to where it meets the left wall of Wee Restorative, make a curious move to gain this and cross over to a ledge on the right.
2. 14m 5b Go right and around the arête to gain the corner. Follow this (poor protection), then traverse right just below the top to finish.

Impacted Wisdom   15m   HVS 5a. H.Cottam, J.Wright. 31st May 2004.
The central corner and abseil line. Follow the corner direct.

Caolas Cul Campaigh Corners:
This is the most extensive area of rock, with several distinct sections, starting from the north-east end of Platform Bay and extending to the north-east tip of the island.

The West End:
Abseil down the first obvious right-facing corner near the junction with Platform Bay.

(The Famous) Sunshine Arête   15m   Severe ***. A.Norton, K.Archer. 31st May 2004.
Traverse left (facing in) from the abseil around two corners. Climb the superb arête.

Dark Corner 15m HVS 5a. H.Cottam, J.Wright. 31st May 2004.
Pleasant climbing up the corner right of Sunshine Arête.

No Toast on Campaigh 15m Severe. K.Archer, A.Norton. 31st May 2004.
The well-cracked slabby face left of Sunshine Arête.

Little Britain Wall:
The next area eastwards. Abseil down the wall to a good ledge which runs its full length.

Little Britain 16m HVS 5a *. A.Norton, K.Archer. 1st June 2004.
Follow the obvious ramp rising from the right end of the ledge.

Aberdoon Stookhoose 16m HVS 5a *. K.Archer, A.Norton. 1st June 2004.
Follow the crack-line direct, easier and better protected than it looks.

Swingback 16m E2 5c. H.Cottam, J.Wright. 2nd June 2004.
The left-facing corner around the left arête of Little Britain Wall. Climb the shallow corner, then continue direct.

Sovay 16m VS 4c. J.Wright, H.Cottam. 2nd June 2004.
The corner at the right end of Little Britain Wall.

The Middle East:
The next section eastwards, reached by abseil down Swing Back.

Northern Sky 18m E2 5b **. K.Archer, A.Norton. 2nd June 2004.
From the bottom of the abseil, traverse left (facing in) to a line of shattered flakes. Climb these over a bulge to a short headwall; pull up and over to finish.

And the Sea Smiled Back 18m E1 5a. A.Norton, K.Archer. 2nd June 2004.
Start 2m right (facing in) from the start of Northern Sky. Tenuous moves up a poorly protected ramp lead to a short headwall.

Geo Mor Campaigh:
The eastern end of the main (northern) tunnel.
Note: *S(limy) Says it All* was a two pitch escape traverse from the entrance of the tunnel back to the right end of Suilean Dubha Wall. K.Archer, A.Norton, 2nd June 2004.

Suilean Dubha Area, The Southern Tunnel:
At its western and landward end the superb rock architecture can be seen forming a curving arch with a small return wall on the south side. A good place when tide or weather rule out other areas.

The Eyes Have It 22m HVS **. A.Norton, K.Archer. 1st June 2004.
1. 6m 5a. From a stance at the right end of the small southern wall, traverse left into the corner.
2. 16m 5a. Traverse left along the lip of the cave using the breaks, to finish up a short corner.

Green Door 15m HVS 5a *. J.Wright, H.Cottam. 1st June 2004.
From the slab at the left end of the arch traverse rightwards to the centre, then finish direct avoiding a loose hold.

Jonah Be Goode 18m E2. H.Cottam, J.Wright (alt). 1st June 2004.
1. 12m 5b. From the bottom of the cave traverse leftwards along the right wall just above sea-level (mid to low tide) by a series of cracks and small slabs to the first blowhole.
2. 6m 5a. Finish by climbing out the blowhole.

The No's to the Right 12m HVS 5a. K.Archer, A.Norton. 3rd June 2004.
From the right end of the return wall, climb the corner and overlaps to finish through a notch.

Whale of a Time 15m HVS 5a. A.Norton, K.Archer. 3rd June 2004.
Traverse left from the starting moves of The No's... for 3m to below an overhanging nose. Pull through this and the next on good holds to the top.

Sarcophagus with the Moves 38m E3 5c, 5a **. K.Archer, A.Norton. 4th June 2004.
1. 18m 5c. From the slab at the western end (common with Green Door), traverse into the tunnel passing two corners until forced to make blind moves down (wet). Take a stance on a ledge directly below the first blow hole.
2. 20m 5a. Step right on to a slab and cross it to its right end. Descend a short wall and cross the easy but slippery slab to the exit. Not possible at high water or big swell.

Suilean Dubha Wall:
The wall between the seaward ends of the two tunnels.
Oblivion Arête (H.Cottam, J.Wright, 2nd June 2004). Climb the arête and grooves trending left, then back right to a worrying exit on big hanging blocks.

CRULIVIG (NB 171 334) Note:
R.I.Jones & J.Sanders climbed Lard of the Pies (SMCJ 2003) and agreed with the note that it is the crag referred to by Andy Macfarlane. The crag is lichenous in its top third and the only line that looks worth climbing is Lard of the Pies, HVS 5a ***, marred by the exit through thick reed grass.

UIG SEA CLIFFS, AIRD UIG AREA, Gallen Head Stack (NB 052 387, tidal):
A fine 25m fin shaped stack lies 400m north of Aird Uig. It is accessible at mid to low tide, by a 70m descent down a steep grassy slope which is best protected by abseil.

Depth Charge 25m HVS 4b. R.I.Jones, J.Sanders. 15th June 2004.
Climb a left-facing corner on the south fin pulling right 2m before the top of the corner to avoid a loose exit. Continue with care to the top. Descent is best by abseil down the route. The name came from the sound of rock being cleared by the leader during the first ascent as it thundered into the sea.

Gallen Beag 1:
These climbs precede those recorded in Gallen Beag 1 in SMCJ 194 p361. Working from the north (left looking in) side of the crag the first obvious corner gives:

S'mad 20m Severe. M. & K.Tighe. 24th June 2001.
The left bounding corner line of the main slab with a choice of corner or groove on the left to finish.

Spanish Windlash 20m Hard Severe *. K. & M.Tighe. 24th June 2001.
The obvious diagonal fault-line running right to left up the face is good entertainment.

The Ruby 20m Mild VS **. M. & K.Tighe. 24th June 2001.
Fabulous climbing up the right bounding arête of the main face. Traverse right from the bottom of Spanish Windlass to the arête. Excellent jugs lead to a ledge and tricky diagonal crack to finish.

Further Adventures in Paradise 20m E1 5b ***. M. & K.Tighe. 24th June 2001.
The immaculate stepped corner to the right/south end of the main wall.

Grooved Arête 20m Severe. M. & K.Tighe. 24th June 2001.
Go right from Further Adventures… Climb a squarish pillar to a ledge at half-height and the grooved arête above.

Swirlpool 20m Mild VS *. M. & K.Tighe. 24th June 2001.
Just right of Grooved Arête is an open corner with a black slab to the right. Abseil down to sea-level and tackle a tricky sloping chimney, a broken corner and a slab-corner.

Magic Geo:
The Crimebusters of the Sea 35m E5 6a **. P.Robins, B.Bransby. 11th June 2004.
A marvellous outing up the obvious weakness in the back of the geo. Starting at the back, climb the left wall to a flake leading into a pink cave. Shuffle and wriggle on outwards and upwards to an easier finish in the wider chimney.

The Eagle Has Landed 35m E6 6b **. P.Robins, B.Bransby. 11th June 2004.
Another splendid journey up the back of the geo, climbing the obvious lower arête, then through the bulge and into the slim finishing groove. The arête is climbed direct and is bold. Going through the bulges is the crux (small cams useful), gaining a block ledge. Step right and go up the pleasant wall and into the finishing groove.

Gimp Route 35m E4 5c **. B.Bransby, P.Robins. 11th June 2004.
Climb the initial corner of The Sorcerer to the ledges, then move left and pull through the bulge, using a flake. Traverse right along a thin seam to gain a ramp which soon becomes a crack, just left of The Alchemist? Go direct to the top.

Screaming Geo:
Bothy House Crack 25m E2 5b. P.Robins, B.Bransby. 12th June 2004.
The obvious off-width that finishes close to the bothy. Cam 5 useful.

Hullaballoo Left-Foot   20m   E5 6a. B.Bransby, P.Robins. 10th June 2004.
A pitch based on Hullaballoo, quite how similar they are is uncertain. From directly below the main corner, climb up and left (fiddly gear) then back right into the corner. Follow this then step left into slim hanging ramp/groove leading leftwards to the top.

Rats Don't Eat Sandwiches   30m   E4 6a ***. L.Houlding, J.Pickles. 9th June 2004.
A very good route which pulls out right from Salty Dog. Start as for that route but traverse right at about 10m to a ledge. Climb the slim groove above to a roof and pull through this to gain a ledge then on to the top.

Damn Your Eyes!   30m   E4 5c. P.Robins, B.Bransby. 9th June 2004.
Starting 5m right of The Screaming Ab Dabs the following route takes a groove-line and provides a good starting pitch for Paranoid Slippers on the tier above. Climb a short corner to a sloping ledge and break. Step left and climb into the main groove, moving left to the vague arête which leads to the main horizontal break. Continue up the slanting groove above, climbing mainly on the left wall (no gear but only 5b).

MINGULAY, Rubha Liath, Geirum Walls:
Seal Clubbing   10m   E1 5c *. G.Latter. 19th August 2004
Start just right of Sealed with a Kiss. Climb up to the right end of the small overlap. Then direct up the wall to finish up the final section of the flake-crack.

Guarsay Mor:
Direct Start to Swimming to America   25m   E2 5b *. N. and P.Craig. 12th June 2004.
Climb up and left round the rib to the left of the belay at the top of the first pitch of Save Our Soles, into a shallow groove right of Lost Souls. Climb this and the wall above direct to a belay below the roof of Swimming to America.

Cobweb Wall:
Unnamed   105m   HVS ***. G.Latter, C.Pulley. 15th August 2004.
Tackles a right-trending groove come ramp system at the right side of the pink veined wall. Start as for Cuan a' Bochan.
1. 50m 5a. From a small ledge below a small overhang, move up to the small overhang. Tackle it on its right-hand side and follow jugs up to a pink bay. Follow bulging rock and a crack on the right-hand side of the pink bay, to an obvious right-rising grey ramp-line. Follow jugs up this to its top.
2. 55m 4c. Follow a series of short corner systems and a broken slab to rejoin the first abseil ledge. Pleasant easy climbing on fragile rock leads to the top.

The South Pillar:
Bill Oddie Eat Your Heart Out   100m   E1 5b *. P.Hemmings, C.Stein. 8th June 2004.
Thirteen meters right of Stugeron on the south face (right of the crest of the point). Abseil 100m to high water level trending rightwards to an isolated section of projecting rock, under which lies a hidden ledge.

1. 25m 5b. From the ledge climb the immediate crack on the right to the top of the isolated rock feature. Climb corners trending rightwards and upwards to a ledge, below a steep wall.

2. 25m 5b. Climb the wall initially on the left, before pulling into the centre to climb flakes and flutes. Follow the natural weakness first rightwards till forced to move into a series of broken corners to a ledge. Traverse rightwards to small ledges and belay below a wall (enjoy the bird life!).

3. 15m 4c. Climb the face above the ledge, trending leftwards then back right up an obvious corner to a large platform. Excellent pitch.

4. 20m 5b. Climb the corner, moving left when the corner runs out (tricky) and pull on to a ledge. Ascend a small wall to a ledge.

5. 15m 4a. Climb pink felspar rock to the top.

Near Stugeron, a large ledge system runs across the cliff at about one-third height. The centre of this ledge supports a large left-facing corner directly below a roof with a prominent crack. The following route is located directly below the central corner of the ledge system.

Unnamed 95m E2 ***. C.Pulley, G.Latter. 16th August 2004.
This route starts on a good ledge, above the high-water mark, with a right-facing corner/chimney at its left hand end. Access is by a 100m abseil.

1 40m 5b. Follow the corner/chimney and its continuation crack over steep ground until a headwall impedes progress. At this point step airily left to a rib. Head more easily upwards, via a short layback crack, to the large ledge and belay below its central corner.

2 55m 5b. Climb the corner to join the roof above on its right-hand side. Move leftwards over the top of the roof and into a short crack/corner that leads to a bulge. From here, undercut leftwards into a prominent right-facing corner. Follow the corner steeply until easier rock leads to the top.

Dun Mingulay, Sron An Duin:
Storm Warning 70m E2 *. R.Austin, R.Durran, G.Latter. 17th August 2004.
Start on tidal ledges at the base of an obvious flake-crack in a black bulge, below and right of the start of Fifteen Fathoms of Fear.

1. 40m 5c. Climb the black flake, move up to another curving flake and climb it to gain short twin cracks leading with difficulty to a good ledge.

2. 30m 4c. Trend leftwards to finish as for Fifteen Fathoms of Fear. A more direct finish should be possible.

PABBAY, Bay Area:
Rebel without a Porpoise 25m E5 6a **. P. and N.Craig. 6th June 2004.
Start in a black groove just left of the blunt rib left of The Herbrudean (SMCJ 2001). Climb the groove for a few metres, then right on to the rib. Climb this to the slab under a band of overhangs. Step right into a bottomless groove, then climb strenuously up and right to a junction with The Herbrudean. Follow this to the top.

Banded Geo:
Geomancer 45m E7 6b ***. N.McNair, P.Newman. May 2003.

Takes a stupendous line to the left of Ship of Fools. Start up a black groove until an obvious traverse can be made out to the roof. Tackle the roof via pockets and a small right-facing flange (crux). Once on the headwall climb up trending slightly left to head for a large pod/flake. Attack the bulge directly above this to reach the capping roof/corner. Escape rightwards along this.

Note: A straightened-out version of The Fool of Ships (E6 6b) was created whilst trying Ship of Fools in 2002. No falls were taken and no pre-inspection.

Allanish Peninsula, Hoofers Geo:
Brother Ray   30m   E5 6b **. R.Campbell, P.Thorburn. 11th June 2004.
The wall right of Sugar Cane Country. Fine climbing though escapable from below the crux. High in the grade and bold. Climb SCC to the start of the crack, traverse right along a break to the centre of the wall before moving up to a pocketed break above (nut runner to the right). Ascend the middle of the wall with difficulty to a good slot (protection) and continue to a juggy flake shake-out on SCC. Stroll up the steep headwall above right end of flake with surprising ease.

JA's Maelstrom   20m   E4 6a *. N.McNair, P.Newman. May 2003.
Takes the flake system between The Fantastic Mr JA and Sugar Cane Country starting up The Fantastic and striking straight up where that route bends left to finish on an arête.

The Poop Deck:
Damnations   25m   E7 6b ****. P.Thorburn, R.Campbell, G.Latter (redpointed). 10th June 2004.
Stupendous sustained climbing, tackling the twin hanging cracks up the centre of the wall. Start up the first few moves as for The Raven, then pull up and left on to the incut shelf above (skyhook in pocket). Make a hard move rocking over to gain the horizontal break above (good runners), and move left and follow the cracks, mainly following the right one to pull into a large break beneath the roof (Cams to 5). Move left to pull rightwards though the roof with very difficult moves to stand on the lip. Continue much more easily directly up the wall above.

Rosinish Peninsula:
Note: N.Morrison notes that Taxi for Tam was done in 2002 not 2003. The route Bouncing Bim, "on the island opposite the camping place" must surely be on the Rosinish Peninsula (which is not an island).

Bay Area:
N.Morrison was on the FA of Irish Rover along with W.Moir, P.Allen and M.Atkins.

MULL, Scoor, Beach Wall:
The Reality Dysfunction   15m   E6 6a. N.McNair. May 2004.
Takes the arête to the left of Waves and White Water. Start on the arête and the drainpipe feature before moving on to the arête proper at half-height with the crux right at the top. Low in the grade but very serious at the top.

Ardtun, Stirk Crag:
O.J.Killer   12m   HVS 5a *. C.Moody, A.Soloist. 15th September 2004.

Right of Gribun Phone Box Vandals are two cracks above a big block. Climb the left-hand crack.

Erraid, Lower Tier:
Fools Gold 8m E2 6a. J.Lines, P.Thorburn. June 2004.
Start below a flying fin left of two main arêtes. Boulder up a seam on to a ledge on the right. Finish up an easy corner.

Red Anvil Chasm (NM 287 195):
Formed by the same dyke as Asteroid Chasm but a further 400m north-west. Probably climbable at high tide.

Red Anvil 15m E3 5c *. J.Lines, P.Thorburn. June 2004.
On its north-east facing wall, climb cracks to the anvil, then take the easiest line out right.

The south-east facing wall has an obvious groove in the centre with a loose block at the top.

Unnamed 8m E3/4 6a *. P.Thorburn, J.Lines. June 2004.
A thin crack starting off a block 4m left of the groove. Awkward to protect.

Paz Irmao 10m E1 5b *. J.Lines, P.Thorburn. June 2004.
A crack 2m right of the groove.

Unnamed 10m HVS 5a *. P.Thorburn, J.Lines. June 2004.
A crack 2m right of Paz Irmao.

Karen's Slab (NM 297 197):
An isolated clean south-west facing slab 300m north-east of the beach.

Sophie 12m E2 5b *. J.Lines, P.Thorburn. June 2004.
The slab. Start up a crack, step right and go up to another crack.

Holly 12m E3 6a. J.Lines, P.Thorburn. June 2004.
A thin slab on left with a hard start.

SKYE

SGURR A'MHADAIDH, The Coir'-uisg Face:
Second-Third Gully/First-Second Gully Combination 260m IV,5. D.Ritchie, M.Shaw, N.MacGougan. 17th January 2004.
1. 40m. Icy steps and chockstones lead under a huge chockstone followed by a short wall to a small cave.
2. 60m. The large cave avoided in summer was climbed direct (crux) followed by easy snow.
3. and 4. 80m. Traverse right over a rib and descend into First-Second Gully, following this to a narrowing.
5. 60m. Climb over several interesting chockstones until above the final difficulty.
6. 20m. Easy snow to the ridge.

SGURR THEARLAICH, West Face:
BC Buttress 110m IV,5. D.Ritchie, M.Shaw. 2nd January 2004.

Good icy mixed climbing taking the buttress between Gully B and Gully C. Start below a prominent groove midway between the gullies.
1. 25m. Climb the icy groove and move up to below a corner.
2. 35m. Climb the short corner above, step right then follow left-trending grooves to a point where a right traverse can be made to gain a prominent jutting block.
3. 50m. Climb straight up reaching easier ground and the main ridge crest.

Vent Du Nord   80m   V,6. D.Ritchie, D.McEachan. 13th February 2005.
This route follows the obvious open groove on the right side of the buttress situated between Gully B and Gully C. Start right of the original route at the point where the base of the buttress turns into the foot of Gully C.
1. 15m. Climb the fault overlooking Gully C to gain a small ledge.
2. 30m. Continue up the open groove above stepping left at a small bulge to gain easier ground. A good pitch.
3. 35m. Move up and left, then back right climbing a short corner directly above the belay to finish up easier ground to the main ridge.

CD Buttress   110m   V,6. D.Ritchie, M.Shaw. 29th January 2004.
A fine route taking the buttress between Gully C and Gully D. Start at the lowest rocks.
1. 40m. Climb broken rocks to gain the foot of an obvious off-width corner-crack. Climb this followed by a second similar corner-crack.
2. 40m. Move straight up for a few metres, then step right gaining a rightwards-rising snow ramp. Follow this to a point overlooking Gully D. Climb a short groove on the left followed by a traverse back right to below the obvious fault splitting the upper wall.
3. 30m. Follow the fine left-slanting crack-line to finish on the main ridge.

Coir' An Lochain (Sgurr Thearlaich):
Aladdin's Route   80m   IV,6.   D.Ritchie, D.McEachan, N.MacGougan. 12th February 2005.
By the summer route, found to be disappointingly short but worthwhile nevertheless. Start below and left of the chimney in a snowy alcove.
1. 35m. Climb an easy angled snowy slab and cross a snow ledge to gain a cave below the main difficulties.
2. 35m. Climb the chimney above with interest to below a huge chockstone.
3. 10m. Surmount the chockstone using the left wall (crux) and climb steeply to finish in the TD Gap.

SRON NA CICHE, The Cioch:
The Gathering   30m   E8 6b ****. D.MacLeod. 8th June 2004.
A spectacular but very serious line climbing the dark underside of the Cioch. The line follows a faint seam leading to an obvious spike in the middle of the wall. Belay on large friends halfway up Slab Corner, at the base of the seam. Hard technical moves lead to a good crimp. Follow the seam for a few moves then break out right on pock-marks with a tenuous sequence leading to good edges and the spike (good rest and first protection). Continue rightwards past a diagonal crack to gain the easy upper slabs.

NEIST, The Upper Crag, Financial Sector:
Above and right of Waterfront (1998) a shorter clean-looking wall has a disjointed crack system on its right.

Robbo's Truss Fund 22m Severe. R.Brown. N.Bassnett, A.Holden. 30th August 2004.
Reach the bottom of the cracks by scrambling up and leftwards through broken rocks to a heathery ledge. Pleasant climbing leads to a large square bay above mid-height. Exit on the right up rock that requires careful treatment.

Island Revenue 25m HVS 5a. N.Bassnett, A.Holden, R.Brown. 30th August 2004.
The clean obvious right-facing corner just right of Robbo's is approached in a similar fashion. Sustained (some would add character-forming) in nature until the big ledge is reached just above the overlap. An easier groove leads to the top.

Immediately right of Terminal Bonus is an impressive right-facing corner.

The Banks of Locharron 30m VS 4c *. R.Brown. N.Bassnett. 31st July 2004.
From the heather ledge climb the corner dodging right only to make use of the massive free standing flake.

Immediately right is a buttress with twin roofs at mid-height. A plethora of routes with alternative starts make good use of this section. Most easily identified is Black Scholes, which takes the dominant left-facing corner and crack straight through the roof. The first route is an eliminate between The Banks of Locharron and Midas Touch which, although offering only 50% independence, gives good climbing. Start just left of the lower continuation crack-line that is Black Scholes.

Days of Gold 30m E1 5a. R.Brown, N.Bassnett. 2nd Sept 2004.
Ascend the left side of a small alcove and continue up and right to a slight recess (joining Black Scholes). Pull over a bulge, then step up left on to slabby ramp. Continue up and then more easily left to gain the top of a large detached block. Move up into the short open book corner. Gain the crack above direct and/or by using the slab to its right. Continue straight up to the left end of the curving overhang, to join Midas Touch. Move diagonally right and up to finish on the highest block.

Immediately right of Shocks and Stares is a right-tilting crack leading into a V-groove.

Redd Sales 25m VS 4c *. R.Brown. N.Bassnett. 31st August 2004.
Start as for Shocks and Stares but continue up and right to the grassy bank below the crack. Step into this from the right but after a couple of moves traverse right, at a flake, until almost in the chimney. Move up on hollow but secure flakes to regain the crack, which is abandoned when the crack widens to use small bolt-ons on the slab. Bridge up the groove to finish.

Chic Hens for Free 28m HVS 5b *. N.Bassnett, R.Brown. 31st July 2004.

Start as for Bridging Interest but step leftwards along a ramp, climbing up to a triangulated jutting fin with a ledge below and on its right. Reach across the shattered cracks to gain the right arête (crux). Move up and back left into a short corner which gives access to fine twin cracks and easier climbing.

The buttress to the right of Shining Path (SMCJ 2000) holds clean walls of rock higher up, above an untidy lower section. The next route gains and climbs a clean right-facing corner in the higher section which is not immediately visible from directly below, but is easily seen from Poverty Point.

Doppelganger   45m   Hard Severe 4b. M.Hudson, J.Sutton, A.Holden. 28th July 2004.
Start 15m right of Shining Path below two small roofs at 3m. Climb past the left end of the roofs and continue over broken columns before taking the front of the rib above to a heather ledge (possible belay). Follow the big corner above past a steepening of jammed blocks.

Lower Tier Note (C. Moody): The January storm has caused many new rock scars along the lower tier. One rock 25m up (over 100kg.) was ripped out of the cliff and left 3m higher up the hill. There are many turfed areas that are now bare rock. The 30m high arch below Wish you were Here (next to One Way Bottle, SMCJ 1999) has been washed away. A Type of Cooker (SMCJ 2001) has been washed away.

Lower Tier, The Euro Zone:
This is the sea-cliff below The Financial Sector. Fulmars might be a problem in the nesting season. Either go easily down the rib below Worm's Eye View and abseil from boulders, or go down steep grass below Terminal Bonus and scamble in. Around the centre of the cliff is a buttress; the traverse round the base of the buttress is tidal. There is a scrambling descent between Still Hot and the Original Descent. The first nine routes finish on a ledge below a 4m wall. A finish was made up this wall by the left side of the large flake, Very Difficult. Other finishes would be possible after removing loose holds.

Still Wet   18m   VS 4c *. C.Moody, C.Grindley. 20th March 2005.
The prominent right-facing corner.

Frozen Turf   18m   Difficult. C.Moody. 26th February 2005.
Left of Yellow Flake is a prominent corner-crack, Still Wet. Climb a left-facing corner crack just right.

Yellow Flake   18m   Severe. C.Moody. 26th February 2005.
Round left of Stormer is a wide crack. Just left of this climb a crack, then a rib. Climb a flake-crack in the yellow rock to a rock scar and easier ground.

Stormer   18m   VS 4c. C.Moody, C.Grindley. 20th March 2005.
Start at the left end of the slabby bay on a barnacle ledge. Climb a crack in brown rock to gain the right side of the rock scar, then continue up the crack-line. Step right below a bulge and finish steeply.

Summer in the City   18m   HVS 5a *. C.Moody, C.Grindley. 20th March 2005.
Good varied climbing. Climb the crack right of Stormer and pull out right. Continue up the slot and pull out right. Move left and finish up the rib on big holds.

Risk of Ice   16m   Very Difficult. C.Moody. 26th February 2005.
Start up and right from Stormer. Climb a short crack, then step left and climb a short corner. Step left again and finish up a bulge.

Summer Time Blues   16m   VS 4b. C.Moody, C.Grindley. 20th March 2005.
Just right of Risk of Ice, climb the crack through bulges to a shelf. Step up left and finish up twin cracks in the corner.

Spindrift   18m   Difficult *. C.Moody. 26th February 2005.
Start 4m right of Risk of Ice. Climb corner-cracks, then traverse left above a steep slab and finish up a corner.

Icefall   16m   Moderate. C.Moody. 26th February 2005.
Start 5m right of Spindrift. Climb a short crack up right, then move left up a corner and right up a shelf.

Staircase Left-Hand Start   12m   Severe. C.Moody, C.Grindley. 20th March 2005.
Start below and left of Staircase at the right side of the pillar, well right of Icefall. Climb a corner-crack to join the original route halfway up.

Staircase   14m   Easy. C.Moody. 29th January 2005.
Start left of the descent. Move up left on huge holds, then move right to finish.

Still Hot   12m   Severe. C.Moody, C.Grindley. 20th March 2005.
Above Staircase are three short cracks. Climb the right-hand crack with a little help from the middle crack.

Original Descent   10m   Moderate.
The crack left of The Banister.

The Banister   12m   Difficult *. B.Taylor. 28th November 2004.
Climb the prominent crack just left of the front of the buttress and continue up.

Wet Soles   14m   Severe. C.Moody. 26th February 2005.
Start at the low point of the traverse at low tide. Follow a barnacle crack and finish up the crack above the block.

Powder   14m   Very Difficult. C.Moody. 26th February 2005.
Start just right of Wet Soles at low tide. Go up twin cracks, then move left to a ledge. Climb a short steep crack right of the block.

Rope Gripper   10m   Difficult. C. Moody. 28th November 2004.
On the right side of the buttress are two parallel cracks. Climb the left-hand one.

Rope Jammer   12m   Very Difficult. C.Moody, B.Taylor. 28th November 2004.
The right-hand crack is 8mm wide.

Poverty Point:

Fifty-fifty   20m   E1 5a *. M.Hudson (unseconded). 4th May 2004.
A prominent rib facing north towards Destitution Point and 10m right of the shaley
cave. If the front of the rib is strictly followed, then protection is very spaced.
Take the crest of the rib on exposed blocky ledges and follow a tapering flake
above in a fine position. Leave the top of the flake (crux) for the final wall.

Fifty-Fifty Left-Hand   20m   HVS 5a *. M.Hudson, B.Birkett. 1st June 2004.
A left-hand variation start reaching the final flake less drastically by cracks on the
left of the arête.

Immediately south of Fifty-fifty is a tall bay of dark-brown rock. Several fine,
non-tidal routes lead from here to a stake belay. A smooth wall with a dark triangular
slot at 3m forms the very left end of the bay.

Black Eye   20m   E1 5b **. M.Hudson, A.Holden, J.Sutton. 27th July 2004.
Pull up the left edge of the wall, with committing moves to reach the dark triangle.
Continue up the wall to a hand-traverse right to reach a crack leading back left to
the top of the tapering flake. Finish as for Fifty-fifty or up a short crack immediately
right.

American Football is Dangerous   20m   E2 5b *. J.Sutton, A.Holden, M.Hudson.
27th July 2004.
Three metres right is a crack-line which steepens to provide a fine layback and
jamming finale.

Thank God for Roger's Aliens   20m   E2 5b *. B.Birkett, M.Hudson. 1st June
2004.
Two metres right again is a leaning left-facing corner with a bulge at half-height.
Climb the corner with a sustained section to pass the bulge.

Flower Power   20m   E3 5c. L.Jones, J.Sutton (yo-yoed). August 2004.
The crack 3m right again, passing a small in-situ flower high up.

Plates of Wood   20m   VS 4c. A.Holden, J.Sutton, M.Hudson. 27th July 2004.
The big dark corner at the back of the bay gives a solid and straightforward line.

Italian Job   18m   E1 5b **. R.Brown. N.Bassnett. 30th October 2004.
This climbs the smooth wall just right of Shelter using cracks on its left edge. A
bold route still awaiting a direct start. Start in the Shelter corner and step up on to
the arête, moving round right to get established on the front face. Sustained wall
climbing leads to a ledge. A left-facing corner above is followed to easy ground.

Note: C. Moody notes that The Man from Ankle (SMCJ 2004, p615) is on an
obvious pillar. The pillar is right of Golden Shower (not left) as you face the cliff.
The pillar is well above high tide.

Destitution Point:
The following routes lie in the short westward facing bay to the north of the Prow,
running from north to south.

Yellow Crack   10m   VS 4c *. D.MacAulay & party. 2003.
Climb the layback crack.

The bay features three shallow corners in the north wall, mentioned but not named in SMCJ 2003.

Haggis   10m   VS 4b *. W. & L.Gordon-Canning. 1999.
The leftmost of the three shallow corners.

Neeps   10m   VS 5a *. W. & L.Gordon-Canning. 1999.
The central corner 3m to the right.

Wee Dram   10m   VS 5a *. W. & L.Gordon-Canning. 1999.
The wall and thin cracks right of Neeps, requiring commitment to start before following an obvious higher crack more easily.

Tatties   10m   Severe *. W. & L.Gordon-Canning. 1999.
Follow cracks just left of the clean rightmost corner. The corner itself is unclimbed.

The corner is bounded on the other side by a rectangular cutaway buttress, which gives good climbing on excellent rock up its blunt undercut arête.

Alien Territory   10m   E2 5c **. R.Brown. J.Holden. 25th September 2004.
Balance up the inverted V-slab and grasp the lip of the buttress. Hand and tiptoe traverse rightwards to good handholds on the right-hand edge. A narrow-width pocket in the bottom corner of the face is vital for protection here. Committing moves gain a ledge above. The wall and slab above are easier but equally fine.

Steaming Entrails   12m   Very Difficult *. W. & L.Gordon-Canning. 1999.
The open black chimney to the right in the corner of the bay.

Pennywhistle   8m   Severe 4c *. N.Bassnett, R.Brown. May 2004. (This line was probably also climbed before but not claimed, by D.MacAulay & party, 2003).
The slab 2m right gives an excellent short route or solo. Keep central for maximum enjoyment.

A short crack just right again is climbed at 5a. Two short broken corners further right are climbed at Mild Severe and Very Difficult. The easiest scramble descent through this area is made down a diagonal ramp line across the top of the Pennywhistle slab.

Long Way Home   8m   Severe 4b. N.Bassnett, R.Brown. May 2004.
The broken juggy arête several metres right on the southern walls of the bay.

Black Chimney   10m   Very Difficult. D.MacAulay & party. 2003.
A tall black groove with a steep finish just right again.

Flea de Wean   14m   HVS 5a *. M.Hudson, J.Sutton. 29th October 2004.
A series of sharp grooves immediately right of the arête. Reachy climbing with minimal gear placements.

Cogless Direct   16m   HVS 5b **. J.Sutton, M.Hudson. 29th October 2004.

Start at sea-level directly below the final corner of Cogless (1998), up the sharp hanging groove immediately to the right of the normal start. An athletic and well-protected combination.

The following lines are grouped around the huge dark sea-chimney visible from the approach, which can be inspected from the landward slopes. Approach by abseil from blocks well back on top of the Prow to small foot-ledges beneath the chimney, and belay on the same blocks.

Squeenius   20m   VS 4c **. M.Hudson, J.Sutton. 29th October 2004.
Start on a dark foot ledge on the left wall of the big chimney. Move up and swing out left over the water onto the front face. Move up on blocky holds and finish up a crack on the right.

Cave Monster   20m   E1 5b ***. J.Sutton, B.Wear. September 2004.
From the same platform as Squeenius, climb the left side of the cave up to a right-facing corner. Good laybacks in the crack lead to a big roof. Pull around this on the left side to good holds. This route may share ground with True Colours (previous SMCJ).

Bleed In Beige   20m   E3 6a/b. D.MacAulay (unsec). May 2003.
Climbs through the triple roofs to the right of True Colours. Start as for Man of Straw but move left on the initial slab at a loose flake, to a blind move left under the first overlap (place awkward protection in the cracks here). Climb through the hanging corners direct.

Across the small cove from Destitution Point is an area of broken pillars accessed by a low-tide scramble or an abseil from above. A short line has been recorded here.

L'Americano   20m   Very Difficult. D.MacAulay, F.McCormick. 8th April 2003.
Climb a forgettable groove / chimney through broken rock.

Foghorn Cove:
The following line lies 10m left of the two deep-water solo lines below the lighthouse climbed by G.Latter in 1999 (SMCJ 2000). It was also suggested by J.Sutton that the existing cracks could be upped a grade to VS and HVS.

Hypertension   15m   E1 5c ***. J.Sutton, L.Jones (both solo). August 2004.
The first line of thin cracks on the steep north-west facing wall. Traverse in from the left to below a small roof. Pull over the roof and follow the steep crack on improving holds.

Baywatch Area:
The next line lies south of the lighthouse steps.

Don't Leave Your Dad in the Rain   20m   Severe 4b *. M.Hudson, A.Holden. 27th July 2004.

Immediately right of Keeping the BOFS.. (1997) is a narrow slab. Pad up the right edge with enjoyable run-out moves higher up.

The Lower Crag, Yellow Walls:
Note: C.Moody notes that for Senora (SMCJ 2004, p616), turn left to Supercharger not right.

TROTTERNISH:
Pop Out Gully   100m   V. M.Fowler, P.Watts. 31st January 2004.
The right-hand gully behind the Old Man of Storr. Deep, atmospheric and rewarding with the crux at the top. The last of the major gully lines behind the Old Man to be climbed.
1. 30m. Two short steps, the second being hard, lead to snow and a pitch in the depths of the gully.
2. 30m. Fine climbing to snow and a large chockstone belay.
3. 40m. A steep ice step followed by difficult climbing on thin ice trending up left to exit on the top by squirming under a chockstone.

FLODIGARRY:
This route is found 5m south of A First for Murdo (SMCJ 2003). Abseil from two boulders half-way down the arête to a massive block in the mouth of a huge recess. This point is about 50m north of Buoy Racer. The route takes a line up the south edge of the clean slab just north of the recess.

Milk Tray Man   30m   Severe *. M.Hudson, M.Price, D.N.Williams. 6th June 2004.
Step off the block and climb through a steep scoop to gain the slab above. Climb close to the left edge of the slab, nicely poised at moments over the recess, to regain the two boulders.

RUBHA HUNISH:
There is a fine series of 30m cliffs along the north-east side of Rubha Hunish, and despite the appearance from above, the routes to date are on immaculate rock with generally good protection. The climbing is similar to Flodigarry, but better.

Middle Stack Area:
This is the clean wall immediately opposite the Middle Stack. Near perfect rock and protection. Abseils and belay are from metal stakes (not in situ). A good reference point is the black ledge used to start the swim to the Middle Stack; the first two routes start from here. The only access to all the routes is by abseil.

The Exit   30m   Severe ***. M.Tighe & party. 18th August 2000.
Probably climbed before by parties returning from the Middle Stack. From the left-hand end of the ledge follow a crack come fault-line directly to the top.

Stage Right   30m   VS 4c **. M.Tighe & party. 18th August 2000.
Climb up to a spike at the highest point of the ledge on the right and make an airy move up and right on to the wall - good flake. Either go diagonally right up the

wall a little way, or hard right a metre or two to gain the vague groove come crack-line which leads to the top.

Looking down the wall from the top of the cliff there are two rocks visible (black topped) above the high tide mark, the one nearest the stack being roughly square with a sloping top and split in the middle while the other looks like a big black rock crystal. There is a triangular ledge with a wee kelp-filled pool opposite the bigger rock, which is dry for all but an hour either side of high tide. Some 10m south from this ledge is a small U-shaped recess with a ledge above the tide line and an immaculate black corner up the left-hand side.

The Planning Department 30m VS 4c ***. M. & K.Tighe, S.Fraser. 20th August 2000.
Climb the perfect corner in the back left-hand side of the bay to exit left at the top on to a rib - a groove come fault line now leads to the top of the crag.

Summer Wine 30m VS 4b ***. M. & K.Tighe, S.Fraser. 20th August 2000.
Climb a short chimney from the left (south) side of the triangular ledge. Go down and left a couple of metres to gain a crack-line which goes up through a beautiful gabbro-like wall to the top.

Clais Dubh 30m HVS 5a **. M. & K.Tighe, S.Fraser. 20th August 2000.
The fine black cleft at the back of the triangular ledge is a struggle to gain. Continue up the chimney until forced out on to the right wall which leads, rather deviously, to the top.

A few metres further north, and almost opposite the black crystal rock, is a large chimney come cave with various ledges around the tide line. The following route takes the left (facing in) exit out of the chimney come cave.

Blue Men of the Minch 30m E1 5b ***. M.Tighe, S.Fraser, A.Wadsworth, I.Lee, J.McClenaghan. 3rd September 2000.
Climb the shallow chimney in the back left-hand corner of the recess. Exit at half-height by a good spike. Avoid the smooth groove above by going left a metre or so where a fault-line leads to the top.

Split Stack Area:
The next crop of routes lie in a rock bay immediately opposite the southerly section of the Split Stack. Access is either by scrambling down a broken gully from the south or by abseiling down the line of the routes - there are good rock belays at the top. There is a huge flat boulder at the southern end of the bay which is lapped by the tide; some bright green lichen lives on top of it. The routes are described from left to right (south to north) starting from the big flat boulder.

The Splits 25m HVS 5b *. M.Tighe, J.McClenaghan. 3rd September 2000.
This takes the left-hand of the two corner come groove lines that are capped by small overhangs and starts just left (south) of the big flat stone. Climb the right-facing corner to the overhang. Pull through on the left (well protected crux) to an easier finish.

Workout 25m VS 4c ***. M. & K.Tighe, J.Cargill. 3rd September 2000.
Start opposite the big flat stone where a narrow chimney come crack line leads to the first overhang. Climb up the outside of the deep crack and overcome the overhang by wide bridging. A smaller overhang above continues the entertainment.

Delicasse 25m VS 4b **. M.Tighe, J.McClenaghan, S.Fraser, J.Cargill. 3rd September 2000.
The route takes a depression just right of the centre of the bay and immediately opposite the south split stack. Pad up the smooth slabby start and a tricky little wall to finish up more broken rocks.

The Narrows 25m HVS 5a **. M.Tighe, J.McClenaghan, I.Lee. 3rd September 2000.
A few metres in from the right-hand side of the bay is a narrow chimney which becomes a crack after quarter height. It gives a classic little tussle.

Bay Back Crack 25m VS 4c **. M.Tighe, J.McClenaghan. 3rd September 2000.
The right-hand corner-crack is guarded by an overhung recess. Climb this, the ramp-line on the right wall, or a combination of the two to reach the upper crack and so to the top.
Note: This is the same route and predates Big Breakfast (SMCJ 2003).

The Non-Stack:
This is a south continuation of the split stacks and is reached by climbing down a few metres into the neck (as for the approach to Split Stack) and back up the other side. The seaward (NE) side of this feature offers a fine crop of well protected climbs on immaculate rock. All routes accessed by abseil to good ledges.
   Having climbed out of the neck, walk southwards the few metres to the top of the cliff. Immediately opposite the neck is a square recess at the top of a chimney come corner-line (Sea Lum). Another corner come chimney approximately 10m to the right is The Prison, and another 10m to the left is Wye Aye Chimney.

Sea Lum 20m Very Difficult *. M. & KTighe, P.Rosher, J.Cargill. May 2002.
The big corner come chimney-line gives a fine little route.

Pods 20m HVS 5a/b **. M.Tighe, D.Fraser. 19th May 2004.
The excellent wall to the left (looking up) of Sea Lum has an obvious peapod crack-line.

Red Buoy 20m HVS 5a/b **. M.Tighe, D.Fraser. 19th May 2004.
South around the corner from Pods, on the seaward face, is an immaculate shallow square-cut chimney with a crack in the back. Sustained and well protected.

Jailbreak 20m Mild VS 4b ***. M.Tighe, D.Fraser. 19th May 2004.
A few metres south of the Red Buoy a crack-line runs through the full height of the face.

Great Escape 20m VS 4b *. M. & K.Tighe, P.Rosher, J.McClenaghan. May 2002.
Just a few metres south again from Jailbreak a big defile runs the full height of the cliff, narrow at the top but a big sea cave below. Wide bridging is followed by a

little wall on the left to a half-way ledge. Continue up the narrower crack above or the groove-line on the left (harder).

Skraa   20m   Mild VS 4b **. M. & K.Tighe, J.Cargill, J.McClenaghan. May 2002.
This and the following routes are to the north of Sea Lum. Starting from the bottom of Sea Lum, Skraa takes a diagonal line up and right across the face to finish at the top of Wye Aye Chimney.

Wye Aye Chimney   20m   Severe *. M. & K.Tighe, P.Rosher. May 2002.
The improbable looking chimney gives a thought-provoking struggle with spaced protection.

Yellow Walls:
North of Wye Aye Chimney is a wall with yellow lichen at the top, and a rounded ledge at about half-height. Two short routes have been done from here taking leisurely crack-lines from the ledge (Yellow Walls left and right, Severe, 2002). The next route starts from a smaller footledge just below the northern end of the rounded ledge, and climbs the seaward arête.

Promptu   20m   Mild VS 4b *. M.Hudson, A.Holden. May 2004.
Traverse 3m right to a shallow groove in the arête. Pad up the arête past a yellow ramp to the final steepening with good positions throughout.

Around the corner from here is a claustrophobic gap between the Non-Stack and the Split Stack. A steep and brooding wall forms the north end of the Non-Stack. The next route takes a line of cracks 2m in from the seaward arête. Abseil down the line of the route from the north end of the Non-Stack.

Émigré   20m   VS 4c *. M.Hudson, D.MacAulay. August 2004.
From the seaward end of the ledges, thoughtful zigzagging (crux) reaches a projecting block at 5m. Follow the cracks above past an open V-groove just right of the arête.

There is a fine chimney-crack up the north end of the Non-Stack.

One o'Clock Crack   20m   HVS 5a/b *. M. & K.Tighe. May 2002.
Abseil down the line of the route from the north end of the Non-Stack or, much better, traverse in from the top of the big flat stone – see next section.

Father's Day   20m   Severe. M. & K.Tighe, S.Fraser, J.Armour. 15th June 2003.
Climbs a chimney in the wall to the south of the North Stack. There is a little wedged chockstone at two-thirds height.

Hoodie Groove   20m   VS 4c. M.Tighe, J.Armour. 15th June 2003.
A few metres in from the left edge of the wall is a wee ledge just on the high tide line but with no belay (abseil rope used). Climb up the groove until it overhangs. Bridge wide and go for the left-hand crack to the top.

Minke   20m   HVS 5a/b **. M. & K.Tighe. 15th June 2003.
Start from the ledge at the bottom of Hoodie Groove. Swing out right and climb an immaculate crack in the wall.

NORTHERN HIGHLANDS NORTH

BEINN DEARG, Coire Ghranda:
Final Destination 130m VIII,7 *. G.Robertson, A.Robertson. 23rd January 2005.
A bold and complex mixed route taking on the challenge of the huge unclimbed wall left of Ice Bomb. Should become icier but may then be even bolder. Start about 20m right of an obvious deep recess/fault immediately right of Tickled Rib.
1. 20m. Climb a diminishing groove up left towards and then round an edge to a perch overlooking the fault, then continue over a couple of steps to a good but cramped belay.
2. 30m. Traverse a slab rightwards on thin ice, then move up and across right again to a delicate step down into a groove. Climb this up to below an obvious black corner with blank slabs on the right. Step left on to the rib, then up directly for a couple of metres before a precarious step left leads to a good belay.
3. 30m. Climb directly up the bulging wall above into an obvious deep groove, then take a crack on the right before stepping back left into the groove above. Follow the groove until strenuous moves lead out left.
4. 30m. Climb straight up slabs for a few metres, then make tricky moves left and up on tufts to an overlap. Climb straight over the overlap and up again into a blind groove (obvious flake runner up on right), then swing across and right into a groove system. Follow the groove system steeply without much in the way of protection to thick ice that leads to a ledge and belay.
5. 20m. Step down and across left into a fault which leads to easier ground and the top.

Note: P.Robertson was also on the first ascent of Cold War.

SEANA BHRAIGH, Luchd Coire, An Sgurr:
Corriemulzie Rib 300m II. D.McGimpsey, A.Nisbet. 18th December 2004.
The fourth from the right of the six ribs (the rib left of Nether Rib). More continuous than the others and with a steeper central step climbed direct at about grade III, although avoidable.

SEANA BHRAIGH, Luchd Coire:
Three parallel ice lines in the centre of the buttress between The Chute and Query Cleft, climbed by B.Davison and D.McGimpsey on 17th February 2005:
Brassica 90m III,4.
Climbs an icy chimney, grooves and short walls left of a dyke-like feature.
Rondo 90m II.
The middle ice line, immediately right of the dyke feature. Surprisingly easy climbing.
White Lady 90m III.
The right-hand line.

BEINN LICE:
Note: A.Bailey & R.McKeddie climbed a frozen waterfall, marked on the 1:50000 map at NC 336 354. About 40m with a 20m vertical section, IV,5 (1990). 10mins

approach, visible from the road. A good combination with Meall an Leithreach (5mins drive away).

RHUE:
Note (I.Taylor): The notorious wide slot on Rhue Morgue takes a Camalot 4.5 or 5. An excellent route at E4 5c **.

ARDMAIR:
Little Toe   30m   E4 5c *. I.Taylor, T.Fryer. 21st July 2004.
A left hand finish to Big Foot. From half-way up the upper wall of Big Foot, swing left and go up a strenuous curving crack to gain the left side of the foot shaped block. Finish straight up Iguana Direct (the crack-line above) or up the right-slanting corner of Big Foot.

Note: I.Taylor notes that Neart nan Gaidheal is described as being right of Unleash the Beast, but is actually to its left. And Friends Retrieval is a right-facing (rather than a left-facing) corner.

CAMAS MOR:
Pirate King   40m   E2 5c. I.Small, A.Hume. 21st May 2004.
Climb the obvious roof slot and arête between Buccaneer and Grapeshot. Start up the arête between Buccaneer and Grapeshot to gain a flake/ramp line and ledge. Move right across the wall above to below the roof. Gain the offwidth slot in the roof (very large Friend useful) and climb it with holds on the right edge. From the ledge above climb final cracked arête initially on the right.

T.W.O.C.   30m   E3 6a. I.Small, A.Hume. 21st May 2004.
Climbs the centre of the steep wall to the right of Hit and Run by a series of diagonal cracks and breaks. Start down and right from the corner of Hit and Run. Follow a thin crack past a wide break, then transfer right to another crack. Go up this on pockets, then right to a further crack. Where this ends, climb directly up breaks to the top.

BEN MORE COIGEACH, Cona' Mheall, Crucifix Buttress:
The Right-Hand Buttress re-named.
Hooded Crack   25m   E3 5c **. J.R.Mackenzie, R.Brown. 30th April 2004.
To the right of Anarchist Crack is a steep slabby wall with twin cracks and an overhung hood, just to the left of the most prominent feature of the crag, a cross-shaped crack. Climb the twin cracks to the hood which provides the strenuous crux. Continue up the short wide crack above to finish. Excellent climbing and good protection.

Crucifixion Crack   25m   E4 6a **. J.R.Mackenzie, A.Nisbet. 9th September 2004.
The centrepiece of the buttress is the straight cross-shaped crack. It provides a splendid exercise in technical jamming. Belay well to the right of the crack. Climb the lower corner, past 'The Guillotine', a mechanically sound but alarming block, to reach and jam up the overhanging crack to the top. Excellent cam protection,

several Friends 3 or similar useful. Possibly three stars and E3 if brushed clear of powdery lichen.

CUL MOR, Creag nan Calman:
Threadmor 120m E1 5b. I.Small, A.Hume. 22nd August 2004.
This route climbs a prominent flake-corner on the buttress right of the foot of the slanting East Gully. Start about 25m right of the gully and immediately of a large black recess.
1. 15m. Move up left on heathery ledges to directly below a left-facing corner.
2. 30m 5b. Move up to the corner and climb directly to a perched pinnacle. From its top pull steeply up a large flake to land on a heathery ledge. Belay to the right at a wide crack.
3. 15m 5a. Climb the wide crack past the grassy pod to easier ground.
4. 30m. Move diagonally right and climb the right edge of a monster flake to a corner below roofs.
5. 35m 5a. Traverse left on a slab below the roofs, then directly up by cracks to easier ground.
Scramble up for 80m to a more level bench. Descent is down the grassy East Gully.

CUL BEAG, West Face:
Kveldro Ridge 200m III,5. E.Brunskill, D.Morris. 26th December 2004.
A winter ascent of the summer route.

Curving Chimney 105m IV,5. E.Brunskill, G.Macfie, D.Morris. 18th January 2005.
Start at the lowest point of the buttress and climb a narrow icy gully up to a terrace leading left to below the Stags Wall (35m). The summer route route was then followed in two pitches without the deviation to the pulpit, mainly up steep turfy grooves and chimneys.

Beagbie 120m V,6 *. E.Brunskill, G.Macfie, D.Morris. 18th January 2005.
This route follows the prominant turfy groove system on the right side of the Lurgainn Edge tower. Start just right of the bottom of the tower and climb up gradually steepening turfy ground and walls to a belay about 5m below where the groove starts to narrow (35m). Climb the sustained and poorly protected groove (50m). Continue up to join Lurgainn Edge and follow this to the top (35m).

REIFF, Pinnacle Area:
Salt Pans 10m E3 6b *. I.Taylor. July 2004.
Climb the wall just left of Earth Shaker to a sloping ledge. Step right and finish up a short hanging corner.

Bouldering Cliff:
Rampant Groove E4 5c **. S.Crowe, K.Magog. 31st May 2004.
Climb The Ramp to near its top, place good cams in the large break, then step left and boldly continue up the hanging groove.

Note: M.Barnard climbed the following on 8th June 2004. The crack immediately left of The Ramp, rising in a series of short steps. Upon reaching the bottom of the last step veer left up a short chimney, leading to the top. It seems very close to The Ramp, but might be a variation finish.

Spaced Out Rockers Cliff:
Misha   35m   E6 6b ***. G.Latter, K.Magog. 26th May 2004.
The central line up the wall, midway between Headlong and Culach. Very sustained. Start 6m right of the arête of Headlong, directly beneath an obvious thin diagonal hanging crack. Weave up first left, then rightwards along breaks to pull back left and move up to the vague crack. Climb this leading to undercut flakes and follow these to gain the break on Spaced Out Rockers… Make hard moves up the wall above (crux) to better holds and a good break. Move out right along this and pull up onto a ledge in the recess (junction with Culach – possible belay). Move out left and continue more easily past large spike to finish. Well-protected – three sets of cams required!

Rubha Ploytach:
The Evil of Spuds   12m   Very Difficult *. C.Angus, O.Gray. 22nd July 2004.
Pull on to the left side of the slab immediately right of The Slide. Trend up and right and finish in a prominent notch.

Rodney's Ramble   12m   Severe **. O.Gray, C.Angus. 22nd July 2004.
Start just left of Touchdown Montana and climb the steep wall to the overhang. Traverse left on good holds to finish as for the previous route.

LOCHINVER CRAGS, Loch Braigh Crag (Ardroe):
Skid Roe   25m   E4 6a. P.Craig N.Craig. 7th April 2004.
Start at an embedded flake, 3m right of the lowest point of the crag. Climb straight up the wall to the left end of the diagonal break that crosses the crag from bottom right to top left. Pull over the overlap via a broken crack system and follow a lichenous shallow gangway right to a pale groove just left of the main roof. Climb the groove to the top.

ACHMELVICH, Middle Tier Crag:
Right of Loch Dubh Slab and close to the loch shore is Waterfall Buttress with an obvious waterfall dropping down its left side. Directly above this and partially hidden from view is Middle Tier Crag while up and slightly right is Ardroe Slab. **Approach:** The easiest approach to Loch Dubh Slab and Middle Tier Crag is to go back down the road from the parking spot for 50m and then take the track to the right. This leads round behind Loch Dubh Crag and back to the loch shore at a small bay just to the left of Loch Dubh Slab. Take a grassy boggy gully on the left to the top of Middle Tier Crag, 20mins.

The crag consists of a 20m tier of excellent gneiss with an overhung base shrouded by birch trees. To right of the overhung section is a blunt arête above some blocks and right again an overhung arrow shaped recess with a hand crack running out to the right.

Windy Ridge   20m   Severe. S.R. and K.E.Charlton. August 2004.

Follow the hand crack up and right for 5m, then move left on to the slab and climb to the top.

Bracken's Dilemma 20m HVS 5a *. S.R. and K.E.Charlton. August 2004.
From the block below the blunt arête swing up and left on to a small ledge. Step right and follow the obvious crack and slabs.

INCHNADAMPH LIMESTONE CRAGS:
Death Rattle 70m E2 5b. J.R.Mackenzie, R.Brown. 6th August 2004.
About 20m left of Acid Rock is a small rowan tree belay. Climb steeply up the wall to its right, past a hole and undercut section. Continue straight up on good grey rock to below a square overhang; step left then back right above it to big holds and the end of the technical climbing which has well spaced protection. Dangerous loose steep ground leads up grass and broken rock to a shallow 'gully' to the right (50m). Continue up easy loose rock up and left to the top (20m).

LOCH GLENDHU, Sundowner Crag:
Note: Sundance Buttress is similar to Until the Fat Lady Sings, as suggested in the new guide, but the second half of the route was further left.

Strictly Ballroom 100m Severe. J.Gillespie, A.Currie. July 2004.
Start 15m to the right of Sundance Buttress. Climb slabs to the bottom of a large overhanging corner, in three pitches. Finish last pitch up wall to right of corner.

The next four climbs start across the river from Sundowner Crag.

River Dance 50m Moderate. D.Jessiman, A.Currie. July 2004.
From the river climb the arête in two pitches.

Dannsa nam Mara 40m Very Difficult. D.Jessiman, K.Bolger, J.Gillespie, A.Currie. July 2004.
Start 10m right of River Dance. Climb cracks to top of wall in two pitches.

Moon Dance 55m Severe. K.Bolger, D.Jessiman, J.Gillespie, A.Currie. July 2004.
Start 15m right of Dannsa nam Mara at red rocks. Trend left for 15m, then straight to top of the wall in two pitches.

Rain Dance 25m Very Difficult. D.Jessiman, A.Currie. July 2004.
Start at buttress 100m to the left of River Dance. Climb the centre of the buttress.

The following climb can be found at NC 288 335, on a small buttress near the bothy, overlooking the river.
Ya Dancer 20m VS 5a. W.Gorman, J.Gillespie, A.Currie. July 2004.
Climb an overhanging wall (hard), then up to a square-cut corner (protection) and on to the top.

FAR NORTH WEST CRAGS, Tarbet Sea Cliffs, Onion Slab:

(NC 161 494).Non-tidal. South-West facing.
A sunny slab, but with some loose rock before cleaning. There are smaller slabby walls farther out, but tidal.

Approach: Park at Tarbet and head north-west through a field and gate. Go up over a knoll to meet a fence, followed to a gate at the top of a gully which leads down to the base of the slab.

Onion Rock 30m E2 5b **. A.Nisbet, R.Brown, J.R.Mackenzie. 10th September 2004.
The left side of the slab is composed of smooth white rock. Climb the leftmost crack-line, which is just right of the white rock until a delicate traverse leads left to the edge. Place poor RP's and move up left on to a sloping shelf. Climb a fine finger crack to the top.

Red Chilli 25m E2 5b *. J.R.Mackenzie, R.Brown, A.Nisbet. 10th September 2004.
A right-slanting line of weakness on the right side of the slab; the rock is not as good but the protection better. Start about 3m right of Onion Rock. Climb upwards to a steepening, then follow a line of handholds rightwards through a bulge to an easier finish.

Tarbet Sea Cliffs, Raven's Crag:
Deep Water Blues, Direct Finish 15m E1 5b ***. J.R.Mackenzie, R.Brown. 6th August 2004.
From the stance above the first pitch an overhanging crack continues straight up the headwall. Climb up to a ledge then climb the crack on generous holds (including a mechanically sound but wobbly jug), jams and protection to the top. A finely positioned and enjoyable stretch of climbing.

Rock Garden Crags, Rockery Wall:
Dianthus 15m Very Difficult *. B. & A.Evans. June 2004.
Seen from the top of Rock Garden Slab there is an obvious pink slab about 100m right, on Rockery Wall. Climb this at its cleanest part, crossing two diagonal cracks.

Flower Power 15m Hard Severe 4b *. G. & K.Latter. 11th April 2004.
Start right of Stone Flowers. Climb right side of the slab to a hanging crack.

Creag Cnoc Thull:
Cnoc Cnoc 20m HVS 4c/5a *. R.Anderson, C.Anderson. 11th April 2004.
A parallel line to Drop 'Em Low. Climb to the left end of the lower overhang and pull up right across this into a groove, which is climbed to the roof. Pull over rightwards onto the slab and climb cracks to the top.

Ridgeway View Crag:
Starry Saxifrage 14m Severe 4a **. K. & G.Latter. 10th April 2004.
The rightmost crack in the slab, just left of shallow groove.

The Silk Glove Memorial Route 12m Severe **. C.Angus, O.Gray. 25th July 2004.

Climb the prominent crack line 4m right of Row the Boat Ashore, with a slight kink leftwards at half-height.

Rodney's Gneiss Route   10m   Severe *. O.Gray, C.Angus. 25th July 2004.
Climb a left-facing corner 2m right again until it is possible to pull on to the arête at half-height. Follow cracks to the top.

C Weed   10m   E1 5b **. P.Armitage, M.Stubbs. 13th July 2004.
Start about 8m right of Row The Boat Ashore up the descent slope. A thin crack runs up through a break at 4m. Climb up through this on small edges, continue up to ledges and finish going left to the top.

Club Moss   15m   Difficult **. K. & G.Latter. 10th April 2004.
The fine blunt rib just above the base of the descent gully at the left end of the main crag.

C Dogs   20m   VS 4b *. M.Stubbs, P.Armitage. 13th July 2004.
Fifty metres left of the main crag is a mossy slab capped by a large roof. Further left of this is a large ledge. Scramble up this to below another small capped roof with a hanging small chimney to its right edge. Climb the slab beneath this roof. Hand traverse right under the roof and pull up into the chimney via a jammed flake. Climb a crack to the top.

Ardmore View Crag (NC 229 519):
The north-west flank of the little knoll to the north-west of Ridgeway View Crag is lined with small slabs and walls. Park off the road in a convenient parking spot just beyond, or before a small stream and walk up and around the shoulder to gain the first rocks in 5mins.

Two Bit Crack   15m   Very Difficult. R. & C.Anderson. 10th April 2004.
This lies on the first slab, starting just left of a V-slot crack a short way above the ground to climbs a vague line of cracks up and leftwards to the highest point.

Moving left and up is a short wall seamed with cracks and then up and left in a corner is a nice pink slab with a thin crack running up it.

Around the Block   15m   VS 4c. R. & C.Anderson. 10th April 2004.
Climb the crack up the left side of the slab, then go up and left around a block into a groove which leads to the top.

Ardmore Crack   15m   E3 5c *. R. & C.Anderson. 10th April 2004.
The thin crack up the slab. Climb Sign of Weakness to the horizontal Friend slot, then move up a short way and place a wire. Return to the horizontal Friend slot and move left to gain the base of the crack. Climb the crack, useful Friend just above the horizontal break.

Sign of Weakness   15m   VS 4c *. R. & C.Anderson. 10th April 2004.
The line of weakness running up the right side of the slab. Climb to a horizontal Friend slot and continue to the top.

Wavy Crack   15m   VS 4c. R. & C.Anderson. 10th April 2004.
The right-slanting crack up the slab just left of the corner.

The Balcony:
A short way to the left is a steep slabby wall with a pleasant heather balcony
running along its base. Two waterworn streaks (often wet) with cracks running up
them are prominent on the left-hand section of the wall. Although the routes are
very close together the climbing is excellent. Routes are described from right to
left.

Space and Time   15m   E2 5b *. R. & C.Anderson. 15th April 2004.
Start just to the left of the obvious crack-line running up the left side of the wall.
Climb a mixture of the clean rock to the left of the crack-line and the crack-line
itself. The climbing and the rock is better 1m to the left but the gear is in the crack.
Move left to the bulge and surmount this rightwards around the nose.

The Sky's the Limit   15m   E3 5b **. R. & C.Anderson. 15th April 2004.
Start just to the right of the grassy ledge which sits just above the ground in the
middle of the wall. Climb directly into a shallow scoop, then move right along a
horizontal break to step up on to this. A tiny hole is located on the wall above. A
skyhook can be placed in this to protect the moves directly past it to reach holds
where a step left gains a good horizontal break. Step up right, surmount the bulge
and finish leftwards around the nose.

Little Star   15m   E3 5c ***. R. & C.Anderson. 15th April 2004.
The thin crack-line in the centre of the wall. Immediately left of The Sky's the
Limit. Climb to the left end of the ledge just above the ground. Go up left on to a
small ledge at the start of the crack. Climb the crack and the bulge to finish.

Starstreak Enterprise   15m   E3 5c ***. R. & C.Anderson. 13th August 2004.
The thin crack up the waterworn orange streak in the centre of the crag is often
wet but when dry it provides a fine little route. Start to the right of the crack and
climb it to the top. A step left just below the upper crack allows good gear to be
placed in the diagonal crack of Gallactica.

Galactica   15m   E3 5c **. R. & C.Anderson. 1st May 2004.
A line based around the thin crack-line up the waterworn orange streak in the
centre of the crag. Climb the left side of the crack until it is possible to reach a
short diagonal slot and go left to more diagonal slots and a diagonal break. Step
left across the arching groove and delicately move up to a small slot, then finish
directly.

Solar Gain   15m   E3 5c **. R. & C.Anderson. 1st May 2004.
A line based around the arched groove toward the left side of the crag. The streak
on the left is slow drying and this is a fine alternative. Climb to the base of the
groove, then go left to a good slanting slot before going up and slightly right to a
horizontal break at the apex of the arch. Climb the thin crack-line above and finish
just left of the widening crack at the top of the crag.

The final two routes take lines up the waterworn pink streak at the left end of the wall, often wet.

Moondust   15m   E2/3 5c ***. R. & C.Anderson. 13th August 2004.
Start at a small flange and climb directly to the slanting slot of Solar Gain before moving up and slightly left to the horizontal break. Step left, then climb directly to the top.

Outer Space   15m   E2 5c *. R. & C.Anderson. 13th August 2004.
Start at the extreme left end of the wall. Attain a standing position in a horizontal slot, step left and climb a thin crack to a ledge on the edge. Climb the right side of the edge to the top.

Oldshoremore:
Seen from the rocks in the middle of Oldshoremore Sands the headland on the south side of the sands consists of a short wall of gneiss leading from the shore to a break about halfway along. From here a black gabbronic intrusion starts from sea-level and increases in height to the right until it forms the full height of the crag before fading into gneiss at the end of the headland. Routes are described from the tip of the headland and the base of the crag can be traversed at low to mid water. After this time, routes can either be reached by abseil or by traversing shorewards from the headland for routes up to and including those on the Black Wall or from an easy descent about 50m from the break halfway along the headland. This descent leads to sea-level and after an initial 'bad step' at the start round an arête, a traverse can be made across the base of a juggy black wall to just before the chimney at the left of the Black Wall itself.

From the tip of the headland a good ledge runs for about 10m below a short bouldering wall to a west facing slab (The Ochre Slab). The right crack is Difficult, the centre of the wall Severe and the left arête Very Difficult. About 10m left of the Ochre Slab is a deep black square-cut chimney (the end of the gabrronic intrusion). Just before the chimney is the Golden Wall which starts from a ledge about 3m above the traverse. On this wall, Stepover (Mild VS 4b) starts from the ledge and then follows the shallow groove/corner leading slightly right. The Arête takes the left arête of the Golden Wall (the right arête of the chimney) at HVS 5a starting from the base of the chimney or VS 4c by traversing in from the chimney above the initial overhang. The left, west-facing wall of the chimney has a Difficult crack and a Very Difficult wall climb up the black rock, starting from the gneiss base. Around the arête to the left is a steep black wall (The Black Wall) starting from a sea-washed ledge. The right arête is Hard Severe (4a), the central crack to the ledge followed by a thin crack/groove is E1 5b, while moving left from the ledge into the shallow groove is HVS 5a (the groove can be reached from below 5b). At the left of the Black Wall is another deep black chimney which marks the end of the low to mid water traverse. This chimney forms the right end of the juggy, black wall leading from the easy descent. The juggy, black wall above the traverse gives a number of routes between Difficult and Mild Severe. Just before the deep chimney there is an obvious overlap about 3m above sea level. The traverse and then the ascent of the overlap and the wall above gives an excellent Mild VS 4b. Routes by S.R. & K.E.Charlton in Summer 2003 and 2004.

Slab above the Road:
Park just before the gate at NC 204 582 and contour the hillside seawards for 80m to reach the base of the slab. The slab is defined by a broken chimney on the left and runs up and right to merge into the hillside. There is a crack running up the centre of the slab which fades towards the top.

Springbank   HVS 5a *. S.R. & K.E.Charlton. May 2004.
Start just right of the broken chimney at a short wall. This leads onto the slab which is followed up and right to about 5m below the top. Climb up an left to gain the top of the crag.

Central Crack   HVS 5a **. S.R. & K.E.Charlton. August 2004.
The central crack is followed to a junction with Springbank about 5m from the top.

Puppy Dog Blues   E1 5b *. S.R. & K.E.Charlton. August 2004.
Starts just right of Central Crack and takes the shallow left-facing corner above. Both holds and protection are at a premium until the corner itself is reached after which the climbing eases considerably.

CREAG AN FHITHICH, Triangular Buttress:
About 60m directly above Russet Wall is Triangular Buttress and right at roughly the same level is a massive gneiss block. Directly above and behind this block is Back Stage. The main face of Triangular Buttress is above a rock ledge above a clear shallow pool and is bounded on the right by a blunt arête starting at about 3m and by a crack on the left. Between these features is another vertical crack which starts just above the rock ledge and runs out on to the upper slab.

Just a Tease   15m   HVS 5a **. S.R. and K.E.Charlton. August 2004.
Gain the hanging arête either direct or from the right and the climb directly to the top.

Straight Crack   15m   VS 4c *. S.R. and K.E.Charlton. August 2004.
The central crack.

Flaming June Crack   15m   VS 4c. S.R. and K.E.Charlton. August 2004.
The leftmost crack

Back Stage:
The main feature is a deep chimney in the centre of the crag. About 5m left of the deep chimney is a short wall below a ledge with a crack running up and left from the right end of the ledge. At the left of the short wall is a shallow wet gully.

Midsummer Sun   20m   Hard Severe 4a *. S.R. and K.E.Charlton. August 2002.
Start up the short wall just to the right of the base of the slanting crack. Climb direct to the ledge, then move slightly right up a faint arête and the follow a shallow groove to the top.

Easy Option   20m   Hard Severe 4a *. S. R. and K.E.Charlton. August 2002.

Start up the short wall directly below the left-slanting crack. Gain this and follow it to its end, then go straight up the arête.

Sandwood Bay:

The following route lies on Crag Two and takes a direct line just right of Marram.

Beach Wall 60m VS *. R.Anderson, C.Anderson. 16th April 2004.
Start on the first rocks at the extreme right side of the sandy beach at bottom of the wall.
1. 35m 4c/5a. Climb directly up compact rocks and thin cracks heading for a shallow corner and thin crack some halfway up the wall. Move up the corner a short way, then out right into the crack, then up right to gain ledges below a small roof. Move up left and around the edge of the steepening to gain large ledges.
2. 25m. Scramble to the top.

The next route lies on Crag One, the first one encountered at the northern end of the beach.

Sandwood Bay Crack 15m E2 5c **. R.Anderson, C.Anderson. 16th April 2004.
A great little route in a stunning setting. Start off the beach at the right side of the crag just left of a steep area of perfect rock. Climb the steep crack past a horizontal break. Scramble down leftwards to descend.
Note: In May 2004 A.Perry climbed a steep juggy 10m crack and the wall to its left, both situated about 50m left of the mini geo mentioned in the new guide, on the wall just to the left of the large overhang.

FOINAVEN, Fourth Dionard Buttress:

There is a mistake in the new guide, in that the route descriptions for Gritstoners Revenge and Badile are the same. This is because they would seem to be the same route given two names. The Fourth Buttress is the most likely location but the line has not been found. The following route is a direct line on excellent clean rock and does not fit their description.

Triskaidekaphobia 130m VS **. D.McGimpsey, A.Nisbet. 13th August 2004.
Climbs clean pale rock in the centre of the buttress. Start at the lowest point of the pale rock.
1. 55m 4c. Climb the pale rock trending slightly right to below steeper rock at a corner with a roof at the base of its right wall.
2. 30m 4c. Climb a shallow groove 5m to the left and continue up walls (well protected) to the base of a ramp (small tree here, well seen from below the cliff).
3. 45m 4c. The ramp is not pleasant so make a tricky move up the wall on the left and finish up slabby ground.

CAITHNESS EAST COAST, Duncansby Stacks:

Little Stack, Seaward Face 12m Mild VS 4b. M.Dent, R.I.Jones. 4th July 2004.
From the left end of the seaward platform climb the wall to the left of an overhang to a ledge at 5m. Traverse right and climb the corner-crack to the top (same as the original route).

Bucholly Castle Stacks, Black Score North Stack (ND 38071 65401):
South East Face Route   30m   VS 4b **. M.Robson, S.M.Richardson. 30th May 2004.
The northerly of the two fine-looking stacks 600m south of Bucholly Castle. Approach by abseiling from fence posts to reach a sea-washed platform below the stack (exposed two hours either side of low tide). Climb the arête on the south-west edge of the stack for 4m, then traverse left along the foot ledge running across the west (landward) face to reach the prominent crack which is followed to the summit. Large cams useful. Abseil descent.

Black Score South Stack (ND 38064 65372):
North East Arête   30m   VS 4c. S.M.Richardson, M.Robson. 30th May 2004.
Approach as for the North Stack and walk across the sea-washed platform to below the north edge of the stack. Climb easily up ledges and the obvious wide open corner to a spacious ledge at the base of a fine black wall. Climb the left-slanting crack for 8m to reach a large ledge on the arête - possible belay (25m, 4c). Tackle the short overhanging wall and mantleshelf on to the mud summit (5m, 4b). Descent: Reverse finishing moves (sling threaded around summit cairn offers some protection) to the ledge on the arête and abseil from a spike and in-situ wire.

North Stack of Martin's Sclaite (ND 38000 65084):
Golden Brown   25m   HVS 4c *. M.Robson, S.M.Richardson. 25th September 2004.
This difficult-looking stack lies 300m south of the Black Score stacks. Approach by abseiling from a fence post just north of a drainage channel to reach a small boulder beach, then swim 15m across the channel to reach the long platform below the stack. Start in the centre of the steep concave south-east face. Climb up on big horizontal bands, pass a roof at one-third height, and finish up the corner above. Descent: From the north-east end of the summit climb down a wide crack on the south-east face for 5m and abseil from in-situ peg belay.

South Stack of Martin's Sclaite (ND 37966 65011):
With Friends Like These   25m   E2 **. M.Robson, S.M.Richardson. 25th September 2004.
Approximately 70m south of the North Stack is another challenging stack. Approach by walking along the platform from the North Stack (exposed two hours either side of low tide). Start in the wide alcove-slot on the north side of the stack.
1. 10m 5a. Climb the left side of the alcove and make an awkward exit to reach a good ledge on the left. Move left to the north-east arête. Friend 4 belay.
2. 5m 5c. Move round the arête and climb the steep wall above (bold) to gain a good ledge.
3. 10m 4c. Climb up and right from the right end of the ledge and climb the north edge to the top.
Descent: Reverse the top pitch for 3m and abseil off in-situ pegs.

AUCKENGILL, Overhang Wall:
Fishy Fingers   9m   VS 4c. R.Wallace, R.Christie. 5th July 2004.
From the 1m step, climb the left-facing corner.

Fishy Surprise 8m VS 4c. R.Wallace (unsec). 2nd July 2004.
Climb the shallow groove between the 1m step and Traction Control.

NOSS HEAD, Pow Feet Stack (ND 37560 54840):
East Face Route 20m VS. S.M.Richardson, M.Robson. 30th May 2004.
The prominent offshore stack in the bay well seen from Castle Sinclair. Approach by descending the cliff to sea-washed platforms (accessible three hours either side of low tide) and swimming a 10m channel to a spacious ledge at the base of the stack. Climb the wall and prominent left-slanting crack on the east face to exit on to a tottering pillar on the south-east arête. Continue up grass and dubious rock to the summit. Abseil from tat around the summit.

Impossible Stack (ND 37460 54790):
A Few Feet Short 25m VSL (Very Severely Loose). M.Robson, S.M.Richardson. 30th May 2004.
The difficult-looking stack 120m west of Sinclair's Bay Stack. Approach at low tide by traversing sea-washed platforms to gain a large flat rock at the north-west corner of the stack. Step across to the stack and climb good rock until a swing leftwards can be made to a ledge. Climb the short wide crack above (large cam useful) and then up steep grass to the summit block. Climb the crack in the west side of the summit block to finish on a rounded mound of mud and bird debris. Descent: Downclimb a few metres and abseil the south-west ridge. (Note, an easier line is possible up the south-west ridge – rotten rock with minimal protection).

WICK SEA CLIFFS, Stack of Old Wick (ND 36890 48540):
Lord Oliphant's Bicycle 40m VS 4b ***. M.Robson, S.M.Richardson. 11th April 2004.
A superb stack 100m south-east of the Castle of Old Wick. Approach by abseiling from fence posts and making a pendulum to ledges at the foot of the landward side of the stack. Traverse right along easy but greasy ledges before moving up to a large ledge on the right arête. Climb a crack and swing left to a large ledge on the arête. Climb up easily until it is possible to move back right to the south-west face. Climb cracks in the middle of the south-west face to the summit. Descent: Abseil from an *in-situ* peg and wire on the landward face.

Salt Water Accelerator Escape Route 40m VS. S.M.Richardson, M.Robson. 11th April 2004.
Takes a line back up the main cliff following the approximate line of the abseil. Climb a short corner to a ledge then climb a left trending line to a large ledge at 20m - possible belay (4c). Continue up a series of short steep walls interspaced with good ledges and move leftwards along the ledge system to top out at the initial abseil point (4b).

SOUTH HEAD OF WICK:
The crag is curiously described and while the rock is different the two walls with the routes described in the guide do give some superb powerful climbing. Routes are described from right to left looking in. Comments on routes in the guide are from N.Morrison.

Chewin' The Fat　8m　E4 6a **. N.Morrison, W.Moir. 8th July 2004.
The rightmost crack-line on the wall with a small white niche at half-height leading to a step in the cliff-top. Technical but with adequate gear. Abseil inspected and practised.

Whiteout　9m　E3 6a. It looks nearer E4 5c (limited gear and flakey rock).

Riding The Waves　9m　E3 6a **. W.Moir, N.Morrison. 8th July 2004.
The 'square wave' crack-line mentioned in the guide. An initial wall gains the left-hand crack. Transfer to the right-hand crack, then back to the left-hand crack at the top. Well protected. Abseil Inspected.

Freeride　9m　E2 5b *. Looks more like E3 5b.

The walls are now broken by the slabby corner of the easy central descent. The next section of wall is short to start with and gains in height after a step at the cliff-top. The shorter section is seemed with cracks and will provide further lines of a samey nature to Wick and Feeble (described below).

Wick and Feeble　9m　E2 5b. N.Morrison, W.Moir. 5th July 2004.
A small ledge juts out at the base of the cliff. Climb cracks directly above the left edge of this to surmount an overlap into an area of more flaky rock split by vertical cracks. Yo-yoed while cleaning on sight.

The Lightness of Being Right-hand　12m　E3 6a ***. W.Moir, N.Morrison. 6th July 2004.
Start up the original line then move right at half-height into the strikingly obvious cracks. Abseil inspected.

The Lightness of Being　12m　E4 6a ***. An excellent route with an awkward top out but surely E4 rather than E3.

The Darkness of Lard　12m　E4 6a ***. N.Morrison, W.Moir. 6th July 2004.
Left of the previous route is an alcove with a corner crack-line running from its left-hand side on to a wall with a hanging right-facing corner above. Powerful moves up the bulging left edge of the alcove access the wall and corner. Abseil inspected and redpointed.

Left of the above route is a vicious overhanging roof crack before the platform drops down a level to a small tidal zone. Across the tidal zone the platform gradually rises up below impressive steep walls, unfortunately formed of poorer rock and lacking significant cracks. At the far end of these walls is a black north-east facing wall with a left-trending diagonal crack on its left-hand side and two left-trending grooves to the right. The routes are described from left to right. They are usually easily reached from the seaward end but, if the small tidal zone is awash, an abseil down the north-east facing wall gives access.

Cheeky Minke　9m　HVS 5a. R.Wallace, G.Richard. 22nd August 2004.
The left trending diagonal crack. Four metres left of Rooh-The-Pooh, Part II,

make awkward moves up the diagonal crack to a ledge, then continue straight up the slab above.

Roo-the-Pooh, Part II   10m   E1 5b. J.Malcolm, R.Wallace. 25th June 2004.
Climb up the middle groove through two small roofs to a ledge. Move up left over two ledges and by a shallow groove to the top.

Second Craic   11m   HVS 5a. R.Wallace, J.Malcolm. 25th June 2004.
Start at the base of the right-hand groove and climb a wall to a crack. Climb the groove by a ledge on the right to finish steeply up the wall.

Minke Magic   16m   E1 5b. R.Wallace, G.Richard. 22nd August 2004.
The south-west end of the impressive overhanging walls has a 2m high ledge which ends with an overhanging corner at its left end. Make difficult moves up the steepening corner using the crack in its rear to a rest below a small roof. Move left to a ledge on the arête, then continue up a slab and over a ledge to the top.

SARCLET, Tilted Ledge:
South of Fishnet Necklace around the arête is another slabby groove.
Fishpaste Breakfast   15m   Very Difficult. R.Christie, R.Wallace. 13th July 2004.
Climb the groove to a nose which is passed on the left.

Oblimov   15m   Severe 4b. R.Wallace, R.Christie. 13th July 2004.
Climb the wall 2m to the left of Yawn to a not so obvious slabby groove which leads to a large flake. Make airy moves by a jug and on to the top.

Hare of the Dowg   15m   Difficult. R.Wallace, L.More, G.Richard. 25th July 2004.
Climb a left-facing ledgy corner 2m left of Bobble to a large ledge. Follow the brown streaks above to a notch in the top edge.

Suckin' on Divids   15m   HVS 5a. G.Richard, R.Wallace, L.More. 25th July 2004.
Starting at the base of Wicker Man, move up a right-trending broken ramp to a ledge at two-thirds height. Head up leftwards to join a faint crack-line that runs through a small roof and follow this to the top.

North from the Tilted Ledge is a 100m wide bay with a jutting headland in the middle.

Lithium Fry-up   35m   HVS 5a **. R.Wallace, R.Christie. 29th July 2004.
The third black corner from the north end of the tilted ledge has a deep black crack at its rear. From a platform at the base of the corner, climb the corner to a steep narrowing. Pull through this to easier ground and continue up the groove to a hanging spike. Move on to the left-hand wall and continue to the top of the corner.

Hats off to the Catman   35m   HVS 5a **. R.Christie, R.Wallace. 5th August 2004.

Start from the platform at the base of Lithium Fry-up. Follow the rising line of right-trending undercut flakes that steepen as they approach a roof. Make awkward moves around the right of the roof to move into a narrow corner, then climb the slab on the right to reach a stance below two corners. Go up the left corner to easier ground.

Directly landward from the north end of the Tilted Ledge is a grey slabby pillar with corners on either side (ND 341 418). Access by abseil.

The Sad Lives of the Rabbit People   35m   VS 4c. R.Christie, R.Wallace. 22nd July 2004.
Start immediately right of the grey slabby pillar from a non-tidal platform. Climb a short narrow chimney to a slab and follow the crack up its left-hand side. Continue up the right-facing corner to a notch at the top.

Chasmic Farce   35m   Severe 4b. R.Wallace, R.Christie. 26th July 2004.
Immediately right of The Sad Lives of the Rabbit People, easily climb a broken slab and groove to a narrow ramp, then continue up the cracked corner.

Harvestmen are not Spiders   35m   Very Difficult. J.Stevenson, R.Christie. 1st August 2004.
A deep chimney to the right of Chasmic Farce.

At the north end of the bay is a 40m wide, 35m high south facing cliff with an overlap running along its left half at mid-height (ND 342 419). The non-tidal ledge at its base can be reached by abseil. In the middle of the cliff is a stunning left-facing overlapping flake/groove system with a generous crack running up its rear.

Silver Surfer   35m   E1 5b ***. R.Wallace, R.Christie. 14th July 2004.
Scramble up an open blocky chimney to reach the base of the flake system. Use the flake to overcome a steep wall, then continue up and left until under a roof. Turn this to the left, then surmount the hollow sounding blocks to finish up the final square corner.

Notes from N.Morrison: For Big Buttress and the bulk of the crags (all barring First Bay and Second Bay) the approach from Sarclet Haven is unnecessarily long. It is possible to drive much closer on the minor road leading to Mains of Ulbster Farm and park level with the south end of the Loch. A direct line south-east to the coast then leads in about 0.5km to the coast at Big Buttress and the natural Arch south of it. The other way is about 1.5km and awkward terrain.
    With regard to Big Buttress a full 50m of rope is needed to get through the stakes and reach the bottom. Walking on Water and Crypt Robber are superb routes.
    The location of Djapana Buttress is wrongly described in that the guide says it can be seen by looking south-east from the top of the headland with the natural arch (which is immediately south of Big Buttress). Djapana Buttress is the NE corner of the headland with the natural Arch and can actually be seen from the top of Big Buttress by looking south-east. There is nothing other than air south-east of the headland with the arch.

ULBSTER, Little Stack of Ulbster (ND 33528 41462):
Combined Operations 20m Very Difficult. S.M.Richardson, M.Robson. 27th September 2004.
This twin-summited stack lies 700m west of the Stack of Ulbster and is easily approached by following the valley southwards from the Mains of Ulbster to the cliff-top and downclimbing a ramp that leads to base of the stack (Difficult). Step across the 1.5m wide channel and climb easy slabs on west side to below a notch separating the summits. Climb a short steep corner up to the notch then continue left up large loose holds to the higher north summit. Descend by simultaneous abseil from the notch.

WESTER WHALE GEO, The Shark's Fin (ND 31980 39960):
Harpoon at a Venture 20m VS 4c *. M.Robson, S.M.Richardson. 27th September 2004.
Approach by descending easy walls and shelves to the south of Wester Whale Geo and swimming 80m around headland to gain east end of stack. Start at the left (west) end of the south face. Climb a short steep wall to a ledge and continue up to the right slanting stepped crack-line that parallels the west ridge to reach the flat elongated summit. Descend by abseiling from large block on summit ridge.

MID CLYTH, Lighthouse Wall:
Son in my Eyes 25m HVS 5a *. D.Porter, D.Moy. 3rd August 2003.
This route starts approximately 4m left of Aqualung where the rock turns darker. Climb the thin left-hand crack to a good platform and niche. Continue direct to an overhang above on the left, and surmount this on the left. Traverse right along the ledge and choose the easiest line up and right.

North of the descent into Lighthouse Wall, there are also a series of short easy routes, which may have been done before. They provide enjoyable soloing. The first three are described left (south) to right (north):

Baby Yella 10m Very Difficult. D.Moy, D.Porter. 3rd August 2003.
The second corner (yellow with lichen) to the right/north of the descent corner.

Black Cleft 10m Severe. D.Porter. 3rd August 2003.
The deep black cleft above a large green puddle.

Don't Give up on me Baby 10m Hard Severe. D.Porter, D.Moy. 3rd August 2003.
Approx 10m north of previous route, very near to the right end of the platform before it drops again to the final section. An easy blocky start leads to a final shallow V-groove with a thin crack at the back.

There is then some scrappier ground, and the following routes are now described from right (north) to left (south):

Tartan Rug 10m Severe. D.Moy, D.Porter. 3rd August 2003.
At the far right end of the access stepped platform system, traverse right along a wee ledge for 6m. Climb a corner-crack system, with a steep corner finish.

Sweetie Wifie   10m   Very Difficult. D.Porter, D.Moy. 3rd August 2003.
The stepped left-facing corner at the end of the access platform.

Old Git   10m   Very Difficult. D.Porter, D.Moy. 3rd August 2003.
The next corner-crack (3-4m from the last route).

Whipper Snapper   10m   Severe. D.Porter, D.Moy. 3rd August 2003.
Just left again, twin cracks in the top half of a short wall. Start beneath a small black overhang and finish up the right-hand crack.

Stolen Arête   10m   Hard Severe. D.Porter, D.Moy. 3rd August 2003.
The left-hand arête of that wall. Stick to the arête all the way, except to finish on the right. No gear.

Fader   8m   Very Difficult. D.Porter, D.Moy. 3rd August 2003.
Two metres left of the arête, move up broken thin cracks to a right-slanting groove just to the left of the arête.

Notes from N.Morrison: An abb rope is needed for the main (Stack) area. Also the approach via the Lighthouse makes for a long circuitous walk when a walk south-east through the fields is quicker. The North Wall including battle of the Bulge and The Fearful Void looks like it needs a good dry spell as there was a small burn flowing over it July 2004.
Two Lost Souls (E1 5b) only gets one star but deserves two or even three.
Silverfish (E1 5b) deserves no stars as it has a nasty start with poor rock and the ground too close for the gear.

Skerry Mor Stack (ND 288 361):
This is the stack referred to in the guide. The stack runs parallel to the cliff face for approximately 50m. Its base is 8m wide and is separated from the cliff by a narrow channel of water for nearly all states of the tide. Access for the daring can be made by a 2.5m jump on to the summit from the cliff at the closest point to the cliff face, however access is more safely gained by abseiling from a block on the cliff top at the south end of the stack to the base of the stack, which is accessible 2hrs either side of low tide.

No More Marlon   18m   HVS 4c. R.I.Jones, M.Dent. 3rd July 2004.
A good exposed route up the south arête. From a tidal ledge on the south end of the stack, climb a short wall to a small terrace, followed by a short section of solid horizontal bands of rock below a vertical wall just right of the arête (Friend 3.5). Pull up this on to the arête in an exposed position, before pulling around this on to the landward wall to climb the arête to the top.

Coulda been a Contender   25m   Severe. M.Dent, R.I.Jones. 3rd July 2004.
From the south end of the stack scramble along ledges on the seaward side to drop down on to the north end of the stack.
1. 12m. Climb the north wall right to a wide ledge at 6m and traverse to a crack-line in the west wall.
2. 13m. Climb the crack-line.

Stack Area - Skerry Mor:
Ron to the Hills   15m   E2 5b. D.Porter, S.Ritchie. 1st May 2004.
Between Freak Power and John's Peel. Gain the top of the Very Large Block via a
thin crack left of centre on its face. Continue up the thin disappearing crack-line
above, finishing into the right side of a niche where the angle and difficulty eases.
Finish easily out of the niche.

Inset Wall:
N.Morrison notes: *Mug's Game* should be described before *Susan* not after it.
Susan is probably E3 5c rather than E2 and is worth stars.
W.Moir climbed a new route left of Theatre of Cruelty at E2 5c.
Frogstroker HVS 5a is overstarred and merits one not three.

Stage Fright   15m   E2 5c. W.Moir, N.Morrison. July 2004.
Climb Bloodhunt to the first ledge. Move right and continue up the thin crack-line
and slot/groove to a ledge. Short corner to the top.

Over the Water:
From Crispy Aromatic Duck, traverse left around the arête and up on to a triangular
platform above the high tide mark.
Mid Clyth Crisis   10m   HVS 5a. R.Christie, G.Richard, R.Wallace. 8th July
2004.
Climb the open overhanging corner to a large ledge on the left. Make an airy step
across to the right-hand ledge, then mantelshelf and stretch to the top of the
overhanging wall.

Left from Mid Clyth Crisis around a jutting arête is the last corner before the
undercut pillar.
World Wide Ebb   10m   E1 5a. R.Wallace, R.Christie. 7th July 2004.
From a platform above the high tide mark, climb a corner until it is split by an
arête, then move up the short overhanging chimney to the left.

Basking Seal   10m   E1 5b. R.Wallace, R.Christie, G.Richard. 8th July 2004.
From the left end of the platform, climb the bulging crack-line using the ledge and
arête on the left, then continue leftwards and finish up a groove in the front of the
pillar.

South Bay:
PFB   10m   VS 4c. R.Wallace, R.Christie. 25th August 2004.
Climb the blank looking corner at the back right of the bay. Not as blank as it
looks.
Super Furry Animal   10m   VS 4c. R.Wallace, S.Ross, R.Christie. 25th August
2004.
Start as for Small North European Mammal to reach a small triangular niche at
3m. Now continue up the left-trending crack with increasingly difficult moves
towards the top.

LATHERONWHEEL, South Corner:
Bedpost   10m   VS 4c. R.Wallace, R.Christie. 24th May 2004.
Climb the arête left of Night Shift directly from the rock pool.

Night Moves   10m   VS 4c. R.Christie, R.Wallace. 24th May 2004.
One metre left of Bedpost, towards the descent, step across the rock pool and climb the crack.

No Coping Out   8m   VS 4c. R.Benton, R.I.Jones. 15th February 2004.
The right, less distinct crack-line left of the deep chimney and right of The Morning Line. High in the grade (but easy to cop out using the arête to the right!).

Winter Blues   8m   VS 4c. R.I.Jones, R.Benton. 15th February 2004.
The crack-line left of The Morning Line. High in the grade.

Sunstroked   8m   VS 4c *. R.I.Jones, R.Benton. 15th February 2004.
Climb the wall 3m left of Shearwater to exit up a V-groove.

Latheron Stacks, Niandt Stack (ND 21255 33075):
Three Step Corner   20m   Severe 4a. M.Robson, S.M.Richardson. 26th September 2004.
Gain the east face of the stack at low tide. Climb three giant steps in the centre of the face and finish up the corner above. Simultaneous abseil descent.

Cleit Thighearn Latheron (ND 20150 32715):
Rosehip Ridge   25m   Moderate. M.Robson, S.M.Richardson. 26th September 2004.
Approach at low tide and climb the south (seaward) ridge to the top. Descend by down-climbing the route.

Cleit a'Chail (ND 19465 32331):
Neptune's Love Funnel   25m   VSL (Very Severely Loose). S.M.Richardson, M.Robson. 26th September 2004.
On the right side of the landward face (accessible at high tide) is a pronounced pillar that is undercut at its base. Climb the left defining crack for 5m, traverse right on to the front face of the pillar. Climb this for 5m then move back left into the crack. Continue up this and the chimney above to easier ground and the top. A challenging route on unstable rock. Simultaneous abseil descent.

ORKNEY, Yesnaby, The Black Dyke:
(HY 221 163). Very Tidal. North-West facing.
Walk to the North end of the car park at the old Military buildings, at the north end of the last building turn and walk west towards the sea. On the cliff top is an unusual black wall separated slightly from the land by a shallow 'trench'. This is The Black Dyke, a 25m high, 30m long headland of black volcanic rock. This is the only example of this rock type on Orkney and gives completely different climbing from the rest of Yesnaby. When dry, this rock gives excellent climbing on big friction holds and at times sparse protection.

Gable End (North)   20m   Severe *. I.Miller, H.Clarke. 26th May 2004.
From the non-tidal platform at the base of the north end of the wall, climb the north facing arête. An escape from above two-thirds height reduces the grade to Very Difficult.

Iain Small on the first winter ascent of Sidewinder (VII, 8), South Trident Buttress, Ben Nevis. Photo: Simon Richardson

Gable End (South)   14m   VS 4b *. I.Miller, H.Clarke. 2nd March 2004.
From the tidal platform at the base of the south end of the wall, climb the south
facing arête of the Black Dyke. Excellent climbing through big bulges with perfect
protection.

The recessed bay to the north holds the continuation of the Black Dyke, where it
runs into the land. This small bay gives the following routes.

Steps   20m   Difficult. I.Miller. 28th May 2004.
Climb up big steps through a small recess, leading up from the seaward end of the
north wall of this bay.

Bigger Steps   20m   Very Difficult. I.Miller. 24th August 2004.
At the right end of the north wall, climb up the bigger steps to an open book
groove, climb this to the top.

Escaping the Rage   22m   VS 4b **. I.Miller, H.Clarke. 26th May 2004.
Climb a very obvious black arête following twin finger cracks which run directly
up the centre of this feature. Beware of the heaving pit, which sits below!!!

Pit Stop   22m   Severe. I.Miller, H.Clarke. 26th May 2004.
An atmospheric route. Starting on the non-tidal platform as for Gable End (North),
traverse towards the black arête to another platform at the base of a cracked slab.
Climb the slab to the top.

The Car Park Buttress:
The Numbtease Dance   20m   Very Difficult. I. & M.Miller, C. & H.Clarke. 3rd
March 2004.
Approx. 8m left of Old Man's Folly, climb a right-trending, left-facing fault on
big holds/small ledges. Finish either direct or continue on the fault to a small niche
and the top.

Brough of Bigging:
The south face of The Brough of Bigging is composed of loose fragile rock. The
first route below climbs the arête at the eastern end of the face, where the rock
steps back to form the broad walkway on to the Brough. Access to the bottom is
by abseil, either into the wee bay to the east followed by some nice sea level
traversing, or by an abseil down the face. Belay points are few on the summit and
a spare 60m rigging rope is required.

Preserve of the Few   20m   XS 5a. D.Sargent, H.Clarke, I.Miller. 5th March 2004.
Climb the very obvious arête at the eastern end of the main face. Climb initially
through an exposed roof and up poor rock to a grassy ledge. Climb directly up
from the ledge on big sandy holds and exit to the right of the jutting nose to the
summit.

At the west end of the south face of the Brough of Bigging sits a recessed bay of
much better rock. The base of this end of the crag is very prone to big seas and
should be approached with caution.

*Looking up from the first pitch of Steep Ghyll, Scafell Crag. The crux pitch is in the upper half of the
gully. Photo: Stephen Reid.*

Wall of Sound   35m   E1 5b. D.Sargent, H.Clarke. 5th March 2004.
1. 15m 5b. Climb the steep crack-line immediately to the left of the huge crack running into the roof of the cave, on good holds and perfect pockets to the huge ledge at half-height. Strenuous!
2. 20m. From this ledge climb the very obvious open book corner-crack to the summit. On poorer rock unfortunately.

Qui Ayre Point, Point Wall:
Deep Blue   10m   E3 5c **. N.Morrison, C.Webb. 22nd July 2004 .
The fine crack-line immediately right of The Cog. On sight. It is worth noting that a calm sea and low tide are needed for many of the routes hereabouts. The walls farther into the bay are a bit more sheltered.

Tower Area:
The Forgotten   18m   E1 5b *. I.Miller, H.Clarke. 4th March 2004.
Climb the thin full-height groove/crack immediately to the left of Bobbin's Groove. Easy at first to a ledge, followed by crimping though a black slab, then strenuous jug pulling up the last steep 6m. Excellent rock and adequate protection.

Note: N.Morrison says The Quarryman is a superb route but E2 5c not E1 5b.

Arch Wall:
Mack the Knife   20m   E5 6a **. T.Rankin, I.Miller. 2nd May 2004.
Climbs through the right end of the roof by an obvious little niche just left of Hajj. Climb the lower wall to the ledge, cross the roof at the apex of the niche and continue up the sustained wall to finish up a thin crack. Ronnie the Axe joins this line just below the thin crack. Another excellent sustained route. Low in the grade. This route could also be started from the ledge and climbed in a big sea.
Note: T.Rankin repeated Ronnie the Axe, agreed with grade and stars, but the indirect line was disappointing. Also repeated Summers End on the False Stack, agreed with grade and quality.

The Langer Huddauf   25m   Difficult *. I.Miller. 24th August 2004.
Start at the extreme right-hand end of the tidal platform at the base of Arch Wall (as for the starts of Wee Lum and Vision Quest.) Climb directly up on perfect rock to gain a sloping ledge, follow the ledge and step up at its highest point. Follow the big hand crack to the top.

Lum Crack   20m   E3 5c **. I.Miller, H.Clarke. 1st October 2004.
Climb the perfect steep hand/finger crack 3m right of the Wee Lum chimney. Access at low tide is by a short traverse to gain Wee Lum. At high tide, abseil in and take a stance on the non-tidal ledge at the base of Wee Lum.

Moss Ghyll Geo:
The geo into which runs the Moss Ghyll stream has a very broken appearance but the north wall holds the following two routes on sound rock and good gear.

Easy Beginings   10m   Difficult. C.Webb, H.Clarke. 25th April 2004.
Climb the full height left-hand crack-line, starting at the seaward end of the pool under the waterfall.

The Limpet Pool   10m   Very Difficult. I.Miller, H.Clarke. 25th April 2004.
Starting to the left or the waterfall, climb the full height crack come fault.

False Stack Area:
A Grand Day Out   10m   VS 4c. N.Morrison, L.Gorham. 18th July 2004.
Immediately right of Wriggle and Grin is a right-slanting groove. This leads pleasantly on to ledges below cracks in an upper wall right of the previous route. Climb the cracks with interest.

Note: Summers Over on The False Stack itself is as good as its 3 stars suggest.

Deerness, Gearsan Walls:
Park at the car park for The Gloup (HY 589 078). Walk down the signposted path to The Gloup. Follow the path past The Gloup and through a style. Follow the path nearest the sea, north towards The Brough of Deerness. Follow the path closest to the sea for about 400m to several small stone wall shelters and cairns on the cliff-top. The largest of these cairns at HY 596 076 marks the most northerly of the routes. The routes are described travelling south back towards The Gloup. Immediately in front of the large cairn is a small headland cut by big grooves either side. The smaller right-hand groove (south) holds the following two routes.

Whales @ Hand   18m   Very Difficult *. I.Miller, C.Webb. 12th July 2004.
Climb the steep full-height crack running up the right-hand side of the groove.

Darkness Descends   18m   Very Difficult. I.Miller, C.Webb. 28th June 2004.
Climb a big corner-crack running up the left-hand side of the groove.

The Art of Grovel   18m   Very Difficult *. I.Miller, C.Webb. 22nd August 2004.
Climb a prominent left-trending ramp, running full-height up the cliffs to the south of the above groove. Nice steep juggy climbing on unusual rock!

From the above cairn walk back along the cliff-top for about 50m to a very damp and green geo. Immediately to the north of this geo, there are two very prominent left-facing corners running full crag height.

Rough and Tumble   18m   VS 4c. I.Miller, C.Webb. 18th May 2004.
This route climbs the larger (left-hand) and more prominent corner.

Immediately to the south of the damp geo the cliff turns 90° to face north. This face is immaculate black rock with four main full crag height cracks. This wall can be easily seen looking back from the cliff tops to the north of the damp geo.

Good Heavens   18m   HVS 5a. C.Webb, I.Miller. 1st May 2004.
Climb the most obvious left-trending hand crack in the centre of the wall. It turns into an open groove in the top half. Strenuous climbing to start.

Joe's Route   18m   E1 5b *. J.Alexander, I.Miller, C.Webb. 17th June 2004.
In the centre of the wall climb a prominent V-groove to a ledge at 14m. Follow a ramp on the left to the top.

Malaise   18m   E1 5b ***. I.Miller, H.Clarke. 10th April 2004.
At the seaward end of the black walls the cliff turns another 90° to face the sea.
This face holds a steep full crag height chimney with an excellent crack running
its full length. Climb this chimney from the non-tidal ledge at its base. Strenuous
and excellent climbing with some sustained moves on the upper half.

A few metres south the cliff turns another 90° to face south. At the landward end
of this face there is a stepped recess around which the following routes lie.

Blackened   16m   HVS 5a **. I.Miller, C.Webb. 28th June 2004.
Climb an excellent steep corner, well protected with excellent jamming.

Crimp for the Big   16m   E1 5a *. I. Miller, C. Webb. 17th June, 2004.
Three metres to the left, climb up the centre of a slab to a square stance. Follow
the holds to another stance below a groove and roof. Pull through the roof and
follow a crack to the top. Devious protection.

Whales @ 20ft   18m   VS 4b. I.Miller, H.Clarke 12th July 2004.
Climb a prominent right-leaning chimney in the centre of the south face on the
black headland.

At the southern end of this recess, the following route climbs the ominous off-
width crack.

No More Pies   20m   Very Difficult. I.Miller, C.Webb. 18th May 2004.
The most prominent feature on this part of the crag is an off-width groove in the
upper half of the wall. Climb up the big steps from the right, climb the off-width
groove and continue up the steps to the top. A bold route.

A farther 50m to the south, just past a further damp geo, is another black north
facing wall with two prominent full crag height grooves.

Gash Bag   18m   Hard Severe *. I.Miller. 30th June 2004.
The larger seaward groove is tidal and rarely dry.

Melange   18m   VS 4b ***. I.Miller, C.Webb. 28th June 2004.
The smaller groove has perfect compact rock with just enough gear (small wires
essential).

Wettened   18m   Very Difficult. C.Webb, I.Miller. 28th June 2004.
Starting at the bottom of an arête to the right of the above, follow good holds and
small steps trending right to the top.

A farther 50m to the south is a narrow north facing black wall, again with two
prominent full crag height grooves. Access to the base is by abseil to a large non-
tidal triangular ledge at the bottom of the seaward groove. Alternative access at
low tide is by walking down the slabs immediately to the south and traversing
along sea-level platforms.

Flying Friends 16m HVS 5b. C.Webb, I.Miller. 28th August 2004.
Climb the left-hand (seaward) skyline arête.

Climb on, Hope! 16m VS 4b **. I.Miller, J.Skene. 2nd July 2004.
From the back of the triangular ledge climb the open-book groove to a small ledge and up through a small roof. At the top of the groove traverse right on a steep wall and pull on jugs past twin roofs to the recess just below the top. Scramble to the top.

Grey to Life 16m Hard Severe *. I.Miller, D.Husband, D.Fox. 2nd July 2004.
From the landward end of the triangular ledge, step around the arête and climb up to a small ledge. Follow the groove to the recess and the top.

South Ronaldsay, Tomb of the Eagles, Old Head (HY 470 834):
The general approach is as for Tomb of the Eagles to Liddel Farm. After which follow the faint coastal path out along the south side of Ham Geo, before turning south for a farther 400 to 500m to the cliffs, which show as three fins of rock running approximately east/west with the climbing on the south side of each one. Climbing is on the usual Rousay Flag that predominates hereabouts. Improbable looking lines and Friend protection are the order of the day. Climbing is good on the North Fin, fine on the Centre and excellent on the South. Routes on the North and Middle Fin were climbed by various Nevis Guides parties during the summer of 2004.

North Fin (15m):
The first major fin encountered when approaching from the north is an island at high tide with access over some slabs below the south face from mid to low tide. *The Giant Steps* (Difficult) run up or down the cliff from here. Just right (east) of the access there are two crack come groove-lines running up the striated wall and forming a V; the left-hand one is *Hook* (Difficult), the right *Line* (Difficult). A few metres right again a plumb vertical crack runs the full height of the cliff – *Sinker* (Very Difficult *). Right again the sea runs under the cliff and the best way to utilize the cliff is to traverse out seawards. *Limbo Dancer* 60m Mild Severe *: choose whichever set of eroded out grooves you prefer and head seawards – helmet mirror handy for watching the feet. Finish up the arête at the far end, or go round the corner at the seaward end where there's an excellent little corner above a triangular tidal pool, *Tri* (Difficult).

Middle Fin:
At 10m this is the lowest of the trilogy, though the climbing is very good. A tidal pond below most of the cliff makes access tricky and the seaward end is best tackled in a calm sea, low tide, or both. For the landward end scramble down a little chimney to the base of a short corner; *Forgotten Friend* (10m Severe *). A few metres right is another, shallower left-facing corner; *Venner* (10m VS+ *). Follow the horizontal fault-line for the next route, which crosses Venner at a one-third height. Keep going right above the pool, then head for the top about 5m; *Rogered* (VS+ **). The next two routes start from the seaward end; *Genser* (10m Very Difficult *). Start from the only bit of clear ledge at the seaward end. A choice of cracks lead to the upper wall end and a finish left or right of a wee beak.

Gansey   10m   Mild Severe   **
Start from the ledge (as above) and tiptoe left beside the pool to a small foot ledge
in the middle of the face. Climb straight up the middle of the face from here on
excellent holds.

South Fin (Saga Wall):
The highest (20m) of the three offers the most extensive climbing on the south
and improbable wall, also a spectacular route through the overhangs on the seaward
end. Access is by abseil or scrambling down ledges from the south-east side, which
brings you to more extensive ledges below the cliff. The most prominent feature
of the cliff is easily seen from here, a spectacular stepped overhang with a crack-
line running up through the middle.

Rattus Rattus   20m   E2 5c ***(?).
The crack-line has been led all bar the last 4m when a top-rope was taken. Still
awaits a clean ascent.

Youthful Enthusiasm   22m   VS 5a **. I.Miller, H.Clarke. 29th September 2004.
Climb the arête (a few metres left of Rattus Rattus) to a left-trending thin crack.
Follow the crack to below a small roof and traverse left. Pull up to a good stance
and climb direct through a seemingly blank section to a continuous crack and the
top.

Left of here is a recessed bay with crack-lines left and right, which both give
pleasant Diffs. Around the corner is the main south facing cliff and just as the
cliff turns the corner there's a square overhang at three-quarters height.

Over the Hill   20m   VS 4b *. M.Tighe, J.Armour. 28th August 2004.
Climb up the groove system immediately below the overhang and make an exciting
move to exit out right on to a little foot ledge below the final little wall.

And More   22m   VS 4c *. I.Miller, H.Clarke. 29th September 2004.
Follow Over the Hill until beneath the large roof, then traverse out left and around
the corner to climb a left-trending crack to the top.

50/50   20m   VS 4c **. M.Tighe, H.Clarke. 8th May 2004.
Below and left of the overhang mentioned in the previous route is another of
similar size and shape. Climb up beneath the overhang trending out leftwards and
using a very prominent 3m vertical slot if required. Pull out on to the face and go
up a shallow left-facing corner for a few metres, passing a tiny overhang just
before the top.

Holding Back the Years   20m   HVS 5a **. M.Tighe, H.Clarke. 9th May 2004.
Just left of the 3m slot, two converging crack-lines create an inverted V. Climb a
groove off the floor, then the striations on up through the V and crack-lines in the
upper wall.

Age Concern   20m   VS 4c **. M.Tighe, H. & C.Clarke, R.Robertson. 15th
September 2004.

A few metres left of the previous route is another slot at half-height. Gain this from below, climb the slot and the wall above.

Senior Moments 15m VS 4b/c. M.Tighe, J.Armour. 28th August 2004.
Start from a ledge at the left hand side of the face, 5m higher than the previous routes. Step out on to the wall from the right-hand side of the ledge and climb up the wall to a diagonal crack just right of the arch.

Life Begins 15m Severe. M.Tighe, J.Armour. 28th August 2004.
Climb the left-hand side of the wall from the ledge.

South Ronaldsay, Hesta Rock:
Hesta Rock is the large headland to the east of The Clett of Crura (ND 466 876). The easiest approach is as for The Clett of Crura. The Hesta rock headland is a rotting mass of extremely loose rock with some steep vegetation. The highest part of the crag is approx. 60m. Running up the centre of the main headland and starting at half-height is a very prominent black chimney. The following route tried to climb this chimney and is recorded as a warning to future explorers. Access to the bottom is by a steep scramble down the grassy slopes to the east followed by a very pleasant sea-level traverse along easy angled slabs to below a large overhanging wall.

Wriggle and Die 120m XS 5a. I.Miller, H.Clarke. 26th April 2004.
1. 30m 4a. From the sea-level slab below the overhanging wall, climb a left-trending ramp on good rock crossing a drainage line and some very greasy rock. Negotiate the drainage line to a nasty step down to a large sloping ledge.
2. 30m 4a. Make a tricky move up on shocking rock to a further ledge and scramble up thick vegetation trending left to a crack-line in the wall at the base of the Black Chimney.
3. 35m 4c. Climb the chimney (insanely loose). After 20m make a terrifying traverse left on to a grassy ramp to a large tottering pillar some 10m up.
4. 25m. Scramble easily up the grassy ramp to the summit.

Clett of Crura:
Ode to my Friend 25m Hard Severe 4b. I.Miller, L.Gorham. 28th July 2004.
Approx. 4m to the left/west of the large groove in the upper centre of the seaward face, climb a faint full height groove up to and through a smaller groove. Top out at the summit cairn.

The Clett:
This small stack is found between The Clett of Crura and the view point at the car park on the main road. Access is by boulder hop at low tide followed by a swim to its seaward face. The stack is an almost exact replica (in miniature) of the Clett of Crura.

Unnamed 12m Severe. L.Gorham, I.Miller. 28th July 2004.
Climb the deep hand crack up the west side of the seaward face, step right at its top to a good stance. Climb the wall directly above on good holds to the top.
Note: Les Gorham was killed during the abseil from this route.

Stronsay, The Vat of Kirbuster:
On the main wall to the right of the three routes in the guide are the following three routes.

Step 2 Arête   14m   HVS 5a. I.Miller, H.Clarke. 1st June 2003.
Start at the bottom of the open book corner to the right of the arête. Climb the corner for a few metres, then traverse left to a small ledge to the right of the roof on the arête. Surmount the roof to a better ledge and follow the arête more easily to the top.

Bleach Blond   14m   VS 4c. S.Herd, K.Kelley. August 2003.
Climb the open book corner to the right of the above route.

Hairdresser   14m   Severe. S.Herd, K.Kelley. August 2003.
The full height crack-line a few metres to the right.

Hoy, Rora Head, Gully 1:
Hewins' Route   35m   E2 5c **. T.Spreyer, A.Hein. 7th July 2004.
Climb the initial finger crack of Mater, then step left and climb between horizontal breaks (crux) to the base of a prominent right-diagonal crack in the centre of the upper wall. Climb this in its entirety, then step right to finish direct.

Banana Transfer Theory   45m   E1 5b ***. A.Hein, T.Spreyer, O.Metheril. 7th July 2004.
Start at the same place as Craa'nest then traverse right along a ledge for 4m to the base of a steep crack. Climb the crack for 5m to a horizontal break, then step right on to a ledge. Go up and right to join Hewins' Route at the bottom of the diagonal crack. Traverse right along a small ledge into the corner of Mater. Climb this until possible to step right on to the arête. Hand traverse right until a deep corner is reached (by Paneer) and finish up this.

St. John's Head:
The headland of St John's terminates as a huge steep stepped arête at its southern end (about 400m from the left arête). This is the largest and most obvious feature on the headland and is easily seen from the Orkney to Scrabster ferry. Access to the route is gained by a scramble from the descent gully along the beach below the main face. A short section below the step main face is only accessible at low tide. Alternatively access by boat in calm seas. The route was climbed in a single 26 hour push with a short bivvy during darkness. A 8m leader fall was taken on pitch 8 and one point of aid used on lead (freed by the second at 5b). Rock quality is in general poor but the location and the atmosphere is truly outstanding, an adventurous and serious route.

Testament to the Insane   475m   XS 5b. D.Fox, R.I.Jones, I.Miller (alt), L.Gorham. 23rd-24th July 2004.
1. 30m. To the left of the boulder beach, directly below the arête, climb a steep grassy slope to the boulder on the horizon.
2. 35m. Scramble easily up the grass to cracks at the right end of a rock band.

3. 40m. Continue up the steepening grass to the base of the wall of the towering arête and a big chimney/groove.

4. 40m 4c. Climb the chimney/groove and pull out left at its top to a sloping grassy stance. Climb up steep grass to another groove, pull out left at its top and follow a short loose corner to a small stance with a peg.

5. 10m. Follow the grassy arête on the right to a bigger ledge at the bottom of a slabby right-facing corner.

6. 40m 4a. From the right-hand end of the ledge, climb the corner to even steeper vegetation, ascend this swiftly to a second right-facing corner and climb this to a good stance.

7. 40m 4c. Climb up trending slightly left to the base of a steep red wall below a huge precarious capping boulder. Traverse right and ascend the steep ramp on better rock to a steep and extremely loose vegetated slope. Climb this delicately to the landward side of another massive perched boulder. Belay in the twin cracks on the wall below it.

8. 45m 5b. Traverse along the grassy ledge to the bottom of the prominent arête, which bounds the right-hand end of the huge slabby wall. Pull around the arête on good holds in an exposed position to gain the base of a left-facing corner. Climb the corner steeply to a grotty ledge (several pegs) below a wide groove.

9. 10m 4a. Climb the wide groove and up grass to a good stance with in situ peg.

10. 45m 5a. Climb the steep right-trending corner through a wee roof to further steep vegetation. Carefully climb the vegetation to a crumbling recess on the left. Climb the centre of the recess to a huge boulder (bivvy on first ascent).

11. 50m. Scramble through deep vegetation to the bottom of the headwall. Belay on the high point of vegetation directly below the huge central fault-line.

12. 25m 4b. Climb the left-facing corner on the left into a cave with a huge block on the floor. Climb through a niche in the roof of the cave to the bottom of a big left-facing corner.

13. 20m 5a. Climb the hand crack 3m to the left of the vegetated open book corner to a good triangular niche. At the back of the niche climb steep hand cracks to a good stance on the left.

14. 45m 5a. Continue up the chimney to a wide grassy ledge above. Traverse along this narrowing ledge delicately to a loose recess. Ascend the recess to the summit.

SHETLAND, Da Grind o' da Navir:

Notes from G.Latter: Many of the routes are much better than the star ratings suggested in the guide, with almost all the routes deserving at least one star. The approach along the coast from the lighthouse takes around 30mins (not 20), and a much shorter approach can be made by taking the turn-off north (signposted Leascole), then turning off left after 0.9 miles/1.4 km to follow an unmetalled road which leads down, through a gate (ignore no unauthorised entry sign) then left again round the back of the cottage to park at the back of the abandoned Fish Hatchery. From here head north crossing three fences (stick to a ridge marked with pipes); then west along the fence to arrive at the crag in less than 10mins.

The South Descent Gully is very straight-forward (not V.Diff.) – about Moderate, with only a short tricky 3m step at the base.

6. *Tenderness on the Block* worth 1*. Replace "block bay to a loose finish" with "move left to finish over ledges up shallow open groove." (Final loose holds removed).

7. *Barnacle Bill* – crux is well protected (small rocks). Positions of this and route 8 should be transposed on the wee map (starts on north-west edge of the prow).

8. *The Raven Banner* worth E1 5b (not HVS), with crux low down moving up from the first cluster of protection. Instead of moving out left at the protruding block, the fine grooves directly above were followed, pulling out left over bulge at top to finish up final easy slab.

11. *The Grindstone* worth 2* excellent rock in fine position. Maybe V.Diff.?

14. *Darklands* worth 1*

17. *The Groove of the Navir* - 15m (not 10m)

18. *Navir Navir Land* – 20m (not 25). Top crack is very steady and not that sustained. Might only be E4 6b – very well protected?

20. *Da Droiltin Tree* worth E1 5b, particularly for final section. Very well-protected, with plenty of good rests.

21. *Nibbek* stunning climbing, possibly worth 4*!??

26. *The Ramp* worth 2*. Crosses some impressive terrain at the grade, on great rock.

Snippek   20m   E1 5b **. G.Latter, K.Finlayson. 9th May 2004.
Good climbing, starting up the right-facing corner round right the edge right of The Ramp. Climb up on to a ledge 3m above the right end of the shelf to belay on glacis just left of the base of the corner. After a short steep start, follow easier upper corners to a large ledge on the left. Step right above a roof and climb direct up thin cracks in the slab on good holds to a short hanging groove. Step right to finish up good breaks.

Eshaness:
Directly beneath the car park is an extensive west-facing overhanging wall above a sloping platform just above high tide level. Head due west from the car park and scramble down easily to a large platform along the cliff top. Abseil from a point just north of a slimy recessed area, at an obvious notch.

Third Stone from the Sun   35m   HVS 5a ****. S.Williams, G.Latter. 5th August 2004.
South of the big corner (abseil point), the most prominent feature is a series of right-facing corners capped by a hanging crack in the headwall. Climb direct to the corner, up this and the next corner to a roof. Pull left through this and continue up the "overhanging potato field" above. Well protected on superb rock throughout.

Solan   35m   E1 5b **. G.Latter, S.Williams. 7th August 2004.
The hanging flake up the centre of the south facing wall just north of the blowhole. Abseil from the south end of the platform to a hanging belay just above the green slime. Climb direct on good holds up to the flake, and up this joyously to meander up the headwall on sharper slightly fragile rock.

Achilles Last Stand   45m   E1 5a **. S.Williams, G.Latter. 9th August 2004.
The huge chimney in the corner right (east) of Solan. Abseil down the right edge

of the south-facing wall to a good ledge at the base of the obvious crack. Climb this a short way, then move into the chimney and follow this with interest, stepping left about 10m from the top to finish up an easier groove.

The Wind Cries… 40m VS 4b ****. S.Williams, G.Latter. 20th April 2004.
Superb steady climbing up the blunt rib and shallow hanging groove immediately west of the blowhole. Abseil down to a good small ledge beneath the groove. Step out left and climb a shallow rib directly, trending up rightwards to gain the groove. Follow this on superb holds.

Scooty Alan 40m HVS 5a ****. G.Latter, L.Fleming. 3rd August 2004.
Another stunning pitch, giving spectacular climbing up the rightmost, most continuous crack system at the right side of the wall. Abseil as for the above route. Move up and climb a short way up the left crack, then move out rightwards on good pockets to the base of the right crack, just above the initial roof. Follow this on fine jams, then directly up the wall above on good pockets to a ledge just short of the top. Pull over a bulge above on to a further ledge, then easily up a final short corner.

No Tern Unstoned 20m HVS 5a **. G.Latter, S.Williams. 22nd April 2004.
The short right-facing corner in the upper half of the large recess just south-west of the blowhole in front of the lighthouse (i.e. just north of the new fence). Abseil down the wall to the right of the corner to a large ledge at the base. Climb the corner, easing in its upper section.

Not Necessarily Stoned, but Beautiful… 45m E1 5c **. S.Williams, G.Latter. 23rd June 2004.
The left-facing corner bounding the left side of the overhanging north wall of the promontory just south of the fence. Climb the corner easily until an impasse just below half-height. Either move out left and follow the crack before returning to the corner, or continue up the corner throughout. At the top, use the flake out right to pull up left, finishing with a difficult mantelshelf.

Cave Crack 40m E5 6a ***. A.Cave, A.Wainwright. 28th May 2004.
The overhanging crack splitting the north facing wall wall just south of the lighthouse boundary fence (just south of Cruel Sea) is a quality challenge. Abseil to ledges 3-4m above sea-level. Reach the crack by a rising traverse from the left (bold), then climb it to the top.
Note: on an attempt at a repeat by G.Latter (failed due to dampness), a direct start was climbed from the ledge directly beneath the route, gained by direct abseil. Better protected.

The next routes are on the projecting west-facing pillar immediately south of the lighthouse boundary fence.

Perfect Groove 45m HVS 5a ****. D.Turnbull, I.Butler. 28th May 2004.
The obvious slim groove and crack in the pillar could pass for E3 but is in fact low in the grade! Top quality. Abseil to ledges a few metres above sea-level. Climb the blank looking wall for 10m to the base of the crack. Follow this to the top.

Near Perfect Arête   45m   HVS 5a **. I.Butler, D.Turnbull. 28th May 2004.
Abseil to slightly higher ledge on the south side of the pillar. Climb up to the arête and follow it to finish up the left wall.

Hanging Crack   35m   E1 5a *. A.Wainwright, A.Cave. 28th May 2004.
Start as for Black Watch. The route climbs the hanging corner in the left arête of the wall. Move up left and pull through a roof into the hanging corner. Follow this to a 'riglos' style finish on surprisingly solid rock.

Saandiloo   35m   HVS 5a **. G.Latter, M.Davidson, C.Nicol, A.Watt. 4th August 2004.
About 100m south of the last described routes in the guide (Atlantic City etc.) is an easy-angled south facing wall (just west of an obvious gravelly area on the cliff-top). The slab at the left side of the crag, breaching the right side of the roof. Abseil down just west of the deep central chimney fault to a small ledge just above high tide. Climb easily leftwards up the slab, then veer right to an obvious deep groove near the right end of the roofs. Climb this to step right to a small ledge and good pockets, then directly more easily up a crack in the final slab.

Tirricks   35m   HVS 4c **. G.Latter, S.Williams, L.Fleming. 30th July 2004.
Abseil down the right side of the wall to a small ledge 6m above the sea and belay to the abseil rope. Follow a slightly left-trending line aiming for an easy hanging groove/flake system leading up to the left side of the capping roofs. Step left to finish up the easy cracked groove.

Pobie Skeo:
The following routes lie on the main south facing wall of the crag and take the obvious main challenges.

The Eyes   18m   E2 5c **. D.Turnbull, I.Butler. 29th May 2004.
Climb the hanging corner to the twin 'Eyes' and an amazing thread. Start just left of the arête as for Stars on 45. Swing right at half-height and make committing moves up and rightwards to an obvious hand slot in the hanging corner. Continue direct to the 'Eyes' then up leftwards to a well-positioned finish on the arête.

Roof Crack Direct   18m   E4 6b **. A.Cave, I.Butler. 29th May 2004.
A tough little number starting in the back of the square-cut cave below the obvious central crack-line. Climb leftwards out of the cave move up to the bulging crack. Hard moves lead to good holds and an easier finish up the crack.

FOULA, Mucklabrek:
Magnus the Brave   75m   E4 **. D.Turnbull, I.Butler. 1st June 2004.
An excellent direct line up the clean white wall near the pinnacle. Start as for Eric the Dead.
1. 27m 5c. Gain the grassy ledge at 4m, then climb direct via a slim left-facing corner to a second ledge. Weave up left, then back right on edges and breaks to a rounded crack. Move up left and go up the clean white wall before being forced rightwards along a break to belay in Eric the Dead.

2. 28m 5c. Climb direct bearing first left to a crack, then back rightwards to the ledge below bubbly rock in the steep wall. Pluck up courage, then take a rising leftwards line through the bulge to a mantel on to a ledge on the right.
3. 20m 5b. Step left, then climb more or less direct to the top finishing up a left-trending flake and a grim pull on to the grass terrace.

Maillie Grooves   85m   E4. I.Butler, D.Turnbull. 30th May 2004.
A grim experience which is harder and much worse than it appears. Start below a series of right-facing corners about 120m from the top of the western descent track.
1. 30m 6a. Climb direct to the base of the first corner via a flared crack (bold). Climb corners and steep cracks to a hard leftwards grovel on to a ledge.
2. 20m 5b. Climb easily leftwards, then up scooped rock before being forced to traverse 6m rightwards to a groove below a steep wall.
3. 25m 6a. Climb up and then bare leftwards via some steep cracks and short corners to another grim thrutch on a belay ledge. Fulmars.
4. 10m 4c. Climb more easily to the top and a block.

NORTHERN HIGHLANDS CENTRAL
No routes here, as a new guide is in preparation.

NORTHERN HIGHLANDS SOUTH

SOUTH GLEN SHIEL, Creag Coire an t-Slugain:
Hong Kong   140m   IV,5 **. H.Chan, A.Nisbet. 16th February 2005.
Climb the direct start to Tipperary (SMCJ 2004) but cross this route and go straight up a groove to an overhung recess (30m). Pass the recess by the rib on the right, then go up left under a steep wall until it is crossed more easily (30m). Follow grooves until the crest of the ridge is joined.

SGURR CHOINNICH (Strathcarron):
Note: The buttress between Chemical Alley and The Bow (see SMCJ 2003, p382), starting just up and right of the base at a steep left-slanting groove was climbed by B.Davison and D.McGimpsey on 18th February 2005. 100m, Grade II.

BEINN BHAN, Coire na Feola:
Weakest Link   150m   III. D.McGimpsey, A.Nisbet. 21st December 2004.
This route is on a left continuation of Suspense Buttress, with its base slightly higher. The only obvious break in a steep lower tier is a groove left of centre on the buttress. Climb a groove through the lowest tier to reach the main groove. This was entered from the left over flakes and followed (45m). Continue up the groove to easier ground (40m). Continue in the same line (45m) to a finish on the left (20m).

Suspense Buttress:
Skinflint   190m   VI,6. A.Nisbet, J.Preston; D.McGimpsey, I.Small. 24th February 2005.

A spectacular line up a groove in the front face of the central lower buttress. Avoid the steep but minor lower tier and start about 15m from the left end of the next tier (this tier is also optional).
1. 10m. Climb a fault with turf leading to a cracked wall. Walk left about 10m to twin cracks in a corner, the only sensible break in the right half of the next tier.
2. 25m. Climb the cracks and their right-slanting continuation, passing the last crack on the right. Walk 5m right to below the main groove.
3. 15m. Climb the initial overhanging section by chimneying and bridging, then go up and right to a ledge on the right of another overhanging section.
4. 30m. Return to the groove and climb it to the final bulge. Move left and back right above this. A final wall is climbed by another move left and back right. Cross the terrace to an embedded flake.
5. 40m. Start up the big groove on the left (the harder version of Suspense Buttress goes up this), then walk right along a ledge (direct may be possible). Climb the buttress above to a ledge.
6. 25m. Climb a groove with a steep finish.
7. 25m. The final groove of Cliffhanger is on the right. Climb a steeper smaller groove to the flat top of the buttress.

Coire na Poite:
Gryphon　130m　V,7. I.Small, D.McGimpsey. 22nd February 2005.
Climbs the front face of the buttress on which Teapot (SMCJ 1994) takes grooves up the left side. Start 5m right of the small cave.
1. 30m. Go up a turfy groove, traverse left and then climb a short hard groove above (crux) to a terrace below a slabby wall.
2. 40m. Climb a right-trending groove, then move out right to a spike. Go up short steps, then traverse back left before climbing up and back right to easier ground leading to a short tower.
3. 30m. Climb a ramp on the right side of the tower to gain its top.
4. 30m. Escape left to easy ground is possible, but continue up the ridge above via short turfy steps.

FUAR THOLL: Note: An impressive route, Sandblaster (VIII,7) was recorded by B.Wilkinson and R.Thomas in March 2005. It was thought to be left of Sandstorm, but this needs checking.

BEN SHIELDAIG　(NG 825 525):
The largest and cleanest of the crags containing some prominent overhangs situated on the south-west slopes of Ben Shieldaig. Well seen from the road and situated just above the tree line. Park about 100m south of the Applecross turn off. The best approach is by way of a clearance on the left but is somewhat unpleasant (about 35mins). The crag is split into three sections. The left section has two large overhangs and is bounded on the right by a groove. The middle section is bounded on the right by another groove with an overhang on the right.

Gateway　35m　HVS　5a *. S.Kennedy, R.Hamilton. 23rd May 2004.
Weaves a line between the two large overhangs on the left section. Scramble up steep heather to the lowest point, directly below the right end of the upper overhang.

Climb a steep crack to some small trees then traverse away left directly below the upper overhang to the exposed left edge. Finish up the easier slab on the left.

Prawn Man   30m   HVS 5a *. R.Hamilton, S.Kennedy. 23rd May 2004.
The prominent groove to the right of the left section. Start in a large recess below the groove, a few metres right of Gateway. Climb a short wall then a slab to a bulge at the base of the groove. Surmount the bulge (crux), continue up the groove and finish up slabs.

BEN DAMPH, Creagan Dubh Toll nam Biast:
Fraoch Groove   450m   IV,4. A.Nisbet (backroped). 14th March 2005
A better and more direct ascent of Erica's Ridge by a line of grooves overlooking the gully on the left (Calluna). Start close to Calluna and go up right to reach the grooves. Climb close to these for three pitches before moving right below the last steep tier to another turfy line. Finish up the easy crest and final chimney as for Erica's Ridge.

Lingo   400m   IV,4. A.Nisbet, J.Preston. 25th February 2005.
The buttress to the left of Calluna. Start just inside Calluna and traverse on to the buttress above the first wall. Go up to a steep band (15m). Climb this and the next band by corners on their right side. Go up and traverse left on to the crest (45m). Continue up the crest for two long pitches to easier ground. Finish up the crest which merges into slopes.

BEN DAMPH FOREST, Kinlochdamph Crag:
War of Attrition   25m   E4 6a *. M.E.Moran, A.J.Moran (on-sight). 30th March 2005.
Climbs the crack/groove line 2m right of the corner with a bird's nest to the right of Ivy League. Very much harder and better than it looks. Go up to a block, swing right into the groove and climb it with sustained interest to an exit on suspect flakes. Finish up an easier flake-crack in the right side of the final arête.

Note: M.E.Moran and J.Preston climbed a direct finish to Hasta la Bista on 13th May 2004. Go up into the recess just left of the prow and make an exciting swing and mantel over a roof to a ledge, then the top (10m, 5c).

Sleeping Dog Climb, Poshpaws Start   14m   Severe. M.E. & A.J.Moran. 4th May 2004.
Makes a pleasant start to Sleeping Dog Climb and routes in the headwall. Climb cracks on the buttress just left of the chimney, moving up and left to block belays below the headwall.

Tiberian Sun   40m   E2 6a *. M.E.Moran, J.Preston. 13th May 2004 .
Climbs a brief but memorable overhanging wall to gain the vice-like groove in the left side of the headwall; protection is good.
1. 14m. As for Poshpaws Start to S.Dog Climb
2. 26m 6a. Gain the wall below the groove from the left and layback boldly into the slot. Bridge leftwards up the groove and finish up a right-facing corner

BEINN EIGHE, Eastern Ramparts:

Tainted Galahad Direct Finish   30m   E3 6a. I.Small, A.Hume, J.Walker. 7th August 2004.

4a. 30m 6a Climb the corner, exit right, then move back left and go directly up to a long narrow ledge with a flake-corner at the right end. Climb a bulging crack in the wall above to the top.

West Buttress:

G.Robertson & E.Tressider climbed West Buttress Diretissima on 27th February 2005, climbing the corner of Senior direct. This gave two more hard pitches, "one of quite goey icy 7 and another of safe torquey 8".

Coire Ruadh-Staca (Pineapple Cliff):

Jambo   120m   V,7 *. D.McGimpsey, A.Nisbet. 19th December 2004.

Right of Midge Ridge is a bay enclosed by overhanging walls. This route takes a right-slanting corner through the walls and leading to a right diagonal line of chimneys. Start on the right side of the bay and climb cracks leading to the corner. Climb the corner and traverse right to a ledge (20m). Climb two successive chimneys leading right (30m). Climb a flake-chimney and a short wall to easier ground. Go up this to a final wall (45m). Traverse right and finish up steep turf.

Chocked   100m   IV,6 *. D.McGimpsey, A.Nisbet. 8th February 2005.

A crack-line just right of Smilodon. Rather close, but the middle pitch is superb.

1. 30m. Climb the initial section of the right of the three chimney systems, then take a slab leading left to below the crack-line.

2. 35m. Climb the crack-line, which leads into the easy gully of Smilodon.

3. 35m. Finish up this.

Quickstep   120m   IV,5. A.Nisbet, D.Preston. 28th November 2004.

The buttress at the far right end of the 'Pineapple Cliff', right of the right chimney system. Five short pitches. Start up a prominent narrow chimney on the left side, facing the rest of the cliff. Staying on the left side, climbs short walls to a corner below a thin pinnacle. From the top of the pinnacle, step left into a steep groove which leads to easier ground. Go down behind a bigger pinnacle and climb a wall on the left before returning right to thread a way amongst finishing short walls.

High on the right (south-west) of the face with the Spidean Lochans, starting at a height of about 780m and finishing on the ridge about 500m west of the top of Spidean Coire nan Clach, is the following route on a dome shaped buttress at NG 961 596.

Bartlett's Dilemma   90m   IV,4. J.Sutherland, A.Gorman. 30th December 2003.

1. 40m. Start just right of the toe of the buttress and go up an icy or turfy gully trending slightly right.

2. 30m. At this point the gully continues easily up and right, but step left and continue up mixed ground until a smooth wall forces a step right around a flake, continue up until below an open chimney.

3. 20m. Continue up towards the chimney and climb it to the top.

Spidean Coire nan Clach:

The Cobbler. 1908 A. E. Robertson Collection.

On Sgurr a' Mhaim, looking East. Date unknown, A. E. Robertson Collection.

North Ridge 100m III,4. V.Chelton, D.McGimpsey, A.Nisbet, J.Preston. 19th November 2004.
The base of the ridge forms an overhanging wall (NG 968 602). Heading up right (west) the right side of the ridge becomes progressively easier. The route takes an obvious line of weakness leading diagonally left with one steep section (potentially very loose) to reach a pinnacle on the crest. The crest soon becomes easy scrambling and walking.

LIATHACH, Path Crag.
(NG 936 573) Alt. 400m.   South facing.
These sandstone crags have fine views over to the Achnashellach hills. Follow the path to the corrie, then go west to the crags, about 40mins.

Lower Tier:
Unnamed 15m VS 4c *. C.Moody, C.Grindley. 7th August 2004.
At the left end of the crag is a shallow gully. Climb a corner-crack right of the gully formed by the left side of a huge block. Step left and finish up an arête.

Foxglove Crack 15m VS 4c **. C.Moody, C.Grindley. 7th August 2004.
Start just right of centre. Climb a right-slanting flake-crack and finish past a small overhang. The wall to the left is black.

Upper Tier:
Unnamed 22m HVS 5a **. C Moody, C.Grindley. 7th August 2004.
Left of centre are two recessed corner-cracks facing each other. Start under the left-hand corner-crack. Move up then right to a ledge, continue up then move left on to a heather ledge. Climb the left-hand corner-crack.

Swirl 20m VS 4c **. C.Moody, C.Grindley. 7th August 2004.
Start towards the right side of the crag. Climb up right to gain and follow a left-facing corner-crack formed by a huge block. Follow an easy slab up right.

DIABAIG PENINSULA, Rolling Wall:
Rolling Baba 20m E2 6a *. M.E. & A.J.Moran. 12th June 2004.
Climbs the walls right of The Ice Bulge; dries quickly after rain. Start as for Beside the Point. Traverse a hand-crack across a steep wall to gain a ramp, then move up and left across an impending wall to good holds and gain a sloping terrace. From a horizontal crack, climb through the bulging wall above on orange quartz rock with a hard crux sequence.

INVERALLIGIN:
Many short routes have been climbed in this area. Descriptions are available if requested. New crags include:
Discovery Rock: (NG 810 570), Alt. 90m. South facing.
A clean outcrop, 15m to 20m high, sited on the Rubha na h-Airde Glaise peninsula above the narrows of Loch Torridon with an interesting variety of routes, ideal for novices.
Big Bill's Crag: (NG 811 568), Partly tidal. South-south-east facing.
A fierce crag, viciously undercut and dipping into the sea, well seen from A896 on the south side of loch.
The Inveralligin Crags: (NG 841 572). comprises of eight distinct buttress features, seven of which are concentrated within a 100m stretch.

Climbers and guides at Sligachan. Early 1900s. A. E. Robertson Collection.

On the West Ridge of Sgurr nan Gillean, looking South. 1905. A. E. Robertson Collection.

CAIRNGORMS

LOCHNAGAR, Black Spout Pinnacle:
The Inhospitable Crack 20m E2 5b. R.Archbold, R.Ross, G.Strange. 24th August 2003.
The prominent crack mentioned in the guidebook description of Black Spout Wall. From a belay at top of Route 2 chimney, climb the obvious left-slanting crack to overhangs. Move left into a recess, then climb a corner and finish over the final bulges of The Link Direct.

Note: N.Morrison notes that the combination of the first pitch of Nihilist and the second pitch of the Extremist gives a very good and sustained way up the cliff with the additional benefit of being just about the fastest drying line on the pinnacle. Probably E2 5b,5b **, 70m.

EAGLES ROCK, The Mid-East Buttress:
Cold Flush 150m II. G.Strange. 23rd January 2005. Start below Shiver and go up rightwards on easy ramps to gain and climb prominent ice runnel through break in upper rocks.

BEINN A' BHUIRD, Coire na Ciche, The Cioch:
Chioch Buttress 100m II. S.M.Richardson. 16th January 2005.
This route climbs the east ridge of The Cioch. Start left of the crest and move up a narrowing snow slope that trends right into a tight V-chimney. Climb this past a constriction and continue up easier ground to the crest. Follow this easily to the top.

Coire nan Clach, Black Crag:
Hombre 40m E2 5c. M.Uceta, G.Strange. 29th June 2003.
A climb on the south end of the crag, well right of Abdel Wahab. Start at a hollow flake above a pointed bollard on an upper grass ledge. Climb up slightly right, then follow a flake-crack to below a slab ramp. Move right, go up past a big spike and continue to a recess below overhangs. Climb up left to a resting position, then make a difficult move to reach easier cracks leading to the top.

BEN AVON, East Meur Gorm Craig:
Near the middle of this half kilometre long west facing broken cliff there are three short compact buttresses. The rightmost is squarish, the centre is steep with a forking crack system and the left has a roof low down on its right.

Backslash 50m VS 4b. R.Archbold, B.Findlay, G.Strange. 1st August 2004. Takes the prominent crack on the squarish buttress. Climb a short corner, flakes, then the fine crack to a ledge. Continue up the crest by an obvious groove.

Fox Crack 50m VS 4c. R.Archbold, B.Findlay, G.Strange. 1st August 2004. The crack-line immediately left of the roof on the left-hand buttress.

CREAGAN A' CHOIRE ETCHACHAN:
Scabbard, Direct Finish 50m HVS 5a. S.M.Richardson, A.S.Robertson. 5th September 2004.
A prominent inverted stepped corner-line directly above the huge spike belay at the top of pitch 2. Pull into the groove above the belay and climb up to a roof. Step left around this and pull into the groove above using holds on the right wall. Continue up the crack above to a good ledge (30m). Finish up easy ground just right of the Dagger corner to the terrace.

STACAN DUBHA:
The Shuttle 150m V,7 *. D.McGimpsey, A.Nisbet. 19th January 2005.
Good climbing but a disproportionately hard crux. Largely by the summer line. Climb the lower tier left of the summer central crack, then scramble to the main climbing. Go rightwards on large flakes, then up to a chimney on the right which leads back left to a terrace below the steepest band. Climb this on its right end; climb up over blocks to gain the gully wall of the buttress and traverse right above the gully until a short V-chimney topped by a flake (crux) cuts back to the crest. Climb this up smooth slabs to an easier upper section.

CARN ETCHACHAN, Upper Tier:
Malicious Midget 80m E2 5c. I.Small, J.Walker. 2nd August 2003.
This route climbs a series of corners and an arête cutting across Poison Dwarf, then crosses the Rock Window to finish up the wall to the left of Crevasse Route.
1. 35m 5b. Start at the foot of the Equinox gully. Follow a left-slanting ramp-line passing below a perched boulder to gain an obvious corner. Climb to a triangular roof, move right on to an arête, then gain the corner on the right. Follow it past a niche to a ledge, then take the corner above to exit left to a large ledge (this final corner is common with Poison Dwarf).
2. 40m 5c. Arrange a side runner in the wide crack of Poison Dwarf, then traverse rightwards above a roof (exposed) to gain the arête. Climb this on the left side to a short groove leading to ledges by the Rock Window. Gain a standing position on the block that forms the Window and step left on to the wall above. Finish by cracks and ledges.

SHELTERSTONE CRAG, Central Slabs:
Note: Icon of Lust (SMCJ 2004) was climbed on 30th June 2003.

COIRE AN T-SNEACHDA, Aladdin's Buttress:
Babes in the Wood 35m VIII,8 **. D.MacLeod, S.Muir. 1st December 2004.
Follow the summer line with increasing difficulty, culminating in a thin crux section at the top of the crack.

Earwig 60m IV,6. J.Lyall, A.Nisbet. 13th January, 2005.
Climbs the right edge of Pygmy Ridge, breaking through the overhanging sidewall behind an ear of rock. Start 8m right of Saturation Point. Climb close under the sidewall (left of a chimney) and through a bulge with a spike. Move left to gain the base of the ear and climb the crack behind it. Move up on flakes to just below a ledge which is on Saturation Point (25m). Step right and climb slabby ground

trending right to reach the right end of an overhanging wall (30m). Gain the crest
of Pygmy Ridge (5m) and either finish up this or escape right.

Fiacaill Buttress:
The Hurting   35m   XI,11 ****. D.MacLeod. 19th February 2005.
Follow the summer line with very sustained hard and serious climbing. There is
groundfall potential on the lower half. M9+ or M10 standard climbing but very
tenuous and blind. FA style: Second attempt following abseil inspection. Gear
placed on lead but no pegs were used and the grade reflects this. Possibly the
hardest single pitch tradtional mixed climb in the world?

NORTH EAST OUTCROPS

BOLTSHEUGH, Lower South (NEO p189):
Trouble Monkey   15m   F7a+ *. T.Rankin. 25th April 2004.
The bolt line through the 3m roof of the cave. Climb a fine boulder problem past
the first bolt on to the ramp. From here it is advisable to clip the next three bolts in
the roof to prevent a possible knee capping on the ramp (long reach or cunning
required). Climb the roof left of the bolts on good but spaced holds to the break at
the lip. Finish up right then left to the lower-off carefully using a jammed block
below the final roof. A fine roof problem on surprisingly solid rock although foot
holds are still friable at present.

PASS OF BALLATER, Western Section, Upper Tier:
Idiot Nation   E5 6b *. A.Robertson, R.Goolden. 12th September 2004.
An artificial but well protected line up the left wall of Little Cenotaph. Start off
the block and climb the thin crack (good microwires) to the break with an awkward
move to enter a niche. From cams in the break, mantel it (crux) using an obvious
sidepull up right to gain a good hold higher up on the arête. Continue up the
hairline crack/flake by another hard balancy move to reach jugs over the top. The
rest on Smith's Arête and the crack of Little Cenotaph are off route.

REDHYTHE POINT, The Gully Buttress (NJ 576 672):
Near the south-east end of the plateau headland, a wide slanting gully with two
enormous chokestones defines a separate buttress. Some good wee climbs on superb
clean rock with good protection. Sections described from south to north.

Bird Poo Wall:
South from the head of the gully, there is an easy scrambling descent with a slabby
buttress just south. This is quite near the mouth of the Tea Cleft, and there is
potential for more easy (and possibly harder) routes, with tricky traverses in at the
base.

Bird Poo Wall   12m   Moderate. N.Everett. 14th September 2003.
Traverse left (facing in) from near the base of the descent into an easy line up jugs
and a crack, stepping left over an overlap near the top. Guano is avoidable.

South-East Face:
High Tide Traverse   25m   4b **. N.Everett. 14th September 2003.
Excellent rock and best with a calm high tide. Cross the groove at the base of the
Bird Poo descent; continue to a slab. Move up a few metres, then swing down on
to an overhanging wall. More good climbing leads round to the base of Rampage
on the East Face.

Wibble   10m   Moderate. S.Muir. 14th August 2003.
Climb the fine slab from the high-tide traverse, then grooves and shelves above.

North-East Face:
Split by Rampage into two halves. Access down Rampage, or via High Tide
Traverse, to good sloping rock at the foot of Rampage.

Break Out   10m   Hard Severe *. N.Everett, I.Martin. 17th April 2004.
Above the foot of Rampage a scroffly overlap looms over the wall. Climb slightly
left, then up onto a crack-laced wall, to cross the overlap just left of its widest
point.

Clean Break   10m   Severe *. N.Everett, S.Muir. 14th September 2003.
From the foot of Rampage, straight up through the thinner part of the overlap and
the wall above.

Rampage   12m   Moderate *. N.Everett, S.Muir. 14th September 2003.
The obvious fine ramp, which in descent is OK but exposed.

Lobster Line   12m   Severe *. N.Everett, S.Muir. 14th September 2003.
Well protected. From the lowest point of Rampage, traverse delicately right, then
up to the obvious crack-line, crossing a shelf (escape possible). Stay in the crack
for a good exposed finish out right.

Gully Wall:
Overhanging the eager chasm, and surprisingly steep. Quite sheltered from showers
but best in good drying weather. Easy scrambling approach down the gully's
northern slabs.

The Deep   12m   Hard Severe 4b **. N.Everett, I.Martin. 17th April 2004.
From the seaward chokestone, place high runners and cross the obvious small
hanging slab to superb positions on the arête. Go up the left side of the arête with
more exposure to the last move of Lobster Line.

Nailbiter   8m   E3 6a. P.Mather. 14th September 2003.
Climb Purple Turtle and place a high side runner. Traverse left into the middle of
the overhanging wall with feet in the big break, hands on low crimps and sidepulls
aiming for a slot in the central crack. Continue direct to the top.

Purple Turtle   8m   Very Difficult. P. & R.Mather. 14th September 2003.
The big overhanging crack climbed largely on its right-hand side. Provides good
steep jug pulling.

What Became of the Monkey?   6m   Very Difficult 4b *. N.Everett, I.Martin. 17th
April 2004.
The entertaining steep flakey line right of Purple Turtle.

Overhanging Wall (NJ 575 672):
This is the obvious overhanging buttress marked on the map in the guide as
"overhanging wall". Access is either via a scramble along the ravine (with a very
awkward move on to the belay shelf below the wall) or by abseil.

Zebedee   10m   E3 6a ***. P.Mather (unsec). 17th April 2004.
This takes the steep flakey crack-line on the right-hand side of the buttress. Use
underclings to pull up into a very small niche. Pull up and left through this aiming
for a great flake hold (crux). Continue up the line of flakes until it is possible to
reach right for yet another fantastic flake. Pull through the top blocky bulge using
underclings.

Rachel's Rescue   20m   Difficult. P. & R.Mather. 17th April 2004.
Follow a traverse line of flakes right off the belay ledge to a narrow ledge. Follow
this (slight descent) until below an open Y-shaped groove; climb the left-hand
branch.

HEAD OF GARNESS (NJ 746 650):
A nice setting on this double headland with easy access, but badly birded in season
and prone to dampness. The grades might be lower with drier rock. Access by an
easy short walk through fields from Mains of Melrose, but ask permission from
the farmer first. Follow a wee path through gorse to a salmon bothy on the east of
the headland. There are good views of the crags from a bit farther on at the top of
the east headland.

East Head of Garness:
Access to this narrow ridge is by the zigzag path down from the bothy, then via an
offshoot on to the slightly loose eastern flanks of the ridge. There is also a steep
rough descent just back from the top of the headland. The rock is good but
superficial looseness remains near the top.

The Black Slab:
The first sizeable face, with the obvious Drainpipe Gully on its south side, and
dominated by a blocky overlap. Scrambling access down rock steps just south of
the gully, to a wee tidal rock bay. The longer routes are inaccessible around high
tide.

The Garnest   14m   Very Difficult. N.Everett, H.Watson. 28th September 2003.
The well protected curving corner bounding the left side of the slab.

Boggle   14m   Hard Severe 4b. P.Mather, S.Muir. 28th September 2003.
Up the middle of the slabby wall starting just right of the base of The Garnest.

Slab 'n' Tickle   14m   VS 4b *. R.Goodier, N.Everett. 28th September 2003.
From the base of the gully, pull on to the right edge of the slab on good holds

(crux). Go straight up the wall left of the arête, crossing slightly dubious blocks after the overlap.

Woggle 10m Very Difficult. P.Mather, S.Muir. 28th September 2003.
From several metres up the gully, up the left-hand corner.

Shougle 8m Difficult. S.Muir, P.Mather. 28th September 2003.
From several metres up the gully, up the short inset corner.

Drainpipe Gully 12m Difficult. R.Goodier. 28th September 2003.
Get mean and dirty in the squirmy chasm.

West Head of Garness:
Access is a scramble along the narrowing west headland, then a Difficult down-climb on the east side to the foot of The Rock Cake. More tricky scrambling across to the seaward headland of The Gateau. Good rock.

The Gateau:
The obvious headland overhangs to the west. can be covered with birds.
A Dream of White Ledges 60m Very Difficult. R.Goodier. 28th September 2003.
Gingerly girdle the Gateau via the guano at mid-height.

GLEN CLOVA, Upper Doonie:
Puffin Bear 7m Very Difficult. S.Holmes, L.Clifton. 31st March 2005.
Start on the left side of a stack of perched boulders. Using a vertical left-slanting crack, climb up and right to the arête. Using a large flake swing round and finish up the front face.

Lower Doonie:
Special Brew, Death Niche Finish 25m E3 6a. I.Small, S.Campbell, C.Cartwright. 6th June 2004.
From the second belay on Special Brew, climb the Furstenburg variation to below the 'death niche'. Enter this precariously (small wires), then exit and climb the blocky arête to finish.

HIGHLAND OUTCROPS

GLEN NEVIS, Polldubh Crags, Pandora's Buttress:
Misadventure 30m E7 6c ***. D.MacLeod. 28th July 2004.
This hard route takes the striking arête below the diagonal cracks of Tomag. Climb up the corner until it is possible to span across to a diagonal crack which comes in from the right on the arête (good protection). Launch up the overhanging arête with increasingly hard and technical moves, culminating in a bold slap for the sloping crack of Tomag. Once established in this, continue up the arête with much easier climbing to the top. Top-rope practice used prior to first ascent, F7c+ difficulty, high in the grade.

Car Park Area:
Notes from C.Moody: *Choke Chimney,* Car Park Crag was missed out of the guide.
Ex-Lax: I.Taylor was on the first ascent.
Bog Crack was climbed by G.Szuca, C.Moody on 18th June 1988.

GORGE CRAG:
Note: A direct finish to All our Yesterdays or Conscription at the same grade, by C.Pettigrew and A.Mackay, 16th May 2004. After climbing to the ledge, instead of traversing the giant flake right to the end of the original route, continue direct up a left-slanting cracked groove above the ledge to the tree belay of Travellin' Man.

CREAG DUBH, Lower Central Wall:
Big Jugs   20m   E2 5c **. C.Pettigrew, E.Currie. 21st May 2004.
A few metres to the right of Man on Fire there is a compact wall capped by a blocky overhang. This climbs the obvious groove through the overhang near its left side. Start directly below the grove. Climb the compact wall to a stance directly below the overhang. Climb the overhang near the left direct using big jugs.

Wee Fried Eggs   20m   E3 6a. C.Pettigrew, E.Currie. 22nd May 2004.
This takes the second cracked groove to the right side of the overhang. Climb the compact wall on the right where the rock is more fractured (still good rock) direct to below the groove. Climb the groove with difficulty and continue to the top.

STRATHNAIRN, Tynrich Slabs, Upper Tier:
Fly Agaric   E2 5b **. S.Clark, B.Sparham, D.Porter. 3rd June 2004.
Between Chanterelle and Scorpion. Start just right of the niche below the right end of the big ledge. Go straight up until level with the ledge and move left on to the end of this. Climb past some weird erosion features and take a faint incut crack diagonally rightwards across the bald convex wall to join Scorpion near the top.

CRAIG A' BARNS, Upper Cave Crag:
Could it be Forever   15m   E4 5c **. N.McNair (unsec). July 2004.
Follow Gotterdamerung and the traverse of Voi d'Lamie for 3m to good nuts approx 4m after the juction of those routes.Then trend left over the bulge to a stonking incut jug. Strike up the wall and step left to finish.

Tiggy McGregor's Moist Adventure   20m   E5 6b *. N.McNair (unsec). July 2004.
Climb Hang Out to the massive runner spike. Traverse 2m left over the slopey ledge immediately up and left of the spike and gain the wall above via a seam to the left of the ledge and a hard move. Bomb up the wall on excellent pockets to gain a pod just below the top and step right to finish.

GLEN OGLE, Dark Side, Concave Wall:
Snipe Shadow   10m   F8b **. D.MacLeod. 27th April 2004.
The central blank concave wall. Technical climbing on finger pockets leads to a desperate crux section near the top.

BEN NEVIS, AONACHS, CREAG MEAGHAIDH

BEN NEVIS, Douglas Boulder:
Right-Hand Chimney VI,7. O.Metherell, G.Hughes. 19th December 2004.
As for the summer route except for pitch 3.
3. 50-55m. Continue up the chimney, turn an overhang on the right rib, and climb up to a recess. Exit left and climb slabs to belay above a second large recess.
4. An exposed rightwards traverse was made to finish up the SW ridge.

Secondary Tower Ridge:
Watery Fowls 150m V,7. S.M.Richardson, I.Parnell. 20th November 2004.
A mixed line between Douglas Gap West Gully and Fawlty Towers. Start 20m left of the icy gully of Fawlty Towers below a steep cracked wall (about 10m right of a steep flake-chimney).
1. 50m. Climb the wall by a series of cracked corners, then move up easier ground.
2. 50m. Move up and left and follow a vague chimney-groove over a steep bulge.
3. 50m. Continue up the groove-line to the crest of Tower Ridge.

The Comb, Note: The Good Groove (VII,7), received its second ascent by S.Halstead and J.Kuczera of Poland who eliminated the rest point used on the first ascent.

Creag Coire na Ciste:
Archangel 110m VIII,7. S.M.Richardson, C.Cartwright. 6th February 2005.
The line of impending corners to the right of Darth Vader. Very sustained and strenuous.
1. 15m. Start 15m right of Darth Vader and climb a steep right-facing corner to a ledge.
2. 20m. Move up and right to a steep corner. Climb this then move right and up to a good stance below the continuation corner.
3. 20m. Climb the right of two grooves to reach a good ledge with a spike on the left. Climb the overhanging wall above (bold) and make a difficult exit on to a narrow ledge. Move up and right across the impending right wall to reach a large ledge system.
4. 30m. Move right 5m and enter an inverted V-slot. Climb this and continue up the contorted chimney-crack above to exit left on to a sloping square ledge.
5. 25m. Climb the overhanging chimney-crack directly behind the belay to reach where the ground eases. Continue easily up snow to the cornice.

Unnamed 110m VII,7. S.M.Richardson, C.Cartwright. 27th February 2005.
A steep mixed climb up the right edge of the wall taken by South Sea Bubble.
1. 30m. Climb the initial ramp of South Gully and belay below a steep groove on the right edge of the wall.
2. 40m. Climb the groove (sustained and strenuous) for 25m to where it fades. Move right on to the arête and move up to a small stance below a short steep wall (and just left of South Gully).
3. 40m. Climb the wall on the left and continue up a short icy gully to exit up the left side of the great snow bowl at the head of South Gully.

South Trident Buttress:
Rattled 100m   IV,5. A.Nisbet, J.Preston. 2nd December 2004.
An attempt on The Rattler, but forced left on to easy ground which will bank out
later in the season. Start as for The Rattler, which starts up the big corner left of
The Groove Climb. Climb a turfy groove right of the corner, then enter the corner
where it becomes a chimney and climb this to a ledge (35m). Traverse the ledge
up left and climb grooves rather close to easy ground to a steep wall (40m). Climb
the wall by a tricky move to a ramp leading right to the crest of the ridge above the
middle tier (25m).

Rattling   115m   V,5. A.Nisbet, J.Preston. 28th January 2005.
A much better version of The Rattler. Climb the big corner of The Rattler, as for
Rattled (35m). Go left until the wall above is broken by a ramp leading to a long
narrow ledge (10m). Gain the ledge and traverse it back right until above the
chimney of The Groove Climb (30m). Cross this route and go up a turf runnel
until a shallow groove leads rightwards through a steep wall into Sidewinder above
its corners (15m). Climb a prominent narrow chimney and its continuation leading
slightly left to the upper crest of the buttress (25m).

Sidewinder   100m   VII,8. I.Small, S.M.Richardson. 8th April 2005.
As for the summer route except the initial chimney was avoided by climbing
easy ground from the left (as for Strident Edge) - the obvious winter way. The
finish may have been close to Rattling. A fine line, strenuous but well protected.

Strident Edge   VI,7. E.Brunskill, G.Hughes. 13th January 2005.
A sensational but surprisingly amenable climb. As for the summer line except that
pitch 2 was split by belaying on a small ledge at 15m. The overhang above was
turned via a spike and cracks on the left wall leading to a break to regain the
groove above. The final pitch was as for Spartacus, the groove right of the arête.

Carn Dearg Buttress:
Trajan's Column   305m   E6 ***. R.Campbell, G.Latter. 7th September 2004.
Fantastic varied climbing up the front face of the pillar right of King Kong's main
pitch.
1. 35m 5a. As for King Kong to the large perched block belay.
2. 25m 6a. Move left, up, then back right to a position above the belay. Continue
right and up to a perch at base of main slab and ascend straight up until possible to
pull round an arête on right on to a sloping ledge in a recess (spike belay on King
Kong 5m higher).
3. 30m 6b. A fantastic wildly-positioned pitch, with devious wandering climbing
and spaced protection. Step down right then make hard fingery moves to gain
good holds in the huge 'boot flake' and more easily up this to small overlap. Make
committing moves out right and up rightwards to a good incut jug, then straight
up past a small useful flake to a rest on the right arête below a smooth uninviting
groove. Traverse hard left into a parallel groove which is followed to a long thin
overlap. Commit right (scary) into the right groove (gear at last!) and make a hard
stretch up right to a good hold on the arête. Continue back left to below the left
side of final overlap, and pull through this keeping close to the left rib leading to

easier ground and the belay common to King Kong and The Bat.

4. 40m 6a. Traverse out left along the obvious fault-line (Bullroar), 10m beyond the crack of King Kong to the crack splitting the slab. Pull over the overlap and climb the slab to a slim smooth hanging groove in the steep wall. Lean out rightwards (crux) to gain two good incut jugs, then directly up the fairly sustained groove above, belaying just above the final capping roof.

5. 15m. Climb easily up slightly left to the base of a small right-facing corner near the right end of the big roof system.

6. 30m 5c. Climb the corner, then move out left into a slim groove and up this, then the fine rib to a good ledge above.

7. 50m 4c. Move out right and up over vegetated ledges to a loose wet corner. Climb this to pull out right on to clean solid rock at a wide blocky crack. Move up left and scramble up leftwards to block belay on ledge.

8. & 9. 80m. Move out right and climb cracks up a slabby corner, then progressively easier scrambling leads up leftwards to the top of the buttress.

The Castle:
Godspell 215m VII,8. S.M.Richardson, K.Cordes. 6th March 2005.
The prominent line of chimneys cutting the headwall of The Castle. Excellent steep mixed climbing.

1. 50m. Start as for The Castle and climb easy snow up the centre of the buttress.

2. 50m. Move left on to easy mixed ground and follow this to a terrace.

3. 50m. The right side of the steep wall above is cut by a short steep icy gully. Climb the gully and continuation corner above to reach the terrace below the headwall.

4. 15m. Climb the chimney past a chokestone in a square-cut recess. A good pitch.

5. 45m. Climb the right side of the recess via an offwidth and steep left-facing corner to a small ledge. Pull over the wall above with difficulty to a terrace (possible belay). Back and foot up the continuation chimney past a chockstone to the top of the headwall. Another excellent pitch!

6. 15m. Finish easily up snow to the top.

STOB BAN (Mamores), South Buttress:
Banjo 200m IV,4. V.Chelton, D.McGimpsey, A.Nisbet, J.Preston. 20th November 2004.
Start at the foot of the fault marked on the diagram in the Ben Nevis guide (p222) as North Ridge Route. The route should be marked farther right. Start up the fault but soon move right to reach steeper ground (35m). Go right and back left to break through a steep wall by a short V-groove about 6m right of the fault (30m). There is now a long smooth V-groove on the right. Climb mixed ground on its right, finishing up the groove or its right rib to reach the North Ridge (45m). Finish easily up this.

Eag Blanc 100m II. V.Chelton, D.McGimpsey. 25th February 2005.
The big groove on the left side of the East Wing. Mostly Grade I with a couple of short, steeper sections.

Ollie 45m IV,4. D.McGimpsey, V.Chelton. 25th February 2005.
The hanging turfy ramp down and left of Eag Blanc. Poorly protected with an awkward wee leaning chimney near the top.

Central Buttress:
Stertor 200m IV,4. B.Davison, D.McGimpsey. 19th February 2005.
The buttress between No Toddy and Central Gully. Follows a line of twisting grooves up the centre which are guarded by a band of slabs at one-third height. Start at the bottom left of the buttress and climb turf leading up and right below steeper ground to a short right-facing groove near the right edge (60m). Go up the groove to a ledge, move left and continue over poorly protected slabs to gain the base of the groove above. Go up this for 10m (40m). Continue up the groove to a terrace, and then gain the next groove by a short nippy corner on the left (30m). The ice in this groove was poor, so a traverse out right to an airy arête led to easier ground (30m). Follow the buttress above to the top (40m).

AONACH BEAG, An Ghaidh Garbh:
The Prisoner 125m V,5 **. A.Nisbet, J.Preston. 30th January 2005.
The fine buttress right of Goblet of Fire. Start at the lowest rocks.
1. 35m. Climb icy steps and blocky grooves in the centre before moving left to below a steep corner.
2. 35m. Climb the corner (crux) and a turfy ramp leading on to the face overlooking Goblet of Fire.
3. 45m. Move left on to a ledge about 10m above Goblet, then climb a turfy crack directly up the face. Where this blanks out, traverse right and return left to continue up the line to the upper crest (joining The Chamber of Secrets?).
4. 10m. A short pitch leads to the upper slopes.

Stob Coire Bhealaich:
Next Janeration 125m IV,4 *. S.Kennedy, A.MacDonald. 27th February 2005.
The buttress approx. 30m left of The Clare Effect contains an open icy gully/ groove. Climb the groove via two short icefalls for 40m then pull out right on to a narrow snow ledge beneath a bulging rock wall (45m). Traverse the ledge rightwards into a groove which leads to an overhung recess. Pull steeply out left into another groove which is followed to the easier upper snow slopes (40m). Steep snow and an awkward cornice (may be avoidable away to the left) leads to the top (30m).

Limbo 95m II/III. S.Kennedy. 6th March 2005.
The easier left hand branch of Next Janeration. Climb the initial icy groove for 40m then take the snow ramp leading out left from the point where Next Janeration pulls out right. Steep snow leads to below the cornice which was outflanked by a long left traverse.

Drive-in Movie 75m III. S.Kennedy, A.MacDonald. 13th March 2005.
The small buttress left of Next Janeration is crossed by a large terrace. Start up a vague recess to reach the left end of the terrace which is followed rightwards to the buttress edge (30m). Step right into the snow ramp of Limbo which is followed until it peters out. Take a direct line up to the problematic cornice (crux) (45m).

SGURR INNSE (NN 290 748):
On the north-west side of Sgurr Innse there is a conspicous crag visible on the approach from the north.

Precarious Wander 55m III,4. J.Thacker, J.McClaren. 18th December 2004.
Start just to the left of the large steep wall at a left-trending ramp.
1. 40m. Follow the ramp-line leftwards with a precarious move, continue up the
leftmost of two corner come groove-lines.
2. 15m. Continue easily up right to scramble up easy ground (ice on the first
ascent).

Mojo 70m II. D.Goodwin. 18th December 2004.
Climb an open gully line to the right of the large steep wall. A short ice step at
half-height. Scramble easily to the top.

MEALL GARBH, Creagan Coire nam Cnamh:
Quiet Running 225m V,6. I.Small, J.Walker. 20th February 2005
Climbs the obvious turfy ramp then right-trending groove bounding the left side
of the Inspiration buttress. Start at a steep narrow chimney directly below the
ramp-line and to the right of Southern Route.
1. 50m. Climb the narrow chimney on ice to a wide ledge and follow the flake-
crack of Inspiration to exit left on turf to reach a belay on the left.
2. 45m. Move back right and go up to a steep crack and bulge on the ramp. Climb
this and the continuation ramp to a block on the left.
3. 55m. Move diagonally right over icy slabs to a snowy bay. Take a narrowing
icy ramp on the left to a steep wall. Go up this on thin ice to gain a right-trending
gully that forms a prominent V-groove. At the top of the groove step right around
bulge to a block. A good long pitch which requires ice on the ramp and wall.
4. and 5. 90m. Climb snow slopes to a cornice finish.

Runs With Deer 230m V,6. I.Small, S.Jensen. 12th March 2005.
Climbs a counter-diagonal line to North Buttress Left Edge, crossing this route at
the large ledge to gain the prominent corner above the huge detached flake.
1. 55m. Start a few meters left of Ledge Route and climb an obvious turfy chimney,
with helpful cracks, to easier ground and belay at the base of the huge detached
flake.
2. 35m. Move left along a ledge and up an icy wall, then step right to gain a V-
groove. At its top bridge right to gain a ramp-line leading to a ledge below the
obvious corner.
3. 50m. Climb the corner to its top and easier ground.
4. and 5. 90m. Climb easier slopes to the cornice.

CREAG MEAGHAIDH, Bellevue Buttress:
Crow Road 200m V,5. S.M.Richardson, I.Parnell. 19th November 2004.
The steep groove-line in the centre of the buttress. Start 90m right of the start of
The Scene at a prominent vegetated ramp that runs up right into steep walls in the
centre of the buttress.
1. 50m. Climb the ramp up and right to below a steep icy groove.
2. 30m. Climb the groove reach a large terrace. Belay by a large rock pinnacle on
the right.
3. 50m. Move up and left and climb a steep icefall to reach an icy groove. Climb
this to its top.
4 and 5. 70m. Move left up mixed ground to gain easy ground and the top.

Pinnacle Buttress:
Eye Candy   200m   VII,7 ***. P.Hostnik, G.Robertson, E.Tressider. 6th March 2005.
A superb route, predominantly on ice, taking the obvious inset corner in the right wall of Smith's Gully.
1. 50m. Follow the first pitch of Smith's Gully, then break out right up a short groove to belay comfortably at the base of the line.
2. 40m. Step left and climb an ice-choked groove then thinly iced slabs to an overhang, Move left again and follow the continuation corner on thin ice to step right to a good belay.
3. 30m. Continue straight up over thinly iced walls, passing a short ice pillar, to belay on Appolyon Ledge.
4. 40m. Above and slightly left is an obvious deep groove. Take the first groove right of this, turning the overhang on the right, then move horizontally right to pull over the bulge at an obvious foothold. Continue straight up turfy walls until an easy snow ramp leads up and left to an icefall overlooking Smith's Gully.
5. 40m. Climb the short but very steep icefall to gain easier ground that leads up and left to a final step and the top (40m).

Extasy   245m   VIII,8. D.Hesleden, B.Sourzac. 4th March 2005.
Start 30m to the left of the Fly Direct at an overhung niche.
1. 30m. Traverse right across a steep slab to a traverse line under a hanging slab. Traverse right to a left-facing corner, then go up this to a small spike 5m to the left of the big flake belay on Fly Direct.
2. 25m. Trend diagonally up and left across a steep wall, go up shallow groove to a ledge, then traverse 4m left to belay on Friends in a roof.
3. 30m. Move left 4m and climb a steep icy stepped groove to exit right up a slab to a large flake.
4. 50m. Climb directly above the belay on ice to a roof. Climb this and pull through a bulge into a left-facing corner; follow this until forced left by a roof up a turf icicle. Climb an easy shallow groove to a flake on Appolon ledge.
5. 30m. Trend right up easy ground to belay 5m to the left of Fly Direct at a large thread, below steep groove.
6. 50m. Pull through a bulge and go left across a steep wall to a flake on the left side of a groove. Climb to the top of the groove (in-situ blade peg), then go left for 5m up a ramp. Traverse diagonally back right above the groove to the left edge of the final snow slope (junction with Fly Direct).
7. 30m. Climb easy snow to the top.

The Moth   380m   VII,8 *. G.Robertson, E.Tresidder. 14th March 2005.
A complex mixed route up the huge wall right of The Fly Direct. On this ascent, the obvious icy line through the headwall (the first natural break right of the Fly Direct/Midge fault) was avoided due to a combination of darkness and very poor conditions on the upper part of the face. Instead, a long and rather unsatisfactory traverse right then back left gained the summit of the Pinnacle. The direct finish would be logical and more in keeping with the rest of the route. Start roughly 50m down and right of The Fly Direct where an obvious terrace leads right on to the face.

1. 30m. Move along the terrace and where it ends step delicately down and traverse the 'turf moustache' strenuously right and then up to the foot of the obvious hooded groove.

2. 40m. Climb the groove to the overhang then traverse left on thin ice to gain turf and then more ice that leads up into an overhanging corner. Bridge up the corner then swing out onto the right wall to a hard mantelshelf. Step back left, move up then follow steep turf rightwards to a sloping ledge system which is traversed hard left to a good flake.

3. 30m. Continue leftwards to gain and follow an iced groove which leads back up right to a small pedestal.

4. 50m. Step right again then gain and follow the obvious line leading up the rib forming left edge of the corner of The Midge.

5. 60m. Follow The Midge to where it goes left to join The Fly Direct.

6. 60m. Move back right, then take a direct line up steep walls and bulges, heading straight for the obvious icy line cutting through the headwall.

7. 110m. Follow the line of least resistance along rightwards, then back up left to the summit of the Pinnacle.

BEN ALDER, Maiden Crag:

Icicles by Bicycle 315m III,4 *. C.Wells, S.Reid (alt). 24th February 2005.
The obvious gully line 15m left of the gully start to Ice Maiden. It lies directly above a long snow runnel and is the centre right of four gullies on this section of the crag, with the Ice Maiden being the right-hand one.

1. 35m. The narrow gully. Belay below a steep icefall on the right.

2. 30m. The icefall (crux) to an excavated belay in the snow scoop above.

3. 50m. Continue up the gully to belay below steeper ice. Warthog turf belay.

4. 50m. Mixed icy climbing gives access to easy ground. Run the rope out to a block belay.

5 & 6. 70m. Easy ground to a gully in the headwall above.

7. 30m. Climb the gully to a stance on the left just before the narrows.

8. 50m. Follow the gully to the plateau.

The top half of this climb is possibly as for Melting Maiden. It would have been possible to climb an alternative finish to the left of the upper gully, but the gully felt like the true line.

The Snow Queen 300m V,5. S.M.Richardson, C.Cartwright. 23rd January 2005.
A long mixed route based on the pillar between Ice Maiden and Witchwhite. Start below the centre of the pillar beneath an obvious groove system.

1. 60m. Climb the groove passing two roofs to a large niche.

2. 30m. Exit right and move up flakes and spikes to reach the start of a prominent left-facing ramp that cuts left across the face.

3. 60m. Follow the ramp to its end where it joins the easy central gully of Ice Maiden. Follow this to a large alcove on the left wall.

4. 50m. Move up for 10m, then move left along a narrow turfy ledge on to the crest of the buttress defining the left side of the face. Follow this, steep and exposed, to a small stance just before the ground eases.

5 and 6. 100m. Continue up the shallow gully above to where it merges with easy mixed ground and follow this to the top.

CREAG DUBH (Drumochter):
I Scream   150m   V,4 *. S.Reid, C.Wells. 25th February 2005.
The narrow icy gully between Swordfish/Neopolitan and The Hex Factor (some 70m left of Swordfish) may be in condition when these big icefalls are not. It gives sustained technical climbing with a minimum of runners.
1. 45m. Climb the right-hand (main) iceline to a big scoop. Continue up the main line above (crux) to an easing under a frightening fringe of poised boulders. Avoid these via the turfy wall on the right.
2. 30m. Scramble to a terrace.
3. 25m. The continuation gully is not without interest – belay on reaching easy ground.
4. 50m. Easy ground, followed by a short icefall on the left.

Choc Ice   60m   II. S.Reid, C.Wells. 25th February 2005.
The ice-filled gully just right of the descent ramp right of Swordfish. Either branch can be taken.

GLEN COE

BUACHAILLE ETIVE MOR, Cuneiform Buttress:
Cunieform Buttress Direttissima   220m   VII,6. E.Brunskill, S.McFarlane 12th December 2002.
The route recorded in SMCJ 2003 as Long Chimney Direct is independent of Long Chimney (which is farther left). A new description:
A serious and direct line taking in the prominent shelf system running up the full length of the West Face. Climb Ordinary Route to the first big ledge (60m). Climb out right from the ledge into a steep groove and continue straight up (Ordinary Route goes up and left) to a prominent cave recess formed by a blocky undercut groove (30m). Climb up right on to a small rocky ledge and step delicately down and right to another capped groove. Climb this for 5m and step right into another groove and continue up this to a ledge (35m). Above is a very narrow chimney, climb this until a flat easy section of the shelf is reached (45m). Continue in the same line up an awkward wide corner-crack and above this make a desperate traverse right for 10m to the obvious ledge below two large detached flakes (35m, a very serious pitch). Climb the flakes and wall above to easy ground beside the descent path to Great Gully (15m).

Broad Buttress West Face, Upper Tier:
M.Dunn notes that scrambling up Great Gully Buttress is an alternative approach, leading directly to Great Gully Upper Buttress, which backs fairly directly on to Broad Buttress West Face. A visit here may allow climbing in the sun all day! For descent, it is better to abseil; there are good anchors just below a small pile of rocks, directly above the Quark routes. The routes are 30m long, including Meson, which is the obvious line about 5m left of the overhang. It is a good line, VS 4c *.

No Meson   HVS 5a **. K.Brookman, M.H.Dunn. 25th August 2002.
Takes the line which runs immediately left of the overhang at 20m (mistaken for

Meson). Climb to a fine steep wall. Take a thin crack (crux) to a ledge. Ascend the corner above.

Strange Quark E1 5c **. M.H.Dunn, K.Brookman. 31st July 2004.
Start just right of the previous route, aiming for the weakness in the overhang. The crack directly below the overhang is often damp but does not adversely affect the climbing. Pull through the overhang with difficulty and layback to the top.

Charm Quark VS 4c *. M.H.Dunn, G.Campbell. 28th September 2002.
Climb directly to the right end of the overhang. Follow a right-facing corner, stepping left on to the arête at the earliest opportunity. Take steep cracks to the top.

Lower Tier: Approach from below is not advisable. Walk about 35m north along the terrace from Meson to another pile of rocks which indicate possible anchors to an abseil roughly down the line of Paladin. Paladin is a good route and takes the obvious line at VS 4c **. Hawkers Crack is also worth climbing at Severe. The rock to the right of Paladin has scope for new routes but is steeper and rather dirty.

Creag a' Bhancair:
Note: The FFA of Carnivore Original Finish should be credited to S.Wilson, T.Marr, Easter 1969.

Tunnel Wall:
The Third Eye 25m F7b+ ***. D.MacLeod. 30th May 2004.
An excellent new line at the left end of Tunnel Wall, taking the pale wall and bulge above. Some difficult moves lead to a boss at the third bolt (rest). A sustained fingery section leads to easier climbing on good holds through the bulge. Another thin move gains the big horizontal and lower-off.

Axiom 30m F7c+ ***. D.MacLeod. 29th May 2004.
A brilliant route taking a parallel line to Admission. Start up The Third Eye to the second bolt. Break off rightwards with increasing difficulty to a hard section on sidepulls to gain good edges in a faint niche (technical crux). More sustained climbing leads through the bulge to a rest. Move up, then rightwards to another difficult section. The finishing section is slightly easier.

Stob Coire Altruim:
Dog Day Monday 100m VI,7 **. M.Bass, S.Yearsley. 21st February 2005.
A fine route which takes the line of hanging chimneys to the right of Cerberus. Start as for Cerberus.
1. 25m. Climb the first pitch of Cerberus to the poor stance, then move rightwards to below an obvious steep slot. Climb this, strenuous, to a peg runner, then move right in an excellent position onto the arête and then up to an obvious and comfortable cave.
2. 25m. Climb the right side of the cave, pull back left into the superb icy chimney line (well protected) which is followed to the start of easier ground.
3. 50m. Follow easier, but very pleasant ground to below the summit.

DIAMOND BUTTRESS:
Koh-i-nor   185m   V,7 *. R.Anderson, R.Milne. 20th February 2005.
A line up the right side of the face.
Start at the entrance to the left branch of Central Gully, a short way up from Direct
Route (winter).
1. 30m. Climb the obvious slabby looking line up left to belay on the edge right of
Direct Route, just below a small crest.
2. 30m. Go up right and climb a stepped turfy corner to just below its top, then go
up and left around the edge to gain ledges leading to a belay at the end of the
girdling ledge.
3. 50m. Climb up behind the belay and step up right onto a ledge, then enter a
recess and swing out right. Go right again into a groove and follow this to ledges.
Continue up the obvious wide chimney and move up to a ledge.
4. 50m. Climb the obvious line up and right onto the edge, then continue above by
a line of turfy iced grooves passing the right side of a narrow, short chimney –
presumably taken by one of the three easier routes that comes up from Central
Gully.
5. 25m. Easily to the top of the buttress.

CHURCH DOOR BUTTRESS:
Flake Route, Right-Hand   190m   V,7 **. R.Anderson, R.Milne. 26th February
2005.
Climbs the right-hand side of the huge flake, starting directly from low down.
Start at the entrance to the right-hand branch of Central Gully.
1. 40m. Climb a short way up the gully and just below the chockstone climb a
series of short, stepped corners on the right wall to snow ledges. Continue to a
belay in the wide chimney where it forks..
2. 25m. Climb the widening left fork over chockstones, then go beneath the huge
jammed blocks into the chimney to emerge on the other side. Belay on the top of
the jammed blocks as for Flake Route.
3. 25m. As for Flake Route, step up right awkwardly, then go up rightwards across
the top of a groove to gain easy ground. Belay on the right as for West Chimney
where it emerges from the hole.
4. 30m. As for Flake Route, up left then take the crack in the sidewall and climb
to the jammed blocks at the start of the Arch. Negotiate the blocks and step down
to belay on the Arch, either at the start or in the centre of the span as for Un Poco
Loco.
5. 30m. As for Flake Route & West Chimney. Traverse the Arch and climb the
shallow chimney with difficulty and continue to ledges. Move left and belay.
6. 40m. Climb the shallow grooves above the belay to reach easy ground.

Note: E.Tressider and I.Lewis climbed a variation to Un Poco Loco on 14th
February 2005. Climb Un Poco Loco crux pitch to where that branches left to go
around the left side of the arch. Instead, follow the obvious shallow right-facing
corner to thread the hole of the arch as the final move! Pumpy and quite hard to
get gear on the crux section, but with good gear before. Hard VII,7.

Crusade   115m   VII,8. S.Chinnery, S.House. March 2005.
Climbs the wall above the start to West Chimney. Very steep and sustained but good
gear. Start about 15m right of West Chimney (about 5m left of Kingpin).
1. 15m. Go diagonally left up snowy ramps to a large square chockstone in the

crack formed by the right side of a large blocky pinnacle. This is directly below an obvious steep, right-facing flake/crack-line and straight above the start of West Chimney.
2. 50m. Climb the flake-line for 25m (crux), then step left at the top to climb steep grooves until a step back right gains a good grassy ledge on the crest of the buttress.
3. 50m. Pull through a bluge to the left and trend up and right on easier ground to reach a steep open corner just to the left of the buttress crest. Finish up this.
Note: Dark Mass probably joins this route during the easy ground on pitch 3.

GEARR AONACH, North Face:
Previous Conviction   160m   VS 4b. J.Bankhead, N.Seal. 1st September 2004.
To the left of the long black corner of Preamble is an area of redder rock. This route takes a faint groove-system up this and continues up the rib to the right of Chimney and Face Route above the slabby ledge. Quick drying.
1. 50m. From a tree belay in the heathery gully underneath the big roof, scramble rightwards on to broken ground and ascend via a short chimney to a stance at the right end of the big roof (might be the same as pitches 1 and 2 of Preamble).
2. 25m. 4a. Move right and step up above the overlap at the first opportunity. Go up a little, then trend right to gain a faint groove and awkward belay in small recess.
3. 25m 4b. Climb straight up on good holds for 10m to small ledge. Step right with difficulty on to a short steep wall, then continue boldly to a slabby ledge.
4. 25m 4a. Avoid the chimney of Chimney and Face Route by the rib to its right to reach a broad grassy terrace.
5. 35m. Trend left through unpleasant terrain to exit via a short chimney. Various other exits appeared feasible, but all were wet, vegetated and loose.

STOB COIRE NAN LOCHAIN, Summit Buttress:
Spectre - Direct Start   E.Brunskill, M.Evans. February 1995.
Below the original traverse in from Scabbard, the Spectre groove-line continues straight down to the bottom of the buttress. This logical direct start climbs straight into the groove-line which is followed up to the original route. Grade is unchanged.

Note: P.Benson and G.Robertson climbed the initial chimney of the original East Face Route direct all the way to the headwall, then continued straight up the obvious clean-cut corner-crack. An outstanding and very sustained icy mixed route, one of the best of its type in Scotland. VII,8 **** given.

North Buttress:
Black Box   100m   IV,5 *. S.Kennedy, A.MacDonald. 19th February 2005.
To the right of Tuberculosis is a large recessed area. North Face follows the groove up the left side of the recess. Dress Circle takes the left-slanting line high on the right overlooking the recess. This route follows a line close to the corner on the right side of the recess joining Dress Circle near the top. To the right of Tuberculosis climb the broken buttress below the recess to a large snow ledge (North Face goes left into the groove from here). Continue up cracks and steep slabs just left of the corner on the right, passing a large flake, to a ledge. Belay on the left at a flake crack below a smooth right-facing corner (55m). Climb the corner and join the final groove of Dress Circle to finish (45m).

AONACH DUBH, Far Eastern Buttress:
The Wong Way 60m Very Difficult. I.Forrest, S.MacFarlane. August 2001.
Climb the first pitch of Yen to reach a grassy ledge. Move right to below a crack-line which lies just left of the chimney-groove which lies left of Turkish Delight. Stiff initial moves quickly yield to good holds and protection as a crack system is gained. Climb steeply until the angle relents and the crack system becomes a deepening groove. Finish up the rib on its left (30m).

Hentai 15m Severe. I.Forrest, J.Lingenhult. 7th August 2004.
On the wall above the buttress, up a slanting groove directly above the start of the descent across to Hole and Corner Gully. Scramble up a few metres from the grassy ledge above the gully then climb left to the left-sloping groove. Climb this to gain a ledge under a small overhang. Step right and pull up on jugs to finish.

GLEN ETIVE, Trilleachan Slabs:
Bumble in the Savannah 195m Severe *. R.Salisbury, J.Hearne, C.Cairney, D.Jackman. 18th April 2004.
A logical route taking the easiest left to right line through some steep and potentially difficult ground, worthwhile despite being climbed in the rain. Good clean rough granite between the grassy bits. Start at the extreme lowest point at the left end of the slabs immediately before the prominent left-hand gully proper. This is about 30m right of Penguin's Paradise.
1. 40m. Climb a slabby wall with two tricky mantelshelf moves, then faint grooves to a small overlap. Climb this and up the cracked slab to a small sloping ledge.
2. 35m. Continue up the cracked slab and trend right on steep grass to good cracks and tree below a prominent rib.
3. 30m. Climb up and on to the rib and follow it without difficulty to a grassy niche.
4. 60m. Move right on to exposed hanging slabs; follow these trending right to gain a short corner. An exposed and poorly protected pitch.
5. 30m. Continue up the slab and then on steep grass to belay below the headwall. Traverse off to the left to gain the left-hand descent gully.
A possible continuation in a superb position is to traverse right across easy vegetated slabs to an arête overlooking the main slabs (near top of Jaywalk?).

Ticked Off 70m VS. S.Kennedy, R.Hamilton. 7th May 2004.
Start below the prominent recess about 15m down and left of the large tree at the foot of Bitten by the Bug.
1. 40m 4c. Pull into the recess which is climbed on the left on gritty red rock to a bulge. Move right to gain an easy ramp which leads up rightwards to below a steepening. Traverse horizontally left along a grassy ledge to reach two short, stepped corners.
2. 35m 4c. Climb the stepped corners, making a delicate move onto the upper slab. Finish up slabs. Descend on the left.

Note: The final corner (pitch 8) of Long Wait Direct was originally climbed as a Direct Finish to the normal route by J.McLean in early 1967 using 1peg for aid. This was freed by T.Marr, T.Sullivan and M.Hosted in late May 1967.

GARBH BHEINN (ARDGOUR), Bealach Buttress:
Right-Hand Gully 100m III. D.Ritchie, M.Shaw. 28th January 2004.
Takes the obvious deep grassy fault to the right of Bealach Buttress Ordinary route.

Bealach Buttress Ordinary Route 100m V,6. D.Ritchie, M.Shaw. 28th January 2004.
A fine route with sustained interest climbed in two long pitches. Start just right of the lowest rocks below the steep slabby front face of the buttress.
1. 50m. Follow grassy tufts rising leftwards then rightwards reaching a smooth slab at half-height. Traverse a few metres delicately left to reach better turf then directly up to some cracked blocks.
2. 50m. Climb the turfy groove on the right to reach the arête and follow this to finish.
Note: Repeated by E.Brunskill and G.Macfie on 1st March 2005 and graded IV,4.

South Wall:
Note: J.Lyall thinks Bodkin (which should be E1) and Poniard share a start. A.Nisbet thinks that Chib is the same as the upper tier of Scimitar. Brogue is probably the same also, because for those who have not done Scimitar, the line appears to be an obvious gap.

Maol Odhar (Creach Bheinn), Coire nam Frithallt.
(NM 882 578), Alt 700m, East facing:
The prominent cliff below the main summit is characterised by two steep buttresses seperated by a deep and narrow gully. The following route climbs the larger left-hand   buttress.

Voodoo Buttress 110m V,6. E.Brunskill, G.Macfie. 2nd March 2005.
Start about 3m up the gully below an obvious turfy groove breaking out left towards the crest of the buttress. Make poorly protected and thin moves to enter the groove and climb it to a recess formed by huge jammed blocks on the crest (45m). Climb the poorly protected and very steep corner directly above (crux) to a large ledge (10m). Continue straight up a wall on to the exposed crest and continue until another sharp saddle of the crest is reached below a steep impasse. Climb on to the small turfy ledge formed by a very loose block and make an exposed traverse rightwards along a foot ledge for about 5m to reach a steep bottomless groove. Climb this to a ledge below a steep wall with a small turfy undercut groove. Climb this continue up and trend left to another recess formed by large jammed blocks (45m). Climb easy ground to the top (10m).

ARDNAMURCHAN, Sgurr nan Gabhar:
Dance of the Psychedelic Lounge Lizards 40m Very Difficult. C.Moody, C.Grindley. 22nd May 2004.
Start at the base of Thor. Climb the rib on the right and continue to the heather ledge. Climb the bold rib on the right.

Smacks of Euphoric Hysteria 30m Very Difficult. C.Moody, C.Grindley. 22nd May 2004.
Climb the slab right of Dance of the Psychedelic Lounge Lizards with a bulge to start. When the slab changes to a wall follow a crack up right.

Note: High Plains Drifter and Solar Wind are the same route.

Creag an Fhir-eoin:
Remember the Sixties? 25m Severe. C.Moody. 25th April 2004.
Climb Claude to the start of the crack, then follow the fault horizontally to the right.

Meall an Fhir-Eoin:
Raging Bull 30m Very Difficult. C.Moody, C.Grindley. 23rd May 2004.
This is on the buttress left of the second pitch of Vulcan. It is split in two by a heather corner-crack. Climb up grass left of Vulcan, then move left to the start of the route. Climb up the middle of the right half of the buttress; there is a bulge at the start.

Meall an Fhir-Eoin, Summit Buttresses:
Note: Barbarella (SMCJ 2003, p418) was done in June 2001, not 2002.

SOUTHERN HIGHLANDS

LOCH SLOY CRAGS:
The following routes were soloed by G.Szuca during the last three years, the harder ones after practice. Approach as for Sub-Station Crag but follow the track uphill for a few hundred metres until at a quarried section next to the road.

Stiff Wellies Severe.
Start at a slabby arête at the right-hand side of the crag. Follow this until possible to move on to the slab on the left. Follow it to a belay on the right (large gear).

Zorg VS 4c.
Start as for the previous route but traverse left past a mossy section into a short groove with a loose block. Bridge upwards and move right on to the slab to finish.

Wee Freebie VS 4c.
At the right-hand side of the crag is an obvious ramp-line running up and left. Follow this past a massive thread, past a bulge and into a corner. Exit using the lower of two traverse lines rightwards past a bulge (crux) and on to the slabby wall. Move left to finish up an easy rib.

Extorsion E1/2 5b.
Start centrally at an obvious black corner. Climb the corner (unprotected) to a move rightwards to exit (Friend#_). Go up and left until at a good flake in the corner. Move right to the higher traverse line to the arête. Go past a bulge and finish up the easier slab.

Katanga E2 5c *.
The black wall on the left.. Start centrally and using a pinch, follow a line of small but positive holds up and slightly leftwards, finishing on to a slab in a corner. Continue up the small headwall past a shallow borehole.

Fred E1 5b/c.
The short green-looking groove at the extreme left-hand end of the crag. Move up to an amazing borehole thread. Go up then right to crux moves traversing to the slab of Katanga. Move down and left to finish at a tree. Poorly protected.

The following routes are on the largest area of slabby rock seen from the approach road, right of and slightly higher than Sub-Station Crag. A large white quartz patch is visible from below but this is on a higher crag. On the right-hand section of the slab of the lower crag are two routes, starting at an obvious white quartz block below the right arête.

Marquee Moon HVS 5a.
Start at the quartz block and surmount the bulge to gain the slab. Using a one finger pocket, move up on to the easier angled slab, which is followed to the top using an arête.

Television E1 5a/b *.
Start just left of the previous route and pull over the bulge (crux) to a good hold (Friend 1). Go up and follow the easier slab to a steepening at the top. Climb this right to left to finish.

The wall right of Marquee Moon is overhanging. Follow this up to the next routes. The rightmost route is Mark of Zoro.

Mark of Zoro 12m E3/4 6a
Start right of Signs of Things to Come. Go up the slab, then move rightwards at the bottom of a crack to a hard move to gain a blocky small foothold on the right-hand end of the slab (crux). Move up to good handholds at quartz, then rightwards to a good sidepull (Friend 1.5). Move left to a good foothold next to a small sapling, then follow the slab and crack rightwards. Unprotected on the lower crux section.

Signs of Things to Come E2 5b **.
The brushed streak up a pocketed slabby wall gives the best route on the wall. Start centrally and follow quartzy holds to halfway, then move left. Hard to protect and a high crux.

Magazine E1 5c.
The wall left of the previous route. Pull over a small overlap and follow quartzy holds to a no hands rest at a block (gear). Pull straight up and slightly leftwards (crux) to finish up the arête.

Bluto Very Difficult.
Start left of Magazine in a shallow corner. Go up the corner to a faint crack-line,

then move left on to the slab. Go up this, then follow easy ground to the final steepening (crux). Hard to protect.

Ten Thousand Light Years from Home   8m   E3 5c **.
Right of the slabby wall of Signs of Things to Come is a small slabby buttress with a slabby right arête. This route takes an obvious cleaned line up its centre. Climb up to the obvious horizontal break at 3m. Move right and reach up with the right hand to a good two finger pocket. Gain the niche up and left, then finish slightly rightwards. Good climbing, poor gear.

Sub-Station Crag:
Silence of the Lambs   E3 6a. G.Szuca, P.Hyde. 1991.
Follows the wall right of Wired for Sound, using protection in that route. Start 5m right of Wired for Sound. Go up to the right-hand side of a ledge. Hard moves up and right lead to a pocket. Layback this on the left, then go and slightly rightwards to undercuts on a small overlap. Go straight up to a horizontal break, then left and slightly down to the in situ belay on Wired for Sound.

BEN VORLICH:
Note: D.MacLeod made a ground up, flashed 2nd ascent of Logical Progression (M10), thinking it was more like M9 given the adjustments in the modern M scale. The gear is still in place from the first ascent in 1999 but is in a poor state.

THE BRACK, Upper Tier:
Note: S.Hall, J.Blackford & M.W.Holland climbed a gully between January Butress and May Route at Grade III on 23rd January 2005 as a continuation of Inglis Clark Arête. Good old snow in the lower section of the gully led to where the gully narrows and steepens to a short chimney. A short iced wall on left, then a good short but steep ice pitch and an easy angled gully led to the top.

BEINN A' CHREACHAIN, Coire an Lochain:
So Where Is The Door And Window Buttress   275m   III,4. E.Brunskill, N.Muir. 22nd January 2005.
This route takes the buttress crest to the right of the main icefall. Start at the next recess down and right of the icefall. Climb the icy right-trending gully for 10m, then break left on to a thinly iced slab and continue up and left to the crest of the buttress (45m). Climb up the steep crest for two pitches (70m) and continue up snowy grooves trending right to easy ground and the top (160m).

Chicken Run   305m   IV,4. E.Brunskill, G.Macfie. 23rd February 2005.
This climbs the prominent icefall (mentioned as unclimbed in the guide) but avoids the hanging pencil of ice. Climb the icefall to a ledge and belay below the pencil of ice (25m). Traverse to the left edge of the ledge and step up and left round the edge on to the steep face. Make a steep and exposed rising leftward traverse to a recess at the right end of a prominent
ledge (30m). Climb straight up into a right-trending shallow gully and climb to the top of this (50m). Continue straight up via icy grooves and steep snow to the top (200m).

The Bells 155m V,5. E.Brunskill, D.Johnson, G.Macfie. 24th February 2005.
The second last buttress up the gully (about 50m up from the top of the rock island) is very steep and rocky. Start at the toe of the buttress and climb shallow grooves on the left of the sharp crest, passing a small snow ledge running rightwards towards the crest. Continue up the grooves until a steep wide ramp runs right to the crest. Climb up this and step right round the crest on to the exposed front face below some large overhangs (40m). Step down rightwards to turfy ledges and go back up trending right to a small sloping ledge with a large jammed block. Climb on to the ledge and make awkward moves round the crest to a small ledge (15m). Continue up the steep turfy groove directly above and continue up turfy grooves and walls (50m). Climb easy snow to the top (50m).
Note: The face to the right of Leucocyte Buttress was climbed at an undistinguished Grade II, with a good finish up the buttress crest right of the central gully. It has been climbed before.

BEINN UDLAIDH:
Fontinalia 70m VIII,9 **. D.MacLeod, S.Muir (both led). February 2005.
An unusual and interesting continental style mixed route with roof climbing leading to a hanging ice fang. Climb pitch 1 of Cut Throat belaying on the right. Follow the thin seam right of the main Cut Throat icicle (strenuous with hard won protection). Continue through the roof above (crux) to swing on to the short hanging fang on the left. Finish as for Cut Throat.

BEN CRUACHAN, Stob Garbh, Coire Chat, Noe Buttress:
Fat Lip Fandango 70m VII,7. I.Small, C.Cartwright. 28th December 2004.
The right-hand of the three parallel crack-lines. Start at the same point as Double Chaser at the right-slanting crack.
1. 35m. Follow the crack rightwards to reach a ledge. From the left side of the ledge step down and around a shield of rock to enter the continuation crack. Climb the crack boldly into a slight niche, then a tenuous exit to a stance.
2. 35m. Follow the icy continuation crack and easier ground into a recess, then pull through a steep wide crack/chimney to the top.

Hats Off 110m V,6. I.Small, J.Walker. 19th December 2004.
A counter diagonal line to Noe Buttress Direct. Start from ledges on the left of and diagonally above that route.
1. 30m. Gain an ice smear. Exit right at its top, cross a small roof to a ledge and from its right end, climb another ice smear. Mixed ground leads to a tricky entry into a flake-groove. Belay at its top.
2. 35m. Climb a flake and gain a wide crack formed by a monster block (common with Noe Buttress Direct). At its top move right to ledges and climb a steep wall to a cramped recess below an overhang. Pull through to a ledge.
3. 40m. Climb short grooves and more broken ground to the top.

Pussy Galore 85m VII,8. D Hesleden, C.Cartwright. 19th February 2005.
The right to left slanting line cutting through Dr Noe. The main feature is a wide crack splitting an overhanging right-facing corner high on the crag. Start at the short left-facing corner right of Dr Noe.
1. 25m. Climb the deceptively steep corner and exit to belay in Dr Noe.

2. 30m. Climb a crack through the left wall to gain then follow the right-facing corner. Exit on to a slab and climb to below the main overhanging corner. Swing right into a higher recess.
3. 30m. Surmount the bulge and continue by a right-trending crack to below the final wall. Cut sharply back left via a flake and continue left to the top.

Cooper Cleft   100m   IV,4. S. Richardson, C.Cartwright. 30th January 2005.
Right of Noe Buttress Direct is an undercut bulging wall slanting upwards and leading into a gully.
1. 50m. Follow the gully up to were it steepens and narrows. Climb the chimney and exit rightwards, then follow the continuation groove.
2. 50m. Climb easily upwards to enter a broad easy-angled scoop. Head rightwards for a col.

Yes Gully (left-hand)   50m   IV,4. S.Richardson, C.Cartwright. 30th January 2005.
The right-hand side of Noe Buttress is bounded by a double gully system divided by a rock fin, similar to though less impressive than the Noe fin. Access to the left-hand gully is barred by a short wall split by a crack. Enter the crack from the right and pull over to enter gully. Continue up the gully to a short steep chimney on the left. Climb this and belay below the top.

Summit Buttress Note: C.Cartwright and S.Richardson climbed three short routes in January 2005.

Drochaid Ghlas:
The following two good routes lie on the slabby left flank of Stonethrowers Buttress.

The Glasscutter   125m   IV,5. D.Ritchie, M.Shaw. 21st December 2004.
Start 25m up and left from the start of Stonethrowers Buttress below a vague rib well right of an obvious offwidth flake-crack.
1. 40m. Climb the fault right of the rib to a point next to the gully of Stonethrowers Buttress, step left, then follow a snow ramp to a steepening.
2. 35m. Climb the short wall (crux) to gain a hanging slab. Climb the slab trending left, then continue up the snowy ramp line above to below a deep chimney.
3. 50m. Continue more easily trending left up the snowy ramp below a prominent jutting block to gain the summit cairn.

The Boxer   100m   IV,5. D.Ritchie, N.MacGougan. 26th December 2004.
Start 10m left of the obvious offwidth crack formed by a huge flake, well left from the start of The Glasscutter.
1. 25m. Climb the open fault up then rightwards to gain the top of the flake-crack. Continue straight up avoiding easy ledges on the left to a cracked wall.
2. 25m. Climb the cracked wall and right-trending corner above to join The Glasscutter above the hanging slab and follow this route for 10m to below the deep chimney
3. 50m. Climb the obvious deep chimney back and footing past a small roof, then follow corners on the ridge crest to the summit cairn. A fine pitch.

Beinn a' Bhuiridh, Coire Ghlais:
Rodgers' Ridge   200m   III. E.Brunskill, G.Macfie. 6th February 2005.
The ridge running up the right-hand edge of the coire. Start at the bottom toe of
the buttress and climb the left edge up steep grooves (35m). Continue up turfy
grooves on the left side of the tower into a steep rocky chimney groove capped by
a large block. Swing out left on to an exposed spike and continue straight up the
steep blocky wall above (20m). Continue up the crest and scramble up easy ground
to the top (145m).

Mush Mush   50m   III,5. E.Brunskill, G.Macfie. 6th February 2005.
This route climbs the chimney-groove system in the middle of the upper left-hand
buttress. Climb a steep rocky corner to enter the main groove (crux) and continue
up the chimney and groove to the top.

LOWLAND OUTCROPS

CLIFTON CRAG, Dirl Chimney Area:
Last Post   8m   Very Difficult. S.Reid, W.Hurford. 14th November 2004 .
The off-width crack-line 1m left of the main crack system of Gramercy makes a
good finish to any of the routes on Hollowstones Buttress. Probably done before.
Climbed on Remembrance Sunday - hence the name.

Twin Cracks Buttress:
Wiggle Direct   E1 5b. C.King, S.Reid. 2nd December 2004.
Follow Wiggle to the junction with Crawl Wall, and then make a long reach up the
arête above to a flake. A second long reach out left across a slab gains a good
pocket, above which a mossy jug enables a pull to the top.

The Slab:
Napoleon   10m   Severe 4a. C.King, S.Reid. 9th December 2004.
The short but stubborn off-width in the right wall of The Corner. Start via The
Corner.

Gorsica   10m   Hard Severe. S.Reid, C.King. 9th December 2004.
The steep juggy arête of the right-bounding buttress of The Slab, finishing left of
the gorse cornice. Start via The Corner.

GALLOWAY SEA-CLIFFS, Balcary Bay:
S.Reid repeated the following route and suggests a new description:
The Cave Traverse   80m   Very Difficult
An interesting traverse, but not without its share of worrying rock. Start in the
large bay at the west end of the main cliffs, immediately under a kissing gate in
the cliff-top path. The peninsula on the east side of the bay is reached by easy
traversing from caves at the back of the bay, then a 10m loose climb leads to the
saddle in the peninsula (30m). Cross to the east side of the peninsula and, traverse
round the corner to the top of a chimney (40m). Descend the chimney to the

cathedral-like cave (10m). The tantalising but water-filled tunnel exiting the cave is unclimbed, and so a return journey by the same route is necessary, with the loose rock section being bypassed by abseil off a pinnacle. Be sure to allow enough time to accomplish the return journey before the tide comes in!

DUMBARTON ROCK:
Negative Creep   10m   F8b *   D.MacLeod. 14th November 2004.
Start up Appliance but break out left after the crux to gain a good sidepull. A long reach gains another big sidepull leading to a desperate crimping sequence to the finishing holds on the ledge. F7c to the last three moves, and the grade is definitely for clipping the belay rather than grabbing!

BERWICKSHIRE COAST, Fast Castle Head:
Note: Urinal Wall is suggested at VS 4c. Pitch 2 can be finished by trending right up the centre of the slab.

The Anchor   45m   HVS *. C.Lesenger, I.Collins. 20th February 1988.
1. 30m 5a. Gain and climb the obvious left-trending fault midway between Atlanta and East Arête to a ledge.
2. 15m 4b. Follow the Atlanta corner direct to the top

Further East Arête   45m   Severe. C.Lesenger, I.Collins. 20th February 1988.
1. 30m 4b. Climb the slab and arête as for East Arête to easy ground but instead of trending left climb a groove directly above to an exposed ledge with a poor block belay.
2. 15m 4b. A ramp on the right leads to the top via a short awkward wall.

Fool's Gold   40m   E1 5a. C.Lesenger, I.Collins. 12th March 1989.
The big left bounding corner of Castle Wall is poorly protected except at the crux near the top.

FIFE, Limekilns, Sentinal Block:
Slow Handclap   12m   E7 6c *. D.MacLeod. 4th Jan 2005.
This serious route takes the smooth and blank looking wall right of Iron Fist. Move easily up to a good hold (poor skyhook possible). Hard and sustained climbing leads directly up the wall to eventually gain better holds near the top. FA headpoint style, F7c climbing.

MISCELLANEOUS NOTES

The W. H. Murray Literary Prize.

As a tribute to the late Bill Murray, whose mountain and environment writings have been an inspiration to many a budding mountaineer, the SMC have set up a modest writing prize, to be run through the pages of the Journal. The basic rules are set out below, and will be re-printed each year. The prize is run with a deadline, as is normal, of the end of January each year. So assuming you are reading this in early July, you have, for the next issue, six months in which to set the pencil, pen or word processor on fire.

The Rules:

1. There shall be a competition for the best entry on Scottish Mountaineering published in the *Scottish Mountaineering Club Journal*. The competition shall be called the 'W. H. Murray Literary Prize', hereafter called the 'Prize.'

2. The judging panel shall consist of, in the first instance, the following: The current Editor of the *SMC Journal;* The current President of the SMC; and two or three lay members, who may be drawn from the membership of the SMC. The lay members of the panel will sit for three years after which they will be replaced.

3. If, in the view of the panel, there is in any year no entries suitable for the Prize, then there shall be no award that year.

4. Entries shall be writing on the general theme of 'Scottish Mountaineering', and may be prose articles of up to approximately 5000 words in length, or shorter verse. Entries may be fictional.

5. Panel members may not enter for the competition during the period of their membership.

6. Entries must be of original, previously unpublished material. Entries should be submitted to the Editor of the *SMC Journal* before the end of January for consideration that year. Lengthy contributions are preferably word-processed and submitted either on 3.5" PC disk or sent via e-mail. (See Office Bearers page at end of this Journal for address etc.) Any contributor to the SMC Journal is entitled to exclude their material from consideration of the Prize and should so notify the Editor of this wish in advance.

7. The prize will be a cheque for the amount £250.

8. Contributors may make different submissions in different years.

9. The decision of the panel is final.

10. Any winning entry will be announced in the *SMC Journal* and will be published in the *SMC Journal* and on the SMC Web site. Thereafter, authors retain copyright.

174 SCOTTISH MOUNTAINEERING CLUB JOURNAL

The W. H. Murray Literary Prize 2005

THE winner of this year's W. H. Murray prize is club member, Graham Little, for his piece on the first ascent of the Lammergeir Spire, a 5350m. summit above the eastern flank of the Miyar Glacier in the Lahul region of India.

Graham's opening lines immediately signal that this is more than a straightforward account of a first ascent : "The ageing process is a matter of compromise, of balancing ambition and ability. To pretend it isn't happening is a sure-fire route to frustration and suffering."

Graham gives us his personal thoughts on the impact of ageing on a lifetime of top-flight mountaineering achievement and how he is coming to terms with that. This is not done in a dry analytical way, but in a style that weaves what at times amounts to poetry into the narrative of what could probably be described as a 'watershed' climb in the author's life.

"As we reverse down the ridge a great bird glides below us, wide wings stroking the air in effortless glide. The ease of the Lammergeir's flight contrasts with my own clumsiness. It is *of* the mountains. I am *in* the mountains."

It is also interesting to note that, like Mick Fowler, a previous recipient of the W. H. M. prize for his article *Climbing In The Cold* , Graham takes the opportunity to point to "climbing as a way of life" as opposed to a competition. "It is very clear to me that mountaineering is not a sport, is not about winning, but is a way of life.

"The walk in, the climb, the walkout – they are the journey of life."

And although Graham perhaps sees himself about to start the long walk out, it seems, judging by the acceptance and understanding displayed in his writing that he will carry the limitations of age comfortably.

Coincidently, this issue of the Journal also has text and photographic evidence of Graham during his 'walk in' period on the first ascent of a route in Galloway in 1968, included in Stephen Reid's fine article *Dungeon Days.*

Also coming in for praise from the judges was Adam Kassyk's *A Tale Of Three Accidents* which, in the regrettable absence of the 'The Accidents' for yet another year, perhaps goes someway to dishing up a portion of Schadenfreud to those feeling the need.

Phil Gribbon also hit the mark with his *Dancing With Sticks* "a delightful and at times thought provoking tale" and as one judge remarked. "Anyone who can wander without contradiction from Pic d'Entard to Chernobyl, to the pier at Mallaig and all while telling the tale of a cowherd's stick deserves a prize."

The limitations of age seems to have been in the air this year as Bob Richardson chose to examine the same theme in his well received piece *The Peak Of The Quarters.* This memoir details an early rebuff from this Highland peak and a return during his Littlesquian 'walk out' period.

"Nearly 50 years later I realised if it were to be done, it were best done soon (if not quickly.)"

One senses however, that unlike Graham, Bob perhaps adopts more of a Meldrewian approach to old age: "The heat, the decrepitude of age and the weight of my pack combined to tell me firmly that my days of scampering the hills had gone and another day like this might just about be terminal – T*he Peak of the Quarters* had taught me two lessons and I didn't much like the second one."

Congratulations again to Graham Little, and for the rest and all the other budding authors out there, there's always next year. The winning article as well as appearing in this year's Journal can also be read in full on the SMC website.

Charlie Orr.

ARCHIVING THE A. E. ROBERTSON COLLECTION

THE Reverend Archibald Eneas Roberston (AER) is celebrated not only as the First Munroist but also as an early and enthusiastic amateur photographer.

With his bout of Munrosis cured, following the completion of his round in 1901, AER turned his energies to photography. In two periods, the early 1900s and the early 1930s, he recorded his activities on the crags and hills of Scotland; his journeys through the glens and islands; his social life, and his travels outwith Scotland and England and beyond. Many of AER's photographs have graced the pages of early volumes of this Journal. They have also been used to illustrate a number of the older District Guides and other, more recent, SMC publications. Through the Journal and the Guides, several of AER's photographs have become iconic images of mountains and mountaineering in Scotland.

My interest in the AER Collection began in the late 1970s. At that time it was my custom to take a regular dram with the late Graham Tiso. On one such visit to his house I found him surrounded by a pile of boxes full of glass plate negatives. It appeared that Graham had just agreed, following the death of AER's second wife, Winifred, to take in the Collection until a more suitable home could be found. The Collection remains to this day in Graham's house where Maude Tiso now acts as guardian and gatekeeper. Back then I knew little of the Collection but, with Graham's permission, I borrowed a couple of the boxes and made some conventional photographic contact prints. I was intrigued not only by the quality of many of the images but also by the range of their subject matter. If these two boxes, chosen at random, contained such delights, then what lay elsewhere in the Collection? However, the limitations of my darkroom and a lack of time meant that there the matter lay, aside from a few desultory conversations with the Club Archivist along the lines that: "Something should be done about AER."

It was not until the Autumn of 2002 that the opportunity to do something arose. Work was no longer a burden on my time and I had finally abandoned the wet darkroom in favour of digital imaging. It seemed that with a bit of effort the Collection could be properly catalogued and digital copies of the images made. Making digital copies would have a number of benefits. Firstly, they would provide an alternative to the original, and often fragile, glass and film negatives; secondly, the images could be digitally enhanced to remove the blemishes accumulated over the years and restored to something close to their original condition; and, finally, once archived, the Collection could be made more easily and widely available. And so it was, with the agreement of the Slide Custodian and the Archivist, that I undertook to catalogue and copy the Collection.

There are two principal parts to the Collection. There is, firstly, a set of glass slides, with positive images for projection, and, secondly, a set of glass and film negatives. The slides are housed in a set of fine wooden boxes, made, it is believed, by AER himself during his woodworking phase. There are 29 wooden boxes, each holding between 50 and 100 slides. The glass and film negatives are stored in the cardboard boxes in which the unexposed plates and film were originally purchased. There are 173 such cardboard boxes, of various sizes, and each holds between 10 and several hundred negatives; (one recently opened box contained no less than 488 negatives). There are, then, probably something like 4000 images in the Collection. At the time of writing, approximately 2250 images have been catalogued and scanned.

In addition to the slides and negatives, there are two other parts to the Collection. There is a number of portfolios of photographic prints and a collection of AER's notebooks. There are 10 large print portfolios and four smaller print albums. The notebooks, 11 in all, seem to have been used by AER to jot down the odd note or thought. Some of the notebooks were designed specifically to record photographic data (*Wellcomes Photographic Exposure Record and Diary*) but AER does not seem to have been particularly punctilious in doing this. Other notebooks contain random jottings, details of days on the hill, the weight of kit carried, the cost of lodgings, the names and addresses of keepers and, as befits a man of the cloth, thoughts of a spiritual and uplifting nature. Neither the print portfolios or the notebooks have been investigated in any great detail in this current exercise.

The first task in cataloguing and scanning the Collection was to set up a database to record details of each image. AER had been fairly diligent in organising and ordering his collection. The majority of the slides are annotated with a description of the image and often the date on which it was made. The boxes of negatives are, similarly, labelled and dated. It is clearly difficult to annotate individual negatives but where the negatives are housed in sleeves or grouped in tissue folders, AER has made pencil notes of their content.

AER's organisation of the Collection has been preserved in the database, down to the position of individual negatives in the boxes. Each record in the database consists of six fields. The first field is a unique identifier which records the type of container the slide or negative is housed in (wooden or cardboard box), the box number and the image number. Thus, CB(S)127-5 is the 5th negative in the small cardboard box numbered 127. The second field simply records whether the image is a slide or a negative. The third field records, *verbatim*, AER's own annotations, if any. The fourth field is used to add to AER's annotations or otherwise describe and identify the image subject matter. The fifth field records the number of the CD on which the image is backed up. And, finally, the sixth field records the number of the contact sheet where a thumbnail of the image can be found.

Each image is scanned at a resolution sufficiently detailed to allow enlargement, if needs be, to a reasonable display size without recourse to the source slide or negative. The image is adjusted to give a good tonal range and any major, and easily dealt with, blemishes removed. Details of the image are then recorded in the database. Once a box has been completed, contact sheets are made with the images as thumbnails, which will allow collections of the images to be conveniently printed and viewed. Once a sufficient number of boxes have been scanned, they are burned onto a CD and copies lodged with the Slide Custodian and the Archivist. Ultimately, it is envisaged that the entire Collection will be available on-line or by way of some portable storage device but the CDs now provide an essential backup to the work in progress. The entire catalogue scanned so far is also archived on an external hard disk.

At the time I undertook to catalogue and make digital copies of the Collection, I had little idea of the scale of the task ahead. What I had fondly imagined to be a few months' work, looks like extending, albeit on a part-time basis, into several years. It has, however, proved to be an absorbing exercise. Each box holds the promise of new and interesting images and working through the Collection has helped to pass many a wet winter's day and dark winter's evening. It has to be accepted that AER was an amateur and that his images cannot be compared with other early mountain photographers such as Sella or the Abraham brothers. Nevertheless, his photographs often show a good eye for composition and a number of his images have real aesthetic value. The technical quality of his negatives may not always be of the best but I have often found his images strangely evocative and moving, despite their imperfections. The Collection is perhaps best known for the mountain images but AER did not confine himself solely to landscapes. Like all enthusiastic amateurs, he carried his camera with him on his travels and recorded what he saw. There are, then, photographs of his social circle and the houses where he stayed as a guest. There are photographs of his various means of transport, tandem bicycle, motor bike and cars, complete with gloved and uniformed chauffeur. There are some fine architectural studies of the antiquities of Rome, with hardly a tourist in sight, and of the cathedrals of England and the Cambridge colleges. And there are images of Highland ways of life and industries long since gone; keepers and their wives in lonely glens; black house crofts at Ardnamurchan and Morar; the herring fleet in Stornoway, and weavers in the Uists.

In the AER Collection, the SMC has been gifted a unique archive, a record of a time when few climbed the hills and wandered the glens solely for pleasure, when a different social order prevailed and when the pioneering activities of the Club were gaining momentum. It is an archive that needs curatorial care and attention. Over the years a number of authors and editors, both from within and outwith the Club, have foraged in the Collection for images to illustrate their work. Perhaps inevitably, the Collection has suffered a little as a consequence. Some images seem to be missing and others have been damaged in transit. On the sleeve of one glass negative, a fine and well kent image of Gearr Aonach in Glencoe, AER has somewhat poignantly noted: "... a perfect Negative! Handle him as if you loved him."

Sadly, the negative has been broken and then crudely repaired with sellotape. It is to be hoped that once this present exercise is completed, then the Collection will have been put on a sounder footing, properly catalogued and made more easily accessible for others to explore and enjoy.

Footnote: Four images from the Collection, taken from those already scanned, have been selected to accompany this article. None of the images have, it is thought, been published before. The first image is a 1908 study of the Cobbler on what looks like a fine Spring day. The identity of the two seated figures in the foreground is not known. The second image is annotated 'On Sgurr a' Mhaim looking East'. It is possible that the photographer in the image is W. Lamond Howie. If this is the case, then AER may not have taken the photograph as Howie was active before AER took up photography. The third image is of a group of climbers at Sligachan in the early 1900s. The gentleman on the left is probably Thomas Meares, AER's usual Skye partner. Next to him is the guide John Mackenzie. The gentleman in the centre is thought to be R. Arnold Brown. The two figures on the right may be other members of the Mackenzie clan, Murdoch and young Rory. The final image is somewhere on the West Ridge of Sgurr nan Gillean and is dated 1905. AER's notebooks have an entry for June 12, of that year recording: "Sgurr nan Gillean by the Pinnacle Ridge and the Gendarme with Meares and John."

John Mackenzie is seated left with, possibly, Rory Mackenzie standing just below him. Kate, AER's first wife, is seated centre. The standing, roped gentleman is Thomas Meares. The seated lady on the right is unknown. We might speculate that Rory Mackenzie had taken the ladies up the Tourist Route and that they are all descending the West Ridge together. How the ladies would have coped with the Gendarme in their heavy skirts is, perhaps, best left to further speculation. I am indebted to the Club Archivist for his help in the identification and description of these images.

David Stone.

A 1948 WINTER ASCENT
By Malcolm Slesser

THERE is so much brilliant climbing done these days, that when I look back at our antics 57 years ago (1948) I am truly impressed at how much climbing technology and skills have advanced. Here is an excerpt, word for word, from my diary of February 15. 1948. What is interesting about it is that we had no guide book, knowing only that we were seeking a way up Central Buttress on the Buachaille Etive Mor. It was my second time on the mountain.

"On the Sunday, Maurice Bramah and myself with an English chap working at the British Aluminium Co. at Kinlochleven set off for a scramble on Central Buttress of the Buachaille. In spite of the cares of life – and there were many that weekend – the lovely weather, warm sunshine and rolling ground mist on the Muir of Rannoch soon brought one to a pleasant frame of mind by its recollection of a previous similar day in the Lost Valley in December 1947.

"We toiled up in a shower of sweat, peeling rapidly the clothes put on earlier for breakfast at Lagangarbh. Maurice, we persuaded to lead and so after the odd scramble on loose rock intermingled with looser heather and snow we arrived beneath our first 'insurmountable' obstacle. There we dallied, chewed the cud, made conventional and time-honoured cracks about leaders and the incidence of their falling off. Finally, with the juice of a dried apricot dripping from the corners of his mouth, up went Maurice. A good lead up a vertical crack. Nos. 2 & 3 looked on not quite unconcernedly, for we had no belay. However, Maurice did not disappointment us and soon we had joined him. The rest of the ascent up to a heather ledge was interesting and in places severe. We were rising high in the buttress now and there occurred an abrupt metamorphosis in the scene. We were suddenly plunged into Alpine rock faces, snow ledges and couloirs. Mist below us and snow everywhere on the higher hills. It had a salutary effect on myself, and my form, which up to now was fit only for a third man on a moderate climb, now rose to the required level. At least I felt up to preventing people falling off – just as well too. A neat lead by Maurice round the right-hand corner and his disappearance caused our last traces of anxiety to disappear and we (i.e. Nos. 2 & 3) lost ourselves in comparative contemplations of Nevis versus Binnein Mor, the latter looking the higher.

"Maurice's perch at the top of his pitch was unsatisfactory. It consisted of (no belay) an arch in the rock face down which dripped an uncommonly large quantity of iced-water drops – most penetrating. From here I body-belayed him while he led the crux in appropriate manner and made it look so easy that (Nos. 2 & 3) were later caught unawares. The crux is a 10ft. groove on small holds made ice-cold by an icy drip from a cornice 100ft. above. There follows a rib traverse up a narrow sloping ledge to reach the only stance and belay. I got up with difficulty and a small margin. No. 3, alas, froze to the rock and then fell off, thereby executing a most commendable acrobatic panegyric in which my rope held easily (good man Tarbuck!) he embedded himself not so elegantly in a snow patch. No time was wasted. In five minutes he had forged a new route up the face and reached us with little more to show for his brief aerial levitation than an inward muttering at the follies of cold fingers and winter rockclimbing.

"The worst was over and with confidant knowledge we pressed on for the top. Once more into an Alpine scene we climbed a sharp snow crest and treaded warily and unroped to join our president George Chisholm. (on Curved Ridge). I suggested Coire Mor for the descent. This presented a magnificent glissade. No limbs were lost, but a considerable number of new seats (patches) will be in demand. We were able to descend to the 1300ft. contour. In all 12 hours of bliss."

1. Maurice Bramah survived Arnhem (as a paratrooper). Later that winter he was to slip on ice while descending Dinner-Time Buttress on Aonach Dubh and died of head injuries.
2. Then primitive and unheated.
3. A Tarbuck knot was all the rage at the time.It was a modified prussic knot whose merit was supposed to be that the knot would slip under load,thus breaking the shock of a falling leader.
4. Obviously, Bell and Harrison's route.
5. George was then president of the JMCS. He died in 2003,an active hillwalker to the end.

IT'S A DOG'S LIFE

By Dave (Heavy) Whalley

I READ with interest a letter in a mountaineering magazine, asking if any dogs have done the Munros and thought it was time to share a small part of a special dog's mountaineering life. My dog, Teallach, (the softest long-haired Alsatian you could ever meet) finished his Munros in 1985 and he had only 12 left for his second time around when he, unfortunately, passed away. I am sure Hamish Brown's dog, Keltie, completed his before Teallach, but Teallach was possibly the second dog to do the complete round and would have been an early Dog Munroist.

The most difficult Munros were on Skye, where we had a great two-day traverse. I have some great photos of him on the Inaccessible Pinnacle. As my rock-climbing ability is limited, getting to the summit with Teallach made it a major operation. However, with the addition of a few extra abseils and help from more talented rock climbing friends, we succeeded. His route finding ability was exceptional, usually vanishing around a ledge to arrive before us above the difficulties.

Teallach made several outstanding walks including two complete traverses of Scotland, a North to South and an East to West – 145 Munros in seven weeks – very hard on the paws! His apprenticeship was spent in Wales where he completed the 14 peaks when still just a pup. He did this hill route on many occasions, learning his basic skills on many of the Welsh classics, besides doing several winter routes here and in the Lakes. During my exile in North Wales, the lesser hills proved good training for Scotland and every six weeks or so we would take a trip to the big hills in the North, this being where he excelled. I have been a member of RAF Mountain Rescue Teams at Kinloss and Leuchars and many long hours were spent on big hill days with the young team members. Teallach's logbook included, the Skye Ridge in two days, 11 full traverses of the South Cluanie (including The Saddle), six complete traverses of the North Cluanie, nine full Traverses of the Mamores, seven full traverses of the Fannichs, three ascents of the Shenavall Six and three ascents of the Affric Munros. In addition, he completed 'The Tranter Traverses' in Kintail and Lochaber *and* was a regular user of the CIC hut, until he was banned by the members.

He was a very accomplished climber on rock and ice and in the end, had to be tied up as he was soloing way beyond my ability to rescue him. Regularly he would meet us at the bottom of the Cioch Slab in Skye, finding his way up from the Sgumain Stone Chute and across Eastern Gully with ease. On one occasion on the Cioch Nose in Applecross, we left him attached to the rucksacks at the bottom of the route. On returning to our kit and having attempted to flee the midges, we found him in the loch more than 2km away, complete with our rucksacks still tied to his collar. He was a regular at Glenmore Lodge, before it was in vogue, until he was banned for annoying too many of the instructors assessing in the Northern Corries at the time. After hearing my shouts while climbing, and thinking I was calling to him for help, many a Winter Leader's assessment was disturbed by Teallach trying to find his way up a Grade II gully. For this I now sincerely apologise to the Principal. The Lodge even sent a formal letter addressed to the MRT at RAF Kinloss, complaining of his abysmal rope work.

Though not a rescue dog, he was superb on the hill and could sniff out a cornice in any weather. His area knowledge was exceptional and he never used a map or compass, always finding the summit and leaving his mark on it! He had two big falls. The first one was on Creag Meaghaidh where he went a 1000ft. in a whiteout. He was out in front as usual and at the over-confident stage in his mountaineering career. After I descended into the Coire expecting to find him in a bad way, I found him okay, a bit shaken and by now very 'cornice aware'. On the second occasion, I left him below Black Spout on Lochnagar. After having an epic on Black Spout Buttress, I was faced with getting off the hill in poor weather, late on a wild winter's night. The only way off was over the cornice down Black Spout Gully. Two following climbers brought the cornice down on top of us – we fell 600ft. Teallach arrived on scene and began digging us out, even though the avalanche had hit him as well. We eventually got back in the wee small hours, battered and bruised.

In those days, snow-holing was fashionable. One night on the Cairngorm plateau after the usual few drams, we all drifted back to our own holes. Just as we were falling asleep, I heard a noise outside and, thinking that it was a raid on our whisky store, sent Teallach out to chase them off. Even though Teallach was a big softy, in the dark and around the snow hole, he must have looked fearsome. Imagine my consternation the following morning, when I went out and found two climbers curled up and shivering. They had left their sacks below Hell's Lum and could not find them. Having seen our light they thought they were safe, only to be met by a huge dog, who would not let them in the snow hole. I brought them in, gave them a brew and walked them off later in the morning, meeting Cairngorm MRT, who were coming to look for our 'lost' friends – another confession.

I rarely saw him tired, only once while completing the Big Three in Torridon, (Beinn Eighe, Liathach and Ben Alligin) the heat got to him and he refused to add Beinn Dearg to the day, heading off down the glen on his own to the vehicle. As he got older like us all, aging began to take its toll. Problems with his hips and back became chronic, but he still loved every minute on the hill. On rescues he was a great asset and was always well behaved. He knew when we had a fatality to deal with, or when the situation was serious and kept out of the way. He found a few casualties in his time and was a warm bivouac partner on many rescues.

After a hill day and back in the bothy, he would always find the new lad's sleeping bag, make himself comfortable in their bag and fall fast asleep. Few were brave enough to move the huge Alsatian and many a novice had a cold night curled up on the floor. Good training for the Greater Ranges! As he got older he would enjoy walking up to the crag and watching our epics on the classic routes, occasionally pinching any food that was left in open rucksacks. Even after a long climbing day he would still be there after 12 hours, waiting for you to come down. He would even know where the descent gully was and meet you. Later on, he developed a love for Sea Stacks and would enjoy the day while we climbed on Am Buachaille or Storr, swimming around the stack, watching what was going on. Every hill loch would involve a swim whatever the weather or season.

Each Friday night he would wait patiently by the Land-Rover ready to go out on the hill, even when his health was failing. He would get upset at not being able to go out at weekends and still sit in the wagon waiting. In the bothies and after a long hill day, he would crawl next to the fire and once burst into flames in the Ossian Youth Hostel after lying too near the stove.

Teallach was an exceptional dog, well behaved on the hill, no problem with sheep or any of the wild life and most of all a great companion. The ultimate Party Leader, always looking after his party, regularly rounding up any stragglers. He was not a just a Munro bagger but an all round 'Scottish Mountaineer'. He used to be able to jump and climb deer fences when in his prime. Unfortunately, he nearly hanged himself when his karabiner caught in the top wire of one fence, much to the consternation of my five-year-old step son who was very worried. I managed to sort it out and Teallach became very aware that his screw gate karabiner should be locked closed at all times. He always wore a screw gate karabiner round his collar and had one terrible habit. When he was thirsty, in the middle of the night. He would head to the toilet for a drink. The noise of the karabiner on the toilet bowl woke everyone.

Even though he died back in 1992, I sorely miss him, what a friend he was, what a life he had.

COLLIE – ACROSS THE BORDER
By Mike Jacob

In last year's Journal, Robin Campbell described how, as a result of his study of previous Journals, he abandoned his youthful opinion that the early climbers were incompetent and wrote that "technical standards - particularly on ice climbs and mixed routes - reached a level in the 1890s that they did not regain until the 1950s".

In support of his contention, he cites: "Harold Raeburn's winter ascents of Crowberry Gully (1898, Buachaille) and Green Gully (Ben Nevis) and William Naismith's winter ascent of the North-East Buttress (1896, Ben Nevis)" – I have inserted the years. To these, perhaps because it preceded them, although normally technically easier, should be added Norman Collie's ascent of Tower Ridge[1] (Ben Nevis, 1894, first with the Lakeland climbers Godfrey Solly and Joseph Collier and then, the following day, with his regular climbing partner Geoffrey Hastings) but, to nit-pick, Green Gully should be subtracted because its ascent was actually in 1906. Today, N.E. Buttress has a grade of IV,4.

Now Robin's statement may seem surprising but, upon examination, is essentially true, although some might argue that the word "regain" in the quotation should be replaced by "exceed". Winter standards may not have risen very much in those 50 years but there is evidence that they were maintained[2]. These, of course, are all Scottish routes but it has recently been pointed out[3] that, across the Border, there was at least one notable winter ascent in the Lake District that adds weight to Robin's assertion – Steep Ghyll (Scafell; Grade V,4) climbed at Christmas 1891 by none other than Norman Collie (with W. Brodie and E. Marshall and not, as previously thought, with G. Hastings and J. W. Robinson in 1890) and the first Grade V route in Britain. This ascent is not to be confused with the controversial ascent of Moss Ghyll in 1892 when Collie used his ice-axe to chip a hold in the rock. Although he contributed articles to various journals,[4] Collie was notoriously reticent about recording details of his climbs; for him, the exploratory nature of climbing took first place and he may also have felt that this particular route was unjustifiably hazardous. The issue of grading is bound to stir debate between the tribes but there can be no dispute that this was a significant ascent by fit and tough Victorian gentlemen whichever side of the Border they happened to be.

Collie, who was on his first visit to Wasdale, had travelled from London by train with his two companions. At the start of the holiday the hotel proprietor, Dan Tyson, was shocked to see them going into the hills in what he thought were their

Sunday clothes but they had no choice as all their luggage had been delayed at
Drigg station. Then, on Christmas Day, the three of them climbed Steep Ghyll in
full winter conditions. Collie later wrote that "it is one of the most dangerous
climbs I have ever made". *(FRCC Journal 1926)*. The party may have been
deceived by the relatively easy start to the gully and climbed to a position from
which they could not retreat, leaving them with no choice but to proceed upwards.
The weather over the next few days continued to be unsettled with strong winds,
low temperatures and snow but this did not deter further exploration of the crags
which included a lucky escape on Pillar's North Climb when the rope, remarkably,
held a long fall by the leader.

Norman Collie was aged 31 at the time of this ascent having started climbing in
1886. His association with Skye and John Mackenzie, and how he became a
renowned world mountaineer and explorer, are well documented[5] elsewhere but it
is worth recalling some of his most significant mountaineering achievements across
other borders.

He had made one visit to the Alps in 1888 (recorded in his application to the
Alpine Club, to which he was admitted in 1893, but apparently not mentioned in
either of his two biographies). By 1895, which was to be a pivotal year, he had
several Alpine seasons under his belt and had climbed the Matterhorn by the
Italian ridge, the Aiguille de Grepon and the Petit Dru as well as first ascents of
the Dent du Requin and the south-west face of the Aiguille du Plan climbed with
C. Slingsby, G. Hastings and A. F. Mummery. It was with Mummery, too, (who,
flying in the face of the Alpine Club's[6] stuffy conservatism, had come to believe
that true adventure lay in self-dependence[7]) that Collie made the first guideless
ascent of the Old Brenva Route on Mont Blanc in 1894.

In 1895 Collie was part of a small expedition led by Mummery (with G. Hastings,
C. G. Bruce – who would lead the 1922 and !924 Everest expeditions – and two
gurkhas, Raghobir Thapa and Goman Singh) which made a remarkable 'alpine-
style' attempt on Nanga Parbat, the most westerly of the 8000m. peaks and, at
8125m., ninth-highest mountain in the world. Situated in British India (now
Pakistan), yet sufficiently distant from the politically-sensitive border areas, it
was comparatively easy of access even then. The party visited the south-east (Rupal)
face and pronounced it "impregnable" and then crossed the Mazeno Pass into the
Diamir valley to reconnoitre. The expedition had been on the mountain for more
than a month when Mummery made his attempt on the summit (Collie, according
to Mummery, appears to have been suffering from the altitude and "*was not keen
on it*") –

*Truly sticking to his principles of climbing light he set on off on August 19th,
accompanied only by Raghobir and equipped with little more than ice-axes, a
tent, some provisions and firewood. Their route was the most direct, straight up
the steep rocky ribs cutting through the menacing seracs of the central Diamir
face. After a night on top of the second rib "excessively difficult" climbing, which
fortunately became easier higher up, brought them all the way to the last break in
the serac barrier at around 6500m. Then Raghobir turned ill and they were forced
to retreat. Now the expedition's hopes rested on finding a feasible way up the last
remaining side of the mountain, the northern or Raikot Face[8]. While the other
members opted for the long way around the Nanga Parbat massif, Mummery
wanted to take a short-cut over the Diama Pass (6227m.)[9]*

between the Diama and Raikot glaciers and perhaps make another attempt on the summit by the Raikot face. Mummery and the two gurkhas were never seen again. On September 13, Collie and Hastings made a three-day trip to reach the camp where they had last seen their companions. However, it was late in the season and there was too much fresh snow to undertake a search and, according to Collie, "*slowly we descended and for the last time looked on the great mountain and the white snows where in some unknown spot our friends lay buried*".

Collie never returned to the Himalaya. In 1897, he accepted an invitation extended by Charles Fay to the Alpine Club to join a memorial climb to attempt Mount Lefroy in the Canadian Rockies. This was successful and the party also made the first ascent of Mount Victoria two days later. Collie was smitten by this virgin terrain and returned to the Canadian Rockies on several other occasions and, by 1911, he had completed 21 first ascents and surveyed and named in excess of 30 peaks (including a Canadian version of Nanga Parbat). This was a unique achievement in a huge and largely unmapped mountain wilderness with arduous access problems. When he returned home after his final visit in 1911 it was to devote more time to his academic work and to his beloved Skye.

However, as President of the Alpine Club in 1920, he became an influential member of the newly-formed Mount Everest Committee and was instrumental in the choice of both Harold Raeburn and Alexander Kellas for the 1921 Everest Reconnaissance Expedition … but this tale of derring-do, if the Editor will allow, awaits a future Journal.

1 Thus prompting W. W. Naismith to write "*the Sassenachs have indeed taken the wind out of our sails … Flodden or even Culloden was nothing to this*". Although often perceived as Scottish, Collie was actually born south of the Border and spent most of his life living and working in England. However, he had joined the SMC in 1891 and, in 1895, Naismith and Collie were together in the party on the first ascent of Castle Ridge (Ben Nevis).
2 The point (which, to be fair, Robin also makes in *The First Scottish Ice Climbers* SMCJ Vol. XXX, 1972) can be illustrated if we take one or two routes from each of the first five decades of the 20th century. I am using modern grading (and ignoring 'grade creep', the process where you discover that routes you completed 20 years ago were beyond your capability), concentrating on Glencoe and Ben Nevis and taking no account of the variability of winter conditions:
1900s – Green Gully (Ben Nevis). 1906. IV, 4. H. Raeburn and E. Phildius
1910s – No significant routes. First World War I (1914-1918).
1920s – Observatory Ridge (Ben Nevis). 1920. IV, 4. H. Raeburn, F. Goggs, W. Mounsey.
1930s – Slav Route/Zero Gully combination. 1936. (Slav Route is VI, 5). J. H. B .Bell and C. M. Allan.
Shelf Route (Buachaille). 1937. IV, 6. W. H. Murray and W. MacKenzie.
1940s – Flake Route (Bidean nam Bian). 1942. IV, 6. G. Scott and F. Cope.
3 In discussion with Stephen Reid, to whom I am grateful for providing help and information. I must also thank his fellow Fell and Rock members, Mike Cocker and Colin Wells, who wrote the research/descriptions regarding the Steep Ghyll ascent upon which I have based my account.
4 *From the Himalaya to Skye*, a collection of his climbing writing based on his visits to the Alps, Norway's Lofoten Islands, Nanga Parbat, Canada and Eire as well as the UK, was republished in 2003 by RippingYarns.com (with all royalties going to the John Muir Trust) and is available both as an e-book and a paperback. Collie also wrote *Climbing In The Himalaya And Other Mountain Ranges* (David Douglas, Edinburgh, 1902. Copies of this book are extremely rare and can be worth several hundred pounds) and he co-authored, with Hugh Stutfield, *Climbs and Exploration in the Canadian Rockies* (also available from RippingYarns).
5 *The Snows Of Yesteryear* by William C. Taylor, 1973 and *Norman Collie, A Life In Two Worlds* by Christine Mill, 1987. A search of the Web throws up several sites with biographical information; however, there are mistakes to be found. For example, one website relates how Collie, in a speech

at the Cairngorm Club's annual dinner in 1925, described his encounter with the Big Grey Man of Ben MacDhui and then, some 12 years later, repeated the tale to Alexander Kellas, a fellow SMC member and accomplished Himalayan explorer/mountaineer. This must have been Collie's second ghostly encounter for Kellas died in 1921 while on the Everest Reconnaissance expedition.
6 Mummery was refused membership of the Alpine Club for several years despite his outstanding Alpine record.
7 Despite this, Mummery's first ascents of the Zmutt Ridge of the Matterhorn (1879), North Summit of the Grand Charmoz (1880) and the Grepon by the Nantillons Face (1881) had all been climbed with guides, which included Alex Burgener on all three routes.
8 Three years earlier the explorer William Martin Conway had studied this aspect of the mountain from Bunji in the Indus Valley and concluded that *"no extraordinary difficulties other than those pertaining to the altitude and the state of the snow appear to bar the way" (Climbing and Exploration in the Karakorum Himalayas,* p.100), a view echoed by Kellas in 1913. Around the same time, a German mountaineering writer and publisher had acquired the German rights to Mummery's classic work *My Climbs in the Alps and Caucasus* which by then included transcripts of Mummery's letters from Nanga Parbat. Thus started the long German/Austrian attempts upon the mountain with, over the succeeding years, multiple tragedies and the loss of many lives before the summit was finally reached up this side of the mountain in 1953 by Hermann Buhl.
9 Jochen Hemmleb writing on the American Foundation for International Mountaineering, Exploration and Research web-site, which also contains excellent photographs and well-researched accounts of the dramatic history of the mountain.

P. J. H. Unna - Research

By Ted Zenthon

My interest in Percy Unna started when I read an article about him in *The Scots Magazine* (October,1991) by Rennie McOwen, in which he thought that Percy's ancestors came form Denmark, as did my own seafaring great-grandfather. It is also interesting to note that Chris Bonington's seafaring grandfather was also born in Denmark. All rather amusing when one thinks of the low-lying terrain of that country.

Percy was born in London in 1878 at 12 Lancaster Gate – a large mansion overlooking Bayswater Road and Kensington Gardens – less than a mile from where I was born in 1921, but in a lowly mews. His father, merchant Ferdinand Unna was born in 1816 in Hamburg as was his mother Friederika (nee Reuben) in 1830. He died in 1950, the year that I was elected to the SMC. Sadly, I never did get to meet him and there are few people still alive who knew him well, so far as his mountaineering activities are concerned. Remarkably few photographs of him appear to have survived.

His keen interest in preserving and contributing to the preservation of the Scottish mountains is very well known. Alex Harrison's article *Reflections in a Diamond,* (SMCJ vol. xxxii 1980), clearly gives details of this and his great generosity. Another insight into his character is a letter he wrote to the editor of the FRCCJ on December 10, 1941:

> *To the Editor of the 'Fell and Rock Journal.'* CAIRNS
> Dear Editor,
> Every member knows that stone walling is a skilled trade, and that it is certainly not easy to build a solid well shaped cairn. Also that some of the old Lake District cairns are fine specimens – notably the slender pillar on the top of Pike 'o Blisco. Whether most of these summit cairns are survey marks or of older standing, I do not know. In any case, they date well back into the last century, as do other marks,

said to have been set up by shepherds. And there a few more already fairly old, such as the Westmoreland cairn, and two tiny ones on Gavel Neese, telling one where to turn off right towards the Napes, and the line of cairns from Esk-Hause to Scafell Pike. All are more or less historic, and should be carefully preserved.

It is the reverse with the untidy piles of stones which have recently sprung up all over the more frequented parts of the Lake District. The intention may have been to help people find their way, but the proper method to do so is to teach them to find their way unaided, even if it means letting them lose it first. This should be encouraged as a matter of public policy, and as a justifiable exception to the miserable principles of Safety First. And is it not useful to be able to find the way in wartime, almost as useful in the army as at sea or in the air? Moreover, these strings of cairns, or rather rubbish heaps, tend to make hikers concentrate on tracks, with the result that almost all the fells are now disfigured with trodden paths, where 40 years ago they were still unscarred. Again in some parts , Bowfell for example, these so-called cairns have become so promiscuous that they fail to show the way at all, but merely form obstructions that trip one in the dark. There is in existence a club, the Gaderene Club, formed for the sole purpose of destroying unwanted cairns. I am an honorary member in so far as that is consistent in a club with no subscription. To justify my membership I have, during the past 18 months, managed to level out from three to four hundred of these ugly piles on but half-a-dozen Lakeland hills, and I appeal to fellow members to complete the work.

On the same principle, some years ago the SMC asked the National Trust for Scotland to discourage directional marks of any kind on its Highland property, and since then the Forestry Commissioners have decided on a similar policy for their National Forest parks in the Forest of Dean and Snowdon district. Perhaps the Fell and Rock might ask the National Trust to do the same in the Lake District.

Yours, etc,

P.J.H. Unna,

10th December,1941.

Clearly, and rightly so, Percy had no desire to see any real change in the mountain landscape, an ethos which now seems to go largely unregarded.

Percy Unna died while climbing alone on the slopes of Beinn Eunaich, near Dalmally and was buried in Pennyfuir cemetery at Dunbeg near Oban.

Alex Harrison recalls:

"The circumstances of Unna's death are curious. The meet was at Dalmally. Unna went there a day or two before the start of the Easter Meet. It was a winter of very hard frost and little snow and when Unna did not return from an expedition a search was made and his body was found at the bottom of a steep slope. It is not known if he slipped or his heart failed. It was arranged that he would be buried at Oban in an afternoon and we all went to find that it had suited the minister and the undertaker to have it in the morning. In some ways it seemed typical of Unna to have it that way. He was buried looking to Ben Cruachan."

I have done some further work on the life of P. J. H. Unna, but unfortunately, old age and failing health have meant that this has not been completed. I have deposited all my research papers along with a family tree in the Club archive – they make interesting reading.

SCOTTISH WINTER NOTES

Three new routes stand out from the 2005 winter season – a technical test piece in the Northern Corries, a bolt-protected climb in the Southern Highlands, and a major addition to Pinnacle Buttress on Creag Meagaidh. These climbs are strikingly different in style, and highlight the variety in the increasingly popular sport of Scottish winter climbing.

Dave Macleod's winter ascent of *The Hurting* in Coire an t-Sneachda was something special. This 35m. high crackline slices through the prominent steep triangular wall on the right side of Fiacaill Buttress and was first climbed in 1991 as a summer E4 6a. The winter ascent was graded a hefty XI,11, making it by far the most difficult winter pitch ever led in Scotland. MacLeod's lead was brilliant, and the resulting route is highly technical and very bold. In rock climbing terms think E9 or E10.

After inspecting the route on abseil, Dave almost flashed the route on his first attempt, but fell off three moves from the top. Scott Muir then top roped the climb, and pointed out to Dave that he had gone the wrong way at the top. Dave returned three days later to settle the score. It was a cold, windy day and recent heavy snow meant the cracks were verglassed. Dave abseiled down to see where Scott had gone at the top, chopped the verglas out of the crucial gear placements, and then led the route. Dave later said the climb was like taking the cruxes of *Happy Tyroleans*, *The Demon*, *The Duel* and *Logical Progression* (considered by many to be Scotland's hardest technical winter routes), making them harder and stacking them on top of each other and then adding groundfall potential. He also suggested that his route may be the "hardest single pitch traditional mixed route in the world".

With his ascents of *The Cathedral* (X,11) last season and now *The Hurting*, Dave has created another facet of Scottish Winter that previously didn't exist. Many climbers will continue to pursue the mountaineering approach, and derive great pleasure from making their ascents ground up and on sight, while others will now be drawn to shorter and more difficult climbs that require some degree of pre-inspection for success. A key element to this new style is that the routes do not depend on pre-placed gear and the bold and serious element that is synonymous with Scottish winter climbing is preserved.

While Dave Macleod's ascent of *The Hurting* attracted universal praise, the creation of Scotland's first bolt-protected winter sports route created a storm of controversy. *Crossroads* (M6) lies on the Upper Tier on Beinn Udlaidh in the Southern Highlands and was equipped and then led by Scott Muir at the end of last year. From a traditional standpoint, placing bolts to protect a Scottish winter climb is the ultimate sin, and the route brought howls of protest.

In other parts of the world, bolts are often used to protect mixed routes, but in Scotland there has always been a strong desire to maximise the adventure and uncertainty when climbing on our relatively small crags. As a result, Scottish winter climbers tend to have excellent on-sight mountaineering skills, while the technical difficulty of our hardest climbs are several notches easier than the top end mixed and dry tool climbs in North America and on the Continent. Scott, who has extensive experience of climbing Continental mixed routes, argues that for Scottish climbing to catch up we need to start developing bolt-protected sports-style winter routes.

Scott Muir is a man of conviction and has shown great courage in going against established tradition by placing bolts in Beinn Udlaidh. From a diversity perspective it seems perfectly reasonable to create bolt-protected winter routes for those that want to climb them, but there are a number of important issues that need to be taken into account.

Firstly, there are the arguments about damage to the environment and stealing opportunities from future generations, but the greatest concern is that bolts will erode the on-sight ethic that many believe to be inherent to Scottish winter climbing

The future of *Crossroads* now rests with other climbers. If it becomes popular with many repeat ascents it will pave the way for other bolt-protected winter routes throughout the Highlands. Alternatively, if the bolts are removed and not replaced, the climb will cease to exist, and it will be remembered as an interesting diversion in the long and varied history of Scottish climbing.

The third route that stands out was climbed in early March during the International Winter Meet. These meets are held every other year at Glenmore Lodge and are jointly hosted by the BMC and MC of S. This year, more than 40 guests from 25 different countries were hosted by 30 British climbers, and the event coincided with the finest winter climbing conditions of the winter. There were dozens of excellent routes climbed during the meet, but the clear standout route was the first ascent of *Extasy* (VIII,8) on Creag Meagaidh by Dave Hesleden and Bruno Sourzac from France. This put to bed one of Scotland's last great problems – the huge 300m. unclimbed wall between *Smith's Gully* and *The Fly*.

Dave had tried this line 11 years earlier, but had ground to a halt after the first pitch. Since then the climb had been talked about by several activists, with some saying that the blank nature of the rock meant that it would not be possible to protect without using bolts. Hesleden and Sourzac had no intention of using bolts, of course, and it was no surprise to hear that the seven-pitch climb was very steep on typically bold Meagaidh mixed terrain, and that five of the seven pitches merited a technical grade of 8.

These statistics suggest that *Extasy* is the most difficult Scottish first ascent to be climbed on sight, and in my view is arguably the most important new route since Brian Davison's ascent of *Mort* on Lochnagar five years before.

Hesleden and Sourzac are no strangers to top-end mixed climbing. Dave is renowned for his skill climbing thin ice and Bruno is one of the world's finest mountaineers. As chief instructor at ENSA in Chamonix, he is the guide that trains the guides, and three days before on the first day of the meet he had demonstrated his consummate skill by leading *Cornucopia* (VII,9) as his first Scottish winter route.

Overall, the 2005 winter season was a difficult one, with few settled periods of weather. Fortunately, a cold and snowy period from mid-February to early March, brought good conditions over much of the Highlands which resulted in some excellent first ascents.

In Glen Coe, Rab Anderson and Rob Milne added two fine routes on Bidean. On Diamond Buttress, they climbed *Koh-i-nor* (V,7) which takes the ramp running up left from the left branch of Central Gully to gain right-trending grooves and chimneys. The following weekend they returned to add *Flake*

Route Right-Hand 190m V,7 on Church Door Buttress. This climbs the chimney up the right side of the huge flake of *Flake Route*.

Simon Yearsley and Malcolm Bass had a great day on the rarely-visited Stob Coire Altruim on the Buachaille, and came away with *Dog Day Monday* (VI,7), a route they'd been eyeing for some time, the superb line of hanging chimneys to the right of *Cerberus*.

During the Winter Meet, Sam Chinnery and top American alpinist, Steve House, had a great day on Bidean, climbing the steep flake-line between *West Chimney* and *Kingpin*. *Crusade* VII,8 is a fine independent line and a great addition to this brilliant high crag. Also of note in the Coe was a direct variation to *Un Poco Loco* by Es Tressider and I. Lewis at hard VII,7, and an excellent direct version of *East Face Route* on Stob Coire nan Lochan at VII,8 by Pete Benson and Guy Robertson.

Farther west, Erik Brunskill and Gavin Macfie had a good find on Maol Odhar in Ardgour with *Voodoo Buttress* (V,6) that climbs the left-hand of twin buttress below the main summit.

The Southern Highlands were the scene of some great new routes. Erik Brunskill made several visits to Coire an Lochain on Beinn a'Cheachain, the least visited of the Bridge of Orchy crags.

The best additions were *Chicken Run* (IV,4), the prominent icefall mentioned as unclimbed in the Southern Highlands guide, which was climbed with Gavin Macfie.

The next day they were joined by Dan Johnson for *The Bells* (V,5), the second last buttress up the gully. This proved to be a more testing affair and with the way ahead uncertain and retreat looking difficult, Brunskill forced an unlikely way through the final overhangs.

Ben Cruachan saw activity from various teams, but the best addition was *Pussy Galore* (VII,8) by Chris Cartwright and Dave Hesleden that takes the left-slanting line of cracks on the front of Noe Buttress. Chris also teamed up with Iain Small for the first ascent of the difficult *Fat Lip Fandango* (VII,7) – a bold and technical route that completes the triptych of corner-lines on the left side of the main cliff.

Nearby on Beinn Udlaidh, Dave MacLeod and Scott Muir added *Fontinalia* (VIII,9), a Continental-style mixed route that takes a thin seam through a roof to gain a hanging ice fang to the right of *Cut Throat*'s second pitch. The protection was placed on the lead and both climbers ensured a full tick by leading the pitch.

Farther north, there were some good new additions in the Central Highlands. Andy Nisbet and Jonathan Preston visited the east face of Aonach Beag and climbed *The Prisoner* (V,5), the fine buttress right of *Goblet of Fire*. Nearby, on Meall Garbh, Iain Small added a couple of good routes with Jason Walker and Susan Jensen. *Quiet Running* (V,6) takes the right-trending groove bounding the left side of the Inspiration buttress and *Runs with Deer* (V,6) is a counter-diagonal line to North Buttress Left Edge.

The very remote Maiden Crag on the north face of Ben Alder saw a couple of visits. Chris Cartwright and I climbed the buttress between *Ice Maiden* and *Witchwhite* to give *The Snow Queen* (V,5), and Colin Wells and Steven Reid climbed the intriguingly named *Icicles by Bicycle* (III,4) that takes the obvious gully line next left of *Ice Maiden*. The same pair also visited Creag Dubh above Loch Ericht and added *I Scream* (V,4) the narrow icy gully between *Swordfish* and *The Hex Factor*.

After Hesleden and Sourzac's ascent of *Extasy*, there were two more big additions on Creag Meagaidh. On the last day of the Winter Meet, Guy Robertson and Es Tressider teamed up with Primoz Hostnik from Slovenia and climbed the thinly-iced hanging ramps right of *Smith's Gully* resulting in the excellent *Eye Candy* (VII,7). Robertson and Tressider returned the following weekend for *The Moth* (VII,8), which takes the huge wall right of *The Fly Direct*, although poor ice in the upper section dictated a right, then left detour through the final headwall.

The event in the Northern Highlands was the first ascent of *Final Destination* (VIII,7) on Beinn Dearg by Guy Robertson and Alastair Robertson. This bold, and complex mixed route, takes the challenge of the huge unclimbed wall left of *Ice Bomb*, in Coire Ghranda and was the scene of a blood-curdling 15m fall when Alastair's tools ripped on the third pitch. Another excellent addition in the Northern Highlads was *Prohibition* (VI,5) in Garbh Choire Mor on An Coileachan in the Fannaichs by Erik Brunskill and Garth Hughes. This takes the S-shaped groove in the buttress right of *Burdock*, and climbs through some unlikely looking terrain with ice hooks in turf for protection.

Beinn Bhan in Applecross came into good condition in February. In Coire na Poite, Iain Small and Dave McGimpsey climbed *Gryphon* (V,7), which takes the front face of the buttress taken by *Teapot*. Two days' later they were back with Andy Nisbet and Jonathan Preston for the first ascent of the spectacular *Skinflint* (VI,6) in Coire na Feola, which takes the groove running up the front face of Suspense Buttress.

Nearby, on Ben Damph, Andy Nisbet climbed the 400m.-long buttresses either side of the gully-line *Calluna. Fraoch Groove* (IV,4) takes the right buttress and is essentially a more direct version of *Erica's Ridge,* and *Lingo* (IV,4), climbed with Jonathan Preston, takes the buttress to the left.

Nisbet and Preston also visited Coire Ruadh-Staca (the Pineapple Cliff) on Beinn Eighe where they found *Quickstep* (IV,5), the buttress at the far right end of the cliff. Andy returned with Dave McGimpsey to climb *Jambo* (V,7), the diagonal line of chimneys to the right of *Midge Ridge* and *Chocked* (IV,6), the superb crackline just right of *Smilodon*.

Also of note on Beinn Eighe was a rare repeat of the superb *West Buttress Diretissima* (VII,8) by Guy Robertson and Es Tressider. They climbed directly up the corner of *Senior* on the lower tier, which gave two more hard pitches of technical 7 and 8.

Across on Skye, Dave Ritchie and D. McEachan had a good weekend in mid-February when they climbed *Vent du Nord* (V,6) the obvious open groove on the right side of the buttress situated between Gully B and Gully C on the West Face of Sgurr Thearlaich. The following day they visited Coir' An Lochain on the same mountain and made the first winter ascent of *Aladdin's Route* (IV,6).

In general, it was a not a good season for mixed routes in the Cairngorms. The cliffs were either bare or covered in deep powder and hoar during the cold weather in February and March. Early in the season, Dave McLeod and Scot Muir made a difficult technical addition to Coire an t-Sneachda with the first winter ascent of *Babes in the Wood* (VIII,8). This summer E2 follows a slanting crackline on the left flank of Aladdin's Buttress and provided a sustained pitch with a thin crux at the top. The line was climbed on the second attempt and was a well known problem that had been attempted before by other parties.

By contrast, it was a good year for new mixed routes on Ben Nevis, and the early highlight was the first winter ascent of *Strident Edge* (VI,7) by Erik Brunskill and Gareth Hughes. This steep VS rock climb on South Trident Buttress is very imposing in summer, and its exposed location makes it look a very unlikely winter objective. Erik and Gareth made their ascent the day after the great storm that wreaked damage across Scotland in the middle of January. Their timing was immaculate, and the strong westerlies brought a huge amount of snow that swamped the Ben's east-facing crags with tons of powder.

Two weeks' later Andy Nisbet and Jonathan Preston also visited South Trident Buttress and climbed *Rattling* (V,5) a fine winter version of *The Rattler*. Gareth made another well-timed ascent early in the season, with the first winter ascent of *Right-Hand Route* (VI,7) on the Douglas Boulder with Ollie Metherell.

On Creag Coire na Ciste, Chris Cartwright and I were particularly pleased with *Archangel* (VIII,7), the line of impending corners to the right of *Darth Vader*. This one had been on our list since 1997, so it was great to finally get it in the bag. We also climbed *The Madness of Crowds* (VII,7), the steep corner system to the right of *South Sea Bubble*. During the Winter Meet, American climber Kelly Cordes and I headed up to The Castle to try the ominous looking hanging chimney that slices through the headwall. This is a prominent line, but it is so steep that it rarely catches much snow. Conditions were perfect, and after I had grunted up the first difficult section, I was treated to a virtuoso performance by Kelly as he stemmed up the overhanging second pitch. Kelly was so enthralled by the climbing that he grabbed the third pitch as well, and on top he enthused that this one route *(Godspell* VII,8) had more than justified his trip over from the US.

After a major thaw that stripped the Highlands bare in mid-March, most winter climbers put their tools away for the season. Typically, the 'lambing snows' arrive in early April, and this year was no exception with heavy snowfalls and very cold temperatures in the middle of the month.

Iain Small and I went up to the Ben to have a look and were surprised to see the mountain covered in fresh powder and hoar. South Trident Buttress looked like a Christmas cake, so we seized our chance and made the first winter ascent of *Sidewinder* (VII,8) the prominent groove line left of *Strident Edge*. We were happy to hang our tools up after this, but the following Saturday conditions were good as well. Gareth Hughes and Tony Stone climbed *Thompson's Route* on No. 3 Gully Buttress, continued up the deep, right-facing corner above to give a fine VII,7 direct finish, and on Stob Coire an Laoigh in the Grey Corries Andy Nisbet slipped in a final new route with Sandy Allan. *Pentagon* (VI,7) takes a steep line up the wall which forms the left side of the rib left of *Taliballan*, and draws a line under what has been a very eventful and fascinating winter season.

Simon Richardson.

100 YEARS AGO. . .

The year began with the Annual Meeting and Dinner in the Caledonian Hotel, Edinburgh on Friday, December 2,1904. President William C. Smith was in the Chair but gave way on the following day to John Rennie, of Wellcroft, Helensburgh; Treasurer Robert Napier reported a balance of £190 13s. 9d.; Secretary Inglis Clark announced nine new members, two deaths and three resignations – a balance of 156 members; and Librarian Goggs (430) and Slide Custodian Robertson (990) enumerated their treasures. Fifty-six members and 23 guests then enjoyed a French menu of oysters, soup, turbot or whitebait, sweetbreads, haggis, roast meat, pheasant, fruit, ice-cream, pastry, and dessert – two courses better than the short commons served up in Glasgow in 1903.

New Year was celebrated at the Loch Awe Hotel, and a muster of 28 suffered dull unseasonable weather for four days. There was no snow below 3000ft. On the 31st, parties climbed the North Face of Stob Dearg from Glen Noe, the Black Shoot of Beinn Eunaich, and had "some fine climbing on the cliff of Stob Garbh from Coire Creachainn" – probably the North-East ridge. At the end of the Meet Morrison, Robertson and Goodeve climbed the central chimney of Meall Bhuiridh, which had defied attempts made at previous Meets here.

In March, the Clark family began a series of visits to the 'Arrochar Alps' with a failed attempt on Elephant Gully of the Brack, returning on July 14, to climb 'Knife-Edge Route' (now Inglis Clark Arête – wrongly dated as 1895 in our guidebook). In April, they explored the cliffs of A' Chrois, climbing half of a ridge left of the Central Gully before finishing by the Gully. A week later they returned with the Walker cousins to climb Pinnacle Buttress (all six on one rope). Later, on May 23, Raeburn and Goggs climbed the Central Buttress (again wrongly dated as 1895). These explorations were amusingly described by Clark in two articles (viii, 309-12 and ix, 19-24)

The Easter Meet (April 20-25) was split between Skye and Kingshouse. On Skye, Secretary Clark had once again arranged a rotating Meet involving hot beds in Sligachan, Camasunary and Glen Brittle, as in 1903. But despite Easter falling a month later, the 19 members and five guests attending once again found the Cuillin in wintry condition and little new climbing was achieved. However, Raeburn and his Swedish guest, Erik Ullén, together with Slingsby and Solly climbed the Central Buttress of the Castles *en route* to Camasunary. This was the first route on this huge face, selected since it was "sheltered from the fierce north-west blizzard which blew all day", and it involved heroic efforts of route-finding in ascent and descent. The party first attempted the South-Central Gully, failing at a huge overhanging pitch. Resuming from the foot of the rocks at 11.40, they made their way up the 1500ft. Central Buttress in under five hours, Raeburn leading the difficult sections in his cloth-soled Kletterschuh. The descent was accomplished by glissading the gully between the Castles and Sgurr na Bhairnich to a point "just before it takes its great plunge down the lower precipices". Then a short wall was climbed to reach Lota Corrie which was traversed to the descent route under Sgurr na h-Uamha. After this, all they had to do was the six-mile route march to Camasunary! This must surely have been one of the most remarkable expeditions in the history of Scottish mountaineering.

On the following day Raeburn and Ullén enjoyed a wintry traverse from Camasunary to Glen Brittle including Garsbheinn to Sgumain *via* the Thearlaich-Dubh Gap. This obstacle "did not look an inviting spot under present conditions.

It was now snowing very heavily – soft, sticky, large flakes that drove levelly through the cleft, and quickly plastered even vertical rocks with white. It stuck also on our faces, filled up our eyes and ears, and drifted into our mouths whenever we ventured to open them. It was especially annoying to Herr Ullén, who is unfortunately obliged to wear spectacles when climbing".

Despite these difficulties, and a stuck abseil rope, the Gap was crossed in 30 minutes, Raeburn climbing the Thearlaich side in gloves. Raeburn observed dryly that: "Arguing from this, ten minutes would be sufficient for a solitary climber, for the delay incidental to the use of the rope would then be eliminated." Although Ullén participated in these exacting expeditions and others, and enjoyed sponsorship by Raeburn, his subsequent application to join the Club was mysteriously unsuccessful. Maylard and Solly traversed Sgumain and the Dubhs at the end of the Meet, failing on the vicious Alasdair *mauvais pas*, an exploit celebrated in the famous poem *Doing the Dubhs,* probably from the pen of Douglas. Two excellent Journal articles by Maylard (viii, 299-303) and Raeburn (ix, 59-70), and a note by Raeburn (ix, 101-2) describe these events.

Eleven members and four guests gathered at the Kingshouse branch of the Meet. No new climbs were achieved, but there was thorough exploration of the Crowberry Ridge and North Buttress. Maclay's article (viii,304-8) set out the topography of the Ridge clearly for the first time. James Gall Inglis recorded the Meet in an excellent (unpublished) photograph.

In May Douglas and Raeburn explored the Berwickshire coast from White Heugh to Fast Castle. Raeburn climbed The Stack (below St Abb's Head) but judged that the Souter was "quite inaccessible" (not climbed until 1967 – by myself and Dave Bathgate). Douglas provided an interesting list of cliffs and stacks in his article (viii, 313-19) as well as alluding to earlier ascents by 'egging' local fishermen described by George Muirhead in his book *Birds of Berwickshire.*

Many members visited the Alps in what was a very poor season and some enjoyed a worse season in Norway. The only expeditions of note were made by Raeburn and Ling, who climbed the North-East ridge of the Ecrins, before moving to Chamonix where they managed the Petit Dru from the Charpoua (bivouac at 11,000ft.) and a solo traverse of the pinnacles of the Charmoz (including the Bâton Wicks) by Raeburn.

In late July two parties (Gibbs and Mounsey in BR 68; A. E. Robertson, Mrs Robertson, Goggs, Morrison and Miss MacDonald – on bicycles) met in Glen Coe and passed a few nights in the Kingshouse Inn. This informal Meet was well described by Gibbs (ix, 9-18), and comprehensively recorded by Robertson's camera. The Church Door Buttress was climbed twice, once by Morrison and Gibbs, and then a few days later by the entire male element of the party. Both ascents involved poorly described variants of the existing route. On the second, Morrison – very much the guiding light of the party – chose a subterranean route: "[Observing] some jammed stones offering a route directly upwards from the middle of this letter-box; wishing, however, to see more of the world, he went right through to the other end of the crack, and, climbing over the jammed blocks, landed on the top. . .The 'Meenister' would have photographed parts of the climb had not the rainclouds descending on the hills not made good work impossible, not to mention the difficulty of getting baggage through the first section – the service as yet not being open for Parcels Post – and with five climbers on 160ft. of rope, there was none to spare for hauling; so the 'bagpipes' – as the camera in a sack with short legs protruding was nicknamed – had to be left at the foot of the rocks."

Haskett Smith and William Garden.

Eric Greenwood and William Douglas.

This comical ascent sounds very like the line of the 1920 Crypt Route, but may be a similar feature lower down the buttress. Elsewhere, two separate attempts were made by Morrison and Gibbs on Abraham's Traverse. Morrison eventually climbed it on a top rope, describing it as "boulder climbing without the slightest possibility of safeguarding the leader after the first few feet". In Robertson's well-known photograph (ix, opp.1) Goggs is shown 'safeguarding' Morrison with a terrifying direct belay. Finally, Goggs and Morrison spent a day exploring the accessible parts of the Dalness Chasm and the rocks above it.

Besides the articles referred to above, the *Journals* for the year published guidebook articles for most of the Western Highlands ranges, and a long and thoughtful piece by Raeburn, *Scottish Snow* (ix, 285-98). Here Raeburn reviews with great care and detail the varieties of snow and ice found and of features such as cornices and avalanches, noting several formidable instances of the latter. He also makes many technical observations about climbing, glissading, ski-ing, etc. His concluding remarks perhaps deserve quotation: "The cultivation of cocoanut-like biceps by any of the modern methods of muscle-growing may possibly be of some use to climbers. But man after all is not a monkey, and if an army may be said to travel upon its stomach, the mountaineer travels, even though the angle approach 80°, mainly by means of his feet. It is to the education of the feet therefore, and incidentally, of course, to the education of hand and eye and brain, that mountaineers should devote their attention. There is no better field for this education, apart altogether from the aesthetic joys to be obtained, than our Scottish Bens in their wintry garb of snow."

The Journal also included obituaries of Joseph Collier and Alfred Williams. Collier, who died aged 50, took part in the well-known tour of Glen Coe and Ben Nevis with Collie, Hastings and Solly, which followed the 1894 Inveroran Easter Meet and culminated in the ascents of Tower Ridge. It was these expeditions, of course, which showed the natives what might be achieved here, and galvanized Naismith, Brown, Tough, etc. into more adventurous climbing. Alfred Williams, the Salisbury artist, was a regular visitor to Skye where he established summer painting camps in Coruisk with his son, Sidney: it is curious that despite these frequent visits, no paintings by Williams of Skye seem to be known.

Robin N. Campbell.

CLIMBING AND COURTING IN NORWAY, 1907.

GIVEN both the scarcity and expense of early climbing literature and ephemera, it was doubly pleasing to recently receive the gift of a photographic album recording a 28-day climbing expedition to Norway entitled, *Norway 1907, August*. The album is large, containing more than 180 black-and-white and sepia-style prints, a few postcards and a small map which appears to have been torn out of a local tourist guide.

Unfortunately, the map is not sufficiently detailed for someone unfamiliar with the country and its mountains to track the expedition route. Some of the prints have pencil captions, and there is a 28-day itinerary, however the handwriting is hard to decipher. This said, the overall effect is highly pleasing and very evocative of that period in climbing, and how one imagines alpine

The Kingshouse Meet, Easter 1905: From left: Walter Nelson, William. Newbigging, Gilbert Thomson, ?, James Maclay, Wm. Morrison, ?, ?, John Grove, ? . Photo: Club collection – James Gall Inglis

The informal Kingshouse Meet, July 1905: From left: George Gibbs, William. Morrison, Miss Macdonald, Kate Robertson, Frank Goggs, Wilfred Mounsey, Archie Robertson. Photo: A. E. Robertson collection

Norway must have been at the time. Tweed jackets and breeches; trilby hats, shirts and, of course, ties; and coiled chest-borne ropes which resemble a doubtful liaison between a clothes line and a MacBrayne' s hawser! Turf-roofed shielings; four-storey, timber clad alpine lodges; a sprinkling of goats; and white-shirted and waistcoated (but tie-less) boatmen in elegant, clinker skiffs complete the picture – almost. For there are also a few group shots of young British and Norwegian ladies early in the album who, as the photographic record unfolds, are soon 'integrated' within the main body of the kirk. One in particular – Phyllis Procter – is never far from the side of one William Douglas (second editor of the Journal). Holiday romance? Or the start of something more permanent? Noting frequent photographs of William Garden and W. P. (Walter Parry) Haskett Smith – he of the first climbing guide to England, Wales and Ireland, with H. C. Hart – in addition to Douglas, I felt that further research might reveal what expedition this was, and where the album had come from.

The album's donor confirmed that Procter and Douglas did marry, with Douglas running a publishing and bookselling business in Castle Street, Edinburgh (Douglas & Foulis). They had two sons, one becoming a London-based impresario. The business closed in the late Sixties, and I understand that two relations (grandchildren?) still live in the Edinburgh area. The donor rescued the album from the fate of the dreaded skip when a friend of the Douglas family was clearing her office upon retirement.

Knowing a little about Douglas and Garden, I then contacted Robin Campbell who kindly supplied the missing links, in the form of an extract from SMCJ vol. X, 1908-9, as follows:

"Mr. Garden, Mr. Douglas, and four friends of the Alpine Club were in Norway in August, when they were favoured with such inclement weather as to put all the rock-climbs of the Horungtinder out of the question. They, however, crossed the Rungs Skar from Vetti to Turtego, and ascended to Dyrhougstinder twice. They also crossed the Justedalsbrae from Fjaerland to Aamot via the Fonsdal, and returned to Fjaerland via Skei, Lunde and the Lunde Skar. The whole party were delighted with Norway, and Turtegro will ever remain in the memory of one, if not in the minds of all, as the most charming spot in the whole world."

As Turtegro was the party's main base, we can assume that the "memory of one" must be that of Douglas, albeit suitably couched in the reserve of the time.

The album is now on permanent loan to friends who are trying to map out the expedition in greater detail, with a view to perhaps visiting the areas involved at some future date.

Ian Hamilton.

Postscript:

A few weeks after receiving the album, my benefactor called to ask if I would like to see a handwritten log of a 'canoe' voyage on the rivers and canals of the English midlands, by one J. G. Stott, dated 1891. He had rescued the log at the same time as the Norwegian album, but knew nothing of the author. Excited at the prospect of photographs of a contemporary canoe, which I thought would be of the classic, beautiful 'Rob Roy' class, I borrowed the album. Sadly, the 'canoe' was actually a double rowing skiff, and the log a somewhat repetitive account of subsequent nights at river/canal side pubs with good beers, but predictable ham and eggs as the main fayre.

A further call to Robin brought confirmation that the skipper would have been Joseph Stott, first editor of the Journal. Given that Stott left Scotland for New Zealand in 1892, the log is probably a record of his last holiday in the UK, and he must have passed it over to Douglas before leaving. On Robin's advice, I advised the donor that most of Stott's papers are lodged with the National Library of Scotland. The log has since been purchased by the Library. I. H.

SCOTTISH MOUNTAINEERING TRUST – 2004-2005

THE Trustees met on August 13 and October 8, 2004.

During the course of these meetings support was given to Miss K. Scott BSES – 2004; British Trust for Ornithology; the Cairngorm Club, (Hut at Muir of Inverey); JMCS Jock Spots, and Andrew Nisbet, New Routes Editor.

Ken Crocket (Chairman) and Matt Shaw retired as Trustees by rotation. The contributions of Ken Crocket and Matt Shaw are much appreciated. In particular, the Trustees are grateful to Ken Crocket for the initiatives he proposed during his period as Chairman, including the Scottish Mountaineering Trust leaflet (which is now available) and joining Scottish Environment Link. The Trust hopes to have an ongoing contact with Ken Crocket in his capacity as the SMC Webmaster.

The present directors of the Publications Co. are R. K. Bott (Chairman), K. V. Crockett, W. C. Runciman, M. G. D. Shaw and T. Prentice (Publications Manager).

The present Trustees are P. MacDonald (Chairman), R. W. Milne, C. J. Orr, W. C. Runciman, A. Tibbs, R. J. Archbold, D. A. Bearhop, D. J. Broadhead, C. M. Huntley and A. C. Stead. W. C. Runciman is both a Trustee and Director and provides liason between the Publication Co. and the Trust. J. Morton Shaw is the Trust Treasurer.

The following grants have been committed by the Trustees:

General Grant Fund

Miss K. Scott BSES – 2004	£250
British Trust for Ornithology	£5000
Cairngorm Club (Hut at Muir of Inverey)	£5000
Grant	£5000
Loan	£5000
JMCS Jock Spots	
Grant	£3800
Loan	
New Routes Editor	£300

Seventy-five Years of the Perth Mountaineering Club

This article is based on an address given at the Seventy-fifth Anniversary Dinner of the Perth Mountaineering Club, held at Mar Lodge on Saturday, November 20, 2004.

Beginnings:
Given the location and proximity to the Highland Line, it is not surprising that there is a long tradition of going to the hills among the folk of Perth and district. The first local organisation dedicated to climbing mountains was the Perthshire Mountain Club, the proceedings of which are recorded from 1875 onwards.[1] This club was a sub-group of the Perthshire Society for Natural Science, an organisation which still flourishes. It is not clear when the Mountain Club ceased to be active, but it was certainly moribund before the First World War. The present Perth Mountaineering Club has no formal links with the PSNS, but the two come together for an annual joint lecture which always has a mountaineering theme.

It appears that after the First World War the SMC was seeking to augment its own membership by establishing branches of the JMCS as 'feeder' clubs. Alistair Cram, a lawyer in Perth, was originally a member of the Edinburgh Section of the JMCS and, as he was the first secretary of the Perth Section, it may be assumed that he was among the principal movers to establish a section in Perth. This took place in 1929. It would, however, be unfair to think that the formation of the Perth JMCS was purely the result of a missionary campaign by the SMC. It may be assumed that there existed in Perth a body of mountaineers who recognised the benefits of sharing and augmenting their mountain skills by forming a club. A club would also, for some, solve the perennial problem of transport to the hills. One notes that all the pre-war meets were by car which says something of the socio-economic status of members, all of whom were male.

As well as being a founder member, Alistair Cram was certainly one of the club's most distinguished members. In addition to notable legal and military careers, in 1939 he became the eighth person to complete the Munros and tops. Then in 1978, along with his wife, he completed a second round of the Munros and tops. But he was not just a hill walker, he had at least one Alpine season before the war and was a mountaineer of sufficient calibre to be considered for membership of the 1953 Everest Expedition. Until his death he was a regular contributor to the 'SMC and JMCS Abroad' section of the SMC Journal, giving details of the trips he and his wife took to many mountainous areas of the world. He attended only one post-war meet of the Perth Club.

Another founder member was Jimmy MacNab. Among MacNab's claims to fame is that he took his Sunday suit and bowler hat on a CIC hut meet so that he would be suitably attired to attend the Kirk service in Fort William on the Sunday. It is not known if MacNab ever repeated this epic, but it seems certain that it is unique to him. The longest-lived of the founder members was Chris Rudie, who died in 1999. He was born in Norway and, unsurprisingly, was particularly involved with skiing and the Dundee Ski Club. Nonetheless, he was active on the hills as a climber and was Hon. President for many years. No one who heard Chris's after-dinner speeches will ever forget their inconsequential, but highly amusing content.

We do not, unfortunately, know a great deal of how these pioneers disported themselves on the Scottish mountains. By modern standards their clothing and gear were primitive, but this does not appear to have curtailed their activities in any way and they were enthusiastically active throughout the year. If nothing else, one can look on the same hills and glens and without difficulty understand why they were attracted to these places.

Post-War:
The first post-war meet took place on November 24, 1946, to Ardvorlich on Loch Earn. This was a bus meet and it was the bus meet that was to characterise the next phase of the club's history. To those who experienced these times it was a 'Golden Age', a special time of primitive equipment, primitive transport, boundless enthusiasm and boundless opportunity. Some pre-war members rejoined at this time, notably Jimmy Grant, Tom Kemp and Walter Pethers, but most post-war members were new to the club. A considerable innovation was the 'lady associate'. These ladies soon made up a significant proportion of the 30-odd who filled Sandy Cameron's bus once a month. To be accurate, Sandy's bus was not the first transport to be used. Tom Kemp was loaned a vehicle by the Bankfoot Motor Co. which he then drove to and from the meet venues, enjoying a day on the hill between bouts of driving. This particular bus was of the war-time utility variety with wooden seats. Imagine travelling from Perth to Glencoe and back on wooden seats – and Tom Kemp *never* exceeded 30 mph! Sandy Cameron's bus, being of pre-war vintage, had the luxury of upholstered seating – no heating of course, but there were travelling rugs provided.

For many, mountaineering in these days consisted of the brief spells of intense activity when one managed to get to the hills. And once there one did not waste the time, but set out, no matter what the weather. In Robin Campbell's words: "These were the days when men were men and a wet day was three Munros.'

Meets were anywhere within a day's bus journey from Perth: Glencoe, Lochnagar, Creag Meaghaidh, Glen Clova and, of course, all the Perthshire hills. Jimmy Grant was the secretary and ran the club virtually single-handed. John Proom was the rock climber *extraordinaire,* but he always had time to take some novice in hand and haul them up their first rock climb. Another interesting character was James Miller who in these days was coming to end of a climbing career which stretched back to the First World War. Among many exploits he had stayed at Maggie Gruer's cottage at Inverey, the legendary lodging for climbers on their way to or from the Cairngorms. James Miller was a tailor and cutter to trade and he wore a very smart pair of breeches of his own design.

It is impossible to do more than mention a very few of the characters and events which epitomise this time. There was Fred Barclay who had been in the RAF Mountain Rescue Team at Kinloss and who, at the end of the day, didn't believe in changing out of wet clothes. Helen Taylor, also known as Little Nell, who drove over the Alpine passes to the Dolomites and back in her bubble car. Nan Miller who became the fifth lady to complete the Munros and then went and married the Town Clerk of Milngavie.

A tradition of the club, established in these days – was that of compleating a round of the Munros. Of the first 100 Munroists, eight were associated in some way with the Perth Club. If the same proportion had been maintained, the Perth Club would now have, at least, 256 members, all of whom would be Munroists!

It was during this period, in 1954, that the club celebrated its Silver Jubilee. A dinner was held at the old Spittal of Glenshee Hotel during the Presidency of John Webster. At the 75th Anniversary Dinner at Mar Lodge in November 2004, there were three members present who had attended the Silver Jubilee Dinner: Nan Rae, Ronnie Rae and Bob Milne. Two others present, John Watt and Iain Robertson would have attended in 1954 had they not been doing their National Service.

If, during this time members had been asked to choose their favourite meet venue, it would almost certainly have been Derry Lodge. As near to the heart of the Cairngorms as one could get by car – and you could drive to Derry Lodge in these days – Derry meets were different in that the club went for the full weekend. From there parties roamed far and wide over the high tops, returning in the evening to a log fire in the lounge and an evening of songs and stories. The best stories were those told by Bob Scott who was resident stalker at Luibeg cottage and who always called by.

The coming of affluence:
Bus meets ceased to be viable in the late 1960s and then began the third and longest phase in the club's history; a phase which is coming or has come to an end. Perhaps the most significant change, after much discussion and wrangling with the other JMCS Sections, was the admission of ladies to full and unrestricted membership of the club. The Perth JMCS also decided at this time take a new name and became the Perth Mountaineering Club, though both titles still appear on the letterhead. At the time of the 75th Anniversary Dinner the club had a female President, a female secretary, a female treasurer, a female meets secretary and sundry female committee members, which suggests that the ladies are fully involved in club affairs. Since the 1960s the trend in Scottish mountaineering towards specialisation has continued, with the mountaineering scene being sub-divided into rock climbers, snow and ice climbers, Munro baggers, etc. The PMC has members who excel in all of these categories and remains a broad church and a home for anyone wishing to go to the hills in pursuit of whatever interest.

With regard to transport, events have moved full-circle and there has been no bus meet for twenty-five years. To start with there was considerable car sharing as there were still members without personal transport, but that is largely gone and most choose to travel independently. At the start of this phase too there was also considerable reliance on access to club huts, and this was a reason for joining a club. But with the growth of independent hostels and better camping gear, club huts have become less significant as a means of staying in the more remote areas, though the PMC continue to make good use of them.

Another development has been the number of members climbing abroad. This has not been directly under the auspices of the PMC which has only had one foreign meet, and that to France.   But members have travelled far and wide and, apart from Antarctica, there is not a continent where club members have not climbed.

So has the third phase ended? Members can find their own transport, can get around without using club huts and because of flexible working hours do not necessarily climb at the weekends. Does this make clubs such as the PMC redundant?

Two reasons suggest that this is not the case.   The first concerns changes which are as yet potential, but which may become of increasing importance. In spite of what politicians say, in all aspects of life we are subject to increasing regulation. Thus club membership may become a means through which we can seek protection from encroachment by legislation and/or those who would manipulate the State against minority interests. For example, the recent Access Legislation has resulted in the formation of Local Access Committees. The PMC is ably represented by Ron Payne on the committee which is responsible for advising on access in Perth and Kinross; but if access now requires a committee, what else might be regulated?

A pessimist might envisage the future requirements of the Health and Safety Gestapo as follows.

Quote: "That hill-going persons within categories a) to f), but not including those holding Alpine Experience Exemption Certificates, Class III, be excluded from ascending above 400m south of the Caledonian Canal or 350m north of the Caledonian Canal, during the months November to March, except when a weather forecast for 48 hours or longer states that wind strengths and ambient temperatures are with within the guidelines laid down by the First Minister's Advisory Committee on Embroidery and Mountaineering" and so on.

It is to be hoped that such a nightmare will be avoided, but the climbing fraternity should be vigilant. Club membership and membership of organisations such as the MC of S become important if climbers have to fight to maintain a congenial milieu in which to pursue their sport.

The second reason for the continuance of clubs such as the PMC is the more significant.   Mountaineering clubs are not just a means to access transport, or huts or any other of the many conveniences they provide. Mountaineers are a wonderfully idiosyncratic bunch and the PMC is no exception. But throughout the last 75 years it has been plain to any observer that the club represented an entity which was greater than the sum of its parts. Members have clearly demonstrated that, whatever their reasons for being drawn to the mountains, membership of the PMC has heightened their enjoyment of them. Solitary mountaineering undoubtedly intensifies the mountain experience and many have enjoyed the hills in solitude. But most have also been members of a group which exulted in a shared experience, whether it was two or three on a rope or rather more striding over moors, along ridges or hunkered down in the lea of a cairn. Moreover, it is always more comforting to say: "Where the hell are we?" than mutter: "Where the hell am I?"

The companionship of the hills is something special. It goes beyond a mere shared interest or being in company with the like-minded.   Mountaineering takes place out of doors in places which are among those least subject to human intrusion. In such an untrammelled environment, often hostile or threatening, often breathtakingly beautiful, we are perhaps more able to know each other, warts and all, to a deeper level than is usually the case. And friendships are the better for it.

The club motto is *Ascendite ascendentes* which has never been adequately translated – 'get up them stairs' will not do. A more appropriate motto for Perth climbers might be the quotation from James Elroy Flecker's, *The Golden Road,* which was adopted by the late Alastair Borthwick for his most excellent book,

We are the Pilgrims, master; we shall go – Always a little further.

Iain A. Robertson.

[1] See J.H.B. Bell in *SMCJ,* xxiii, p 308; also R. N. Campbell in PMC, *Millennium Journal,* p 19.

Virtual Adventure

The death a few years back of former *Scotsman* editor Sir Alistair Dunnett brought me to read his wonderful book *Quest By Canoe* written in 1951 (recently republished as *The Canoe Boys*) and referred to in an appreciation of his life by his partner in this adventure James (Seamus) Adam. The book describes in a wonderfully easy prose style a true seat of the pants, taste it and see, adventure, involving these two young men purchasing canoes of questionable seaworthiness, and setting off on a trip round the often hostile water of the Western Isles of Scotland.

"Any sort of sea would constantly search its way through the deck lacing, while we were to know many an occasion when it would break solidly into the cockpit itself." – *Quest by Canoe.*

It is just this type of adventure and exploration of both landscape, and perhaps more importantly, of self, that is increasingly denied the youth of today. Denied in the name of safety, of prudence and the perceived need to worship at the altar of an ever burgeoning, cossetting and costly 'outdoor industry'. An 'industry' which would have you believe that those of us who have an aversion to throwing money into its coffers and being certified by its courses, should stick very much to the well walked paths of life.

When Alistair and his pal were doing their thing, I would imagine they would look at a map, decide whether or not they should take a raincoat, and off they would go. OK perhaps I exaggerate, (slightly!) but you can bet your bottom dollar that there weren't 20 or so glossy Outdoor Monthly Mags telling them that to have any chance of success would entail expenditure which, in present day terms, would probably have been enough to buy them a small house. Neither would they be burdened with the extra cost and worry over which of the hundreds of canoe courses they would have to go on, without which, is now deemed to make close acquaintance with the grim reaper almost inevitable.

"We had never seen canoes at close quarters until a few weeks previously, and our only experience of handling them had been on a recent Sunday afternoon on the Forth and Clyde Canal." – *Quest by Canoe.*

We now live in a culture where the vast majority of people would never consider taking a physical risk of any sort and the small minority who do, want to do so in safety. Bit of a paradox that, oxymoron even, a 'safe risk', no such beast I think. And herein lies the problem.

Let's move for the moment from the sandy blue inlets of the west coast to the mountains of Glencoe. Here, duly kitted out in your latest Gore-Tex 'must haves' as advertised in 'Ever Decreasing Outdoors' monthly, you sign up for a winter mountaineering course and by the end of the week, courtesy of a large dent in your Visa Card, superb weather and the company of two radio controlled guides to provide a psychological safety net, you and your girlfriend/boyfriend/partner have climbed Crowberry Gully a 1000ft. ice-climbing test piece on Buachaille Etive Mor. After returning to your jobs in the city, your new found ability, coupled with a high disposable income, makes you an easy target for an advert in yet another glossy and before you know it you have 'climbed' to the summit of Mont Blanc in the company of 20 or 30 other 'out on the edge' types roped to some grumpy French guides on a percentage from the travel company. (If you have a spare 20 grand they'll take you up Everest apparently). Finance, or to be more precise, lack of it, was not such a problem for the 'Canoe Boys'. "Here we were now, afloat, and our total cash amounted to four shillings and sevenpence." *Quest by Canoe.* I don't think that this sanitised, plastic, and apparently safe 'adventure' (what happens when you've done the courses and the guides aren't there and the weather's not quite like the brochures) quite fits in with Sir Alistair's ethos. It may go some way to exploring the physical landscape, albeit in a perfunctory manner, but as far as journeying through that all important 'inner landscape', it doesn't even begin to scratch the surface.

'Our steel has rusted in the night,
We fail unless we make it good.
Seek increase of our little might,
And gather up our hardihood.'
– *Quest by Canoe.*

Anyone fancy a 'virtual reality' canoe trip round the Western Isles? **CJO@ARMCHAIR.ADV.CO.UK**

MUNRO MATTERS

By David Kirk (Clerk of the List)

With a further 217 names added to the List between April 1, 2004 and March 31, 2005, I have not had to worry too much about lack of material to use for this year's report. Again I must thank all the people who wrote to me. The List of this year's Compleationists are as follows. As before, the first five columns are number, name, then Munro, Top and Furth Compleation years.

3120	William John McAllan	2004			3167	James Philip Higginson	2004
3121	Jane Wilmot-Smith	2004			3168	Jillian Karima Higginson	2004
3122	Chris Jones	2004			3169	Mike Atherton	2004
3123	Steven Kirk	1996			3170	Trevor W. Mitton	2004
3124	George Pumffrey	2004			3171	Duncan Stirling	2004
3125	Ann Macleod	2003			3172	John Forester Thom	2003
3126	Keith Millar	2003	2003	2004	3173	Julian Kirk	2004
3127	Peter Collins	1996			3174	Ian Hamilton Rodney	2004
3128	Anthony Lang	2004			3175	Mike Elrick	2004
3129	Richard E. P. Spencer	2004			3176	Graham Pascall	2004
3130	Neil Henderson	2004			3177	Dave Crosher	2004
3131	Duncan J. MacPherson	2003			3178	Bruce S. Davidson	2004
3132	Nicholas J. L. Gardener	2004		2004	3179	Mike Knox	2004 2004
3133	Jenny Lingenhult	2004			3180	Robert Sleight	2004
3134	Steve Coutts	2004			3181	Pauline Sleight	2004
3135	Margaret Tees	2004			3182	Jon G. Moss	2004
3136	Richard Speirs	2004	2004	2002	3183	Barry Smith	2004
3137	R. Lazenby	2004			3184	Nancy C. Cox	2004
3138	Chris Dobson	2002			3185	Jeffrey J. Cox	2004
3139	Alan J. Winchester	2004			3186	Jan Crawshaw	2004
3140	Mark W. Phillips	2004			3187	Alison Philip	2004 2004
3141	Peter D. Cottam	2004			3188	Bill Strang	2004 2004
3142	Steve Chambers	1994	1995		3189	Nigel Horsfield	2004
3143	Michael Pearce	2004			3190	Alistair Drummond	2004
3144	Kathryn J. Osborne	2004			3191	Stewart Byrne	2004
3145	Rodger W. Osborne	2004			3192	Gregor Yates	2004
3146	Adrian R. Proctor	2001			3193	Elaine Anderson	2004
3147	Rosalyn Clancey	2004			3194	Gail Crawford	2004
3148	William Rawles	2004			3195	Richard Tait	2004
3149	John Smith	2004			3196	Jim Wallace	2004
3150	Marion Smith	2004			3197	Margaret F. H. Hodge	2004
3151	Eric Grant	2004			3198	Michael Cates	2004
3152	Roger Gregory	2003	2004		3199	Jane Rendall	2004
3153	Ewan Grant Finlay	2004			3200	Adam Middleton	2004
3154	Di Hollow	2004			3201	W. Keith Hamflett	2004
3155	William Casey	2004	2004	1998	3202	A. Fiona D. Mackenzie	2004
3156	Jonquil Mary Boyd	2004			3203	John Anderson	2004
3157	Stuart Boyd	1997			3204	Margaret Roberts	2004
3158	David A. Bunting	2004			3205	Avril Hedges	2004
3159	Chris Wilson	2004			3206	Wilma Tully	2004
3160	David Bridges	2004			3207	Allan Gibson	2004
3161	Barry Arthur	2004			3208	Colin Robertson	2004
3162	Margaret Parker	2004			3209	Glenda Robertson	2004
3163	Neil Willcox	2004			3210	Robert F. Waterston	2004
3164	Brian N. Jones	2004			3211	Margaret Squires	2004
3165	Andrew Joynson	2004			3212	Derek Robertson	2004
3166	Roger Chappell	2004			3213	Charles Murray	2004

3214	Allan Adam	2004	
3215	William John Robinson	2004	
3216	David K. Lygate	2004	
3217	Kenneth Ratcliffe	2004	
3218	Margaret A. Minards	2004	
3219	Willy Slavin	2004	
3220	Mike Carter	2004	2004
3221	Derek Jewell	2004	
3222	Craig Robertson	2004	
3223	Guy Dewhirst	2004	
3224	Mike Dennis	2004	
3225	Liz Baran	2004	
3226	Timothy Chappell	2004	
3227	Gordon Hendry	2004	
3228	James Overstone	2004	
3229	Rosemary Bailey	2004	
3230	Mark Whitehouse	2004	
3231	Tim Brett	2004	
3232	Dougal Drysdale	2001	
3233	Irene Macgregor	2004	
3234	Stephen Hunt	2003	2002
3235	Alan Adrian	2004	
3236	Senga Adrian	2004	
3237	Steven A Elliot	2004	
3238	Michael Hetherington	2004	
3239	Helena Brigginshaw	2004	
3240	John M. Foster	2004	
3241	Andy Pearson	2004	
3242	George Henry Shearer	2004	
3243	Simon Grove	2004	
3244	Wilhelm Schroder	2002	
3245	Peter Stewart	2003	
3246	George Ferguson	2004	
3247	Roderick J. B. Rhodes	2004	
3248	Alison Fox	2004	
3249	Carmel Smith	2004	
3250	Ian Smith	2004	
3251	John A. Strain	2004	
3252	Tony Wilcox	2004	
3253	Keith Jackson	2004	
3254	Brian Lee	2004	
3255	Colin Marsh	2004	
3256	Bob Allison	2004	
3257	Roger Greeves	2004	
3258	Alan R. Binns	2004	
3259	Alison Smith	2004	
3260	Jean Cowan	2004	
3261	Chris Ottley	2003	
3262	David Law	2004	
3263	Eddie Wilkinson	2004	
3264	Jeanie Clabbie	2004	
3265	Peter Wilson	2004	
3266	Gerry McKenna	2004	
3267	Susan Davidson	2004	
3268	Tony Viveash	2004	
3269	Peter John Robertson	2004	
3270	Vincent Conlon	2004	
3271	Kevin Murray	2004	
3272	I. S. Halliburton	2004	
3273	Jim Hewson	2004	
3274	Harvie W. Brown	2004	
3275	John Higgins	2004	
3276	Ann Aitken	2004	
3277	Elaine Swain	2004	
3278	Les McPhail	2003	
3279	John Millar	2004	
3280	Dr. M.E. Buchanan	2004	
3281	Muriel Thomson	2004	
3282	Ray Thompson	2004	
3283	Paul Conroy	2004	
3284	Chris Ridgeway	2004	
3285	Lindsey Ridgeway	2004	
3286	Bill Roberts	2004	
3287	Marion Craig	2004	2004
3288	Duncan Craig	2004	2004
3289	Robert J. Kinnaird	2004	
3290	Judith K. Scott	2004	
3291	Donald P. Morrison	2004	
3292	Donald Malone	2004	
3293	Paul Ormerod	2004	2004
3294	Philip J. Taylor	2004	
3295	Colin Young	2004	
3296	Colin Lesenger	2004	
3297	Emma O' Shea	2004	
3298	Manuel Lapp	2004	
3299	Martin Snijders	2004	
3300	Gordon Scott	2004	
3301	Reg Willis	2004	
3302	Martin Dey	2004	
3303	Neil Campbell	2003	
3304	Francis Kelly	2003	
3305	Janet Pitt Lewis	2004	
3306	Clive Smith	2004	
3307	Neil Thompson	2004	
3308	Phil Lancasterm	2004	
3309	Paul Myers	2004	
3310	Dennis MacGillivray	2004	
3311	Alexander D. Spalding	2004	
3312	Jane O Dochartaigh	2004	
3313	Paul King	2004	
3314	John Albiston	2004	
3315	Stuart Malpas	2004	
3316	Ian Maitland	2004	
3317	Adele Struthers	2004	
3318	Crawford Cumming	2004	
3319	Brian Billington	2004	
3320	Alistair Morrison	2004	
3321	Karen Parker	2004	
3322	Derel Capper	2004	
3323	Janet Capper	2004	
3324	Martin Tull	2004	
3325	Stan Work	2004	
3326	Robert W. Kerr	2004	
3327	Mike Nieman	2004	

SCOTTISH MOUNTAINEERING CLUB JOURNAL

204

3328	Dave Bonnett	1999
3329	Morna Forrester	2004
3330	Simon Mills	2004
3331	Douglas Wilson	2004
3332	Rob M. Speed	2004

3333	Martin Banfield	2004
3334	John C. Calder	2004
3335	Robert O. Duncan	1999
3336	Niall R. Duncan	2001

One of those unusual coincidences occurred on Sgor na Ulaidh on April 24, last year. Chris Dobson (3138), having left his wife lower down on the Glen Etive approach, was powering up towards his final summit, when out of the mist, he came upon around 30 people, also approaching the summit, but from the Glen Coe direction. This turned out to be the summit party of Steve Coutts (3134). Steve and Chris summited together.

Also managing to get 30 people on their final top were Steven Elliott (3237) and Peter Wilson (3265), on Na Gruagaichean. Steve's biggest day during his round was 19 Munros in the Glen Sheil area in 24 hours. Peter did the north side only, to get a haul of 12. A further '30 on Top' day was achieved by Elaine Anderson (3193) on Meall nan Tarmachan. She reported several real ptarmigan on top too, and someone even brought a stuffed one – she didn't say if it was originally alive. The greatest number of people on top for a Compleation this year goes to Sister Margaret Minards (3218) and Rev. Willy Slavin who managed 42 on Ben na Lap. Irene MacGregor (3233) on Creise, had 10 Munroists among her 27 summiteers.

An unusual double compleation of Munros and Tops was completed by Richard 'Tricky' Spiers (3136). He traversed the Corrag Bhuide ridge of An Teallach to meet up with 25 people on Bidean a Glas Thuill. After celebrating his final Munro, he tramped alone over to repeat his first Top, Glas Mheall Liath. Following a further traverse of Bidean, he then completed his Tops on Glas Mheall Mor.

Compleat Munro rounds, while based overseas, are not common. This year, Margaret Tees (3135) did just this, while based in Ireland. She was wondering if she was the first woman to do this, and I expect she is – unless you know better of course. Also travelling from afar, we had the third claimed Dutch compleation this year by Martin Snijders (3299). The Scottish mountains are so highly thought of in the Netherlands that he needed to delay reporting due to having to give Press interviews and appear on local TV and radio. Despite the distance travelled, Martin managed to get 30 onto his final summit, to be met by Hamish Brown (62), who had heard about the ascent and climbed the hill from the other side. Manuel Lapp (3298) from Freiberg in Germany reports needing 16 trips to compleat. As well as the scenery, the reason he keeps returning is that: "In Scotland, the people like their own mountains and they understand people who do the same."

Niall Campbell (3303) needed to race to finish on Beinn Bhuide, just days before being posted to Germany with the RAF. He came upon a film crew on his descent, and discovered that they were shooting, of all things – *Eastenders*.

With a start in 1935, and compleating on the remote Mullach nan Dheirhgain in 2004 at 80, this year's *Munrois Longius* is Robert Waterston (3210). Partners compleating together are often mentioned, however a letter which I received from Nancy and Jeffrey Cox (3184 and 3185) has allowed me to invent yet a further 'Bad Latin' category. They are this year's *'Munrois Longius con Matrimonium'*. At compleation, Nancy was 71 and Jeffrey was 69. Furthermore, it was Ladhar Bheinn they chose. Kathryn and Rodger Osborne (3144 and 3145) did every summit together and are now sharing their second round together. Six couples have completed two rounds together, but I don't expect that many have shared every summit. Also sharing virtually every Munro with a trusted partner was Richard Spencer (3129), who did all but some of Skye with his dog, Guy. Guy is even the main subject of the final summit photo. A further joint compleation of Munros and Tops was achieved by Alison Philip and Bill Strang (3187 and 3188), when they topped out on Moruisg with 20 friends. Steven Kirk (3123) had his wife as company on Mull's Munro, but could very easily have ended up with a further family member – just days after they got down she gave birth.

Also finishing on Ladhar Bheinn was Chris Jones (3122) who gave himself the additional handicap of combining his last Munro weekend with his stag weekend – it's lucky he got on the hill at all.

I often get letters from people lists other than those in Munro's Tables, but I have never had someone ticking 'airfields' before! This is what Somerset-based Barry Arthur (3161) is doing. Barry got 33 people up Ben Chonzie in May 2004, but only 32 walked down – his son paraglided off the top. Also being given a fly-past was Eric Grant (3151). As he was ascending from Glen Nevis to traverse over to Aonach Mor, a pair of golden eagles soared right past him.

A compleation of Munros, Tops and Corbetts was recorded in a single letter by Steve Chambers (3142). He completed the Tops on the Basteir Tooth in 1995, but needed to return and do Knights Peak in 1999, before he felt he could record. Still, he was pleased to have a fine pair of peaks for his Top compleation.

Two people compleating together is quite common, but having three together is less so. There were two triple compleations this year, one all male, the other all female. Margaret Roberts (3204), Avril Hedges (3205) and Wilma Tully (3206) finished on Sgurr Alasdair, and Jim Hewson (3273), Harvie Brown (3274) and David Law were on 'Ben Mull'.

When people look up Ken Crocket's final summit photo-library in the SMC web-site, it is often hard to tell which hill is featured without reading the caption. Ann Macleod's (3125) friends made sure everyone would know who was doing what, where and when, by unrolling a 10ft. x 3ft. professionally produced banner above her head for the summit pictures. As well as taking unusual things up final hills, Paul Myres (3309) managed to take someone with a very unusual job. It was his uncle – the Ilkley Town Crier. This gentleman had composed a poetic piece to Paul, which he delivered in typical manner on the summit. Also receiving a poetic offering was Stan Work (3325) whose brother presented him with a framed copy. The poem appeared in the Moray Mountaineering Club newsletter, and its last verse is:

> But never mind, the year's drift by,
> Stob Ban you see against the sky,
> Is this the one or is there more,
> Not for you – it's 284.

No one reported having to drag a ball and chain up their final summit this year, but Gordon Scott (3300) was made to carry a friend's son, a 10-year-old, up Sgurr Dearg of Beinn a Bheither. More than 20 people watched him suffer, including two who had flown over especially from Oman.

The Inn Pinn always produces some good stories for this report and this year is no exception. Colin Marsh (3255) finished his last three Munros on the same day – the round of Coire Laggan, finishing with Alasdair – and all that on his 50th birthday too. As Colin was negotiating the abseil from the Inn Pinn, his wife arranged the 20 or so onlookers on Sgurr Dearg to sing, *Happy Birthday.*

A rather unusual tale came from John Millar (3279) – it was his first Munro! He was camping in Glen Brittle and decided to scramble up the hills, knowing nothing of the Cuillin's reputation, or even having heard of the Inn Pinn. When he saw the pinnacle, he initially tried the short side, but failed. He then managed the long side, but had a bit of trouble getting down the same way. His next Munro wasn't for another 22 years, and only after that did he realise that he had already done the hardest one.

Also having an amazing first Munro day was Michael Hetherington (3238). He did the Cairngorm 4000-ers. He did them, however, by walking in from Aviemore, and that after getting the train in the wee small hours from Perthshire. His penultimate Munro trip was also a 14-hour day, walking in to Knoydart from Kinloch Hourn and back, aged 70. Brian Billington (3319), who completed on the Buachaille in July 2004, 42 years after starting, remembers meeting two men on Sgurr Ruadh in July 1962, one of whom was on his final Munro. Brian still has a photo of the men, and would be happy to pass it on to them or their family – please contact myself for Brian's address. Only six men are listed as compleating in 1962.

Charles Murray's (3213) brother deserves a mention. He faithfully accompanied his brother on his day of triumph on Chno Dearg, despite his boots not having seen daylight in four years. On the way up, he had to tie them together with bandages, and on the way down, as the soles fell to bits, he had to turn them upside-down and bandage the uppers to the soles of his own feet. Also with odd things on his feet was Keith Jackson (3253), who did the whole lot (including the Inn Pinn) in Wellies – the only footwear suitable for the Scottish bogs – in his opinion. Apart from Keith, there was no mention of any Fancy Dress Munroists this year, however Helena Brigginshaw (3239) was surprised to meet a masked man, clad all in black, as she reached her final summit, Angel's Peak. She was even more surprised when presented with a box of Milk Tray. Apparently, he had approached via Glen Feshie and had been texting a member of her party to ensure a suitably timed meet up.

Extended trips to all Munro summits are always of interest, and to finish this piece, I feel due congratulations must go to Emma O'Shea (3297), who did them all but Beinn Heasgarnich in 1999 solo (apart from Meg, her Border Collie), in a four-month trek for MacMillan Cancer Relief. The reason that she missed one out was because the "weather was very poor".

AMENDMENTS

The following have added to their entries on the List. Each Munroist's record is shown in full. The columns refer to Number, Name, Munros, Tops, Furths and Corbetts.

Number	Name	Munros	Tops	Furths	Corbetts
1137	Mike Weedon	1989	2003	2004	2002
1040	James Gordon	1992	1994		1998
			1996		
			1998		
			2000		
			2004		
1401	Alan Bellis	1995		2004	2002
1080	Jeffrey C. Stone	1992			2004
1238	R. J. Anderson	1993	2003		
1796	John L. Robinson	1997	2003		
1797	Elaine Stewart	1997	2003		
1798	Colin P. Watts	1997	2003		
2438	Morag Barclay	2000	2003		
2579	Isabel M. G. Watts	2001	2003		
634	Bill Miller	1987	1998	1991	1992
		1988			
		2004			
2021	W. R. Strachan	1998			
		2004			
494	Terry Butterworth	1987	2004		

No.	Name				
		2004			
1045	Steve Fallon	1992	1993		
		1994			
		1995			
		1996			
		1997			
		1998			
		1999			
		2000			
		2001			
		2002			
		2003			
		2004			
1419	Donald W. W. Smith	1995	2004		
23	*M. Hutchinson	1955	1955	1970	1992
		1992	1998		
		1998			
		2004			
2266	David S. Norrie	1999			2004
3220	Mike Carter	2004	2004		
2373	David M. Raw	2000			
		2004			
359	Alf Barnard	1984	1985		
		2004	2004		
2412	Dave Windle	2000			2004
1318	Catherine S. Gray	1994			2004
1319	Robert P. Gray	1994			2004
1113	Kenneth Oliver	1989	1991		2003
		1996			
		2004			
775	Peter Malone	1990	1995		2004
		2004			
2342	Anthony P. Weetman	2000	2004		
2281	James A. Thomson	1999	2004		
225	Alan L. Brook	1980	1980	1978	2004
		2002	2002		
1246	Janey Brogan	1993			2004
1247	David Brogan	1993			2004
204	Christopher Bond	1980	1986	1986	2004
262	Roger J. C. Robb	1981	2003		2004
		2000			
3152	Roger Gregory	2003	2004		
1801	Lindsay Boyd	1997	2002		2004
		2000			
		2002			
118	Diane Standring	1973			2004
3136	Richard Speirs	2004	2004	2002	
1317	Leigh Sayers	1994			
		2003			
568	Charles L. Scott	1987			
		2004			

As ever, people who wish to register a Compleation or an Amendment, or make any necessary correction to the List, should send a letter with a stamped addressed envelope to me at:

Greenhowe Farmhouse, Banchory Devenick, Aberdeenshire, AB12 5YJ.

If you wish a certificate (for either a Munro or Corbett compleation), please make sure you enclose an A4 sae. If a certificate isn't required, and an e-mail address is given on a received letter, I can speed up return of information, by e-mailing back.

Have a great day on the hill.

David Kirk

Clerk of the List.

Iain Robertson reports: The Munro Society enters its fourth year with a healthy membership which appears to have stabilised around the 120 mark. The year's two official events were the Annual Meeting at the University of Stirling and the Annual Dinner at Blair Atholl. The Stirling meeting saw the public launch of Mountain Quality Indicators (MQIs). Official representatives from groups – SMC, John Muir Trust, Scottish National Heritage and the National Trust for Scotland gave a positive welcome to the concept.

The next and challenging stage will be to extend the database of scrutinised Munros to the point where it will be possible to monitor alterations in their physical and ecological state and so determine their well-being or otherwise. In the evening the annual Munro Lecture was given by the irrepressible Jim Curran, who demonstrated that life is still good for the "middle-aged mountaineer".

The dinner at Blair Atholl was held concurrently with an exhibition of mountain paintings and photographs in the Banvie Room at Blair Castle. This lasted for 10 days and preceded and succeeded the dinner. The Banvie Room is at the exit from the Castle and has to be traversed by all visitors. In addition to the pictures, the case was set out for an extension of the boundaries of the Cairngorm National Park to include Highland Perthshire. This is a matter of considerable importance to the community in Blair Atholl and the Munro Society, which shares this view, was concerned to show common cause with the local people. Speaker at the dinner was Ian Smith, depute editor of *High* magazine, who eloquently demonstrated that the fascination of mountains is a multi-faceted passion with infinite scope for individuality.

As part of the effort to extend the Society's archive, video interviews have been arranged with some of the older Munroists, not necessarily members of the Society. The first properly edited interview is due to be screened at the 2005 Annual Meeting at Birnam. This is with Jim Cosgrove (Munroist 56) from Kirriemuir and now in his 90s. Further interviews will be screened when they have been edited. The Society's archivist is very keen to receive material dealing with Munros or Munroists and the archive is lodged in the A. K. Bell Library, Perth, where it is available for study by interested parties. The Archivist may be contacted at Glasgow University Library, Hillhead Street, Glasgow, G12 8QE.

All other communications should be addressed to: Eleanore Hunter, Secretary, 12 Randolph Court, Stirling, FK8 2AL.

Easter Meet 2005. Photo: Dick Allen.

It's a dog's life – Teallach on the Mamores. Photo: Dave 'Heavy' Whalley.

IN MEMORIAM

MALCOLM STIRTON SMITH j1954

Mac Smith died in Aberdeen on December 22, 2004 aged 83, a remarkable Aberdonian and Cairngorms character. As my wife, Jenny, said before his funeral: 'There will never be another Mac. He was a man of many parts."

Tom Weir and I went ski-touring with him on a few days at Luibeg in 1949-52, and I came to know him well after returning from Baffin Island to Aberdeen, when we shared the top storey of 10 The Chanonry from autumn 1953 to spring 1955. Many a topic we discussed in our North-east Scots tongue – mountaineering, polar regions, philosophy, religion, geomorphology, entomology, books on Scottish hills, and their authors.

In *The Scotsman*, I wrote: "Mac Smith will long be remembered as a remarkable Aberdonian and Cairngorms character. He had a breadth of interests more typical of the 1800s than the 1900s. Joiner, naturalist, entomologist, conservationist, photographer, humanist, bibliophile, jazz enthusiast, Bass connoisseur, argumentative debater, competent all-round mountaineer and ski-mountaineer alone or in company, Nature Conservancy warden who became the Warden of St Kilda and made an annotated collection of its invertebrates, writer of articles in the *Etchachan Club Journal,* and author of the best climbers' guide ever produced in Scotland."

After war service as a gunner, he became a joiner in the shipyard of Hall, Russell and Co. A keen entomologist, he went on field trips with the Northern Naturalists' Club, and he and a few workmates began to climb on Sundays, travelling by bus on Saturday afternoons and walking far to camp or bothy. A good observer, Mac was the main explorer, reconnoitring on almost every weekend and developing unrivalled knowledge of every cliff on the Aberdeen side of the Cairngorms. His special favourites were the corries of Beinn a' Bhuird, Ben Macdui and Braeriach, but as an all-rounder he also appreciated the glens. In short summer trips he and friends went farther afield to climb in Skye, Dauphine, Chamonix, and twice at Cogne.

Mac enthused his friends, and as a keen second gave encouragement and information on the route ahead. Sometimes he could be grumpy, quelling incipient bombast with a few effective words and a scornful look. I recall an evening meeting of Etchachan Club members at an Aberdeen café when Sandy Tewnion pontificated at length to five of us. When Sandy paused to draw breath, Mac said: "You're welcome to your opinions, Sandy," neatly ending the tedious homily without causing offence. To most folk, however, Mac was retiring, even shy, and eschewed any fuss made on his behalf.

Our flat drew many evening visits from climber friends. Tom Patey often slept on a camp-bed in my room, after discussions about climbing, interspersed with tea and listening to Mac's records of traditional jazz. I bought a US army jeep for £100, and Tom often persuaded Mac and me to come to Ellon and join him on his home sea-cliffs of Longhaven. On the first trip, Tom took on his rope two Ellon girls who had been his schoolmates. After they were up, I asked Mac if he wished to go first, but he waved me into the lead with a confident: "I'll field ye!" While I climbed and then brought him up, there came a stream of comments about the rock, the route ahead, and the standard of each move, a Mac characteristic. There followed many trips to the Cairngorms and coast. The jeep often carried six of us with rucksacks, reaching a top speed of 35 mph as it roared up Deeside, but smashing through snowdrifts that stopped cars or buses.

Mac Smith.

Philip 'Bish' McAra. Photo: Alan Scott.

Mac was not fast on rock or when walking and skiing, but had staunch staying-power. I recall a phone call late on the night of April 12, 1954, from George Roberts, then Aberdeen co-ordinator of mountain rescue, who was gathering local climbers for a rescue and asked Mac and I to come. Two members of Moray Mountaineering Club had fallen at Chokestone Gully in the Garbh Choire on April 11, one suffered compound fractures to both legs, and his mostly unscathed companion raised the alarm. Mac and I drove to Derry Lodge where we met George with a few Aberdeen climbers, and we set off in darkness. In the Lairig Ghru we met the RAF Mountain Rescue Team coming from Speyside, and then walked up Garbh Choire in falling snow to where Alan Balch lay in a sleeping bag, beside a doctor who had given him pain-killing drugs. After sledging him down snowdrifts, we carried the 15-stone casualty for seven rough wet miles to Derry at 5 p.m. Despite little sleep, Mac was still fresh and in no hurry to return to Aberdeen. For an hour we strolled in the pinewood as wood-pigeons cooed and mistle thrushes sang, a contrast from our long struggle earlier in the day.

Since 1951, Mac had been writing notes for a possible climbers' guide to the Cairngorms, and under Patey's influence this idea began to take shape. On November 28, 1953, Tom Weir gave a lecture to the Cairngorm Club. Next morning, I drove up Deeside with him, Patey, Mike Taylor and Bill Brooker, and we climbed Eagle Ridge. On the way back to Aberdeen, Weir brimmed with enthusiasm about a guide. He would ask the SMC to authorise the work, with Patey, Mac and Taylor as editors and others helping. The SMC agreed. Proposed by Weir, these three and I became members and attended the 1954 dinner in Edinburgh. Though a member for more than 20 years, Mac avoided later meetings, being generally averse to big gatherings.

Later, he became guide author, helped by Patey, Taylor and others. It was typical of Mac's modesty that he referred to himself as 'The Editor'. He generously acknowledged: "Without the aid of T. W. Patey, the Editor's constant associate in the venture from 1954 to 1956, this guide could not have been written."

The SMC published the guide in 1961 and 1962, two little red books with drawings of cliffs. Mac's work had been a labour of love, assessing every phrase and editing repeatedly.

Previously, most mountaineers thought Scotland had good climbs only in the West. Mac demolished this notion, describing many fine routes on scores of tall granite crags beyond remote glens in the UK's snowiest hill-range. Nowadays, it is taken for granted that the Cairngorms are nationally important for climbing on rock, snow and ice. Also, his guide was the first to use winter grades, after Aberdeen climbers found summer grades inadequate for classifying winter routes. Winter grading is now general.

Around 1960, Mac became a Nature Conservancy warden. In *The Highlands and Islands*, F. Fraser Darling and J. Morton Boyd portrayed him as 'The Warden of St Kilda' on Plate XX, and referred to Smith (1963), *A collection of invertebrates from St. Kilda between 1961 and 1963*. He contributed a few articles to the *Etchachan Club Journal*:- A 'lang' lauf (Anonymous 1954), *The blues and the ballad* (1955), and *What's in a name?* (1996), the last one reprinted in the *SMCJ* of 1998.

His notable style extended to everyday letters. In December, 2001, he sent me one in which he recalled Tom Patey and "those glorious moments of hilarity at the Chanonry when, climbing the stairs, I heard gales of laughter coming from you. Mystified, I entered your room to find you sitting on a chair, convulsed in non-stop laughter at Tom kneeling in the buff, frantically searching through his vest, pants, shirt and trousers stretched out on the floor for the flea he had picked up on the bus".

New editions of the guide give more routes, but Mac's guide stands out for elegance and good observation. The recent edition praises it as a 'masterpiece'. Such it will remain.

Adam Watson.

IN THE late Fifties Mac's hill companions were Kenny Winram, George Davidson, Bertie Duguid and Gordon Leslie. Most hill folk at that time reached Braemar on the Strachan's bus which left Aberdeen at 3.15 on Saturday afternoon. Very few people at that time had the five-day week. First port of call would be the Bruachdrine for High Tea and then across the road to the Fife Arms.

By closing time (9.30) Mac's table was covered in empty Bass bottles. Their evenings in the Fife were spent discussing just about everything – entomology, religion, politics, their favourite places in Scotland and the Alps. They could also talk for hours about the merits of bottled Bass. The Fife barmen knew better than to go farther than just taking the top off for them, because they all had their own special way of pouring. I have watched fascinated by Bass-pouring demonstrations. Put the bottle neck right to the bottom of the glass and pour very slowly, one of the gang would say. "Na! Na!, said Mac, "pour it slowly on to where your thumb is holding the glass."

I think the stuff was terrified to come out of the bottle in case it appeared cloudy. If someone poured a cloudy Bass there were hoots of derision and uncomplimentary remarks on his pouring method. Of course, the unfortunate recipient, in order to save honour, marched up to the bar and demanded another – telling the barman his beer was off.

If truth be told, I think they drank it so fast the beer didn't have enough time on the shelf to settle.

By the late-Fifties Mac had virtually stopped rockclimbing but spent a lot of time in the Cairngorm corries looking for beetles and sometimes walking up to Coire Etchachan or Sputan Dearg with Davie Reid and myself pointing out what he thought would make a good route. He seemed to know just about every nook and cranny in the whole Cairngorms. He imparted his knowledge to us young ones in a quiet, modest fashion as was his manner.

I think at this time he was probably a bit jaded with rockclimbing after having spent recent years chasing Patey around the cliffs in order to produce his excellent guide books. He was starting to enjoy his long, solitary days looking for, and recording, the beasties of the Cairngorms.

One Saturday, early in 1959, I met Mac on the 3.15 bus and we spent the three hours chatting about the hills – home and abroad. He told me all about his favourite place in the Alps – Cogne in the Gran Paradiso area, and also of the trips to Chamonix with Tom Patey, Mike Taylor, Sticker Thom and Freddie Malcolm. You should get yourself out there, he said. So that July, Reid and I hitched to Chamonix during our Trades Fortnight holiday managing to spend three days gazing at the Aiguilles before hitting the road back.

After I got back I met Mac at Luibeg and told him I had been to Chamonix. He thought that was great, but later on that weekend he sort of gave me a row when he found out that I had never been to Skye. Sometimes you just could not win with Mac.

He certainly did not suffer fools gladly. Mac could be quite abrupt with someone who questioned his gradings of the Cairngorms climbs.

Once, I innocently became the recipient of one of his withering looks – of which he was a master – when I said that Braeriach Direct should be graded harder than V.

Diff. There's nothing wrong with the grading, he said, and his look implied that there was something wrong with my climbing.

However, soon after, I was speaking to Dick Barclay, who along with Ronnie Sellers and Mac, had made the first ascent of Braeriach Direct.

I told Dick that I had asked Mac about the grading and said: "Mac must have found it very easy."

Incredulously Dick replied: "When we took Mac up the crux the rope was so tight we could have plucked it like a fiddle string!"

Needless to say I never again mentioned the climb to Mac.

When Mac joined the Nature Conservancy his various postings meant he lost touch with some of his Aberdeen friends and it was not until he became the warden at the Sands of Forvie, Newburgh – just north of Aberdeen that he came back into the fold.

He took an intense interest in what the Aberdeen climbers were doing and was constantly amazed at the quality of slide shows at the Etchachan Club's winter meets which he eagerly attended up until a year before his death. On numerous occasions he spoke of his admiration for enthusiasts like Greg Strange, Simon Richardson and Andy Nisbet.

A few years ago after one of the slide shows at the Blue Lampie, Mac and I were invited round to a nearby climbers' flat for an extra, late drink. There we met Graeme Livingstone (The Brat) who was fascinated by Mac's tales of St. Kilda etc., and was moved to say: "He is a sharp cookie."

He certainly was.

Derek Pyper.

UNLIKE Adam ánd Derek I was never fortunate enough to spend any time with Mac in the hills. I was part of the next generation of North-east climbers who came along in the 1960s. To us, Mac was already a legend, immortalised in the writing of Tom Patey and author of our two-volume red bible. Like the copy of Alexcander's District Guide which Mac carried with him throughout the war, his Climbers' Guide Book was our inspiration. We were so pathetically smitten by the Cairngorms that we sometimes played a game in the bothy at night which involved identifying a climb from lines read out of the guide. "An inch by inch struggle throughout" will be familiar to local climbers, being the apt description of the first ascent of The Dagger on Creagan a' Choire Etchachan.

In the 1970s, during the anarchic period of the Etchachan Club, I got to know Mac a little better as he, Sandy Russell, Kenny Winram and Bill Brooker regularly formed the old guard at the monthly meetings held in the University rooms. By this time, Mac had completed his stint at Tentsmuir Point and was working at Forvie Reserve at Newburgh.

After retirement, Mac was retained on contract by the Nature Conservancy to survey the broadleaved woodland of the North-east region. This resulted in many Sites of Special Scientific Interest being added to the list. He said of this three-year period: "Heaven, I was in heaven and no longing for the hills."

In the 1980s I started work on a history of climbing in the Cairngorms, which, incidentally, should have been written by Mac himself. Naturally, he was one of the first people I visited, although visited was not quite the right word. He was living in a flat at the foot of Craigie Loanings and in all the 10 years or so he helped me with the book I was never once permitted to cross the threshold of that smoke-stained doorway. I soon found that the quickest way to contact him was to drop a note through his letter box, return home, then wait for him to phone from his nearest call box. Goodness knows what he had in that flat? Initially, he was cagey about the grand project as he called it, but when he realised I wasn't doing a Micky Spillane he became very enthusiastic. As each chapter was completed, he read through the text, ostensibly to check for historical accuracy, but he could not resist marking it like an old English teacher. It came back with more red ink on it than original text. As you can imagine, we often had much debate over fairly trivial matters. It was his help and encouragement that kept me going.

Three years ago Mac moved into his sister's house, and last summer, after he had a spell in hospital we had a fine evening, looking at slides and photos, and talking about the hills and the war. He even played some of his favourite jazz pieces, including *Squareface*. During his recent session in Aberdeen Royal Infirmary in November, I saw him several times. On my last visit I took a current issue of a glossy climbing magazine which contained an article on four classic Scottish winter climbs, including Route Major on Carn Etchachan which Mac had climbed with Tom Patey nearly 50 years ago. Mac had been pretty miserable in hospital, but this time his spirit was high as he was going home the next day and looking forward to taking a short walk. In less than three weeks his heart finally gave out.

Greg Strange.

PHILIP 'BISH' McARA j1987

ON JANUARY 29, 2005 the club lost one of its most individual of members with the passing of Bish McAra.

Bish took to the hills from an early age initially through hill walking but, while still at school, turning to climbing. In typically unregulated fashion he explored with school friends the esoteric pleasures to be had in climbing and developing Neilston quarry. Attendance at Strathclyde University brought new friends and, with the acquisition of a motorbike, the rock climbing accelerator was opened up full. After University the group of friends from there became subsumed into the Rannoch Mountaineering Club.

Bish's interests were wide and varied. So diverse were they that it was not until Bish was hospitalised following a serious car accident in January 2003 that separate groups of friends came to realise that there were in fact parallel universes of interests and friends in which Bish alone was the common factor. Walking, skiing, snow boarding, mountain biking, motor cycling, car driving, even caving (admittedly limited generally to Stoney Middleton in post pub sessions). All means of getting to, getting up, getting down or even getting under the hills were strictly on limits. In addition there was his interest in model building, paragliding and music. His grand passion, however, was climbing and this you had to understand in order to begin to understand Bish at all, assuming you could ever understand him in the first place – he was unremittingly lateral.

Bish's life and thinking were undertaken at escape velocity, it was a rare event not to encounter a unique Bish insight or tangent on anything. It could be hard to follow at times but always worth the effort, as the perspective offered breathed life back into a world often turned a little flat. As he once famously described the conclusion to a glorious day on the Ben. "It was fantastic man, fantastic, on a flat day you can see America."

Once you had recovered from Bish's slightly kaleidoscopic view of things you encountered a warm, endearingly old-fashioned and highly engaging personality.

His hospitality was limitless. Stopping by at his house was likely to turn into the offer of a Bish crafted curry, a few beers and an overnight stay. He struggled with the idea that there should be some regulation to the size of a group of people he should be with, not least because Bish enjoyed a good story. He was a raconteur blessed with both a unique delivery and a wealth of material from across the face of the planet on which he could draw with only the slightest provocation.

His adventures, for such they were, took him to the Alps, Greece, Spain, Italy, Germany, America and Antarctica. A climbing guidebook for Bish was as a red rag to a bull. He found it difficult to bridle his enthusiasm for climbing and the expression of that enthusiasm. Limb-flaying off-widths that would see the McAra temperature to near fever pitch. Many a leader lost in contemplation of a teetering, delicate crux has had their reverie of stone interrupted by the arrival of Bish at the crag in a lather of anticipation, "beef it man, beef it", "wrok man, wrok", etc.

Absence of someone to climb with, whether that be due to bad weather, (others not always sharing the full extent of his passion to climb whenever physically possible) geography or whatever, defined for Bish the rationale behind soloing. It was rare for a good day to pass and for him not to be out there. The stories of Bish adventures are legion.

What might not have been apparent to some was the Edwardian edge to the man. He loved the Clyde, Millport in particular, and the glory days of the steamers (boats, not the Rannoch). He crafted exquisite steam models of the vessels of yesteryear often based on nothing other than a photograph. These he built with the utmost care encompassing radio controls and home made copper boilers (pressure tested in the bath of course). His vocabulary and manners, once you stripped away the contemporary overlay, could be quite old-fashioned. Expressions such as "Please pass on my regards to..." were common parlance. A piano enjoyed pride of place in the house. He was what might best be termed an enthusiastic piano player. This reflected his interest in music which spanned from classical through 70s glam rock and punk rock, 80s new wave, all the way through to Zombie trance.

He was also fiercely proud of being a member of the SMC. The club lapel badge used to adorn the fur helmet for many years. He enjoyed the traditions and the history underlying the club.

Bish died in Glencoe doing what he loved most, being in the hills. He leaves behind his wife, Rhona and his girls, Rhiannon and Meghan, and all the rest of us.

I remember when rock was young...

John Dunn.

This obituary arrived too late for inclusion in last year's Journal.

WILLIAM B. YOUNG. j.1953

I FIRST met Bill in January 1952 when each of us was stranded in Crianlarich Youth Hostel during the weekend of the great gale that destroyed the Stranraer-Larne Ferry with great loss of life. One of us convinced the other (I'm not sure which was which) that conditions were just right to do Y-Gully on Cruach Ardrain. Yes, conditions were just right for the climb but we paid for it when we stuck our heads out the top of the gully. Realising we would have to crawl off the summit, one of us, almost certainly Bill, he was streets ahead of me in lateral thinking, had the brilliant idea of climbing back down the gully! So began a friendship that lasted just more than half-a-century.

If ever a person can be described as having served an apprenticeship in hillwalking it has to be Bill. The journeyman in Bill's case was his uncle. Long before he was interested in joining a club, and starting while still a schoolboy, Bill was being introduced to the hills of Scotland by his uncle, a lover of the hills in his own right and a hillwalker of unquestioned ability. Together they covered the length and breadth of Scotland with their hillwalking so that when we teamed up together

Bill was by far the more experienced of the two. Neither of us had much experience in rockclimbing or in winter climbing but, as was the custom in these days, we taught ourselves by setting ourselves targets every time we went into the hills, the next target always being that little bit harder than the previous one. This way of learning, of course, can have unexpected consequences! For a time, we had a reputation for being benighted. On one winter occasion we had to rope down in the dark from Crowberry Gully junction after failing to exit the left fork and finding that the bus had gone on without us (though two members had stayed behind 'just in case'); on another we spent the night out on the Eastern Traverse of Tower Ridge, and on another we finished a winter ascent of Observatory Ridge in the dark, finding when we got back to the CIC Hut that our 'friends' had commandeered our sleeping bags for their greater comfort. Bill took great pleasure in recovering our bags. One could get away with that in these days for there were few mountain rescue teams ready to charge off if one was only a few hours overdue.

We had three trips to the Alps – two in Chamonix and one in the Bregaglia. I would have needed Bill to list the various climbs we did during these seasons for my memory serves me ill. However, two incidents stand out in my memory. The first was possibly a case where vaulting ambition might have led us beyond our competence. We wanted to climb the Grand Couloir of the Aiguille Verte – why we wanted to do that I cannot remember but it may have had something to do with the magic 4000m! Preparing for our trip the night before, we heard that there had been an accident in the Couloir – a party of aspirant guides had come under sustained stone-fall and there had been fatalities. The bodies were brought down and laid out for the night under the sloping slab covering the old Couvercle Hut. When we saw these bundles we looked at each other – words were not needed. We never did climb the Verte. The second occurred at the end of one of our trips to Chamonix. With two days left we decided to walk up Mont Blanc. After spending the night at the Tete Rousse Hut we went by the Aiguille du Gouter and the Dome du Gouter to the summit. The weather was turning bad with visibility down to a few hundred yards when we reached the Vallot Hut on the way down. When we were brewing up we were approached by an elderly English couple who asked if we would share the cost of a guide to get us all down the mountain, for one of the other two occupants of the Hut was none other than the famous French guide, Lionel Terray. It was not going to be cheap. With the traditions of the Club pressing on our shoulders we nobly responded that we wanted to finish the descent under our own steam, but a more compelling reason was that at that stage in our holiday we hardly had two francs to rub together. For years afterwards we conjectured as to what might have happened had that situation presented itself at the beginning of the holiday when we had some money in our pockets. It would have been quite a tale to have told our club-mates – we climbed with Lionel Terray.

Bill was probably never happier than when he was in the hills but this emotional characteristic was never very obvious. I never heard him say: "I love the hills" for that was not his style. I never heard him make expression of inner feelings about the beauty of the mountains or of the challenge they posed or suggest that the hills had in any way moved him. In this respect – expressing his own emotions – he was a very private person, though in all other respects he could fight his corner with passion and conviction. But as one got to know Bill on the hill, one could detect chinks in that reserve regarding his personal feelings about the hills. When a person walks the hills in all weathers, when his enthusiasm shows no signs of diminishing, when he treats every hill regardless of its altitude with respect, when he seeks to capture every nuance of shade or colour on camera, then one is entitled to assume that he has an enduring love for the hills. That was Bill. He had little time for the character development model as applied to mountain craft and blamed the education system for distorting the sport. I, being a member of the educational establishment, was often the recipient of Bill's trenchant criticisms. He was condemnatory of those books that set out to describe how to get up every hill in Scotland for it was the unknown or the unexpected that he most relished. A hillwalker *par excellence* he took little interest in Munro bashing – I doubt if he himself knew how many he had climbed.

Bill would not have described himself as a rockclimber or as a snow and ice climber but he would have been satisfied and pleased to be described as a mountaineer. One becomes a mountaineer as a result of time spent on the hill in all weathers on rock and ice and snow, exercising judgment between caution and risk. It is not simply an outlet for athletic activity but a genuine craft as well as a genuine enthusiasm, making an infinite variety of demands of strength, endurance, nerve, will and temperament on the participant. Those of us who knew Bill will recognise that as an apt description of the man. Mountaineering was a way of life. It was a total experience – best pursued from a tent or a snow hole or a cave or a mountain hut. I cannot recall, nor could I imagine, Bill on a climbing trip based in a hotel.

A recent memory of Bill will always stay with me. It happened during the Centenary Yacht Meet. We landed at Loch Scavaig heading for Sgurr na Stri. Bill chose to stroll up the path to Loch Coruisk. It was a glorious day, brilliant sunshine and no wind. As I went up the hill I could look back and see Bill as he made his leisurely way up to Coruisk. He stopped here and he looked there and occasionally stopped for longer spells to take what I presumed were photographs. He was in the heart of the mountains again and the Cuillins at that. Having known Bill for more than 50 years I knew exactly what was in his mind.

DMC.

HARRY TILLY j.1940

The death occurred last February of (Tobias) Harry Tilly, aged 96. He had been a member of the Scottish Mountaineering Club since 1940, and was the elder brother of Charles Tilly, also an SMC member from 1945 until his death in April 1992.

Harry Tilly was a solicitor in practice in Hartlepool, Co. Durham, joining his family firm called Temperley, Tilly and Hayward, when his grandfather and father were the senior partners. They both died in 1931-32, so that as soon as Harry qualified as a solicitor, he became the senior partner in the firm, until his retirement in 1971. His brother, Charles, also became a partner when he qualified. The firm still continues under the name of Tilly, Bailey and Irvine, and two of Charles's sons are now members of the firm.

In his younger years, Harry was a keen mountaineer, climbing in the Lake District, Scotland and the Alps. During the Second World War, he was in the RAF and was posted to serve in India. In between combat operations, his mountaineering experience was used in helping aircrew who were suffering from battle fatigue, to recuperate by leading them on expeditions in the Himalayas. After demobilisation he returned to the family law practice.

In 1952 he was part of a small expedition to the Himalayas, and was short-listed for the 1953 Everest expedition under John Hunt. He declined that opportunity modestly saying that he did not think his climbing skill was of the standard that would be required if the expedition was to be successful.

On his retirement, he and his wife, Diana, whom he had married in 1955, moved to live in Southern Tuscany, where he developed a great love of Italy and its art and architecture. He 'retired' entirely from mountain climbing, though he always loved walking in the country. In 1987 they moved back to live in Sussex until his wife died in 1996. Harry then returned to live in his hometown of Hartlepool where he remained fit, active and cheerful until his sudden death.

He never took a very active part in the SMC though he attended some New Year and Easter meets in the early 1950s.

E. G. B.

JOHN SMITH

AT FIRST, I couldn't believe it. John Smith, builder of the Naismith Hut, killed in a car accident on the Ullapool Road. Here was a man who had done a header off the Naismith roof, managed a repeat off the Lagangarbh Barn roof, and lived to tell the tale. What a man – indestructible – or so I thought.

I remember, during a site visit, saying to him that he really needed someone to help put on the crinkly iron roof, but merely received a smile and a shrug of the shoulders. John was like that – an individual in all things and redoubtable with it. At the time, I admitted to a personal interest in his welfare as I was supposed to be the 'safety officer' for the site works, having signed a new-fangled bureaucratic form to prove it. I don't suppose John gave a docken for that bit of paper.

John had his priorities in good order and often took time off during the week for various Highland activities; one site visit was adjusted to much later in the day so that he could come down from a bird watch at Handa Island. Site meetings were enjoyable affairs – relaxed and affable – and soon I was able to extend the length of time between visits knowing that everything was in good hands. There were times when I fussed about building details, particularly those concerning the roof and mentioned the matter several times, only to receive smiling and somewhat evasive replies. I really didn't need to bother – the finished roof more than came up to my expectations.

John completed the Lagangarbh Barn roof in nine days. This was a remarkable time given the indifferent weather conditions and a gale somewhere in the middle of the work. He did the job single-handedly, apart from a little portering of materials by members of the huts sub committee at the beginning and end of the contract.

Next time you are in the Naismith, look at the staircase and appreciate the craftsmanship. That part of the building is a memorial in itself. John cared more about quality than reward – and not many in the building industry can say that today.

John Smith, Master Builder, the club is indebted to you and I feel privileged to have known and worked with you.

Douglas Niven.

PROCEEDINGS OF THE CLUB

The following new members have been admitted and welcomed to the Club 2004-2005.

JOHN T. H. ALLEN (65), Retired school-teacher. Killin.

MARK ATKINS (44), IT Engineer, Kemnay.

AlASDAIR BUCHANAN (23), Trainee Mountain Guide, Edinburgh.

DAVID BUCHANAN (56), Software Consultant, Edinburgh.

MICHAEL CARROLL (41), RAF Mountain Rescue, Leuchars.

RICHARD Jewell (30), IT System Support Specialist, Lennoxtown.

JONATHAN I JONES (33), Mountaineering Instructor, Aviemore.

ROBERT MCMURRAY (24), Traineee Solicitor, Kirkcaldy.

HENRY T. M. METHOLD (43), Mountaineering Instructor, Fort William.

DAVID J. WEBB (51), Professor of Medicine, Edinburgh.

The One-Hundred-and-Fifteenth AGM and Dinner

ONCE again we returned north. The suitably antiquated ,but recently refurbished, Victorian pile that is the Ben Wyvis Hotel within the appropriately Victorian setting of the village of Strathpeffer was the venue. The afternoon sessions quickly propelled us out of our reverie of nostalgia into the 21st century with excellent presentations from Rob Milne on (some of) the seven highest summits prior to his attempt on the seventh of the seven in the 2005 season, and a riveting talk, slides and video session from Scott Muir on Dry Tooling Technique. This was a revelation to most of us and a few grey heads were scratched amid murmurings of "what next" around the room, but the presentations were superb and clear evidence that the Club encompasses all variants across the spectrum of climbing from the traditional to the ultra modern.

The AGM was its usual mixture of the bland and the controversial, but finished commendably quickly in just over an hour. The charging of professional guides for use of huts, wind farms and the proposal to erect a statue of Norman Collie adjacent to the Sligachan Hotel were among the more controversial issues discussed, in the finest traditions of the Club, inconclusively. The tragic death in a road accident of John Smith who carried out the work on the Naismith Hut and Lagangarbh barn was noted.

The splendid banqueting hall of the Ben Wyvis did justice to our large gathering and the quality of the meal was up to standard both in quality and quantity. President, Peter MacDonald, conducted the proceedings with appropriate gravitas and charm in equal measure. In addition to welcoming our new members and presenting the W. H. Murray prize to Robin Campbell (entitling him to a free dinner), he especially welcomed Eric Langmuir and John Mallinson the first ascentionists of Spartan Slab on the 50th anniversary of the first route on Etive Slabs.

Our guests from kindred clubs were welcomed and subjected to gentle character assassination from Ronnie Robb in inimitable Aberdonian style. They were Moira Broadhead from the LSCC, Scott Smith of the JMCS, Gary Wardrop of the Cairngorm Club and Clive Rowland representing the Fell and Rock. Our principle guest was Denis Gray who gave a characteristically humorous address recalling the halcyon days of a few decades past, particularly the exploits of Tom Patey, Bob Grieve and yes – Robin Campbell. The club song received its customary lusty rendition, redolent with emotion as usual and ably led by Curly Ross with Robin Campbell accompanying. Curly also treated us to a few other favourites, and other musical entertainment on the pipes was provided by Iain MacLeod. The new President, Colin Stead, was invested with the Club Regalia followed by the usual crack extending into the wee sma' oors.

A fine weekend was rounded off on the Sunday for most of us with some fresh air in fairly typical early December weather, the new President leading a small, but select, team to the summit of Bienn Laith Mhor Fannaich.

Next year's dinner location has been left to the discretion of the committee and no doubt the traditions of the Club will be upheld regardless of the venue.

Bill McKerrow.

Easter Meet 2005 – Dundonnell

EASTER was early this year but our hopes for snow on the mountains went unfulfilled. The meet was held at Dundonnell Hotel with a cool easterly wind and a mixture of cloudy and sunny days. Light-hearted banter surrounded the photographic competition, which was won by John Hay on condition that he shared the prize of a bottle of malt with the members!

Members climbed Beinn Dearg, An Teallach, Meall Gorm and An Coileachan, Mealla' Chrasgaidh, Sgurr nan Clach Geala and Sgurr nan Each, Beinn Dearg Mor, Ghobhlach, Cull Mhor, Sgurr Breac and A' Chailleach, Sail Mhor, Sgurr Fiona and Bidean Ghlas Thuill. On his way home Rob Milne, in training for Everest, climbed the three Corbetts Beinn Dearg Bheag, Beinn Dearg Mor and Beinn a' Chaisgein Mor, plus the Graham Beinn a' Chaisgein Bheag from Gruinard. Dave Broadhead and Des Rubens climbed several routes on Raven and Loch Tollaidh crags.

Those present: President Colin Stead, Robin Campbell, Brian Fleming, Peter MacDonald, Malcolm Slesser and guest Jane King, Iain Smart, Dick Allen and guests Chris (President of the Wayfarers' Club) and Pauline Kenny, Paul Brian and guest David Stone, Dave Broadhead, Robin Chalmers, Mike Fleming, John Hay, Colwyn Jones and Ann MacDonald, Bill McKerrow, Rob Milne, Roger Robb, and Des Rubens.

Dick Allen.

JMCS REPORTS

Glasgow Section: Although the JMCS Glasgow section has seen only a small increase in numbers to 111, the popularity of club meets has continued to grow. Tuesday and Thursday training sessions at the Ibrox climbing wall and fortnightly Thursday night pub meets remain popular.The weekend meets in Scotland and England have also been well attended.

Despite the lean winter, members made the most of the good conditions when they occurred and ascents were made of *Smith's Gully* on Creagh Meagaidh, *Point Five* and others. Last summer the wet weather restricted most to hill walking, mountain biking, or lowland crags. Memorable ascents included the *Diabeg Pillar*, *Burning Desire* at Ardmair, *Hamish Teddies* at Craig A Barns, and other quality cragging at Sheigra and Reiff.

A number of club members travelled abroad. Brian and Heike visited Costa Blanca at Christmas, Lofoten (Norway) in June, the High Sierra of California in August, and Fontainebleau at Easter and again in October. Fontainebleau also proved popular with other club members, given the availability of cheap flights from Glasgow and more reliable conditions than Dumbarton Rock!

Richard Jewell and Jo Thurlow visited Rätikon in July for two weeks (East Switzerland bordering on Austria). They report a fantastic area for Alpine sport climbing (routes from 80m. to 800m.), all on superb limestone with some bolting. They completed quite a few routes between V and VIII (F7a) on Kirchlispitzen and Sulzfluh including the classic Galdriel (400m., VIII) on the Kirchlispitzen. A good walking area too – very quiet. They recommend the Pardutzhütte as a base for any interested climber (check out http://www.kcr-online.ch if you have a dictionary).

Matthew Dent and Richard Jewell visited Lundy for a week in August, describing "a trad. Heaven – a must for any lover of coastal adventure climbing. We completed around 20 routes from HVS to E4 including *Citheron* (E4) – one of the best routes of its grade I've ever climbed, and a repeat of the classic *Controlled Burning* (E3) – three weeks before it was reclaimed by the sea".

The Club president Ann MacDonald had a busy year when she and Colwyn Jones (Hon. President) went ski-mountaineering in late April 2004, and skied both up and down the isolated 4000m. peak in Italy, the Gran Paradiso, in fantastic powder snow. A day later they went up to the Panossiere Hut and ascended the Tournelon Blanc (3707m.). Next day the group ascended the Combin de Corbassiere (3715m.) and the Petit Combin (3672m.). An attempt on the Grand Combin was aborted because of poor conditions (i.e. there was no ski track to follow).

Last July, Ann MacDonald and Colwyn Jones plus two SMC members flew via Iceland to Constable Point in Greenland. They used a chartered helicopter to get into the mountains of Liverpool Land on the East Greenland coast. From the camp on the glacier they all successfully climbed Tvillingerne (1447m.), the highest peak in the range, plus another adjacent peak of similar height. However, poor weather with heavy rain and poor visibility prevented them from leaving camp on many days and the remainder of the good weather was used to walk to the Innuit settlement of Scoresbysund (Ittoqatoormiut). The rock of the southern part of the range was very poor quality for climbing and many of the scree slopes over the passes were very unstable due to global warming melting the glaciers. The actual glacier travel presented few objective dangers at that time of year. Owing to the heavy rain the flight back to Iceland on August 7, was delayed.

Last November, after coming 52nd in the Karrimor International Mountain Marathon, Colwyn Jones and Ann MacDonald flew to Malaga in Spain for some winter rock at El Chorro. It was a splendid, if intimidating, venue and the pair succeeded in climbing each day on the vertical limestone. Weather was good. David MacDonald and Neil Marshall also visited Spain for autumn sport climbing.

New Zealand was visited by three club members last year. Jeremy and Dee Morris spent a year there, occasionally working but mostly travelling and exploring the walking and climbing opportunities, and learning to ski. Sport climbing venues were visited in both the North and South Islands, and accessible alpine rock and ice were enjoyed at the Remarkables ski field. Paul and Jenny Hammond also visited the country in December, enjoying the walking and hot springs.

Officials elected: *Hon. President,* Ann MacDonald; *Hon. Vice-President,* Scott Stewart; *President,* Claire Gilchrist; *Vice-President,* Vicky Stewart; *Secretary,*

Jeremy Morris, Flat 0/2, 13 Wilton Drive, Glasgow G20 6RW; *Meets Secretary,*
Iain Sneddon; *Newsletter Editor,* Dave Eaton; *New Members Secretary,* Jo Thurlow;
Treasurer, Richard Jewell; *Coruisk Hut Bookings,* John Fenemore, 7 Campsie
Road, Lindsayfield, East Kilbride, G75 9GE; *Coruisk Hut Maintenance,* Alex
Haddow; *Committee Members,* Paul Hammond, Matt Munro, John Porter.

Jeremy Morris.

Perth Mountaineering Club (JMCS Perth Section)

Last year marked the 75th anniversary of the Perth Mountaineering Club, and
saw another thriving programme of meets and a membership active both at home
on club meets and independently farther afield.

The majority of the year's 14 weekend meets were well attended. A particular
success was the annual dinner meet held at the Loch Maree Hotel in November
2003. The hotel offered a very reasonable deal on accommodation, so all 37 attendees
treated themselves to some unaccustomed creature comforts. The highlight for many
was a boat trip across the Loch on the Sunday, landing at poetically named Funeral
Point to climb Beinn Lair and Beinn Airigh Charr.

There were two meets to Skye during the year. The first to Coruisk in May and
then later to the Glen Brittle Memorial Hut in September. Those attending the former
definitely had the best of the weather, with many superb climbs and scrambles
undertaken from the less visited side of the Cuillins.

Several members enjoyed spending the Easter weekend at the Naithsmith Hut at
Elphin. The superior quality of the accommodation offered by the SMC was much
appreciated. Despite mediocre weather, a two-car shuffle enabled a fine long traverse
of remote Beinn Leoid to be made.

The summer camping meets were all particularly well attended. The first was the
June backpacking meet to the Fisherfield area. Several members demonstrated great
resilience by notching up an impressive number of new Munros and Corbetts despite
poor weather. The river crossings also became an adventure in their own right.

The Club hosted the joint meet for the JMCS with the July camping meet to
Achinaird Sands at Achiltibuie. Several members of the Glasgow JMCS were able
to join us for a weekend of mixed weather, but one when dry spells lasted long
enough for some rock climbing to take place.

The Club's now traditional family meet took place at Gairloch Sands in August.
It was a season of torrential downpours – the results of which closed the A9, forcing
lengthy detours on some participants. However, there was wall-to-wall sunshine on
the Saturday when three members completed a fine traverse of An Teallach in near-
perfect conditions, rounded off with a dip in the burn on the way down.

Meanwhile, younger attendees and 'parents-on-duty' had a most enjoyable day
on the beach – also basking in shallow waters. All in all, the only 'fly in the ointment'
seemed to be the rather ferocious midges.

October brought a new departure with a meet to Low House on Coniston. Those
attending very much enjoyed exploring the more compact Lake District hills and
discovering the local crags.

Two members, Irene MacGregor and Phillip Taylor completed their Munros during
the year, and Chris Bond completed his round of the Corbetts.

The joint meeting of the Perthshire Society of Natural Science and the
Mountaineering Club was as usual held in January, and Dave Hewitt was invited as

a guest of the Club to speak on the subject of the first 100 Munroists. It was interesting that several of them were sitting in the audience.

Officials elected: *President,* Mike Aldridge; *Vice-President,* Irene MacGregor; *Secretary,* Sue Barrie, Glensaugh Lodge, Laurencekirk, Aberdeenshire, AB30 1HB 01561 340673; *Treasurer,* Pam Dutton; *Newsletter Editor,* Des Bassett; *Meets Convener,* Beverly Robertson; *Committee Members,* Phillip Taylor, Ray Lee, Willie Jeffrey and Chris Hine.

Edinburgh Section: Membership is currently 87, including eight aspirant and nine associate members. Rock climbing, winter climbing and hill walking are the main activities, with ski-mountaineering and mountain biking also popular.

The section holds midweek meets at the Heriot-Watt climbing wall during winter and various crags around Edinburgh in summer. Traprain and Aberdour are the most popular outdoor venues, but there are also visits to crags farther afield such as Dunkeld, Kyloe and Berry Hill in Northumberland. The wet weather alternative is the Ratho Adventure Centre. Members also gather at Alien Rock on a Monday night.

The highpoint of the summer 2004 weekend meets was a visit to the Glasgow Section's Coruisk Memorial Hut on Skye in June. Inclement weather did not stop a mass ascent of the classic Dubhs ridge. Other well-attended meets were held at Raw Head Hut in Langdale and Salving House in Borrowdale.

The winter meets began with hill walking at Muir of Inverey cottage near Braemar in early January. Wild weather stopped the planned climbing on Lochnagar but presented an opportunity to try out a Rustchblock Stability Test on the snow. Poor weather similarly blighted our next meet at The Smiddy.

By the middle of February the weather had improved to give great climbing conditions for meets at Blackrock Cottage in Glen Coe and the Ling Hut in Torridon. Teams were out on Glover's Chimney, Emerald Gully and March Hare's Gully among others. Unfortunately, the arrival of southerly winds and mild weather meant winter conditions rapidly disappeared, and the Easter meet at the CIC Hut saw disappointing conditions. The consolation was a visit to the most reliable ice in Scotland at the Ice Factor.

Members have visited a number of different areas abroad. Hot rock continues to be popular, with visits to France and Spain.

Members continue to visit the Alps in winter for ice climbing and skiing, taking advantage of the direct flights from Edinburgh to Geneva, and were active in the regular alpine venues of Chamonix and Zermatt during summer. Outside of Europe two members visited Argentina to climb Aconcagua and another spent a month in summer on a climbing expedition to Kyrgyzstan.

The Annual Dinner took place at the Kenmore Hotel. An excellent meal was followed by a memorable speech from MC of S President and SMC member John Mackenzie.

John's speech highlighted the ups and downs of a climbing career with a particular focus on unintended adventures. It was quite a departure from the more usual catalogue of impressive ascents but none the worse for that. Much laughter and applause showed the audience greatly appreciated his contribution to a successful evening.

The section's huts continue to be popular with both members and other clubs. The traditional Hogmanay at the Smiddy was well-attended this year. Committee members are still being kept busy with deliberations regarding the future of Jock's Spot cottage.

The Joint Eastern Section SMC/JMCS slide nights have continued to be interesting events with speakers on a wide-range of subjects associated with climbing and mountaineering. The slide nights take place at 7.30pm on the second Tuesday of the month from October to March. This year the venue has shifted to the South Side Community Centre at 117 Nicolson Street.

Andy Nisbet started the slide nights off with an interesting lecture on *Mostly winter climbing in mostly the North-West Highlands.* Other speakers have included Neil Boyd on the North Face of the Eiger and Des Rubens on the Anglo-Scottish Vilcanota Expedition to Peru.

The slide nights also have a social aspect, with dinner beforehand at the New Bell Inn Restaurant. Thanks go to Des Rubens for all his efforts in organising these evenings.

Officials elected: *Hon. President*, John Fowler; *Hon. Vice-President*, Euan Scott; *President*, Brian Finlayson; *Vice-President*, Patrick Winter (also Meets Secretary); *Treasurer*, Bryan Rynne; *Secretary*, Neil Cuthbert, 25 Plewlands Gardens, Edinburgh (secretary@edinburghjmcs.org.uk); *Web Master*, Davy Virdee; *Smiddy Custodian*, Helen Forde, 30 Reid Terrace, Edinburgh; *Jock Spot's Custodian*, Ali Borthwick, 2 Aytoun Grove, Dunfermline. *Ordinary Members* – Susan Marvell, Stewart Bauchop.

London Section: Last year was another active and varied year for the club.

Membership is steady at about 40 and attendance at meets is variable as usual, with anything between three and twenty members present. Our program of monthly weekend meets follows a traditional pattern starting at our club cottage in Bethesda in January and moving North to Scotland for the winter months.

The January 'Presidents meet' was well attended and members managed most activities ranging from rock climbing in the sunshine at Hollyhead to winter scrambling and mountain biking. This diversification appears to be a trend, with members taking advantage of the conditions to choose between a variety of mountain sports including skiing, biking, walking, climbing and sailing.

Meets are scattered throughout the UK (as are our members) and we had successful meets at Bethesda, our club cottage; Glencoe Youth Hostel; Bosherton, Pembroke; Orpheus Caving club hut, Derbyshire; camping in Buttermere with the kids and climbing in Borrowdale.

The varied meets were well attended except the washout that was Scotland in March.

Highlights included some exceptional weather this year – sunny rock climbing in January (Hollyhead mountain), great Scottish ice conditions in February and a hurricane in June on Idwal slabs.

We hosted a group of 12 from a walking club at the Co-op who were subjected to Idwal slabs in the pouring rain – and said they enjoyed it!

We had members in the Bregaglia Alps and a sailing trip around Rum and Knoydart that included white-out conditions on Ladhar Bheinn in May. We can also report that the approach descent to Gogarth is as treacherous as ever and although we had members giving demonstrations at E2 we also had a member demonstrating the 'lob' from the path – 'big Steve' Senior took a 30ft. free-fall onto the steep bracken with little more than a stiff neck – rather dampening enthusiasm in our new members. We can recommend the Orpheus caving club for both their hospitality and convivial hut in Derbyshire. We intend to visit again and take them up on their offer of sub-terranean adventures.

Our cottage in Bethesda is improving slowly and steadily thanks to the dedicated efforts of a few handy members and this year we have a marvellous new shower room which is a great improvement and a major asset for mixed groups or kids. Speaking of kids, two meets this year were 'family' orientated – camping in Buttermere and a party at our cottage – both went well with mixed conditions and boundless enthusiasm from the youngsters. Good prospects for increasing membership in 10 years.

Our Annual Meeting was held in Llanberis in November and was well attended. Biking and scrambling being the order of the grim day and the evening's proceedings electing most of the same officers.

Officials elected: President, John Firmin; Treasurer, David Hughes; Secretary, Chris Bashforth; Hut Custodian, Rod Kleckham; meets responsibility shared among the committee.

Our web-site has been off-line this year as we re-vamp it and look for an alternative host and 'webmaster' – an update will be provided as soon as we can confirm the new details.

Chris Bashforth.

SMC AND JMCS ABROAD

Antarctica – Vinson Massif, January 2004

Rob Milne reports: Antarctica is all cold, except when the sun shines and it shines all the time in January and so, my great adventure mountain climbing in Antarctica was more balmy than barmy.

Thirty motivated climbers and guide gathered in Punta Arenas, Chile just after New Year. All had the seven summits in mind. I had joined an Alpine Ascents group of 17 for an ascent of Vinson Massif (16, 067ft.), the highest mountain on the continent of Antarctica. Most of the clients had limited mountaineering experience, but this was meant to be an easy and fun trip.

After the usual few days of delay waiting for good enough weather to fly, we were on our way. Our feet rested on jet fuel barrels down the middle of the giant Russian cargo plane as we tried to sleep. Just before landing we all dressed in our cold weather gear, expecting –25°C temps when we got off the plane. Anticipation was only tempered by our fear of the cold when the plane finally slid to a stop on the 11-mile long bare ice runway. We need not have feared, since the fog rolled in as we landed and it was only just below freezing. By the time we had walked the 1km to the Patriot Hills camp, most of us were overheating. Welcome to balmy Antarctica.

The next morning, or should I say after we had some sleep in our sunny tents, the fog had lifted and we were flown to Vinson base camp in two Twin Otters. I had run into Di Gilbert at Patriot Hills where she was working as a camp manager. Di lives in Aviemore, so it was a real surprise to meet a virtual neighbour at the bottom of the world. She told me that Heather Morning, a member of the current SMC committee was the base camp manager at Vinson.

Heather met us as we jumped off the plane and I gave her a big hello hug. Obviously not recognising me, she hugged me back. Then I told her who I was and we shared another welcome hug between two SMC committee members at the bottom of the world. We landed in brilliant, sunny weather. Tents went up with bare hands and the evening finished with a few glasses of wine on Heather's 'sun porch' watching the midnight sun work its way around the sky.

Next morning the work started as we hauled sleds five miles up the wide flat glacier to Camp 1. Even with partial fog it was roasting hot on the glacier. I was down to minimal thermal underwear and didn't wear gloves. My biggest worry was getting fried by the hole in the ozone layer! Balmy Antarctica. Loads dumped, snow walls were built and we sauntered back down the glacier in thick fog. The midnight sun blazed as we feasted in our 'Posh House', a parachute like cover over a pit we had dug in the snow to make a great dining and socialising tent.

The next few days were spent carrying loads to the next camp, then moving to the next camp. We were soon above the glacier fog and into bright hot sunshine. The views just got better and better as we ascended to 12,000ft. I was still roasting on the glaciers and had hardly worn gloves for four days. Either Antarctica is balmy, or my hands have become used to the cold after 20+ Scottish winters.

Heather had been stuck at base camp the whole season, watching all the others make the top. Finally, she got permission to take a few days off and try for the summit. Before we carried to high camp, she skied up to join our group for dinner. She was going to share my tent, but when she heard about my legendary snoring, opted to sleep in the Posh House instead.

Although our groups were in rope teams, Heather was moving unroped on her skis. She walked just in front of me from Camp 1 to the High Camp and so two committee members passed a sunny day in Antarctica talking about Scottish climbing and comparing the headwall to the Goat Track. Although Di had reported it as much the same, we felt the headwall was much longer and steeper. But still pretty tame by Scottish standards.

By summit day we had been on the go for five straight days. But the weather was perfect and rather than risk losing this window, we pushed for the summit. Heather skied off early while we were getting roped up and disappeared up the glacier for the top. Our three rope teams moved at a comfortable pace. The wide glacier at 14,000ft. was like a sun oven and we were all roasting. Balmy Antarctica. For once I wore my gloves, I thought my hands were getting too much sun!

We were just over two-thirds of the way up when Heather came skiing down. "Rob, there is a nice Scottish like ridge to the top," she enthused. She had easily ticked the top in great weather and was zipping back down to camp. As far as we knew she was the first woman to climb the mountain moving independently and the first to ski down. 1000ft. below the summit and various members were starting to feel the effects of 15,000ft where the spin of the earth made it feel more like 16,000. We dropped ski poles and worked up a steep snow slope. Halfway up, I became the first member of the team to punch a leg into a crevasse! My axe had plunged through and as I stepped back my leg went in to the hip. No matter, I widened the whole for the others to see and kept going.

The summit ridge was great. A few steps of Grade I/II with a great view, big drops and no wind. Seemingly without effort, we were all standing at the top of the bottom of the world and, in spite of a slight breeze, I still didn't need my down jacket. Lots of photos for sponsors meant we had to queue to stand at the highest point. Although it was a straightforward descent, it was a 12-hour day and everyone felt pretty tired. Elated we feasted into the wee hours. (There is no night, remember).

After a rest day, it was time to move back to Base Camp. I and a few others were keen to climb a second peak, so a group of four of us set off for Mount Shinn, the third highest peak in Antarctica. We had to pay a price for this, we still had to descend to base camp the same day. This meant a 2000m. descent from the summit to base camp.

The four of us cruised the snow fields of Shinn, corkscrewing around to the opposite side. We were rewarded with great views of unclimbed faces on Tyree, the second highest peak. Superb challenges for future generations. The peak is rarely ascended, so no one was sure where to go. Vern Tejas, the head guide said we went up a ridge on the opposite side. But once we got round there, we found wide mixed faces, but no ridge. So we went further round. Still no ridge. So we went farther round. Finally, we decided to just climb the mixed face. At Grade II, we had a great time with the feeling of going where no man had gone before. We called the new route the 'Fakawe', as in 'Where the Fakawe'. The weather held and we had great views of Vinson, Tyree and the ice cap. Getting two peaks done feels so much better than one.

The descent from high camp was just hard work. The ones that didn't climb Shinn were ready to bolt for home and had headed off quickly. Whatever they left we had to carry, making for heavy but not unfair loads. Long before we got down, they had arrived and been picked up by the Twin Otters. But it was pleasant to arrive to a relatively empty camp. Thick fog had rolled in as we descended so, while having dinner in Heather's base camp radio tent, we discussed whether we would be stuck there for weeks.

Next 'morning' was still foggy so over a French toast breakfast we again discussed whether we would be here for many more weeks. It was looking like we might pay a high price for getting a second summit. But I had done my fifth of the seven summits.

But then the fog cleared, the sun blazed and Heather reported: "They are in the air!" A mad rush to pack camp before the planes arrived, stripped to thermal underwear in the intense sun. Balmy Antarctica.

Back at Patriot Hills, it was cold and windy. We needed only a 12-hour good weather window to get back home. The others were still wanting to bolt for home. I was happy to explore the local hills. By the third day of waiting some were getting desperate. Satellite phones were in constant use. One guy was busy rearranging meetings. I learned to make an igloo. One was worried about getting home for a birthday party. I played cricket on the ice with the British lady who had set the record for the fastest solo to the south pole (42 days!). And I found the stash of frozen wine in the big snow cave. We tried an all night dancing party with Heather and I trying (and totally failing) to teach the others the Gay Gordons. It got hot in the eating tent from all the dancing, so the Congo line out the door and across the ice seemed a good idea at first. Luckily, we all got back into the tent before we got cold again.

Finally, the wind dropped, the plane arrived and we were headed home! And my most stark memories are of 24-hour sunshine and balmy Antarctica.

Russia – Elbrus 2005

ROB MILNE reports: Looking back, it was silly to get stressed at the exceedingly long delay getting our visas checked on entry to Moscow, we still had to wait for our two backpacks. Little did I know at the time that we would have to wait days days for them! We had an enjoyable night exploring Red Square and watching the vibrant night life, assuming we would have our back packs the next morning.

Two days later, my 20-year-old son, Alex, and our Russian minder, Igor, undertook our first acclimatisation walk – by riding up a chairlift. Mt. Cheget (3410m.) gave great views of Elbrus and the Baksan valley as well as a chance to stretch our legs. In spite of promises that our backpacks would arrive soon, there was still no sign of them. Luckily most of our gear for the ascent was in our two duffels. It was time for the move up the mountain, so we rented back packs, sleeping bags and crampons from a local shop, everything else we had or could make do without.

The next disaster was that the first stage of the cable car was not working. So we had to walk for more than an hour to the start of the second stage. What us, soft? Luckily the second stage was working fine and we were soon on the snow. But again, a problem, the final stage of the chairlift to Garabashi Station (3750m.) was not working. A quick tenner to the snowcat driver and we had a most enjoyable ride almost to the site of our first camp.

It was only midday and camp was set, so we took a short walk up to the burned out Priyut 11 Hut for more acclimatisation. Distances were very short and we were feeling good. We had to resist the urge to go up quickly, after all we were above 4000m. on our first day.

Day two on the mountain dawned clear and sunny. More time was spent looking at all the fantastic peaks across the Caucasus then looking at our peak. The move to high camp was easy and by midday we had flogged up the snow cat tracks and had camp set at the edge of the lava flow (4500m.). For the next stage of acclimatisation, that afternoon we walked up to the Pastukhov Rocks (4700m.), virtually the same height as Mt. Blanc with far less effort. For Alex, it was his first time on real ice wearing crampons. Easy walking, but not a place to trip. Luckily he learned fast! We watched the long lines of guided groups going up and down like snail lines doing their acclimatisation. Early the next morning, we heard the snow cats bringing the American groups back up. They had already walked that far once, so why not ride the second time?

Dawn of the third day and it was already summit time. We avoided the worst of the cold by starting when the sun rose. It was clear that we were fit enough to go quickly and didn't need a 3am start. I always find it a lot easier to avoid the cold starts.

Soon we were up to the Pastukhov Rocks. The part above is probably the crux of the ascent – a thousand foot steep snow slope – featureless and boring. We were each in our own private hell, pacing slowly uphill and breathing hard. Igor fell farther and farther behind, but Alex and I were feeling good. We rested on a sunny rock and waited for Igor. Our fitness from climbing three Corbetts before going to Russia was paying off nicely.

A short traverse and we were in the saddle between the two summits. The wind was light, it was sunny and warm, so Igor opted to sleep while Alex and I went to the top. The final steep slope can be very dangerous if icy. At 18,000ft. it is not a place to trip on your crampons. Luckily, there was enough snow to make walking secure and we moved up well. I knew I was now close to the sixth of the '7 summits', so I turned up the pace on the final slopes. Thoughts of Everest and dealing with higher altitude filled my head as I pushed my pacing and breathing.

The summit (5642m., 18,620ft.) was almost an anti-climax. Summits are always great howevers! We had to wait our turn to take photos on top and people were getting tired of waiting for us to finish all our photos. A sure sign of a popular mountain. It clouded in on the descent. The long slope above the Pastukhov Rocks was nerve-racking. A slip could mean a death slide, and one couldn't see how far was left to go. Eventually, we reached the rocks and the easier slopes for a well-earned nap at the tent.

Next morning dawned bright and clear again. Great views of fantastic Alpine peaks. I kept thinking what a shame that we came only for a week and missed some great climbing opportunities. Ah well, chairlift was working and soon it was beer and vodka time. As for our backpacks, we got them at the Moscow airport just an hour before we flew home.

India

Brian Davison reports on Miyar Nala 2004: A four strong party from England and Scotland (Graham Little, Jim Lowther, Brian Davison and Kevin Kelly) visited the Miyar valley in India during May 2004.

The area offers large granite walls in a mountain setting. Various parties have been to the area since the first visit by an Italian team in 1992. Most teams have established base camp at the snout of the Miyar glacier and climbed in the adjacent valleys. Previous trips have given a variety of names to the side glaciers which already have local names. We journeyed further up the Miyar Glacier to the junction with the Jangpar Glacier which was explored and found to offer some impressive mountain big wall potential.

May was found to be too early to attempt technical rock climbing as ledges held much snow from an unseasonably late fall (the heaviest for 25 years!) which was melting and flowing down the rock walls.

Two snow routes were climbed. A ruc-sac dropped after the completion of the difficult climbing forced a retreat short of the summit of one peak. Three rock routes were climbed on slabs and spires nearer base camp:

Christina Peak, 5420m (GL, JL 14 May) by south face at PD.

South face of Pt5960m, (BD, KK) retreat from 5800m after dropping a ruc-sac.

Lammergier Spike 5350m (GL, JL 22May) Alpine D.

First Ascent of two 600m+ rock routes at UIAA VI on slabs above Khai Got on east side of Miyar Nala (BD, KK).

Many of the currently available maps of the Miyar Nala and the glacier area are generally small scale and often of poor quality. The sketch maps produced by the Slovenian and Italian expeditions while useful are often not very topographically accurate. Some of the heights claimed for peaks climbed are exaggerated.

The outline map of the Jangpar Glacier is more accurate although peak heights are only accurate to +/- 70m.

There is also mounting confusion over the names of the glaciers that lie to the east of the Miyar Nala/Glacier. Dali Got below the snout of Miyar Glacier has been the site of several expedition base camps and as such is a useful reference point. The following names have been used, the favoured versions (which are often local names) are given first followed by alternatives.

Glaciers linking to the Miyar Glacier:
Jangpar Glacier (no alternatives) – the final glacier to join the Miyar Glacier (about 6km above Dali Got at its snout).

Glaciers not linking to the Miyar Glacier:
Dali Glacier (Spaghetti Glacier, Thunder Glacier) – Lies directly above Dali Got.
Chhudong Glacier (Tawa Glacier) – Lies just over 1km down the valley from Dali Got.
Takdung Glacier (Nameless Glacier) – Lies 4km down the valley from Dali Got

Greenland
Southern Kangerdlugssuaq Expedition 2003

BRIAN DAVISON reports: From July 23 to August 15, eight British climbers visited the mountains on the south side of the Kangerdlugssuaq fjord. Base camp was at approximately 1700m. in the snow basin at the head of the Nordre Parallelgletscher and Sondre Parallelgletscher.

This was reached using a ski equipped Twin Otter chartered from Iceland. From this base camp a number of sledge trips were undertaken into the mountains in the area. Members of the expedition made a total of 35 probable first ascents of unclimbed peaks during the three weeks in Greenland. Weather was generally very good for the first two weeks with more unsettled weather occurring during the third week.

Paul Walker of Tangent Expeditions organised freighting of equipment and food as well as accommodation in Iceland. As part of this deal we were offered a rifle which we did not take and pulk sledges, but more importantly a satellite phone. VHF radio, emergency beacon and flares were also included. Paul was extremely helpful and also supplied us with aerial photographs of the area, a useful addition to the maps.

There have been two previous expeditions to the south side of the Kangerdlugssuaq fjord at 68° 30° North on the east coast of Greenland. The first in 1990, led by Stan Wooley, was flown in using a ski equipped Twin Otter which landed at a higher elevation, farther inland and closer to the ice cap. The group then divided into two teams which both undertook impressive and independent ski and sledding trips bagging many of the highest spot marked peaks in the area. Realising the potential of the area and the prospect of good granite, Phil Bartlett, a member of the 1990 trip, led an expedition in 1998 which landed on the glacier to the north of Redekammen. Members of the expedition climbed that mountain and several to the north west toward the Kangerdlugssuaq fjord.

Personnel: Brian Davison (SMC), Pete Nelson, Graham Robinson, David Wilkinson (SMC), William Church, Pete Brooks, Clive Dandridge, Michael Pettipher.

Bill Wallace reports: In April this year, myself, Dick Allen and Peter MacDonald visited the mountains north of Tasiilaq (until recently called Angmagssalik) in East Greenland. We were accompanied by John Howell, Helen Phillips and Ian White, three friends from previous ski-mountaineering exploits.

To take account of the possible effects of global warming and, hopefully, ensure good powder snow, the group left for Greenland on April 3 – three weeks earlier than previously.

Our food had been sent off more than three weeks in advance and its arrival had been confirmed by the carriers. The airport staff, however, assured us that it had not arrived! Fortunately, we were able to purchase some replacement food at the small local supermarket at Kap Dan and were generously given some freeze-dried meals which were up to four years out-of-date.

In good weather the following day we helicoptered to the Tasiilaq Mountain Hut which is well appointed and accommodates up to 12 in a very dramatic position, with many rock peaks which would provide excellent rock climbing in summer. From the hut we dragged sledges to the Karale Glacier. No ski activity was possible for the next two days due to mist and flat lighting, but thereafter, we had four days of excellent weather and climbed several peaks.

The good weather continued next day when we returned to the hut. The following morning a blizzard and very poor visibility delayed our start. We did, however, have to set out as we had only three days in which to reach Kummiut on Angmagssalik Fiord and rendezvous with the helicopter. Continuing poor visibility and avoiding a 200ft. ice dam restricted our progress to 10km.

Our tents were battered that night by strong gusts and heavy, wet snow and the following night by a prolonged gale and heavy rain. Despite this we reached Kummiut on schedule. The bad weather grounded the helicopter and so the journey to the airstrip at Kulusuk was completed by the soggy six on a small fishing boat at a considerable saving in cost.

Although this year, unlike three years ago, we did reach the Karale Glacier, the weather is unpredictable and extra time must be allowed for.

South America
The Anglo-Scottish Vilcanota Expedition 2004

DES RUBENS reports: This expedition to Peru was highly successful, despite the elderly nature of the participants. We were 50% Scottish and 50% English although all SMC members. Myself, Steve Kennedy and Dave Wilkinson flew from Edinburgh to Newark (New York) on July 9. Here we met Geoff Cohen, presently domiciled in Washington DC. Newark is a good place to buy whisky so having met the expedition's needs, we boarded a direct flight to Lima. A brief bivvy in a secluded corner of the airport and early next morning we were flying east to the ancient Inca capital of Cusco. Here we were met by our agent, Angelina, and whiskied – sorry whisked – off to a small hotel.

The Vilcanota is a relatively small range situated about 60 miles from Cusco. A minibus journey of several hours over an execrable road took us, along with our cook and assistant, Domingo and Quintino, to the village of Tinqui. The following day, nine horses appeared. A day-and-a-half of beautiful walking took us to base camp (4600m), an idyllic grass cropped bowl, surrounded by fine peaks. We were surprised to find a large Slovenian team *in situ*. However, they were leaving shortly, although not before we had shared a precious bottle of our Glenlivet. To the west of base camp were the Colque Cruz range and its attendants, our main area of interest; west and south were the Cayangate group, while more directly south were the Jatunhuma group.

Most of the peaks in the Colque Cruz range had initially been climbed from the far side. It was easy to see why. From our forays, we could see that the far from seductive steep faces of the main peaks were further defended by heavily contorted glaciers. Unsurprisingly, there was no shortage of new ground.

After several days of acclimatising forays, we set off for the main objective, the unclimbed south face of Colque Cruz 1, (6102m), the highest peak in the area. This approach required some route-finding and an unpleasant glacier. Once across this dry glacier, we made good progress up an ice corridor between Ichu Ananta, an outlier of Colque Cruz 1 and the main glacier which descends from the Colque Cruz peaks, (numbered 1 to 6). Before long we were forced onto this glacier where we encountered deep snow, which the Slovenians had warned us about. We put up our bivvy tents and set off early next morning up the crevassed glacier towards the south face. The snow varied between calf and waist deep, with several steep 'bottomless' sections. Eventually, after several hours of struggle we encountered better snow on avalanche debris below the Colque Cruz 1 face.

Although the face appeared technically within our capabilities, the vast depth of snow adhering to it made an attempt out of the question. Although initially disappointed, the fine unclimbed peak of Ichu Ananta (5720m) was close by. This gave a worthy consolation prize. The aspect of its slope gave much better going, and a few hundred feet of ascent from the col between it and Colque Cruz gained a fine ridge with a honeycombed arête, swings of the axes on good ice and some delicate rock traverses. We gained the summit at about 4 pm.

For our next forays, opinions as to objectives diverged and we split amicably into two pairs. Geoff and Dave made a first ascent of Ninaparaco, (5930m) a 'top' of Jatunhuma 1, but a very worthy objective in its own right. The ascent of the north face of the mountain involved rock pitches up to severe, Grade 3 ice and careful route finding to gain the summit from the face without have to traverse a difficult ridge. Moreover the route was exposed to some serac danger.

Steve and I made the first ascent of the Scottish Spur, a fine ridge descending towards base camp from the eastern part of the Colque Cruz range. The crux of the ridge involved two pitches with bad snow and steep ice, about Scottish 5. Unfortunately, having overcome the difficult section to reach easy ground, the snow continued to be very bad and prevented us from reaching the watershed. However, some fine technical climbing had been achieved.

We rejoined after four days absence and enjoyed some idling. Finally, Steve and I enjoyed a wonderful day on a minor peak of the Cayangate, with magnificent views of the Colque Cruz range.

After a night of drinking in Tinqui with the arrieros (horsemen) and the kitchen lads, we returned to Scottish soil on August 8, having enjoyed an excellent trip in every respect.

Further details appear in an article in *The Scottish Mountaineer*, June edition of this year.

Acknowledgements to the Mountaineering Council of Scotland, the Mount Everest Foundation and the BMC for financial support.

I make a few tentative observations, based on this single visit.

Ridges are difficult. Faces of suitable aspect may be better alternatives.

Snow does not consolidate readily.

The weather was generally excellent, but there had been unseasonable heavy snow before we arrived.

The use of an agent was most helpful and recommended.

Some trekking was being done in the area, particularly round Ausangate, the highest peak in the area which dominated our approach march.

Cusco is a wonderful city and a good place to spend some time acclimatising.

Theft is still a problem, although most Peruvians are friendly.

Any members interested in further information are welcome to contact me.

The Alps

PETER MACDONALD reports: Miles Watson and I had a week in the Valais Alps in September 2004. Our first two nights were spent at the Dix Hut from which we traversed Mont Blanc de Cheilon, climbing the East Ridge from the Col de la Serpentine and descending by the *voie normale*.

The next day we moved to Zermatt and up to the Rothorn Hut, from which we climbed the beautiful Ober Gabelhorn via the Wellenkuppe, returning the same way.

After that the weather deteriorated, so we drove round to the Val d'Anniviers and found accommodation in the picturesque village of Grimentz, where we spent the last day exploring the Glacier de Moiry.

An enjoyable trip, with only a few people in the huts and fewer on the mountains at that time of year.

Cordillera Vilca Norte, Peru – Des Rubens with the Scottish Spur in the background. Photo: Steve Kennedy

REVIEWS

The Villain – The Life Of Don Whillans: Jim Perrin. (Hutchison, 2005, hardback, 320pp, ISBN 0-0917-9438-2. 18.99.)

To undertake the writing of any biography is a considerable and all-consuming challenge: to have any chance of success the author must live, breathe, eat and sleep the very soul of his subject but still retain an objective detachment. This remorseless requirement needs to be sustained in unremitting, assiduous research, hunting through a miscellany of paper, journals, books and the mythology of hearsay, lost in a maze of dead-ends, mercilessly stripping fact from fable.

Then comes the creative process – the hardest part – seeking the inspiration to craft the galaxy of elusive words tumbling around in the mind into the expressive, enduring prose that captures both the essence of the subject and the reader's imagination. The scale of this task of distillation and interpretation leaps from Alpine to Himalayan proportions when the subject is none other than the legendary Don 'The Villain' Whillans. It is a lonely, balancing act upon a taut high-wire, the invention forever constrained, just like that of a portrait painter. In the void beneath, should you lose concentration, there is a spider's web masquerading as a safety net. This trap has many silky threads; inaccuracies, irrelevancies, a lack of balance, poor presentation and, in particular, a self-indulgent intrusion by the writer's own persona, much in the way of an over-zealous referee in an otherwise free-flowing football match.

Jim Perrin manages to tread this narrow line with skill, sensitivity and honesty. He passes no meddling judgments upon the actions of his subject although he must have been sorely tempted at times, but more of this later. Jim was originally commissioned for this biography shortly after Whillans's death in August 1985 and, a few years on, he wrote an article *Opening Up The Whillans Box*[1] in which he described this task of sorting through the stacks of press-cuttings, taped interviews, written recollections and – handled "with a shiver of excitement" - Don's diaries and correspondence. Production of the book, it seemed, was imminent … but it didn't happen.

The reason given by Jim for this delay in publication of nearly two decades is that "certain scruples led me to the conclusion that it should not be published during the lifetime of Audrey Whillans, Don's widow, who was a good-natured, long-suffering woman of whom I became very fond".

Despite her wish that the story be told "warts and all" Jim has stood by his principles although, surely, she must have harboured suspicions given her husband's history of crude philandering. Jim has tackled this potentially touchy topic with integrity: he demonstrates quite clearly that Whillans was a "sexual opportunist" and that there were marital infidelities (and I suspect that there was a lot more that Jim could have divulged) but manages to avoid any kind of salacious scandal-mongering. Audrey comes over as a forbearing and tolerant wife, and the public airing of the instances of her ill-use by Whillans would surely have deeply hurt the feelings of a proud woman.

If this biography has any weakness, it is in the sense of a missed opportunity, with Audrey's death, to probe more deeply into her relationship with Don. Since, when he was provoked or in a drunken rage, Don seems to have lived by the maxim "if you've got a problem, hit it" it would have been significant to know if she had ever suffered any physical abuse and felt intimidated by him or whether

Steve Kennedy above Base Camp. Colque Cruz 1 (6102m), highest peak in the Cordillera Vilca Norte, behind. Photo: Des Rubens.

Geoff Cohen and Steve Kennedy on reconnaissance. Photo: Des Rubens.

he managed to curb this side of his temperament. So, while the most significant of his climbing partnerships eventually foundered, Audrey managed to stay the course and I wonder how?

This is not a book of gloss, in any sense, nor need it be - there are no colour photos of breathtaking mountain scenes, for example, or a shiny jacket cover. Most of the (black and white) photos are from the Audrey Whillans's collection and, I assume, previously unpublished. There are some early climbing snapshots – for example, of Whillans in 1951 repeating the Joe Brown classic of Elder Crack, Curbar Edge, the rope hanging directly from his waist with no protection. Close study of the photo of Don's last rock climb, and Bill Peascod's last moments, Great Slab on Cloggy in 1985, shows that he still tied the rope directly round his waist while Peascod wears the famous Whillans Harness (from which the royalties had become a mainstay of Don's income). There is a misprint in the caption for Brown's Eliminate, Froggatt Edge, giving it a technical grade of 5G and, on p.176, SMC stalwarts might raise an eyebrow at the list of "so-called 'Senior Clubs'." I think a photo showing the routes on Clogwyn Du'r Arddu, the arena for much of the exploratory activities described in the text, would have been beneficial. There is an illustration, too, of the perils of quotation, for on p.297 Leo Dickinson awards Mark Spitz an extra Olympic swimming gold medal.

Jim Perrin is a climber and the author of several books – and winner of the Boardman/Tasker prize for his biography of John Menlove Edwards. Although he may have his critics[2], should you doubt his ability to capture atmosphere then could you better this description of camping in a dreich Glenbrittle?

"A necessary and traditional part of every mountaineer's apprenticeship, it comprises wet clothes for a fortnight, swirling mist, slippery basalt where you expected frictional gabbro, topographical confusion, searing drops, anxious descents, endless clammy hours spent swatting midges and avoiding contact with the tent fabric as you gaze out at the waves soughing in from a grey sea on to the grey shingle of a Hebridean beach"

The book opens high on the South Face of Annapurna with Don Whillans and Dougal Haston, who was later to consider his partner the best mountaineer in the world, poised for their 1970 summit bid.

"The intensity of expectation from both without and within that is operating on these two men is extraordinary." And Perrin justifiably identifies this as a pivotal moment in their lives. While Haston was to go on to film-star status after his success on the S.W. Face of Everest in 1975, for Whillans "from Annapurna's summit, it only remained to go down" and it is this strange reversal and the nature of the enigma that was Don Whillans that makes the story such compelling reading. Ironically, it was Haston who was to close the door finally on Whillans's Everest ambitions and thus was he elevated to what most of us perceived to be "outlaw status", a role for which "he was available, and he was formidable, with his piercing blue eyes and forearms like hams, and he had been rejected, and he was funny and cutting and disrespectful, and the B-team, which in effect is all of us, began rather to pamper him and court him and love him".

Don Whillans was born, in 1933, into the Adelphi district of Salford, an area of filthy, narrow streets and his formative years were those of any alley-kid – scrambling and playing by the dirty river Irwell (known as the Inkwell), smashing milk bottles with catapults and, especially important for a physically small boy, fighting – and so the stubborn, self-reliant, and tough character developed. The author treats his subject with an understanding surely instilled by the same mean slums of Greater Manchester and a similar route to the liberating hill-country of the Derbyshire Peak District which Don took, often on his own, in his early teens.

The chapters describing Whillans's progression from novice rock-climber to 'Rock and Ice' supremo, with their nostalgic overtones of a more adventurous, unregulated time – was it really that long ago? – are full of atmosphere. I particularly like the aptness of the comparison between the Whillans character and the gritstone of his native northern crags. Jim Perrin imparts a sense of objective regard, not just for Whillans, but for Brown and all the other climbers involved in the surge of standards at the time; for example, the inclusion of John Streetly's tense account of the first ascent of Red Slab on Cloggy – "Even to this day perhaps the boldest lead relative to contemporary standards of difficulty ever made on a British cliff" – will make you reach for your chalk-bag, if you would use one.

With respect to Scotland, there's a fresh view of the Whillans relationship with the Creagh Dhu, especially John Cunningham and the gamesmanship between them, and the circumstances (again!) of the first ascents of Sassenach and Centurion. Although the Rock and Ice may have ruffled some Scottish feathers (including those of an eagle in Glencoe with a catapult) the balance was certainly redressed when Don, referring to one of the hardest and most dangerous climbs of his career, a very icy South Pillar of the Marmolata di Penia, said that "it came nearest to the real hard Scottish winter climbs", and they climbed it without axes or crampons. Lithe and powerful, Whillans was to become a widely respected and highly accomplished alpinist who "learnt to assess risk with an unerring instinct" and Perrin gives an intelligent re-appraisal of some past misconceptions.

For example, the well-documented rescue of Brian Nally on the North Face of the Eiger, where Don's mountain 'savvy' enabled them to cut out the reverse of the Hinterstoisser Traverse, has tended to portray Nally in an unfavourable, incompetent light but Jim generously argues that he "deserves not only sympathy…but also far more credit than he has ever been given".

The West Face of the Blaitière, the Walker Spur[3], the Central Pillar of Freney on Mont Blanc, the West face of the Petit Dru, the Bonatti Route on the SW. Pillar of the Dru, the Cassin Route on the North-East Face of the Piz Badile, all either first or early ascents accomplished in his 20s with various companions – and many more. Then on to South America, the Himalayas and Chomolungma (Everest[4]).

It was "a wholehearted commitment to mountaineering" which seemed to be heading for the stars but, in the end, foundered. Despite the appeal of his gruff sense of humour and his many strengths, did the dogmatic and inflexible attitudes which he could scarcely hide, and something as simple as domestic laziness on expeditions[5], alienate his companions and prevent him achieving the public status that he craved? Jim Perrin presents the case that, despite his impressive mountaineering legacy, the Whillans approach was "focused more nearly on reward than delight … and in that lies his individual tragedy, if we wish to see it as such".

Finally, from 'The Whillans Box' article: "I don't think the climbing world knows why it so revered Whillans, but for me it glimmers into definition in an image where the harshness, the reductive pragmatism, exploitive isolation, strength, kindness and presiding sense of justice combine… I've ended up liking him in spite of myself."

If you don't like the use of footnotes in this review then you won't like the book, for there's more than one instance where they take up most of the page, and this is acknowledged in the Preface. However, it does allow Jim to add some personal comments and extra information. I don't find it intrusive and how else would you learn about the murder of Slim Sorrell, Joe Brown's early climbing partner, for example?

Jim admits that the book was extremely difficult for him to write, made especially distressing in the final months of its completion by the death of his son[6], to whom the book is dedicated. It is a fine memorial.

[1] For the uninitiated, the Whillans Box was a sturdy frame-tent first conceived by Don and Vic Bray on the Towers of Paine expedition to Patagonia in 1962. Relatively easy to erect on steep faces "it was to prove very useful on all the major British Himalayan expeditions of the 1970s". It not only provided hut-like shelter but the roof was supposed to act as a solar trap to melt snow during the day. However, in the context of the book, it was also a container the size of a small cabin-trunk, formerly the property of Don Whillans, housing all the material upon which Perrin based his work. The veiled reference to Pandora's Box should also be borne in mind. Incidentally, I am adopting, here, the Perrin rationale for footnoting "to contextualise without interrupting narrative flow".

[2] Jim, high on a cocktail of drugs, once soloed Cheddar Gorge's 'Coronation Street' and then had the temerity to write about it. This, along with stories of wild partying (especially with Al Harris), his association with the anarchic climbing scene in Wales in the late 1960s and beyond, and his forthright political views, have provided ammunition for his detractors, judging by the barbed side-swipe 'Jimlove Menwords' which I have seen used.

[3] Incidentally, on the pages of this Journal (2002, No.193, p.9) C. Bonington is erroneously credited with having been in the party in 1959. It was in 1962 that he and Ian Clough climbed both the Walker Spur and the Eiger North Face. The latter ascent infuriating Whillans who perceived it as a betrayal.

[4]. I suppose that all Whillans fans know about the famous retort to Felix Kuen on the fraught S. W. Face of Everest expedition led by K. Herrligkoffer, first related by Mike Thompson in 'Out With The Boys Again'. Jim Perrin doubts the veracity of the story because there was no football World Cup in 1972. However, this witticism is just too good to be relegated to the sin-bin and, in its favour, the fact is that West Germany dumped England (3-1 on aggregate) from the European Championships in the Spring of that year.

[5] On the Torre Egger expedition of 1973/74, Whillans, struggling to complete the carry between camps, surprised his companions by deciding to stock his intermediate camp from a higher one downwards…

[6] Will Perrin who took his own life at the age of 24. Ed Douglas wrote an obituary for the 'Guardian' newspaper (which can be viewed at www.guardian.co.uk/obituaries).

In the Ghost Country: Peter Hillary and John Elder (Mainstream Publishing, 2004, 341pp, six b/w photographs, £15.99, ISBN 1 84018 835 9).

In 1998 Peter Hillary set out to ski to the South Pole with two companions. Relationships rapidly disintegrated to the point where the three men barely spoke to each other, and he retreated inside his own head, keeping imagined (or perhaps real) company with people and places from his past – his ghosts. Many were friends who had died in the mountains, including tragically his mother and sister.

The expedition was an ambitious project, but essentially misconceived in terms of purpose and execution, and dogged by too many problems. The book too is ambitious but suffers from similar shortcomings, of concept, content and execution. *In the Ghost Country* is a collaboration between Hillary and Elder, an Australian journalist. Hillary's first person contribution is indented in fragments of varying length into Elder's third person descriptive text, which forms the bulk of the narrative. And here lies an immediate problem. Books written by two authors are usually a professional writer's account of events experienced by a (presumably less articulate) adventurer. But this book tries to deal not just with events, but with memories, feelings, visions and imaginings. Elder has to get inside Hillary's head, and perhaps the latter's experience has passed through too many filters by the time the reader is confronted by Elder's words on the page. In the end it is Elder's book, rather than Hillary's.

Are Hillary's 'ghosts' visions, hallucinations, or just memories, even daydreams? There are references to Shackleton's 'fourth man' but the reader is left guessing, and doubting. Despite the often traumatic nature of his experiences, Hillary's 'ghosts' come across as random wanderings across the landscape of his mind, largely anecdotal, with little insight beyond the recollections themselves. One is left with the feeling that he has never really come to terms with his experiences, and at one point he very honestly admits that he is unable to express feelings – rather a drawback in dealing with this type of subject matter.

The account of the trip is interleaved with extensive commentary on Scott and Shackleton, restating the notion of their era of the heroism and nobility of great deeds of exploration and adventure. This contrasts with the reality of a thoroughly miserable, gruelling and even cynical experience. The compromises resulting from patronage and sponsorship are evident, and the notion of unsupported polar exploration is contradicted by the availability of resupply and rescue. Personal relationships are at the heart of good expedition writing, but the animosities between the three adventurers leave a sour taste, and the suspicion that the author's own perspective can never be impartial. Hillary's own character must have been shaped by the tragedies he has known, but the reader is left with little more understanding of him, than the fact that he has experienced these tragedies. The shadow of a famous father looms large, but is just that, a shadow. The relationship between polar travel and mountain climbing is touched on often, but hardly explored. These are all potentially fascinating questions, but the raw material provided by Hillary's ghosts is never really exploited.

The text is liberally sprinkled with quotations and epigraphs from Homer, Sartre, T. S. Eliot and Tennyson, providing a veneer of erudition which sits uncomfortably with Hillary and Elder's own contrasting styles. The former's is anecdotal, at times almost prosaic given the disturbing and painful experiences he is trying to address. Elder's writing jumps from unimaginative journalism to overlong streams of consciousness stuffed with repetitive concepts and peculiar metaphors. In truth, much of the content is depressing, as the reader contends with the brutal hardships of the journey, the traumatic events of Hillary's past, the lack of positive human relationships, the awkward style or the growing realisation that the entire concept (book and expedition) fails to fulfil its potential. There were simply not enough positive redeeming features to counterbalance the grinding misery and resolve the emotional pain, and perhaps it was on account of this that I was extremely relieved when the expedition finally reached the south pole and I reached the final page.

Adam Kassyk.

Mountains of the Mind – A History of a Fascination: Robert MacFarlane, (Granta Books, paperback, 306pp, 8.99.)

O the mind, mind has mountains...
Gerard Manly Hopkins. c.1880

In this unique book Robert MacFarlane presents us with mountains both as physical/ geological construct and, as the title would suggest, the mental construct of modern man.

His very persuasive standpoint being, that mountains and our attitudes towards them owe as much to mindscape as they do to landscape.

MacFarlane cleverly blends the two in a progression from 16th century 'terra incognita' and a 'There be Dragons' mentality, through the 'sublime' mountain worship of Shelley, Ruskin *et al,* to the scientific endeavors still linked with mountaineering at the beginning of the 20th century, arriving finally at the noble pursuit of mountain climbing and the consequent courting of danger as a laudable end in itself. And all this, running in parallel with the acknowledgement of 'Deep Time' inherent in the ongoing decoding of geological encryption.

His description of landscape and geological forces in what he calls 'The Great Stone Book' is fascinating and is achieved in such a way that it is both simple and at times poetic in its rendering of information more normally associated with the technically prosaic.

He is eclectic in his literary references with quotes ranging from Petrarch to Simpson - Joe and all points in between, sampling freely from poetry, prose, diary and letter. He also draws heavily on the artistic endeavors of many across the ages and it is in this department that the book displays what is, for this reviewer, its only weakness, poor quality photographic reproduction.

Mountains Of The Mind could be said to be truly, and indeed literally, visionary in its conception and MacFarlane has succeeded in telling a wonderful tale of the evolution of the mountain world in the consciousness of modern man.

C. J. Orr.

Life and Limb – A True Story of Tragedy and Survival Against the Odds:- Jamie Andrew. (Portrait, hardback, 306pp, ISBN 0-7499-5007-2. £17.99).

The majority of Journal readers will be well aware of the plight in which the two Jamies found themselves, clinging to hope in desperate circumstances on the North Face of Les Droites in January 1999, after a successful winter ascent. An epic of enormous proportions ensued that tragically was not to have the ending we all would have wished. This compelling and dramatic account by Jamie Andrew of the personal battle to survive and deal with the aftermath of the tragedy is gripping stuff. I found it difficult to put down and this for me is a rare occurrence.

Jamie recounts climbing the route with Jamie Fisher in worsening conditions to the point where retreat became impossible. The close bond between the two clearly comes across as they shared the icy Breche for five days and nights in freak, horrendous weather, praying to be rescued and reunited with friends and family. Through the thoughts of his girl friend, Anna, Jamie gives a moving account of the emotions of those anxiously waiting for word of their safe return from the security of the Chamonix valley.

There are many heroic efforts in the book that inspire and leave the reader in awe. What the two Jamie's went through is beyond comprehension. The rescue itself was nothing short of audacious and committing. The desperate emotional position Anna and both climbers parents found themselves in when they waited for word of who had survived and who had perished is powerful. The high drama on the mountain is replaced with the struggle to survive severe frost bite and resultant surgery in the internationally renowned Chamonix hospital. The coming to terms with the loss of a close friend and the nightmare of becoming a quadruple amputee. The subsequent journey of recovery and determination to overcome the seemingly impossible has to be read.

Jamie's writing is very personal and honest and not short of humour. It is peppered with amusing moments that perhaps acted as a coping mechanism in the darkest of hours. The long, lonely days and nights on the Breche des Droites are punctuated with trips back in time to memorable outings to the Lakes, Cuillins and Cairngorms in much more pleasant and enjoyable circumstances.

Jamie's achievements following the accident are remarkable and include getting back up the Ben and climbing and skiing in the Alps. He also possesses the strength of character and motivation to run the London Marathon for charity in under six hours. Running a marathon is tough enough with all four limbs fully functioning, never mind covering the 26.2 miles on carbon fibre prosthetic legs. Since the publication of this book Jamie has made an ascent of Kiliminjaro and he and Anna have become proud parents.

When pushed to write this review, it was done so with some reluctance, not because of a lack of willingness, but because of a worry that I wouldn't do it justice. Talent with the pen has never been considered a personal strength, however, I can read. I found this a most enthralling and inspirational book and one that I would very much recommend to others.

Niall Ritchie.

The Joy Of Climbing: Terry Gifford, (Whittles Publishing, 2004, paperback 192pp, ISBN 190-444-5063, 15.00)

Being editor of a climbing journal, the resounding clunk heralding the arrival of a review book tends to lose its excitement after five years. And it is a very rare occasion indeed that the first skim through the pages results in the newspaper being cast aside and the rest of the morning spent captivated by the volume on offer. *The Joy of Climbing* by Terry Gifford is one such book.

Much of climbing literature suffers from the fact that it tends to be formulaic and quite frankly boring. The intricate moves and wrinkles of a rock face are only of abiding interest in themselves as lists in a guidebook and it is only when one places them in the context of landscape and perhaps more importantly mindscape that they can truly captivate and inspire. Terry Gifford achieves this admirably in what could arguably be called a new genre in the literature of climbing.

His use of language in evoking place and emotion is of the first order and I include his poetry in this. I accept that many people on seeing any verse form immediately turn the page but even the uninitiated will not fail to get something from his works.

This is a book full of humour, of history, companionship, life, death and joy, written by a man at ease with himself, with his climbing life and with the craft to convey the real joy of climbing to his readers.

C. J. Orr.

OFFICE BEARERS 2004-2005
Honorary President: William. D. Brooker
Honorary Vice-President: Douglas Scott, Gerry S. Peet
President: A. Colin Stead
Vice-Presidents: Desmond W. Rubens, David J. Broadhead

Honorary Secretary: John R. R. Fowler, 4 Doune Terrace, Edinburgh, EH3 6DY. **Honorary Treasurer:** John A. Wood, Spout Close, Millbeck, Underskiddaw, Keswick, Cumbria CA12 4PS. **Honorary Editor:** Charles J. Orr, 28 Chesters View, Bonnyrigg, Midlothian EH19 3PU. **Convener of the Publications Sub-Committee:** Rob W. Milne, Four Winds, Westfield, near Bathgate, West Lothian, EH48 3DG. **Honorary Librarian:** Ian R. Angell, The Old Manse, 3 New Street, Largs, Ayrshire, KA30 9LL. **Honorary Custodian of Slides:** Graeme N. Hunter, Church House, Gill Croft, Easingwold, Yorkshire YO61 3HH. **Honorary Archivist:** Robin N. Campbell, Glynside, by Fintry, Stirlingshire, G63 0LW. **Convener of the Huts Sub-Committee:** William H. Duncan, Kirktoun, East End, Lochwinnoch, Renfrewshire, PA12 4ER. **Custodian of the CIC Hut:** Robin Clothier, 35 Broompark Drive, Newton Mearns, Glasgow G77 5DZ. **Custodian of Lagangarbh Hut:** Bernard M. Swan, 16 Knowes View, Faifley, Clydebank, Dunbartonshire, G81 5AT. **Custodian of the Ling Hut:** William Skidmore, 1 Kirkton Drive, Lochcarron, Wester Ross, IV54 8UD. **Custodian of the Raeburn Hut:** Gerry Peet, 6 Roman Way, Dunblane, Perthshire, FK15 9DQ. **Custodian of the Naismith Hut:** William S. McKerrow, Scotsburn House, Drummond Road, Inverness, IV2 4NA. **Committee:** Jamie R. Andrew, Heather Morning, Ronnie Robb, Donald J. Ballance, Adam Kassyk, Alex Runciman, Ann Macdonald, David Nichols, Chris Ravey.

SMC Internet Address – http://www.smc.org.uk SMC e-mail: smc@smc.org.uk

Journal Information

Editor:	Charles J. Orr, 28 Chesters View, Bonnyrigg, Midlothian EH19 3PU. (e-mail: charliejorr@hotmail.com).
New Routes Editor:	A. D. Nisbet, 20 Craigie Avenue, Boat of Garten, Inverness-shire PH24 3BL. (e-mail: anisbe@globalnet.co.uk).
Advertisements:	D. G. Pyper, 3 Keir Circle, Westhill, Skene, Aberdeen AB32 6RE. (e-mail: derek@pyper.fsbusiness.co.uk).
Distribution:	D. F. Lang, Hillfoot Hey, 580 Perth Road, Dundee DD2 1PZ.

INSTRUCTIONS TO CONTRIBUTORS

Articles for the Journal should be submitted before the end of January for consideration for the following issue. Lengthy contributions are preferably typed, double-spaced, on one side only, and with ample margins (minimum 30mm). Articles may be accepted on floppy disk, IBM compatible (contact Editor beforehand), or by e-mail. The Editor welcomes material from both members and non-members, with priority being given to articles of Scottish Mountaineering content. Photographs are also welcome, and should be good quality colour slides. All textual material should be sent to the Editor, address and e-mail as above. Photographic material should be sent direct to the Editor of Photographs, address as above.

Copyright.Textual matter appearing in the Miscellaneous section of the Journal, including New Climbs, is copyright of the publishers. Copyright of articles in the main section of the Journal is retained by individual authors.

SCOTTISH MOUNTAINEERING CLUB
SCOTTISH MOUNTAINEERING TRUST

HILLWALKERS' GUIDES
The Munros	£20
The Munros CD-ROM	£40
Munros GPS data disk – from SMC website	£10.48
The Corbetts and Other Scottish Hills	£19
The Corbetts and Other Scottish Hills CD-ROM	£30
North-west Highlands	£22
The Cairngorms	£17.95
Central Highlands	£17.95
Islands of Scotland including Skye	£19.95
Southern Highlands	£16.95
Southern Uplands	£16.95

CLIMBERS' GUIDES
Arran, Arrochar and Southern Highlands	£14.95
Ben Nevis	£19.95
Glen Coe	£20
The Cairngorms Vol. 1	£10.95
The Cairngorms Vol. 2	£11.95
Highland Outcrops	£17.50
Lowland Outcrops	£20
North-east Outcrops	£18.50
Northern Highlands Vol. 1	£12.95
Northern Highlands North	£20
Scottish Winter Climbs	£19
Skye and the Hebrides (Two Vols)	£19.95

SCRAMBLERS' GUIDE
Skye Scrambles	£15.50

OTHER PUBLICATIONS
A History of Glenmore Lodge – e-book from SMC website	£5
Munro's Tables	£15.95
A Chance in a Million? Avalanches in Scotland	£14.95
The Munroist's Companion	£16
Scottish Hill and Mountain Names	£9.95
Ben Nevis – Britain's Highest Mountain	£14.95
Ski Mountaineering in Scotland	£12.95

Prices were correct at time of publication, but are subject to change.
Visit our website for more details and to purchase on line:
www.smc.org.uk
Distributed by:
Cordee, 3a De Montfort Street, Leicester LE1 7HD
Tel: 0116 254 3579 Fax: 0116 247 1176 www.cordee.co.uk
These publications are available from many bookshops and mountain equipment suppliers

SMC HUTS

The SMC operate five huts all of which are strategically sited in or adjacent to areas of outstanding mountain scenery.

CIC Hut – Ben Nevis
Lagangarbh – Glencoe
Raeburn – Laggan, Dalwhinnie
Ling – Torridon
Naismith – Elphin, Sutherland

Bookings should be made to the relative Custodian, through Club Secretaries or via individual membership of the Mountaineering Council. Popular times (e.g winter weekends at CIC) may require booking well in advance.

All huts are fully equipped and users require only their sleeping bags. Cooking, heating and lighting facilities are inclusive in the charge.

The Naismith Hut, as featured, is in a splendid location to explore the hills and routes of the North West.

SCOTTISH MOUNTAINEERING CLUB JOURNAL BACK NUMBERS

169 – 1978 – £8
171 – 1980 – £8
176 – 1985 – £10
177 – 1986 – £10
178 – 1987 – £6
180 – 1989 – £6
181 – 1990 – £6
182 – 1991 – £6
184 – 1993 – £6
185 – 1994 – £6
186 – 1995 – £6
187 – 1996 – £6
188 – 1997 – £7
189 – 1998 – £9
190 – 1999 – £9
191 – 2000 – £10
192 – 2001 – £10
193 – 2002 – £10
194 – 2003 – £10
195 – 2004 – £10

Indices for Volumes 28, 29, 30, 32, 33 are available at £1 each and the cumulated Index for Volumes 21-30 at £2. Postage is extra. They may be obtained from Derek Pyper, 3 Keir Circle, Westhill, Skene, Aberdeenshire, AB32 6R

Trust us to keep you in the mountains.

Polly Murray, Adventurer, Tiso sponsored athlete

Tiso have been specialising in outdoor clothing and equipment for over 40 years. So before you step out, step into Tiso.

£13.95

ISBN 0-907521-76-2

9 780907 521761 >